VOL. 35
VIZ Media Edition

Story and Art by
RUMIKO TAKAHASHI

English Adaptation by Gerard Jones

Translation/Mari Morimoto
Touch-up Art & Lettering/Bill Schuch
Cover and Interior Graphic Design/Yuki Ameda
Editor/Ian Robertson

Editor in Chief, Books/Alvin Lu
Editor in Chief, Magazines/Marc Weidenbaum
VP of Publishing Licensing/Rika Inouye
VP of Sales/Gonzalo Ferreyra
Sr. VP of Marketing/Liza Coppola
Publisher/Hyoe Narita

Printed in the U.S.A.

Published by VIZ Media, LLC
P.O. Box 77010
San Francisco, CA 94107

VIZ Media Edition
10 9 8 7 6 5 4 3 2 1
First printing, October 2008

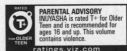

RATED
T+
FOR OLDER TEEN

PARENTAL ADVISORY
INUYASHA is rated T+ for Older
Teen and is recommended for
ages 16 and up. This volume
contains violence.
ratings.viz.com

VIZ
mEDIA

www.viz.com

store.viz.com

INUYASHA

VOL. 35

VIZ Media Edition

STORY AND ART BY
RUMIKO TAKAHASHI

CONTENTS

SCROLL ONE
PROTOTYPES
7

SCROLL TWO
MORYOMARU
25

SCROLL THREE
CORPSES
43

SCROLL FOUR
STOLEN OBJECTS
61

SCROLL FIVE
THE FORGOTTEN FIANCÉE
79

SCROLL SIX
PAST INDISCRETIONS
97

SCROLL SEVEN
FORGIVENESS
115

SCROLL EIGHT
THE ACOLYTES
133

SCROLL NINE
GORYOMARU
151

SCROLL TEN
THE DEFORMED ARM
169

THE STORY THUS FAR

Long ago, in the "Warring States" era of Japan's Muromachi period (Sengoku-jidai, approximately 1467-1568 CE), a legendary dog-like half-demon called "Inuyasha" attempted to steal the Shikon Jewel—or "Jewel of Four Souls"—from a village, but was stopped by the enchanted arrow of the village priestess, Kikyo. Inuyasha fell into a deep sleep, pinned to a tree by Kikyo's arrow, while the mortally wounded Kikyo took the Shikon Jewel with her into the fires of her funeral pyre. Years passed.

Fast-forward to the present day. Kagome, a Japanese high school girl, is pulled into a well one day by a mysterious centipede monster and finds herself transported into the past—only to come face to face with the trapped Inuyasha. She frees him, and Inuyasha easily defeats the centipede monster.

The residents of the village, now 50 years older, readily accept Kagome as the reincarnation of their deceased priestess Kikyo, a claim supported by the fact that the Shikon Jewel emerges from a cut on Kagome's body. Unfortunately, the jewel's rediscovery means that the village is soon under attack by a variety of demons in search of this treasure. Then, the jewel is accidentally shattered into many shards, each of which may have the fearsome power of the entire jewel.

Although Inuyasha says he hates Kagome because of her resemblance to Kikyo, the woman who "killed" him, he is forced to team up with her when Kaede, the village leader, binds him to Kagome with a powerful spell. Now the two grudging companions must fight to reclaim and reassemble the shattered shards of the Shikon Jewel before they fall into the wrong hands...

THIS VOLUME A new crop of demons is plaguing the land. The more demons are killed, the more humanlike they become. This progression culminates in a battle between the gang and Moryomaru, Hakudoshi's new and fearsome creation. Can Koga and Inuyasha stop their in-fighting long enough to battle a common enemy?

CHARACTERS

INUYASHA
Half-demon hybrid, son of a human mother and demon father. His necklace is enchanted, allowing Kagome to control him with a word.

KAGOME
Modern-day Japanese schoolgirl who can travel back and forth between the past and present through an enchanted well.

NARAKU
Enigmatic demon-mastermind behind the miseries of nearly everyone in the story.

MIROKU
Lecherous Buddhist priest cursed with a mystical "hellhole" in his hand that's slowly killing him.

KOGA
Leader of the Wolf Clan, Koga is himself a Wolf Demon and, because of several Shikon shards in his legs, possesses super speed. Enamored of Kagome, he quarrels with Inuyasha frequently.

SANGO
"Demon Exterminator" or slayer from the village where the Shikon Jewel was first born.

SCROLL 1
PROTOTYPES

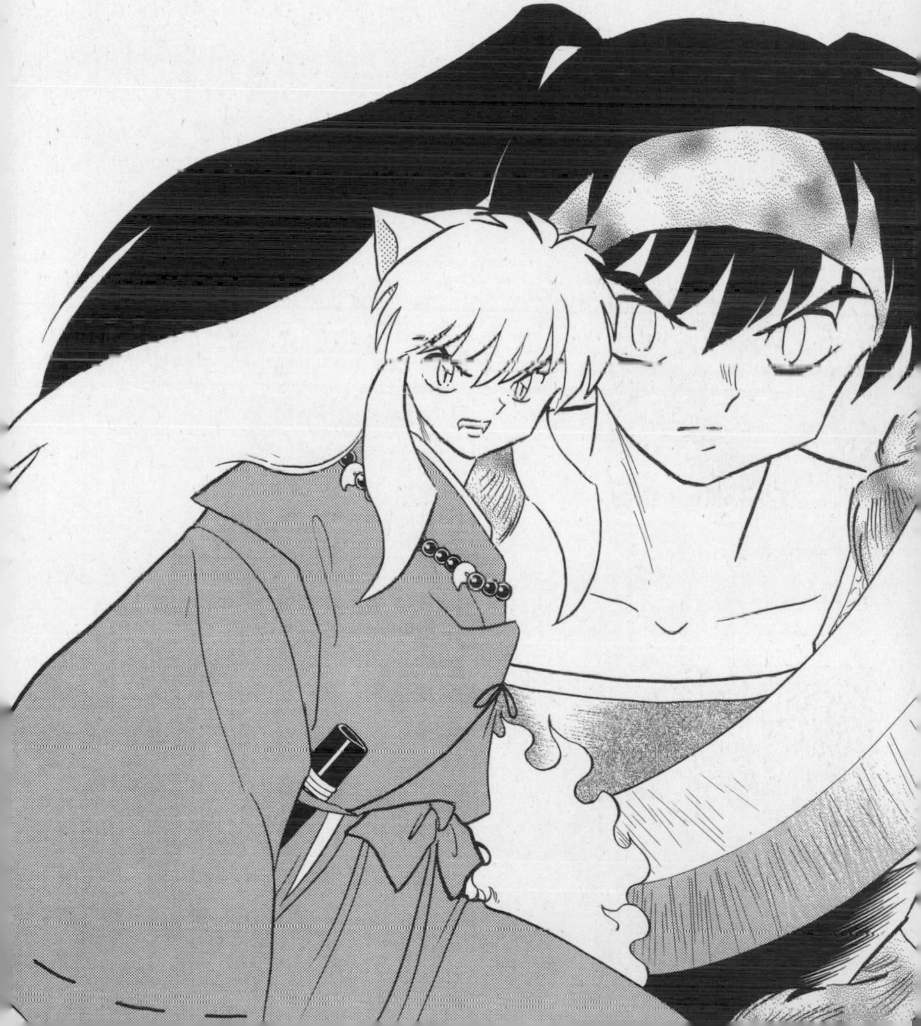

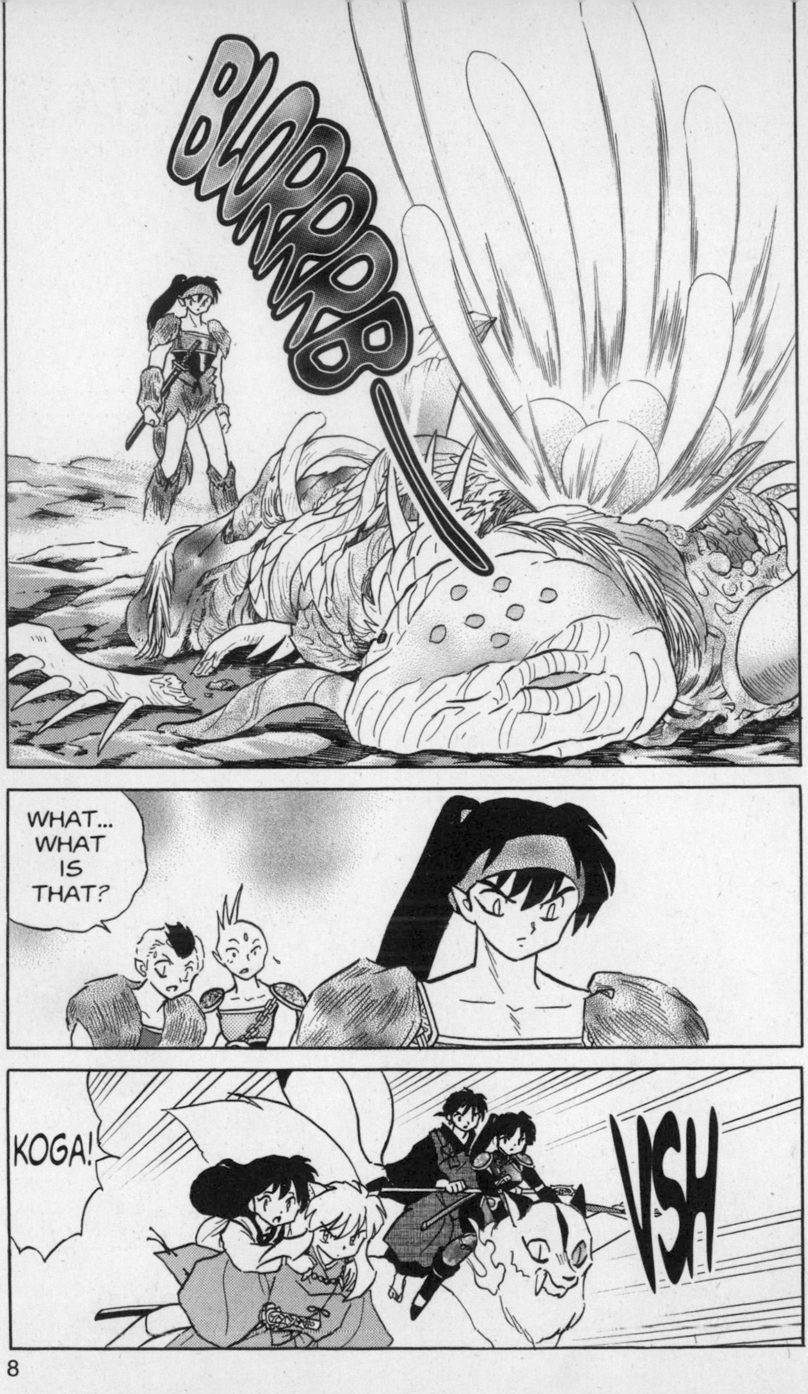
BLOOOOOB
WHAT... WHAT IS THAT?
KOGA!
VSH

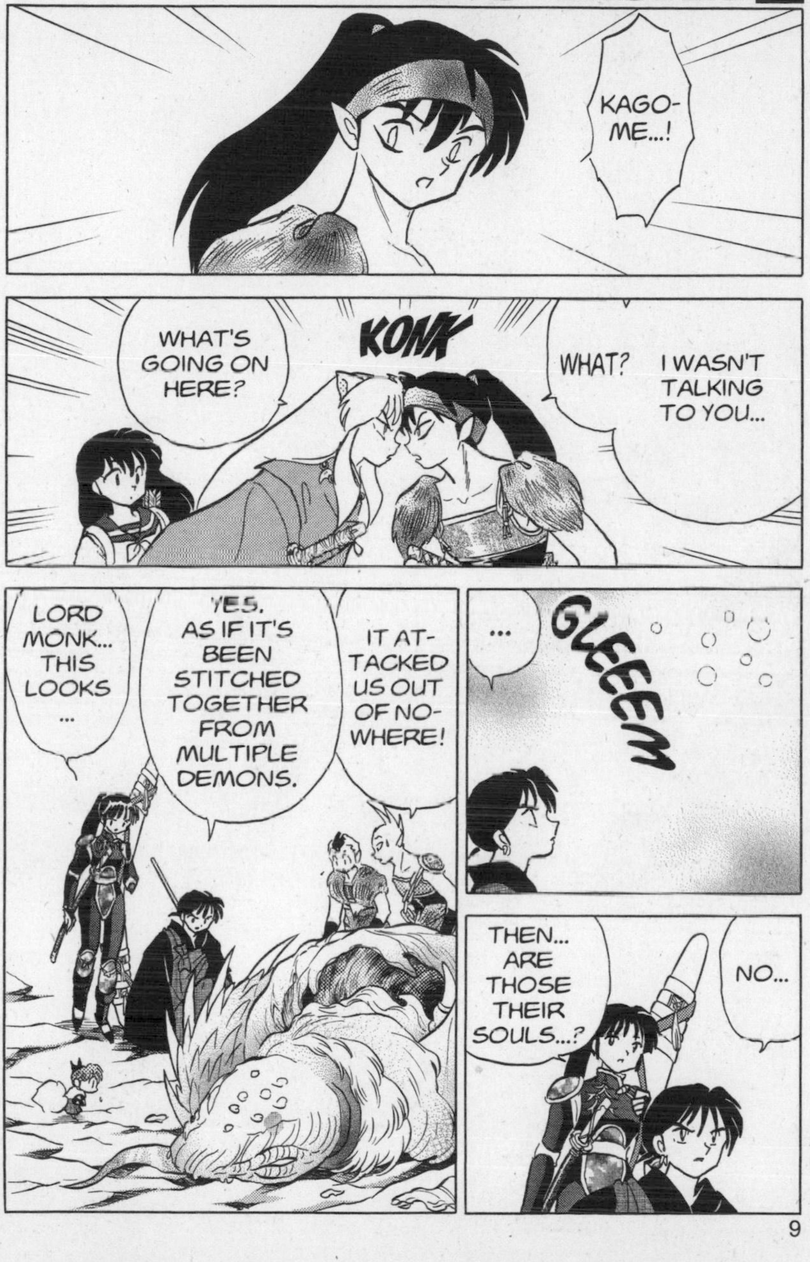
KAGO-ME...!
WHAT'S GOING ON HERE?
KONK
WHAT?
I WASN'T TALKING TO YOU...
LORD MONK... THIS LOOKS ...
YES. AS IF IT'S BEEN STITCHED TOGETHER FROM MULTIPLE DEMONS.
IT AT-TACKED US OUT OF NO-WHERE!
...
GLEEEM
THEN... ARE THOSE THEIR SOULS...?
NO...

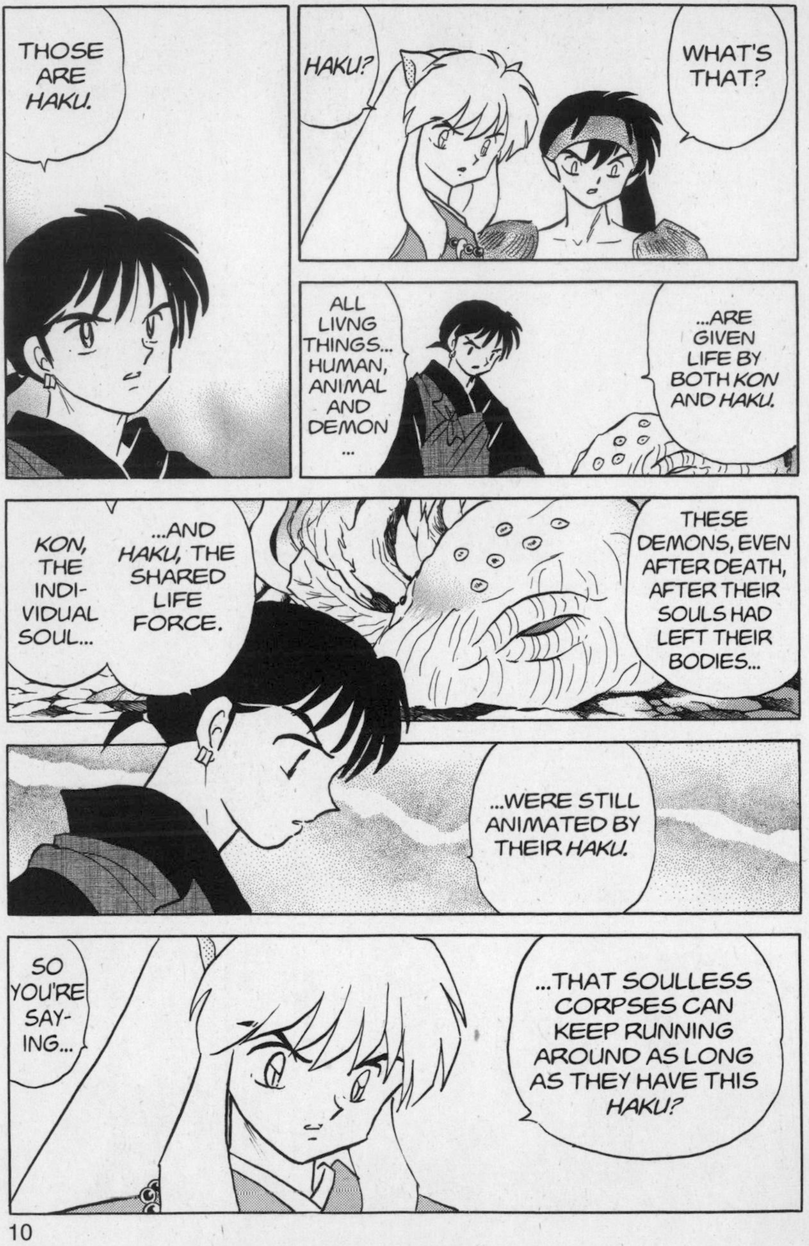
THOSE ARE HAKU.
HAKU?
WHAT'S THAT?
ALL LIVNG THINGS... HUMAN, ANIMAL AND DEMON ...
...ARE GIVEN LIFE BY BOTH KON AND HAKU.
KON, THE INDI-VIDUAL SOUL...
...AND HAKU, THE SHARED LIFE FORCE.
THESE DEMONS, EVEN AFTER DEATH, AFTER THEIR SOULS HAD LEFT THEIR BODIES...
...WERE STILL ANIMATED BY THEIR HAKU.
SO YOU'RE SAY-ING...
...THAT SOULLESS CORPSES CAN KEEP RUNNING AROUND AS LONG AS THEY HAVE THIS HAKU?

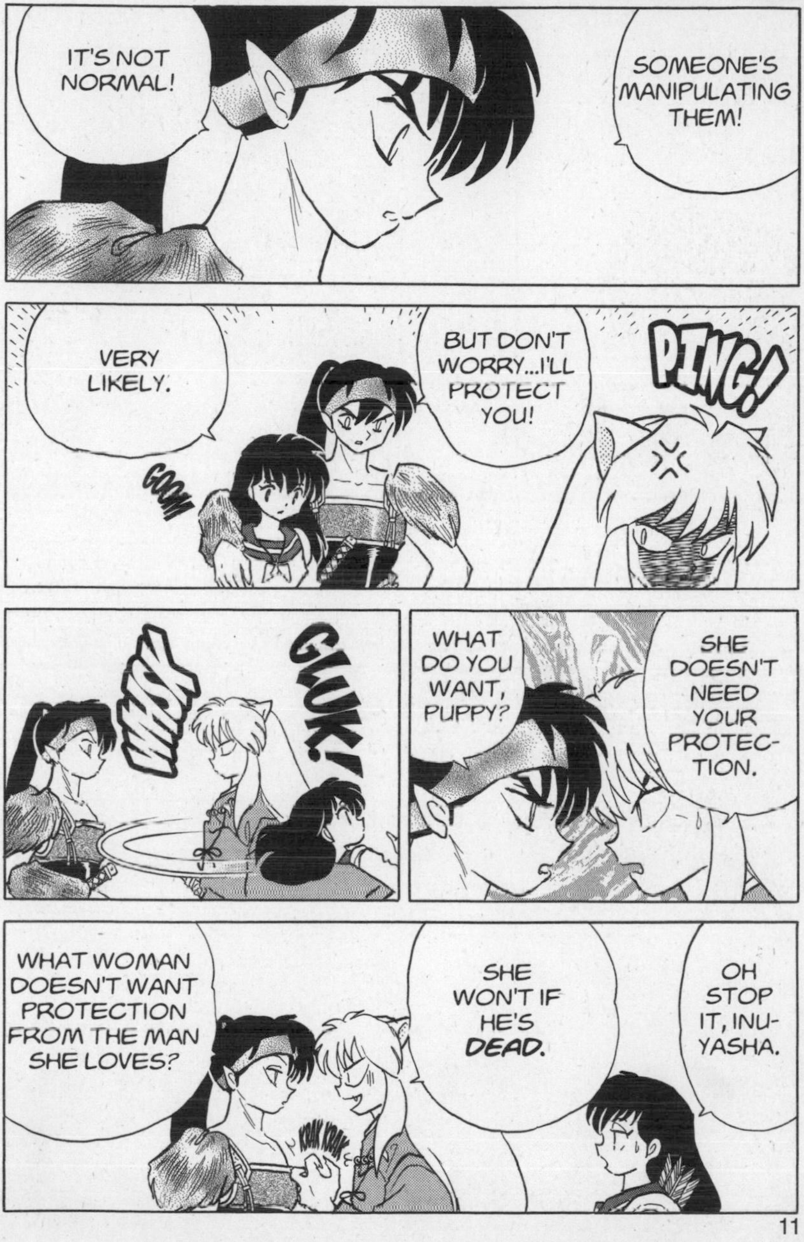
IT'S NOT NORMAL!
SOMEONE'S MANIPULATING THEM!
VERY LIKELY.
GOOM
BUT DON'T WORRY...I'LL PROTECT YOU!
PING!
WHISH
GLUK!
WHAT DO YOU WANT, PUPPY?
SHE DOESN'T NEED YOUR PROTEC-TION.
WHAT WOMAN DOESN'T WANT PROTECTION FROM THE MAN SHE LOVES?
KRAK KRAK
SHE WON'T IF HE'S DEAD.
OH STOP IT, INU-YASHA.

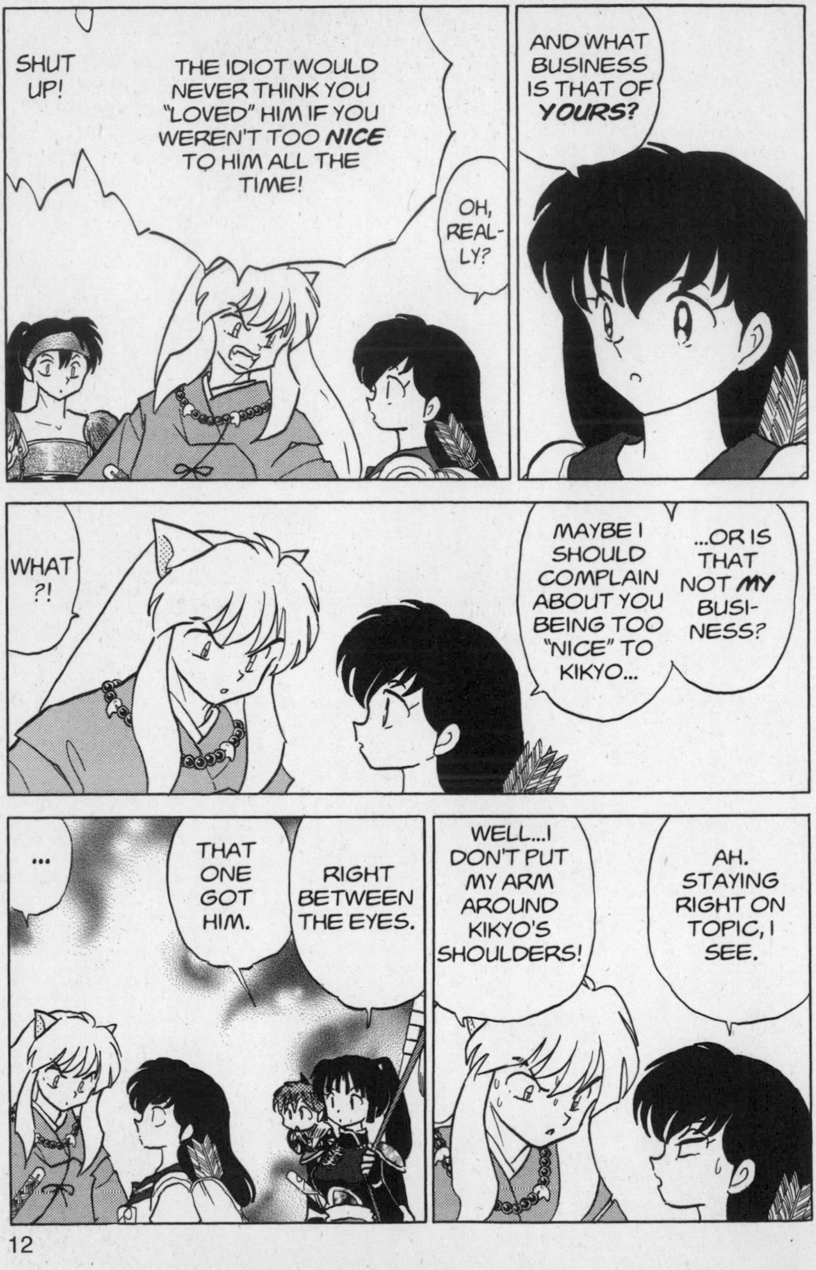
SHUT UP!
THE IDIOT WOULD NEVER THINK YOU "LOVED" HIM IF YOU WEREN'T TOO **NICE** TO HIM ALL THE TIME!
OH, REAL-LY?
AND WHAT BUSINESS IS THAT OF ***YOURS?***
WHAT?!
MAYBE I SHOULD COMPLAIN ABOUT YOU BEING TOO "NICE" TO KIKYO...
...OR IS THAT NOT ***MY*** BUSI-NESS?
...
THAT ONE GOT HIM.
RIGHT BETWEEN THE EYES.
WELL...I DON'T PUT MY ARM AROUND KIKYO'S SHOULDERS!
AH. STAYING RIGHT ON TOPIC, I SEE.

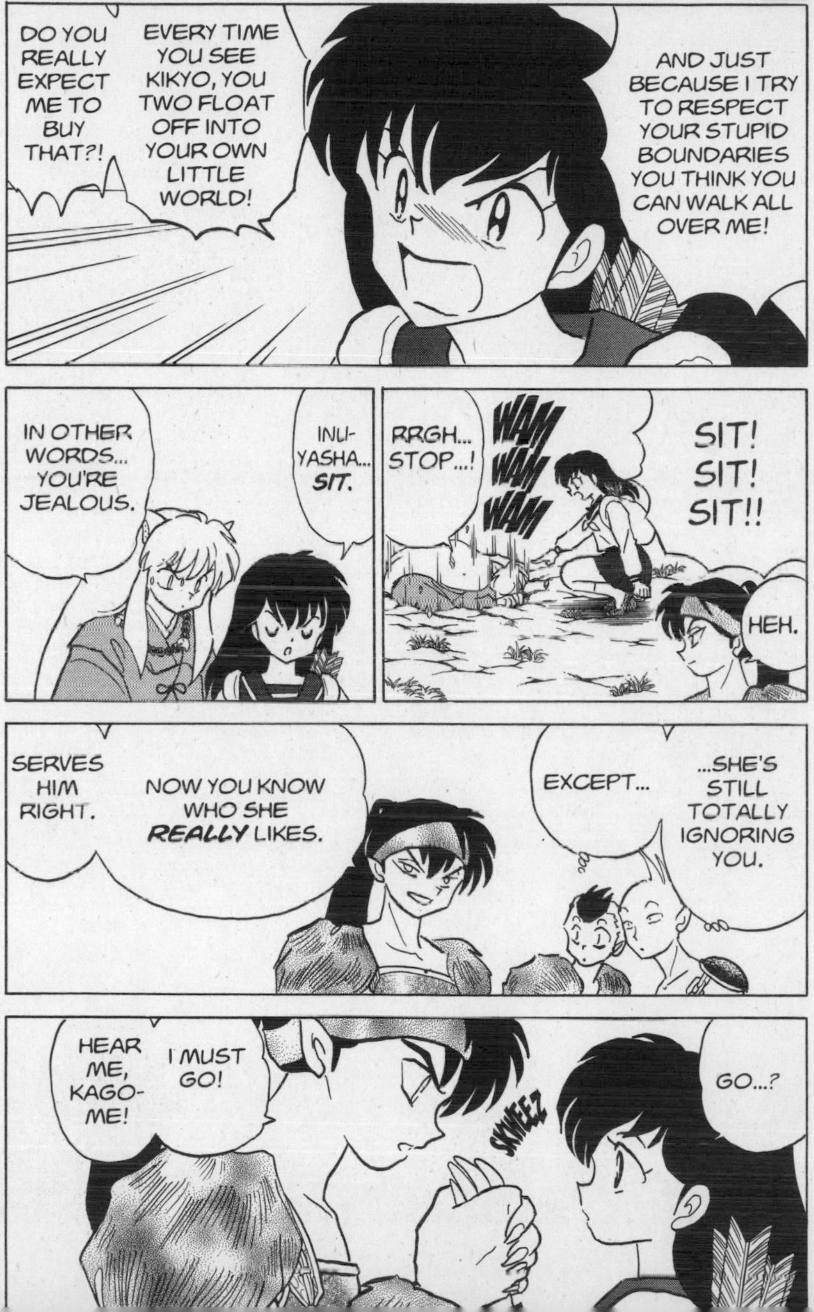
DO YOU REALLY EXPECT ME TO BUY THAT?!
EVERY TIME YOU SEE KIKYO, YOU TWO FLOAT OFF INTO YOUR OWN LITTLE WORLD!
AND JUST BECAUSE I TRY TO RESPECT YOUR STUPID BOUNDARIES YOU THINK YOU CAN WALK ALL OVER ME!
IN OTHER WORDS... YOU'RE JEALOUS.
INU-YASHA... SIT.
RRGH... STOP...!
WAM WAM WAM
SIT! SIT! SIT!!
HEH.
SERVES HIM RIGHT.
NOW YOU KNOW WHO SHE REALLY LIKES.
EXCEPT...
...SHE'S STILL TOTALLY IGNORING YOU.
HEAR ME, KAGOME!
I MUST GO!
SKWEEZ
GO...?

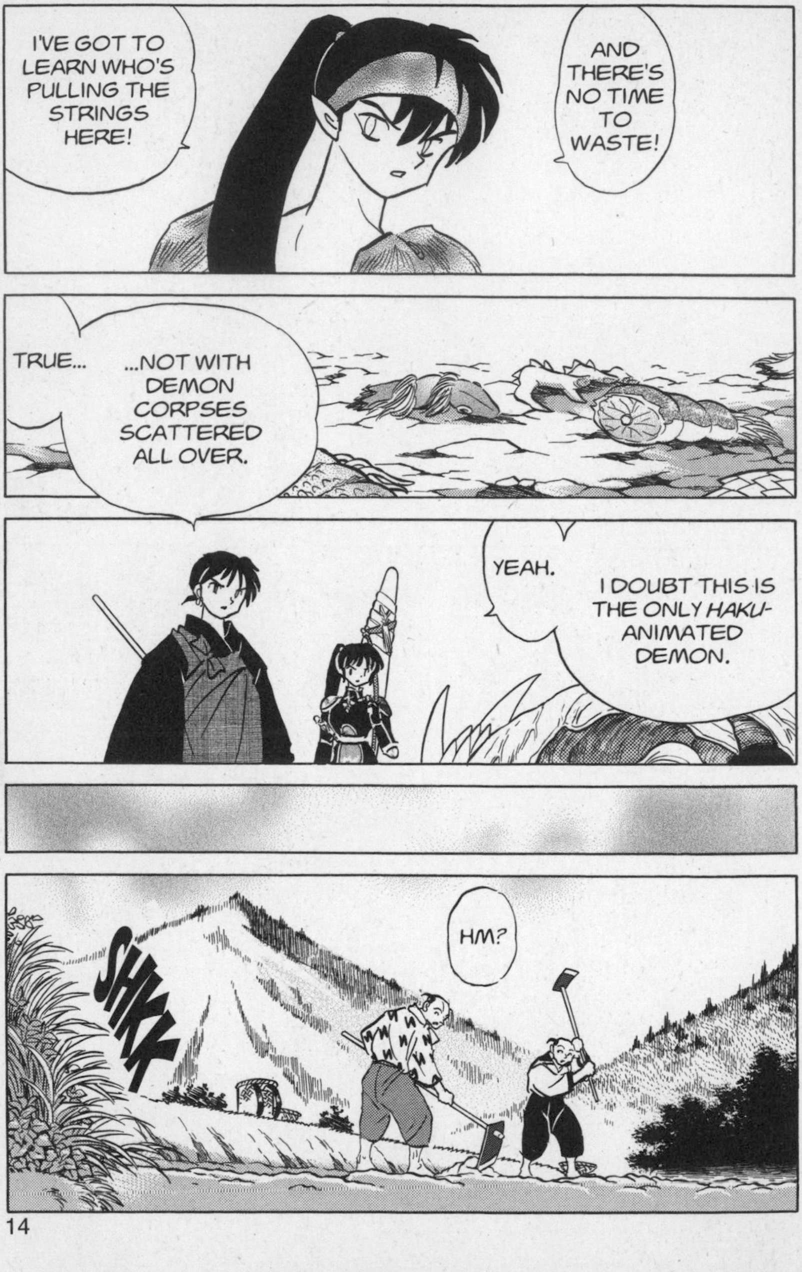
I'VE GOT TO LEARN WHO'S PULLING THE STRINGS HERE!
AND THERE'S NO TIME TO WASTE!
TRUE...
...NOT WITH DEMON CORPSES SCATTERED ALL OVER.
YEAH.
I DOUBT THIS IS THE ONLY *HAKU*-ANIMATED DEMON.
SHKK
HM?

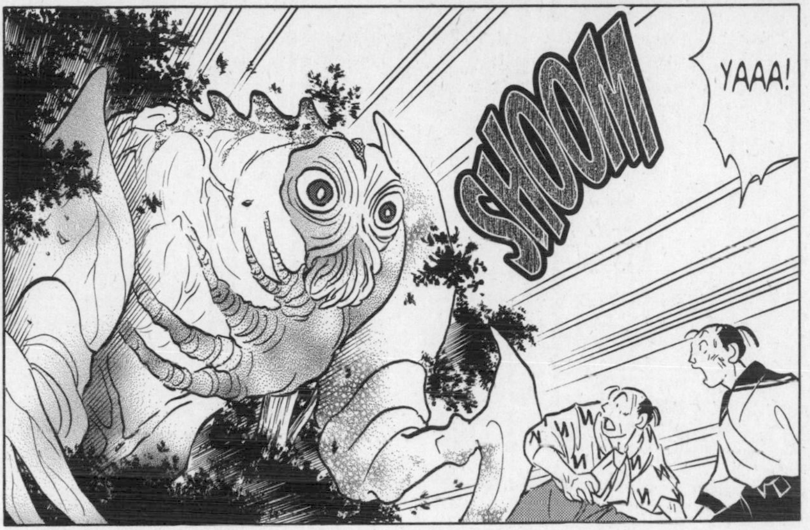
SHOOM
YAAA!

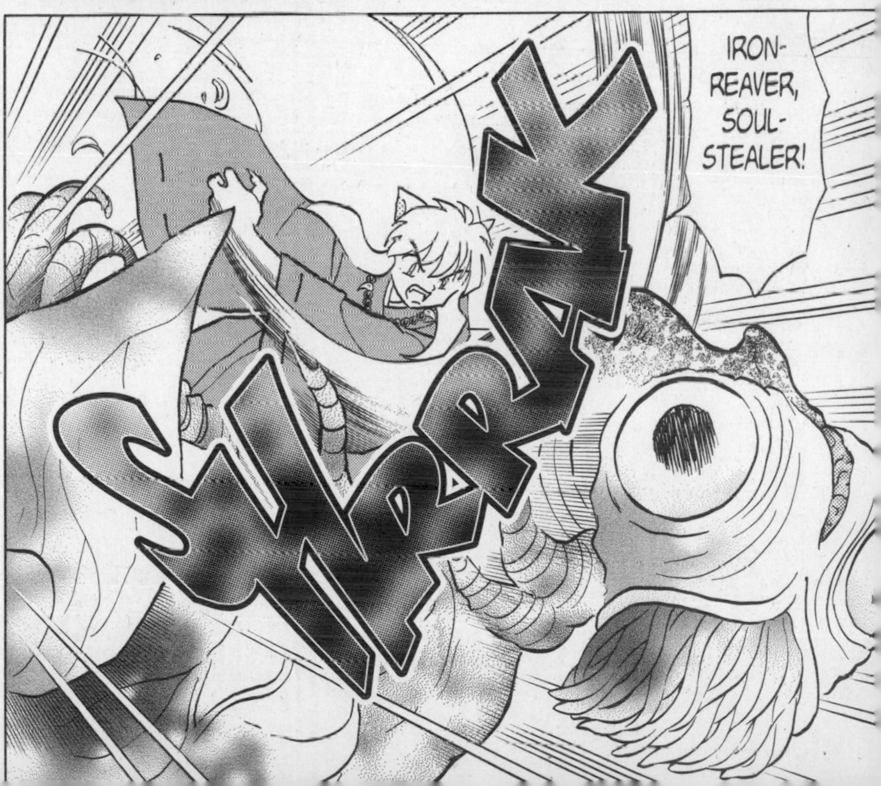
IRON-REAVER, SOUL-STEALER!
SHRRAK

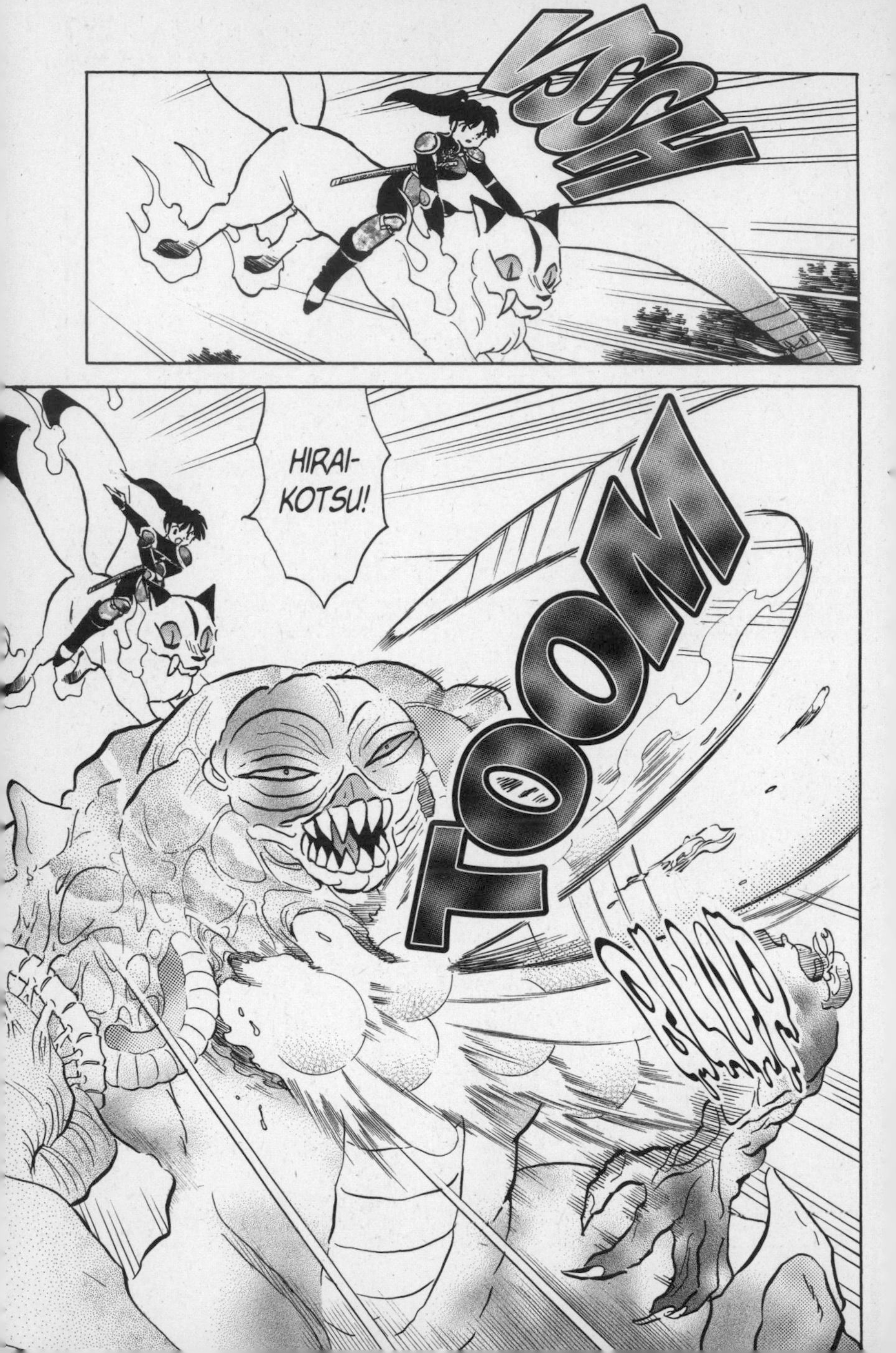
VASH
HIRAI-KOTSU!
TOOOM

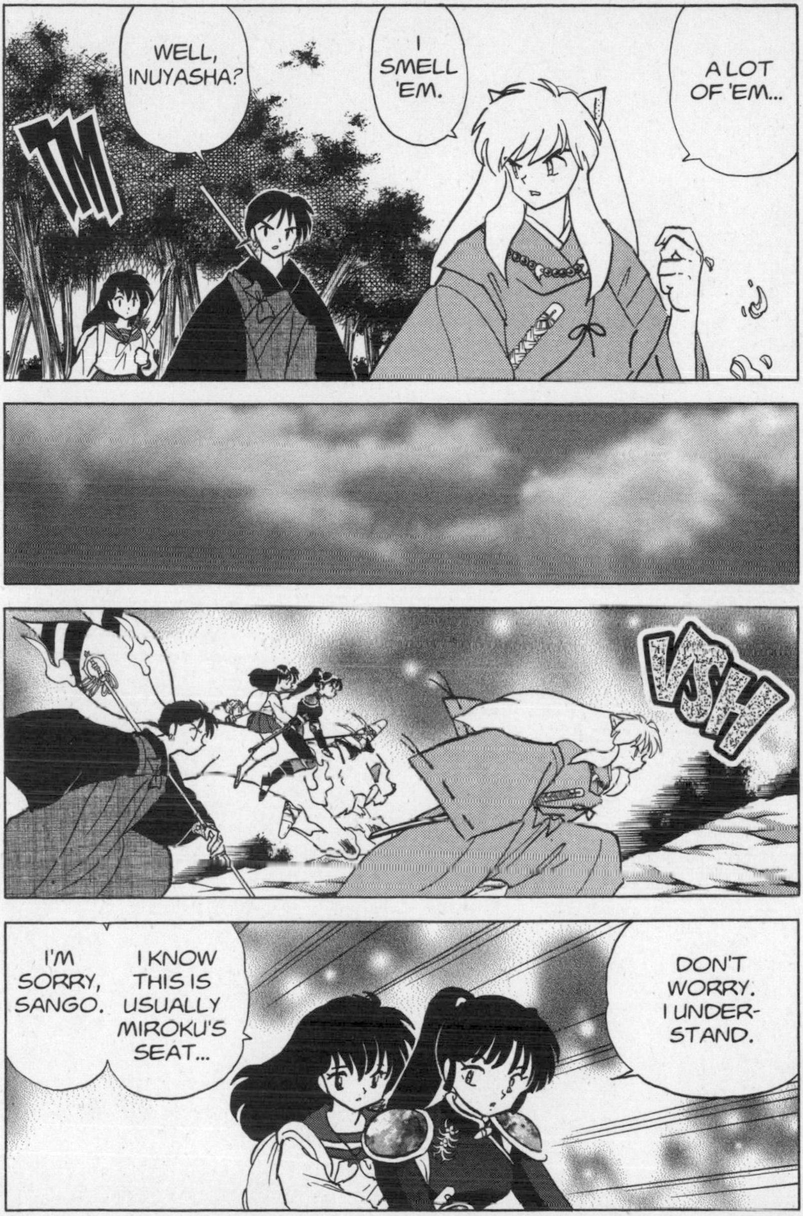
WELL, INUYASHA?
TM
I SMELL 'EM.
A LOT OF 'EM...
VSH
I'M SORRY, SANGO.
I KNOW THIS IS USUALLY MIROKU'S SEAT...
DON'T WORRY. I UNDER-STAND.

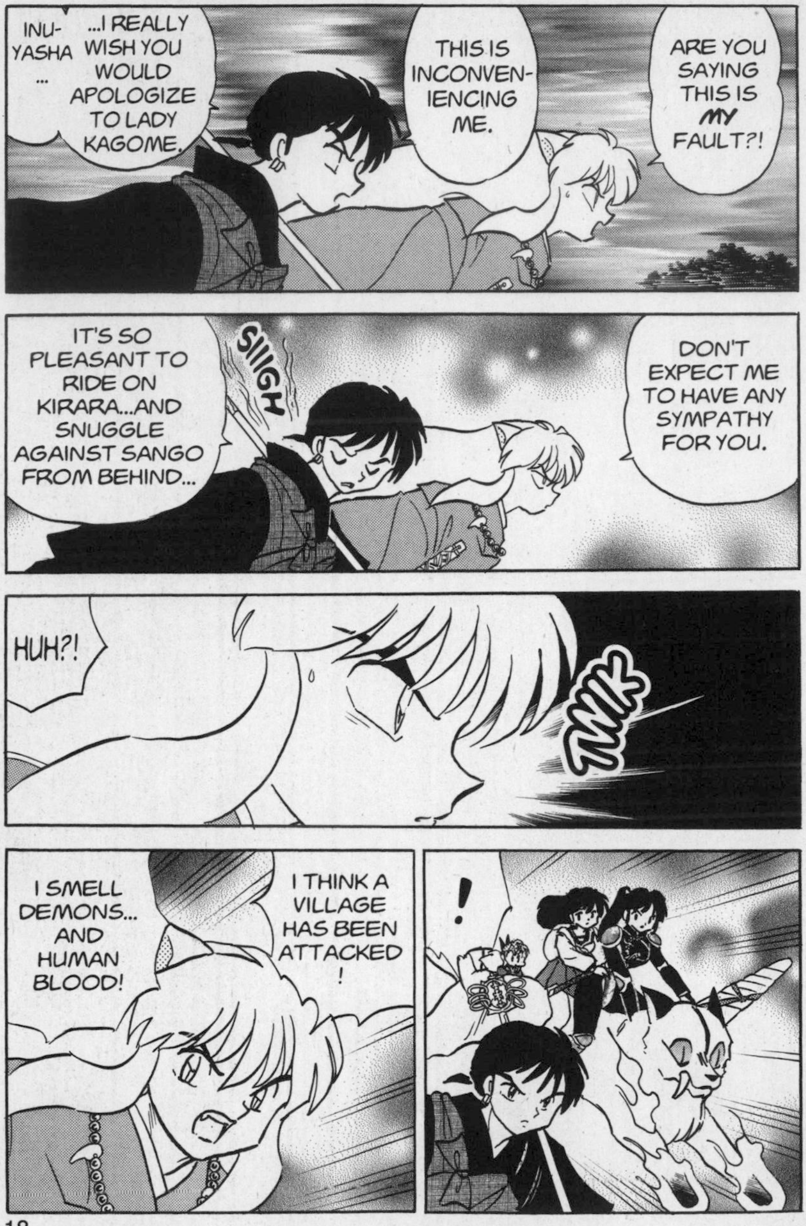
INU-YASHA ...
...I REALLY WISH YOU WOULD APOLOGIZE TO LADY KAGOME.
THIS IS INCONVEN-IENCING ME.
ARE YOU SAYING THIS IS MY FAULT?!
IT'S SO PLEASANT TO RIDE ON KIRARA...AND SNUGGLE AGAINST SANGO FROM BEHIND...
SIIIGH
DON'T EXPECT ME TO HAVE ANY SYMPATHY FOR YOU.
HUH?!
TWIK
I SMELL DEMONS... AND HUMAN BLOOD!
I THINK A VILLAGE HAS BEEN ATTACKED!
!

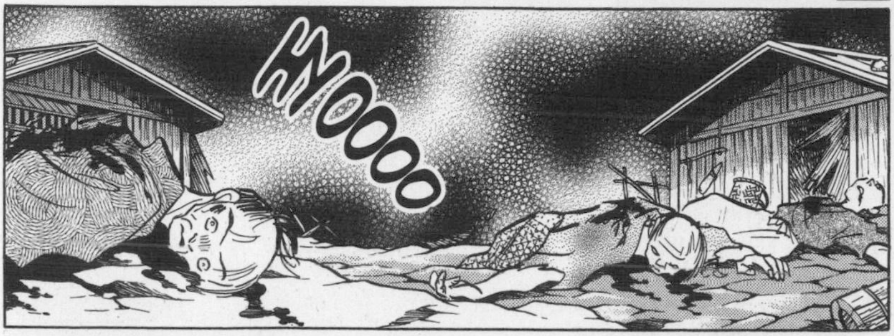
HYOOOO

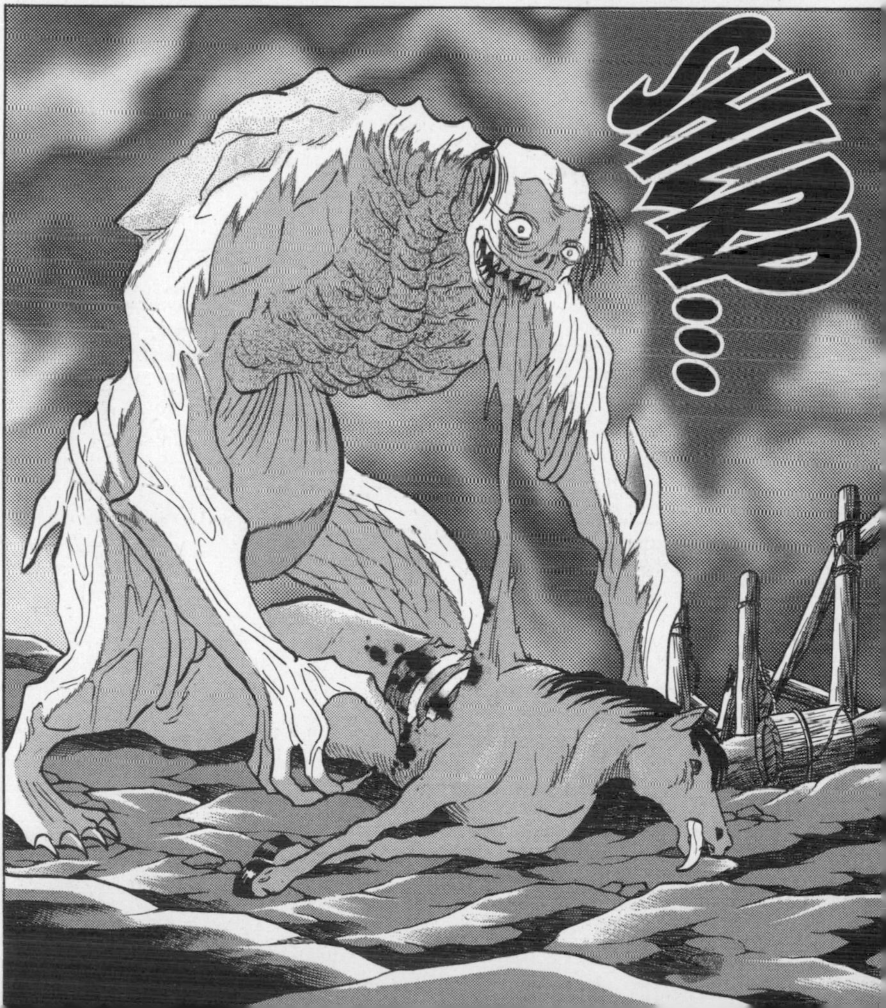
SHRP...

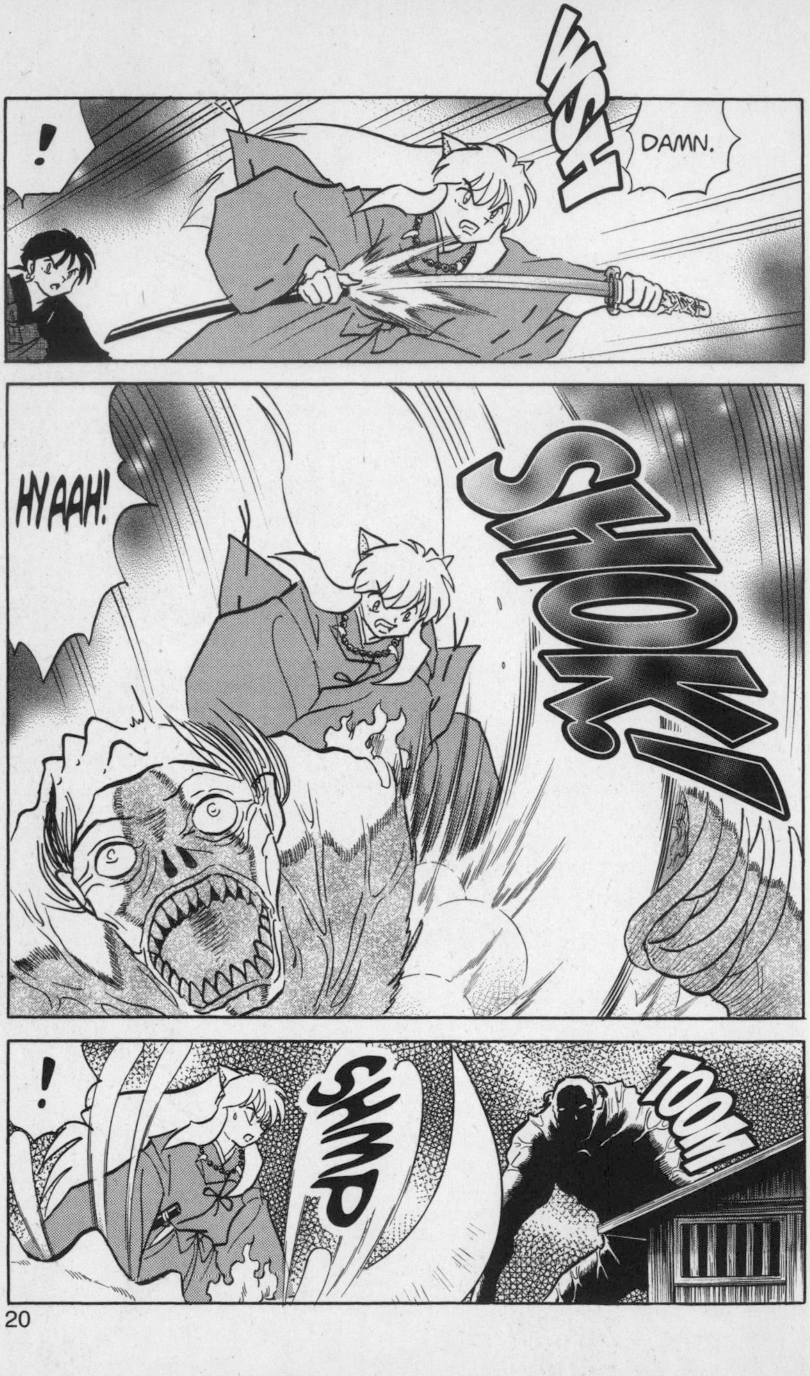
!
WSH
DAMN.
HYAAH!
SHOK!
!
SHMP
TOOM

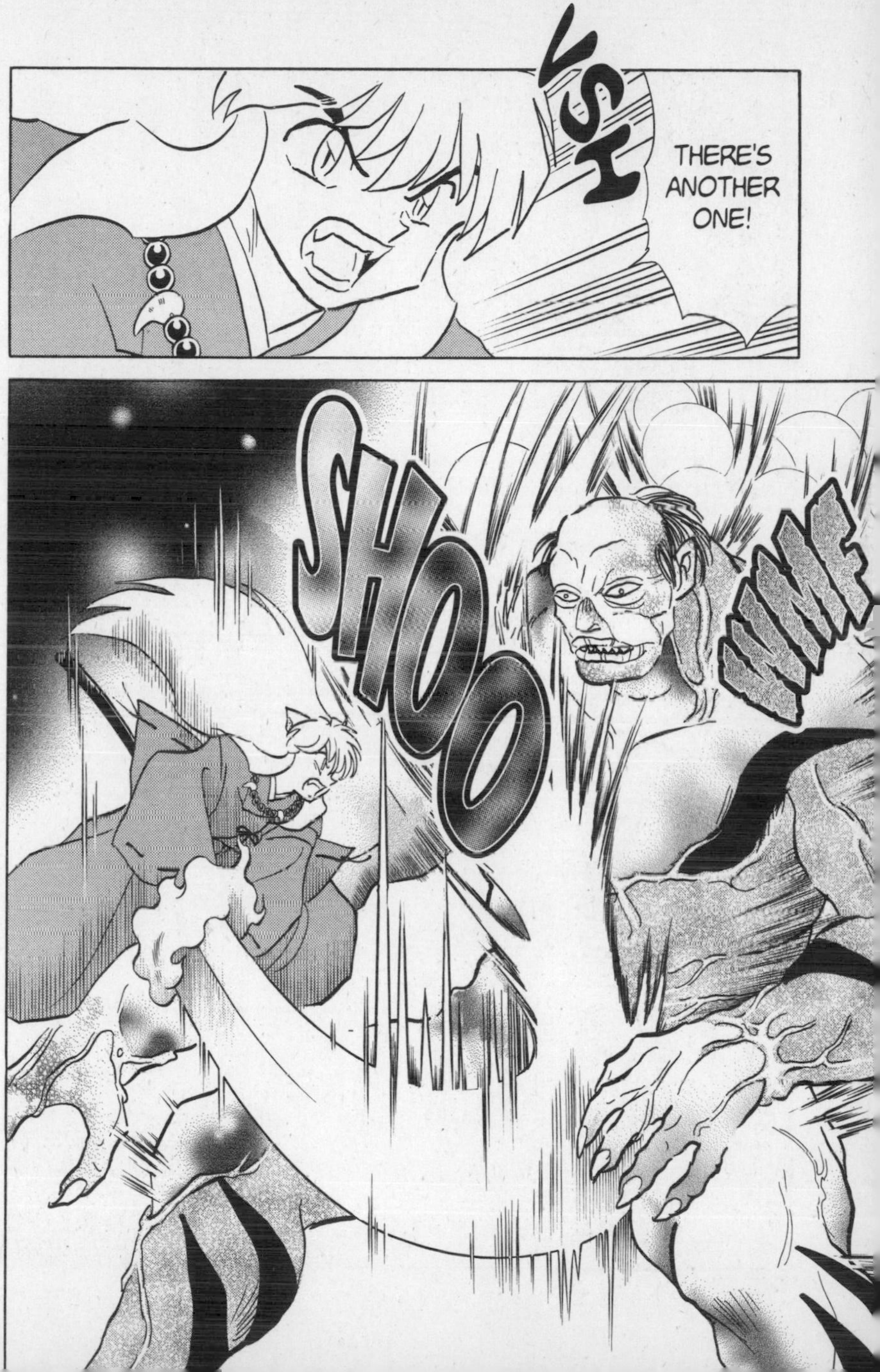
VSH
THERE'S ANOTHER ONE!
SHOOO
WMF

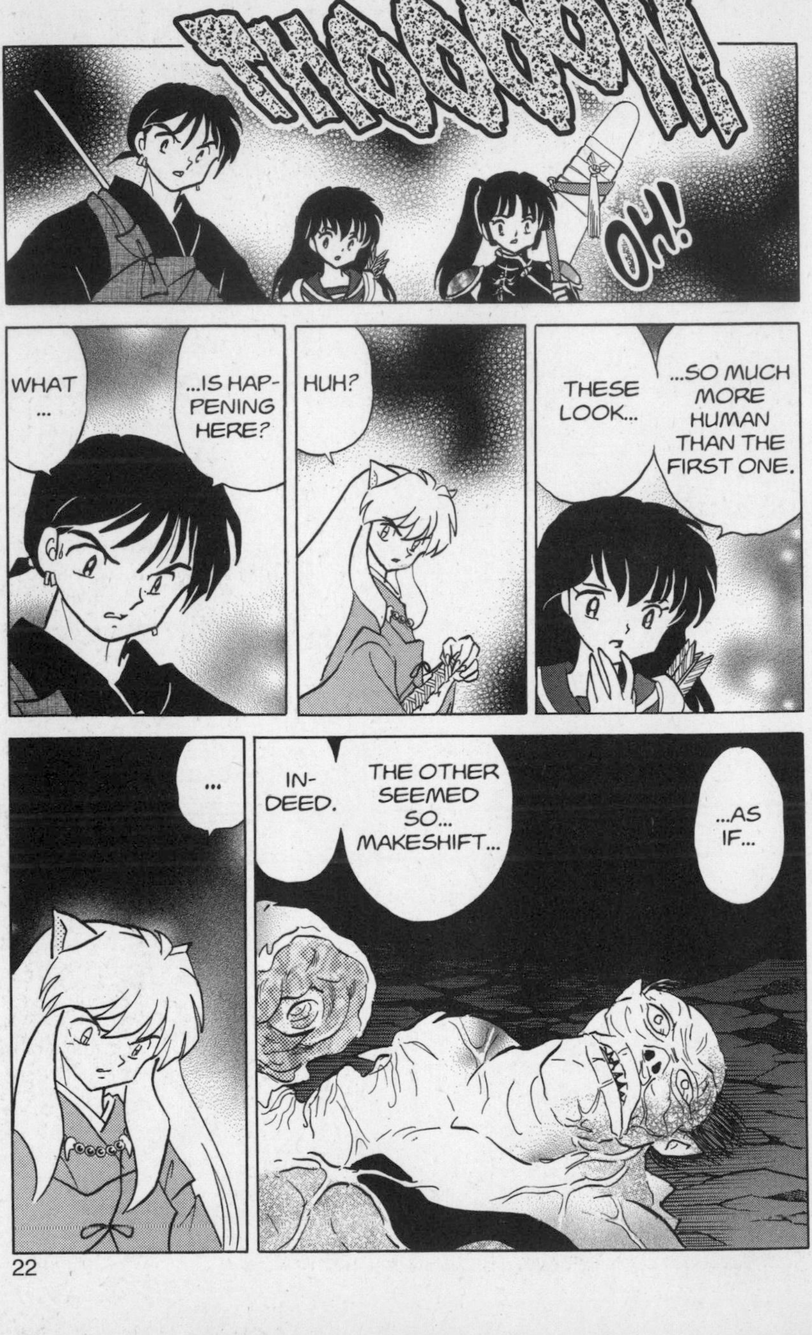
THOOOOM
OH!
WHAT ...
...IS HAPPENING HERE?
HUH?
THESE LOOK...
...SO MUCH MORE HUMAN THAN THE FIRST ONE.
...
INDEED.
THE OTHER SEEMED SO... MAKESHIFT...
...AS IF...

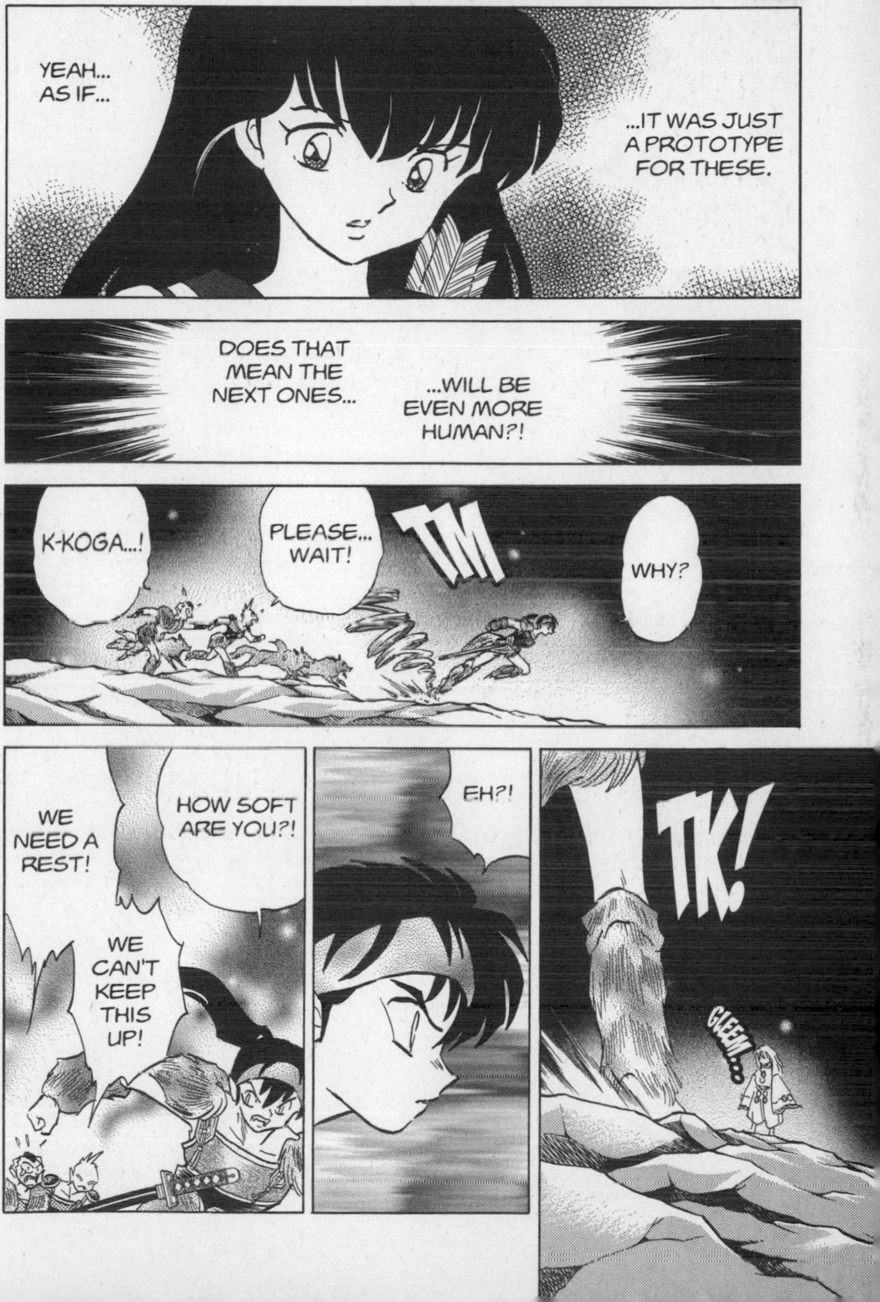
YEAH... AS IF...
...IT WAS JUST A PROTOTYPE FOR THESE.
DOES THAT MEAN THE NEXT ONES...
...WILL BE EVEN MORE HUMAN?!
K-KOGA...!
PLEASE... WAIT!
TM
WHY?
WE NEED A REST!
HOW SOFT ARE YOU?!
WE CAN'T KEEP THIS UP!
EH?!
TK!
GLEEM...

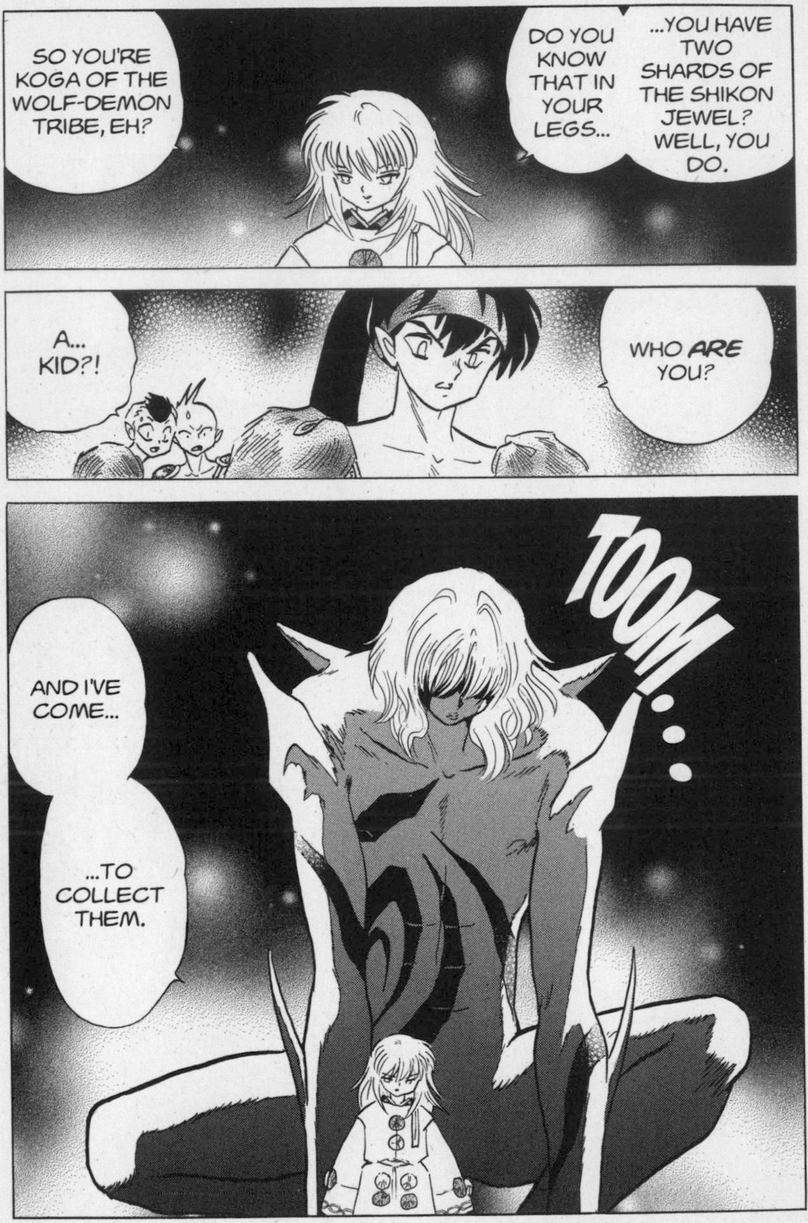
SO YOU'RE KOGA OF THE WOLF-DEMON TRIBE, EH?
DO YOU KNOW THAT IN YOUR LEGS...
...YOU HAVE TWO SHARDS OF THE SHIKON JEWEL? WELL, YOU DO.
A... KID?!
WHO ARE YOU?
AND I'VE COME...
...TO COLLECT THEM.
TOOM...

SCROLL 2
MORYOMARU

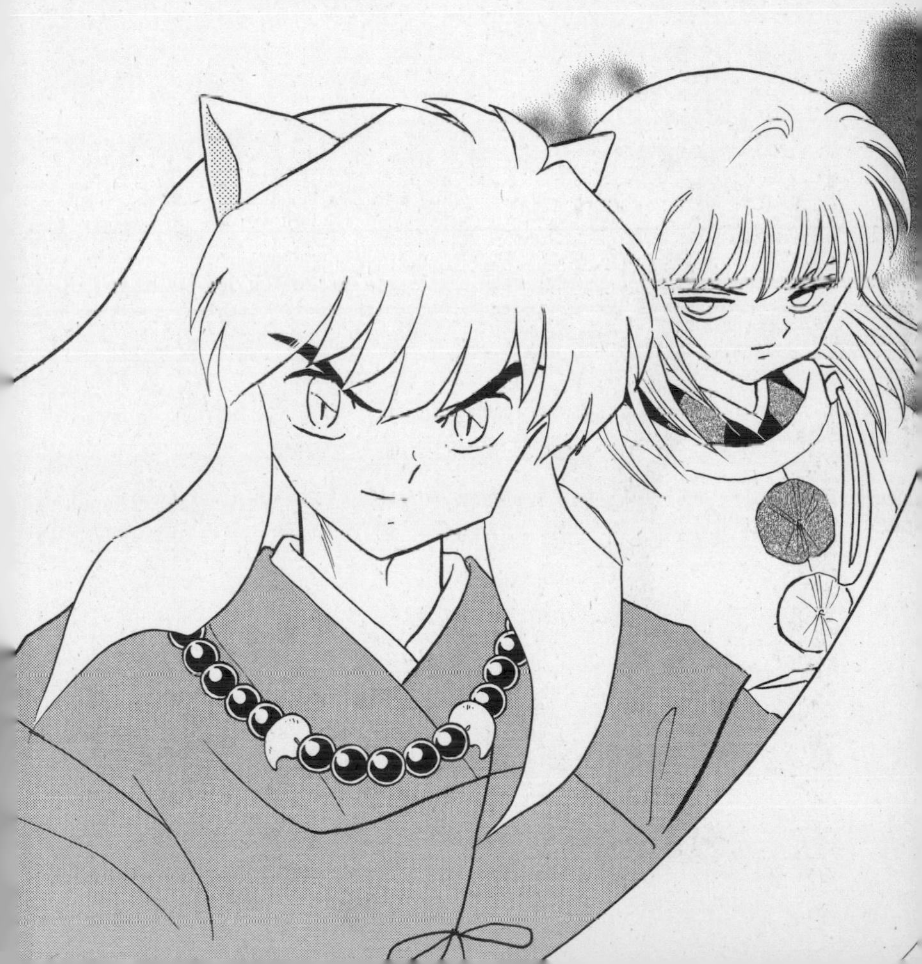

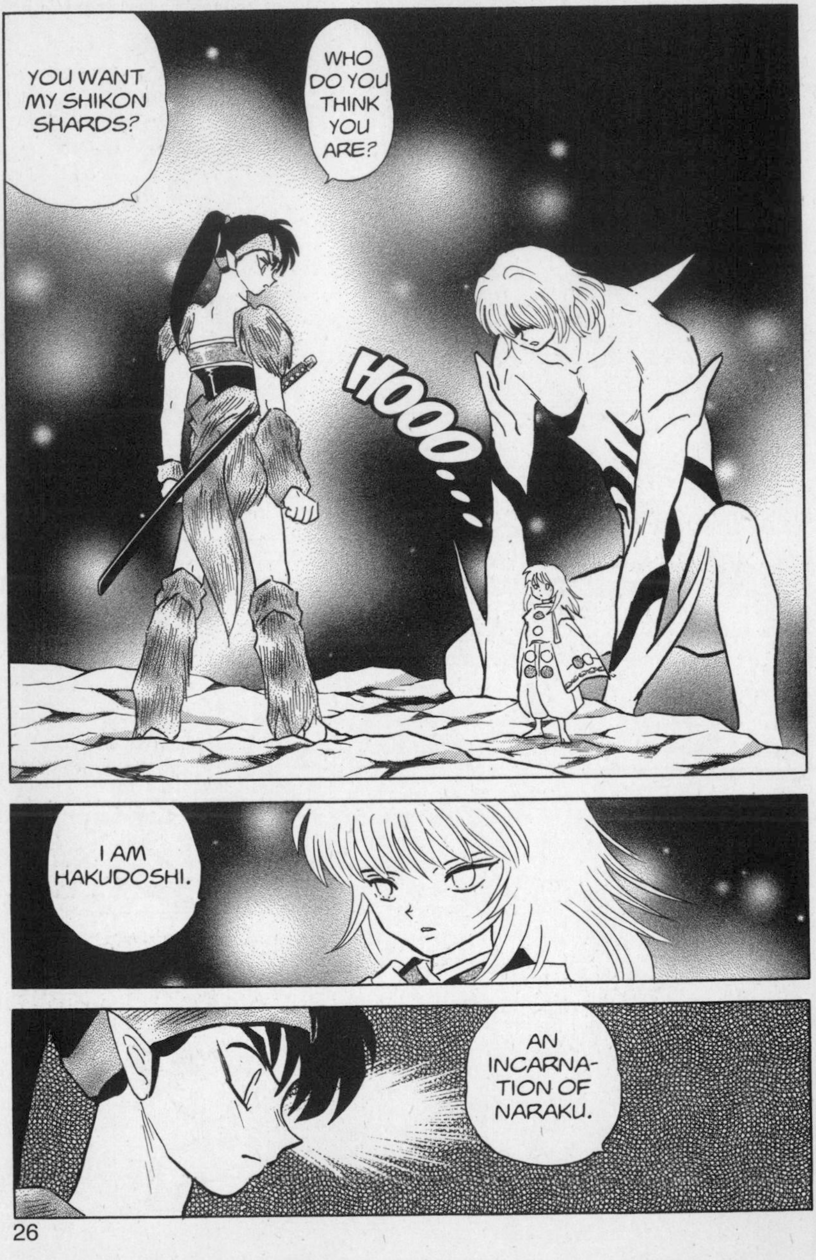
YOU WANT MY SHIKON SHARDS?
WHO DO YOU THINK YOU ARE?
HOOO...
I AM HAKUDOSHI.
AN INCARNATION OF NARAKU.

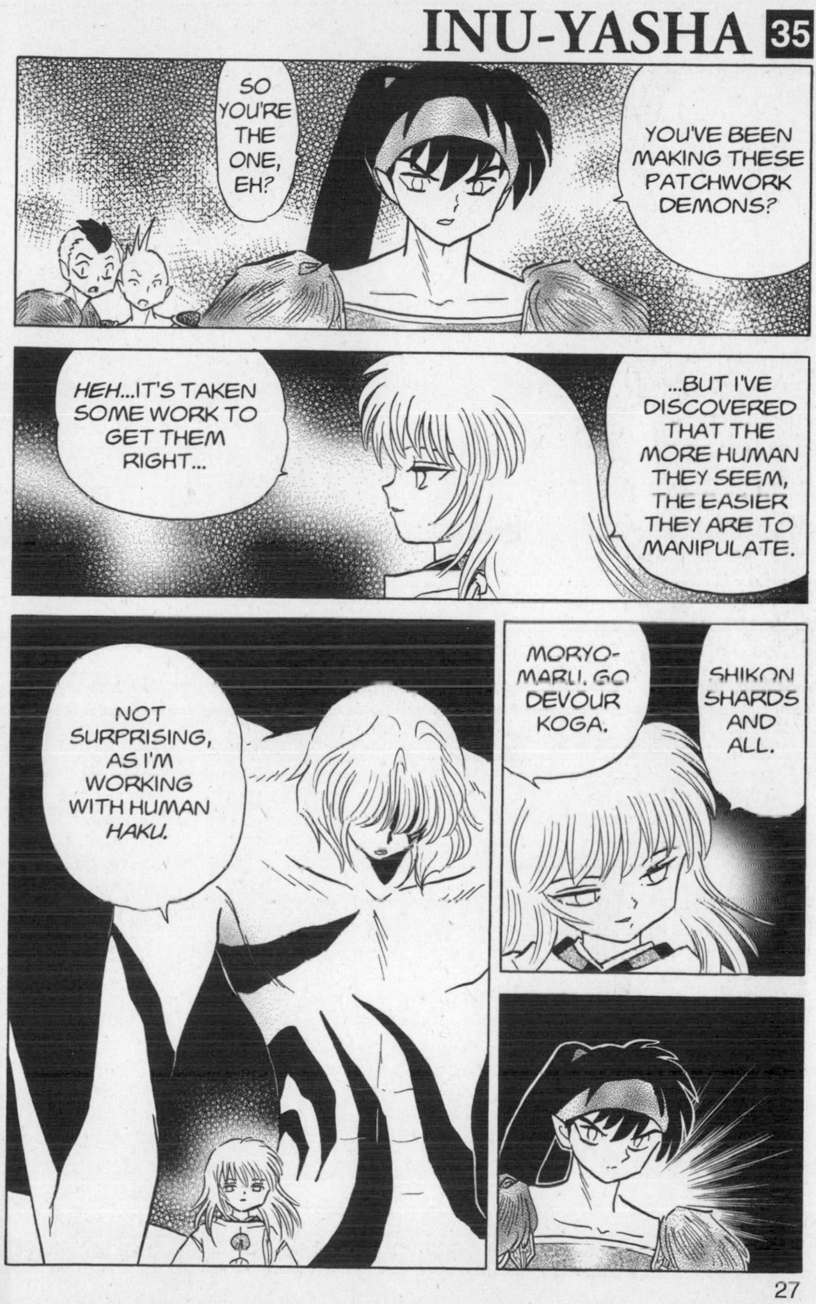
SO YOU'RE THE ONE, EH?
YOU'VE BEEN MAKING THESE PATCHWORK DEMONS?
HEH...IT'S TAKEN SOME WORK TO GET THEM RIGHT...
...BUT I'VE DISCOVERED THAT THE MORE HUMAN THEY SEEM, THE EASIER THEY ARE TO MANIPULATE.
NOT SURPRISING, AS I'M WORKING WITH HUMAN HAKU.
MORYO-MARU, GO DEVOUR KOGA.
SHIKON SHARDS AND ALL.

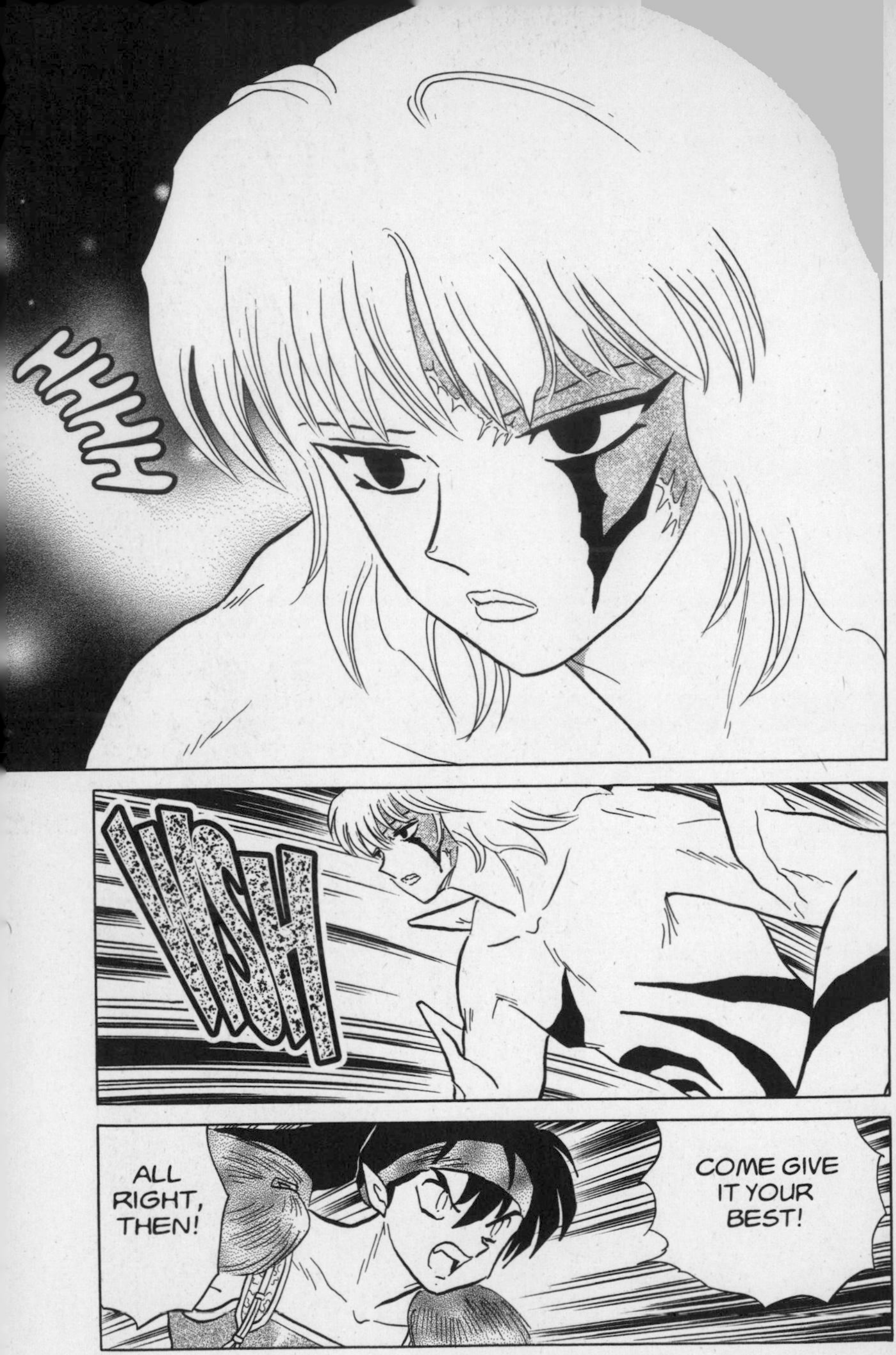
HHHH
WSH
ALL RIGHT, THEN!
COME GIVE IT YOUR BEST!

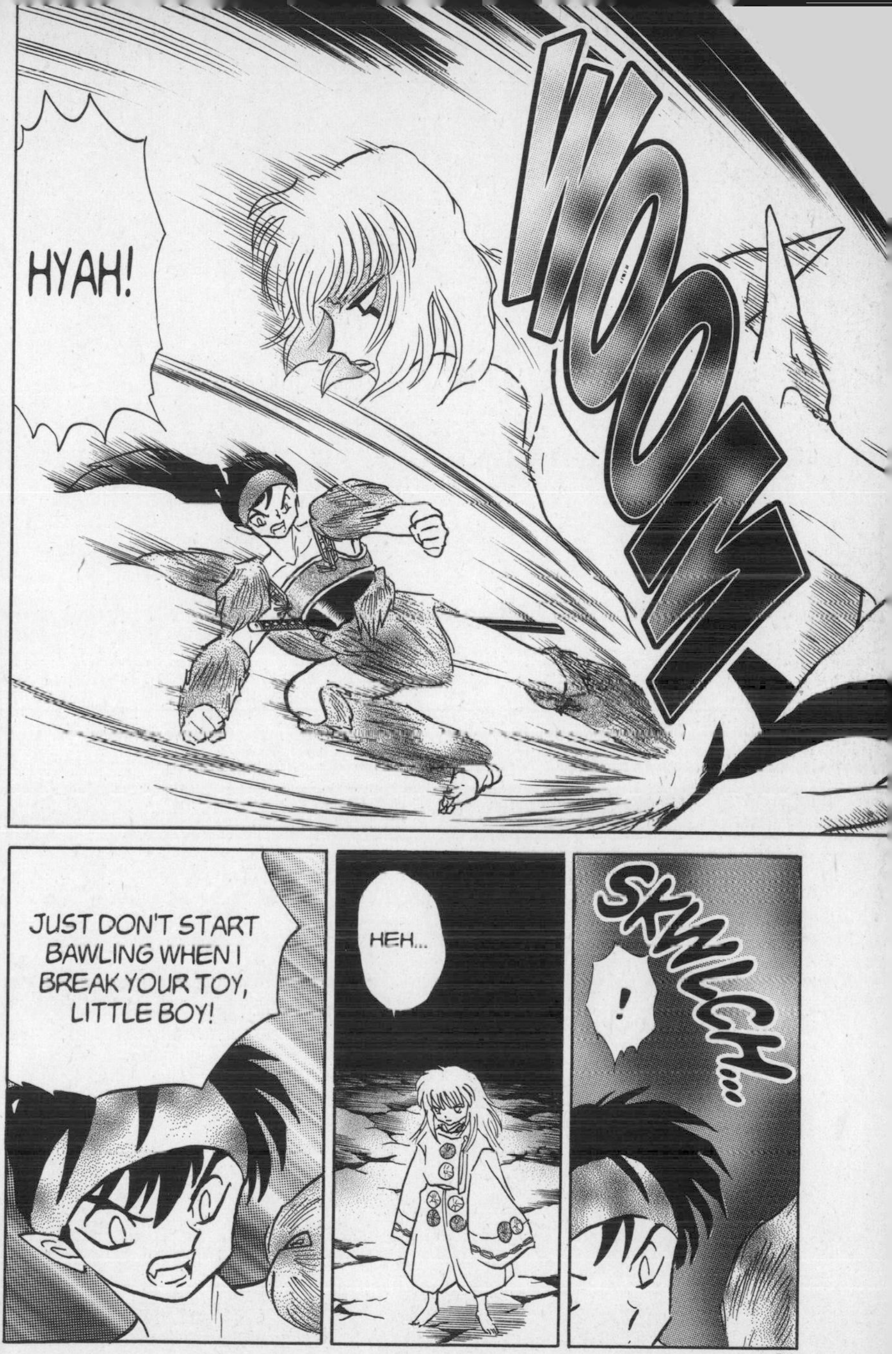
HYAH!
WHOOSH!
JUST DON'T START BAWLING WHEN I BREAK YOUR TOY, LITTLE BOY!
HEH...
!
SKWLCH...

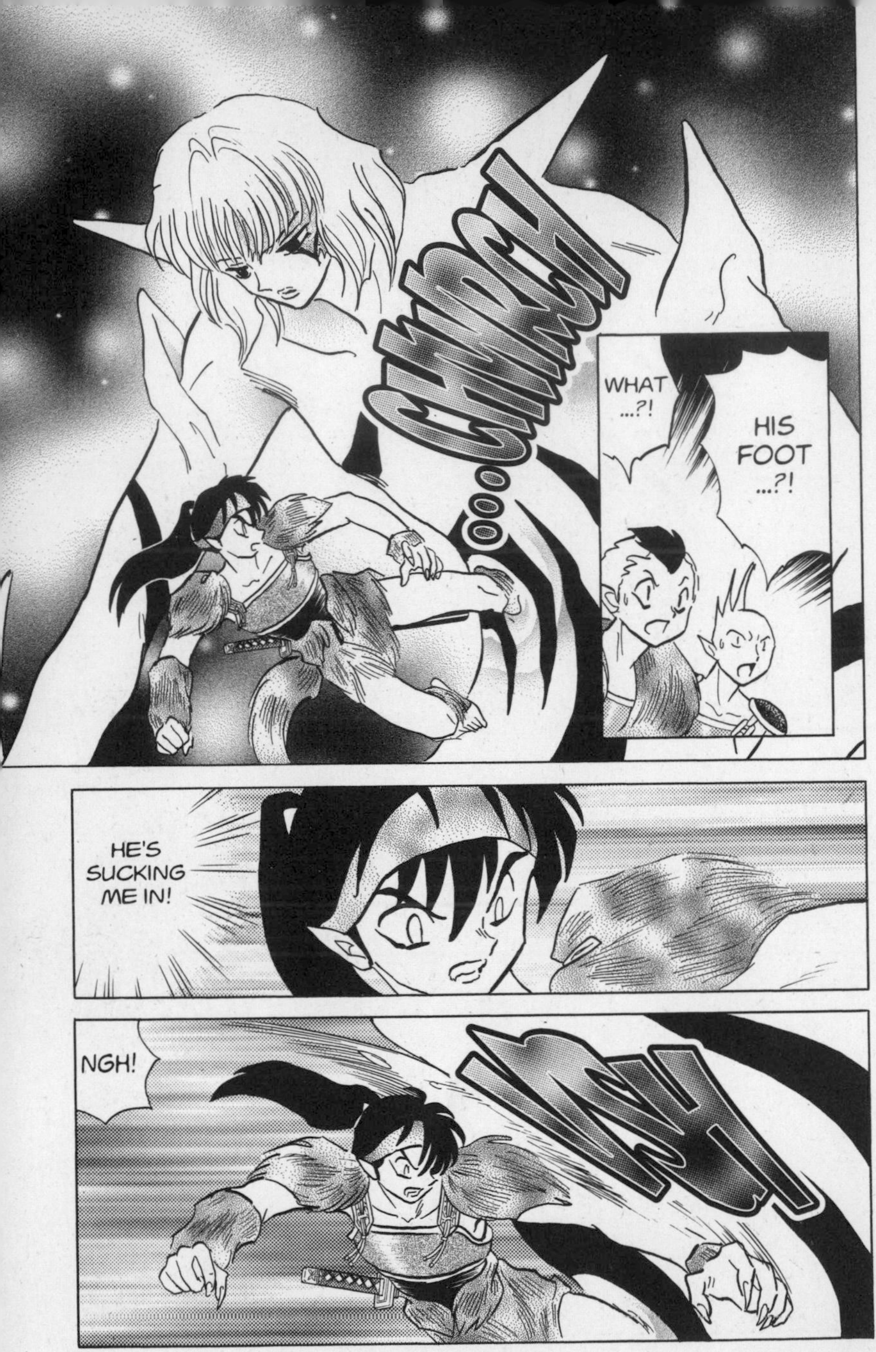
WHAT ...?!
HIS FOOT ...?!
HE'S SUCKING ME IN!
NGH!

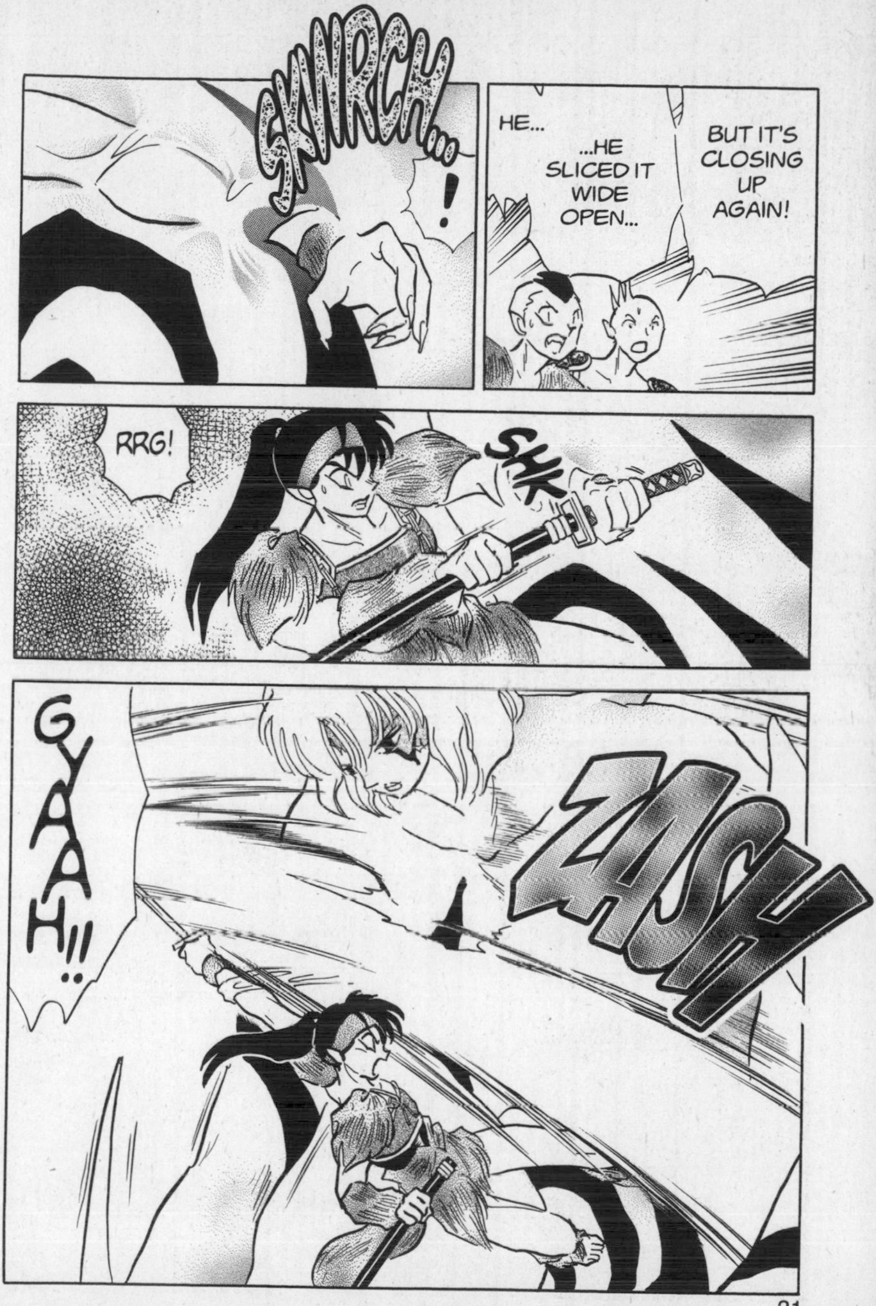
SKWRCH...
!
HE...
...HE SLICED IT WIDE OPEN...
BUT IT'S CLOSING UP AGAIN!
RRG!
SHK
GYAAAH!!
ZASH

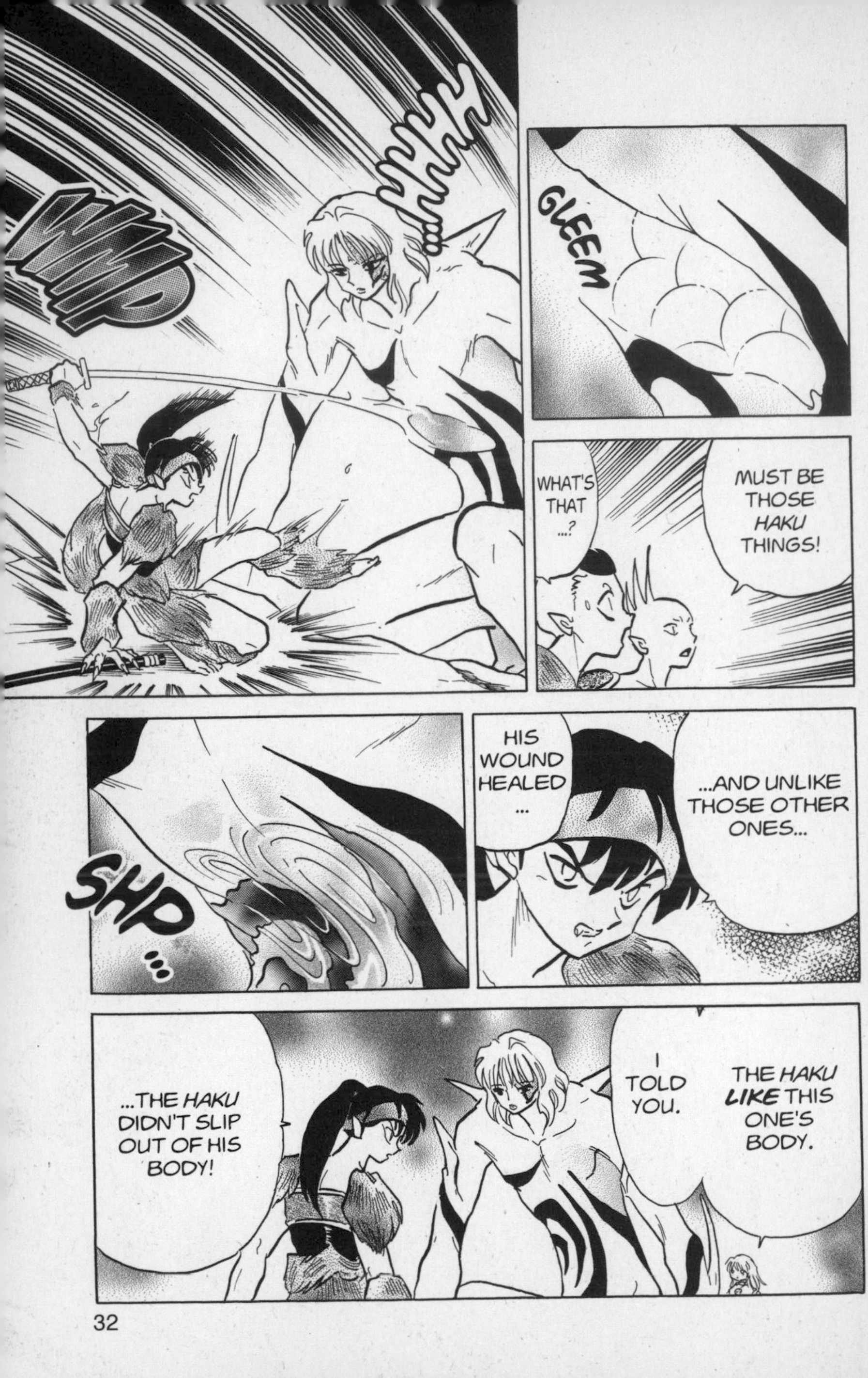
WMP
THUNK...
GLEEM
WHAT'S THAT ...?
MUST BE THOSE HAKU THINGS!
SHP...
HIS WOUND HEALED ...
...AND UNLIKE THOSE OTHER ONES...
...THE HAKU DIDN'T SLIP OUT OF HIS BODY!
I TOLD YOU.
THE HAKU LIKE THIS ONE'S BODY.

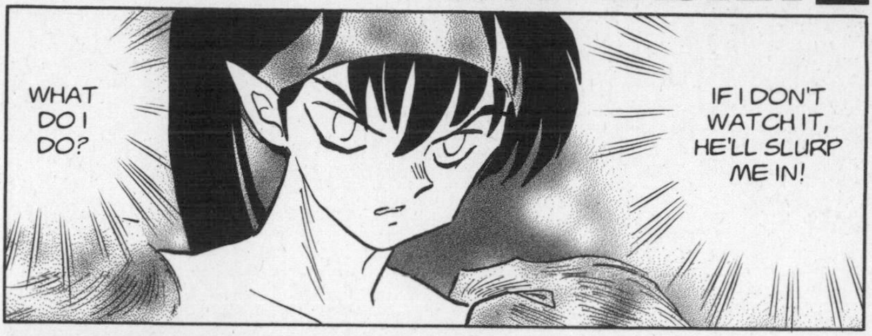
WHAT DO I DO?
IF I DON'T WATCH IT, HE'LL SLURP ME IN!

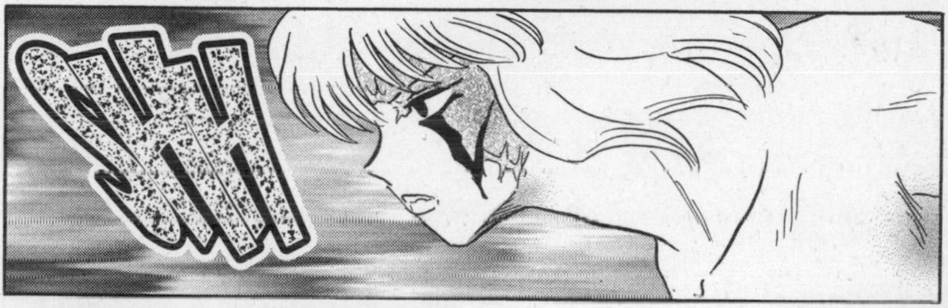
SHH

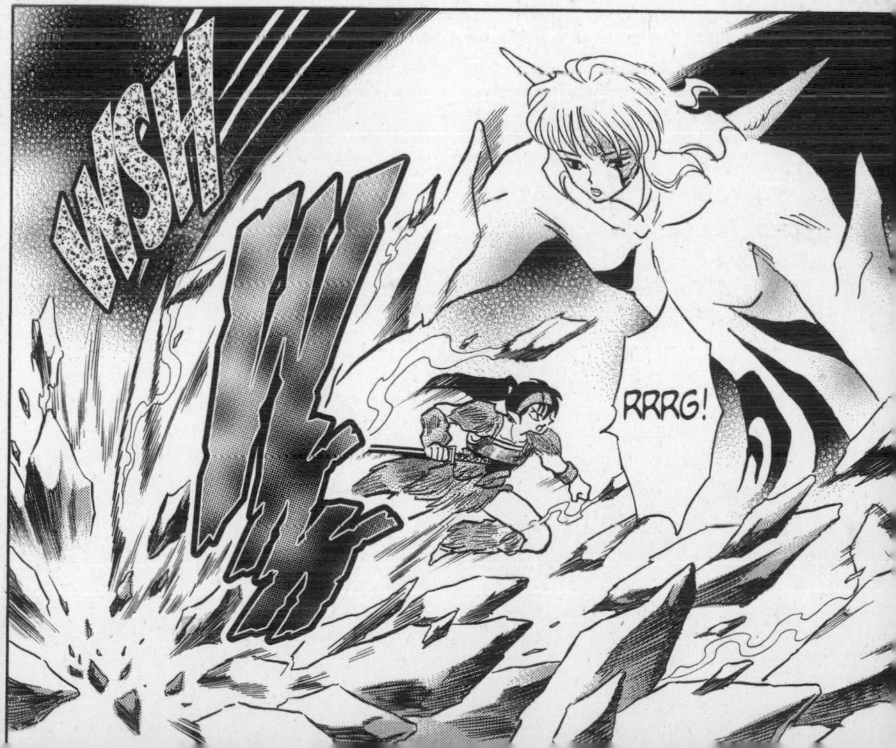
WSH
RRRG!

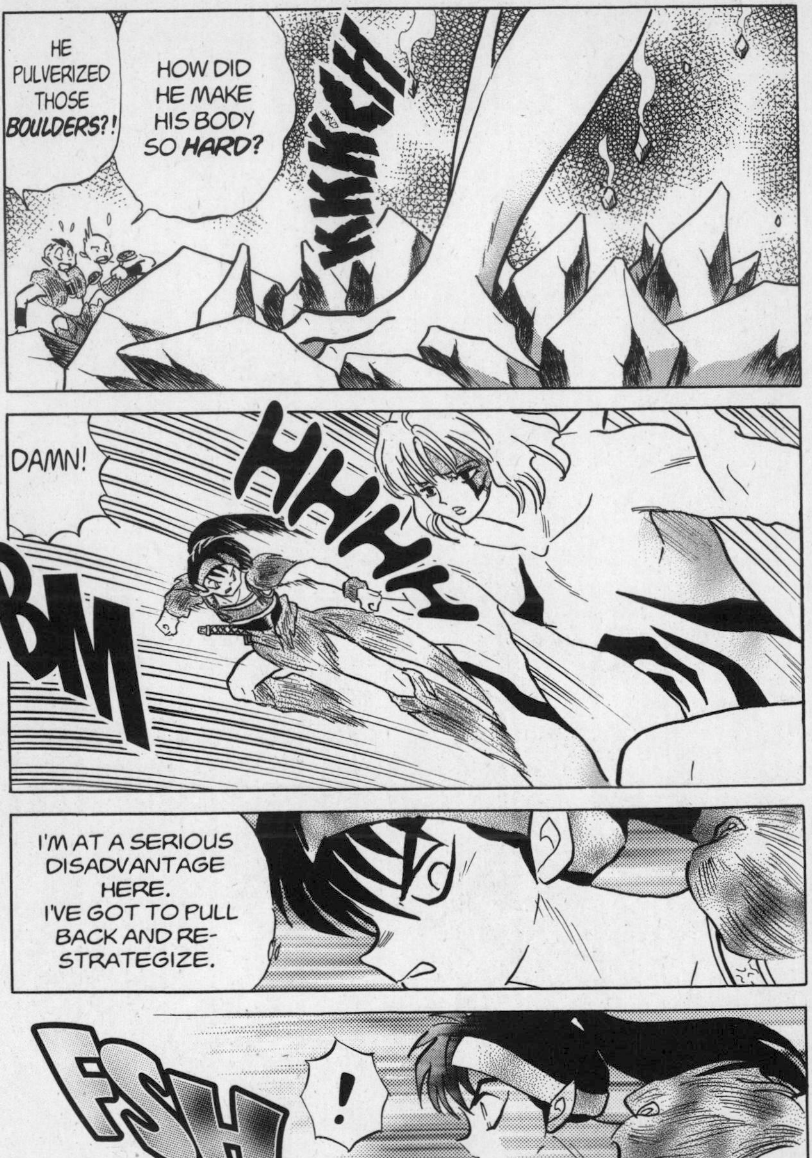
HE PULVERIZED THOSE BOULDERS?!
HOW DID HE MAKE HIS BODY SO HARD?
KKKKCH
DAMN!
BM
HHHH
I'M AT A SERIOUS DISADVANTAGE HERE. I'VE GOT TO PULL BACK AND RE-STRATEGIZE.
FSH
!

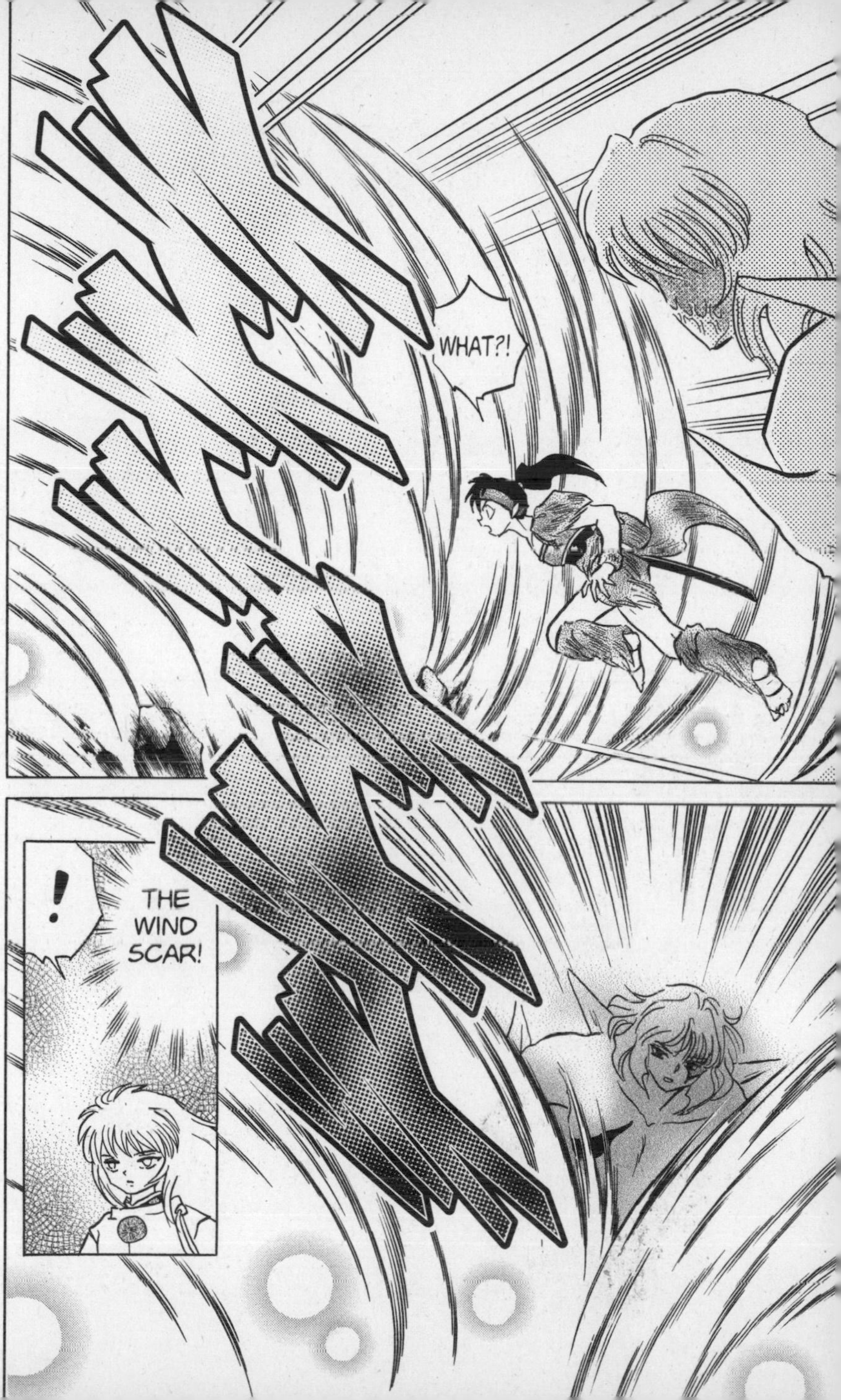
WHAT?!
!
THE WIND SCAR!

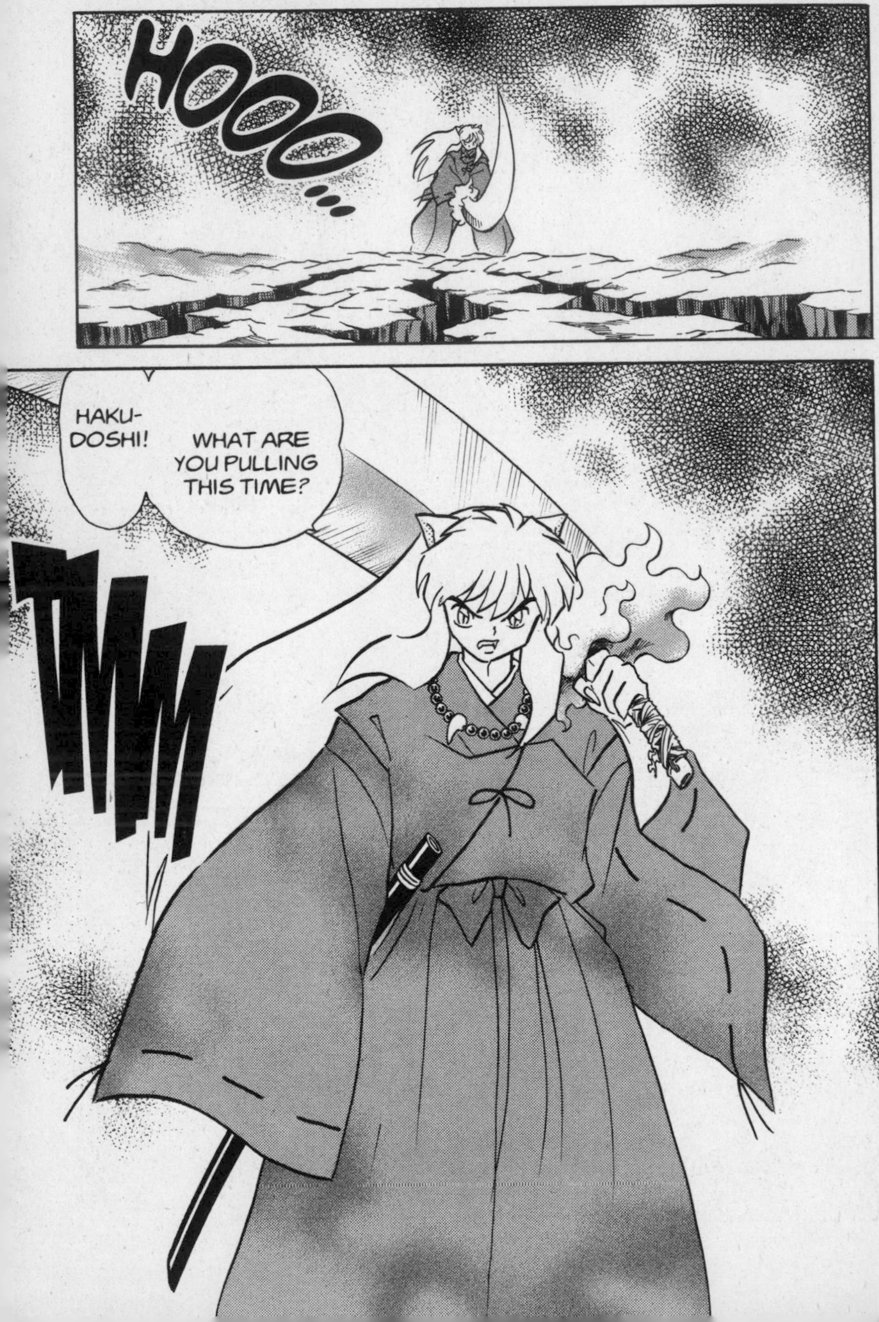
HOOO...
HAKU-DOSHI!
WHAT ARE YOU PULLING THIS TIME?
TMMM

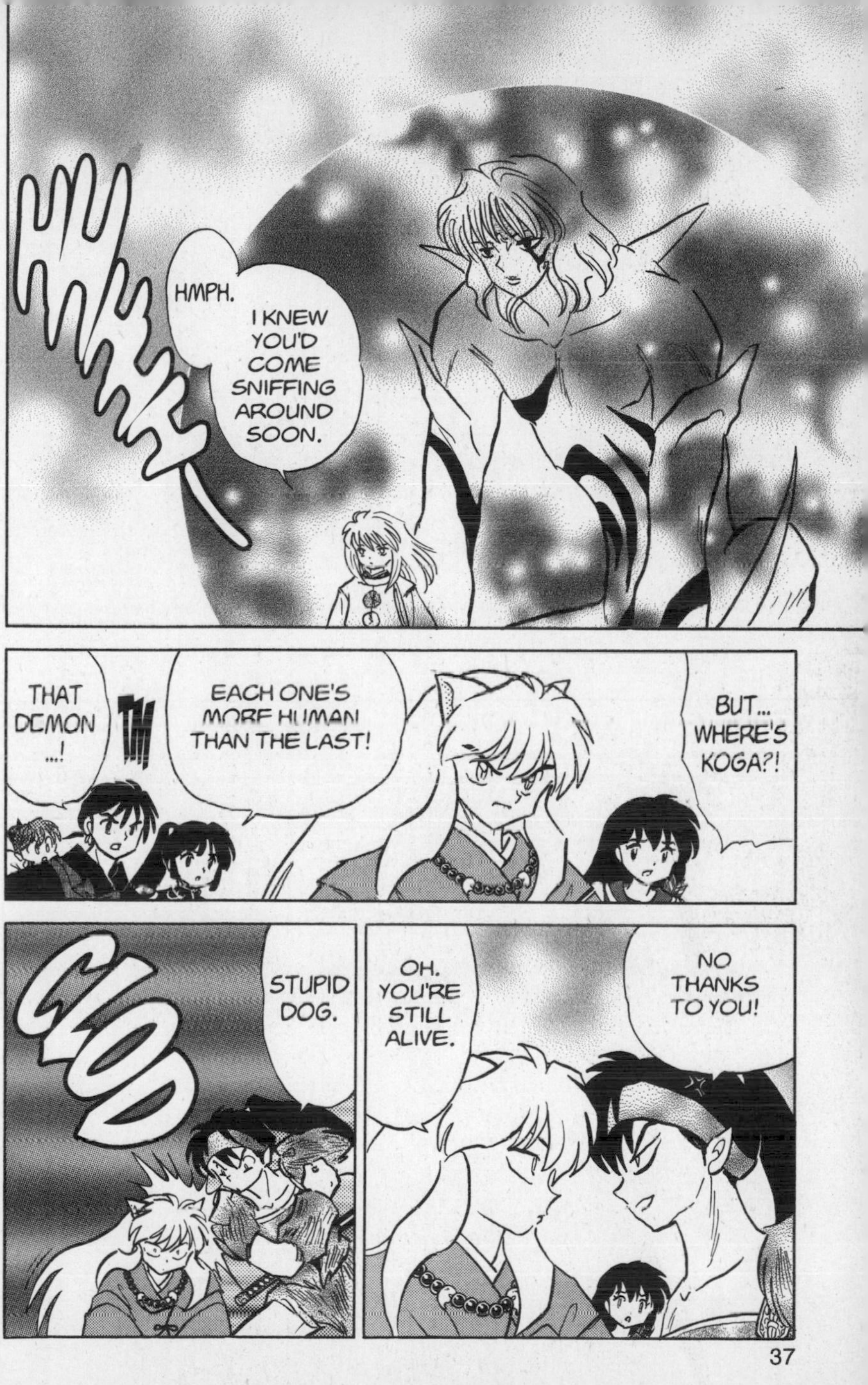
HMPH.
I KNEW YOU'D COME SNIFFING AROUND SOON.
THAT DEMON ...!
EACH ONE'S MORE HUMAN THAN THE LAST!
BUT... WHERE'S KOGA?!
CLOD
STUPID DOG.
OH. YOU'RE STILL ALIVE.
NO THANKS TO YOU!

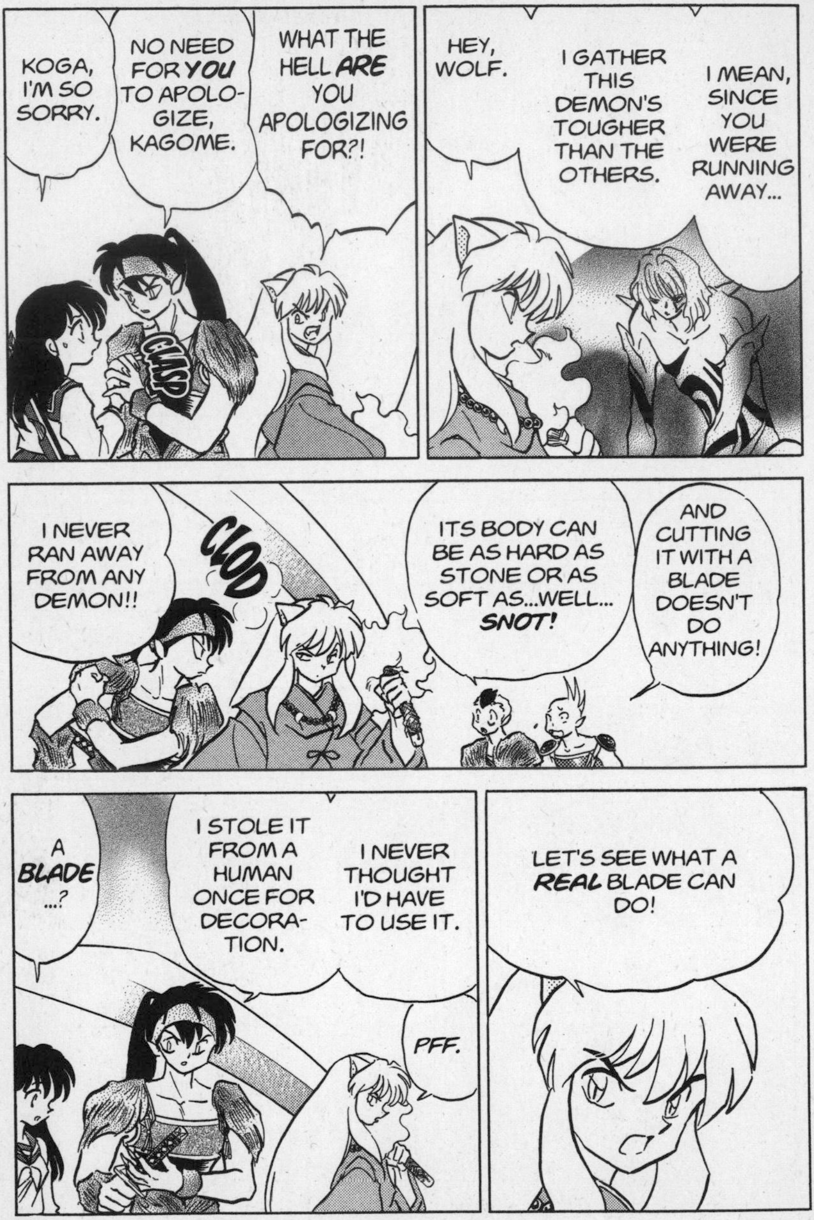
KOGA, I'M SO SORRY.
NO NEED FOR **YOU** TO APOLOGIZE, KAGOME.
GLASP
WHAT THE HELL **ARE** YOU APOLOGIZING FOR?!
HEY, WOLF.
I GATHER THIS DEMON'S TOUGHER THAN THE OTHERS.
I MEAN, SINCE YOU WERE RUNNING AWAY...
I NEVER RAN AWAY FROM ANY DEMON!!
CLOD
ITS BODY CAN BE AS HARD AS STONE OR AS SOFT AS...WELL... **SNOT!**
AND CUTTING IT WITH A BLADE DOESN'T DO ANYTHING!
A **BLADE** ...?
I STOLE IT FROM A HUMAN ONCE FOR DECORATION.
I NEVER THOUGHT I'D HAVE TO USE IT.
PFF.
LET'S SEE WHAT A **REAL** BLADE CAN DO!

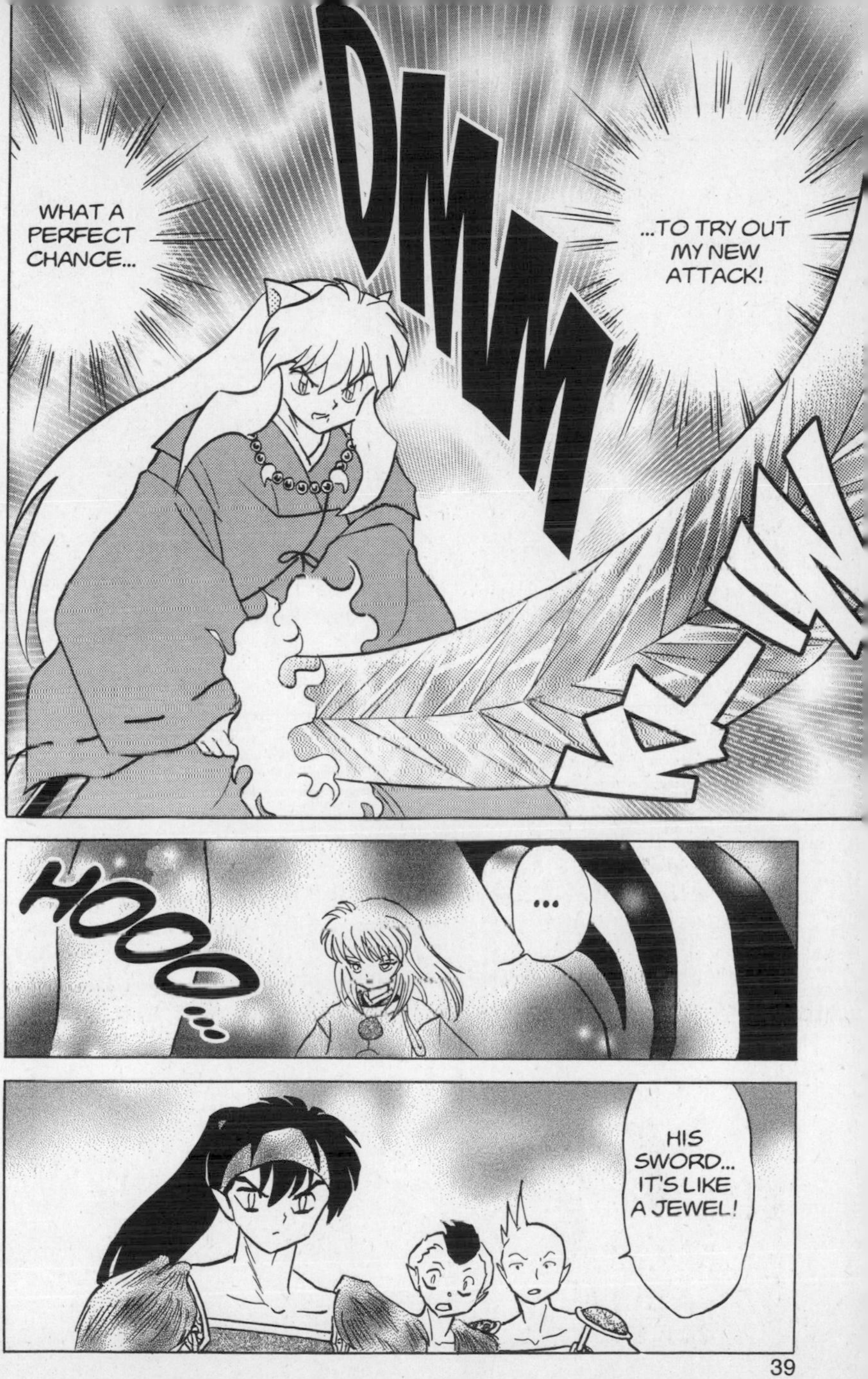
WHAT A PERFECT CHANCE...
DMM
...TO TRY OUT MY NEW ATTACK!
KRIIN
HOOO...
...
HIS SWORD... IT'S LIKE A JEWEL!

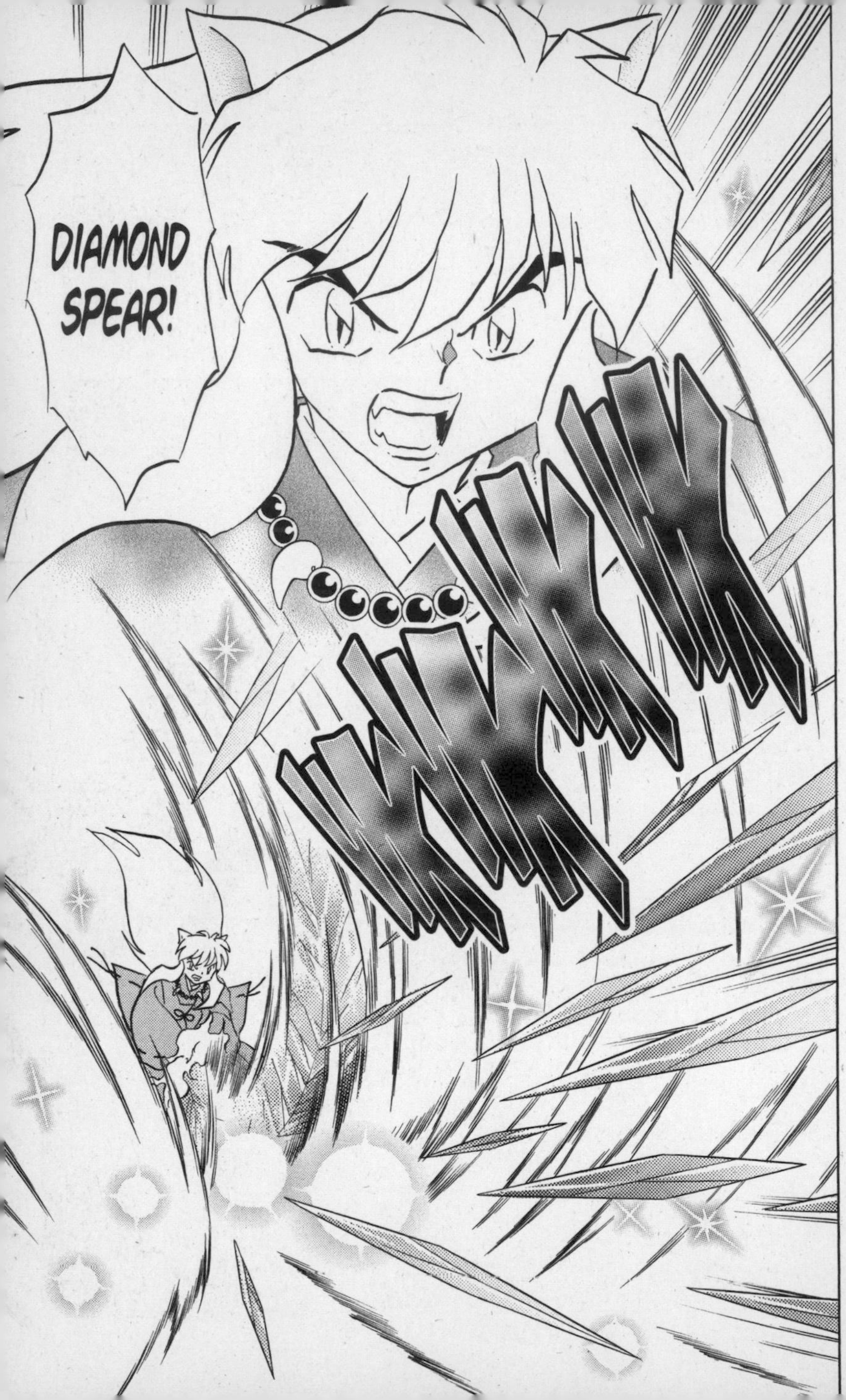
DIAMOND SPEAR!

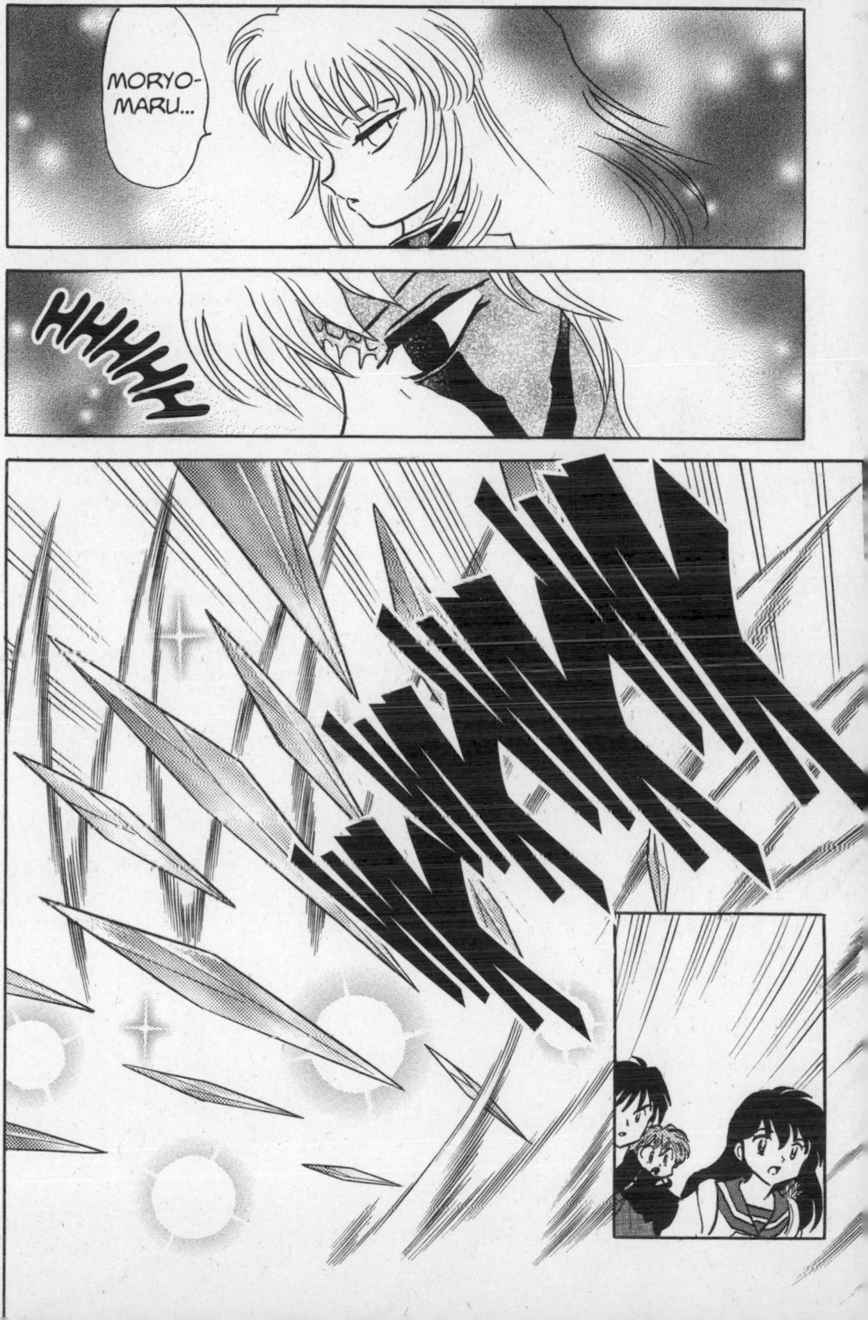
MORYO-
MARU...
HHHHH

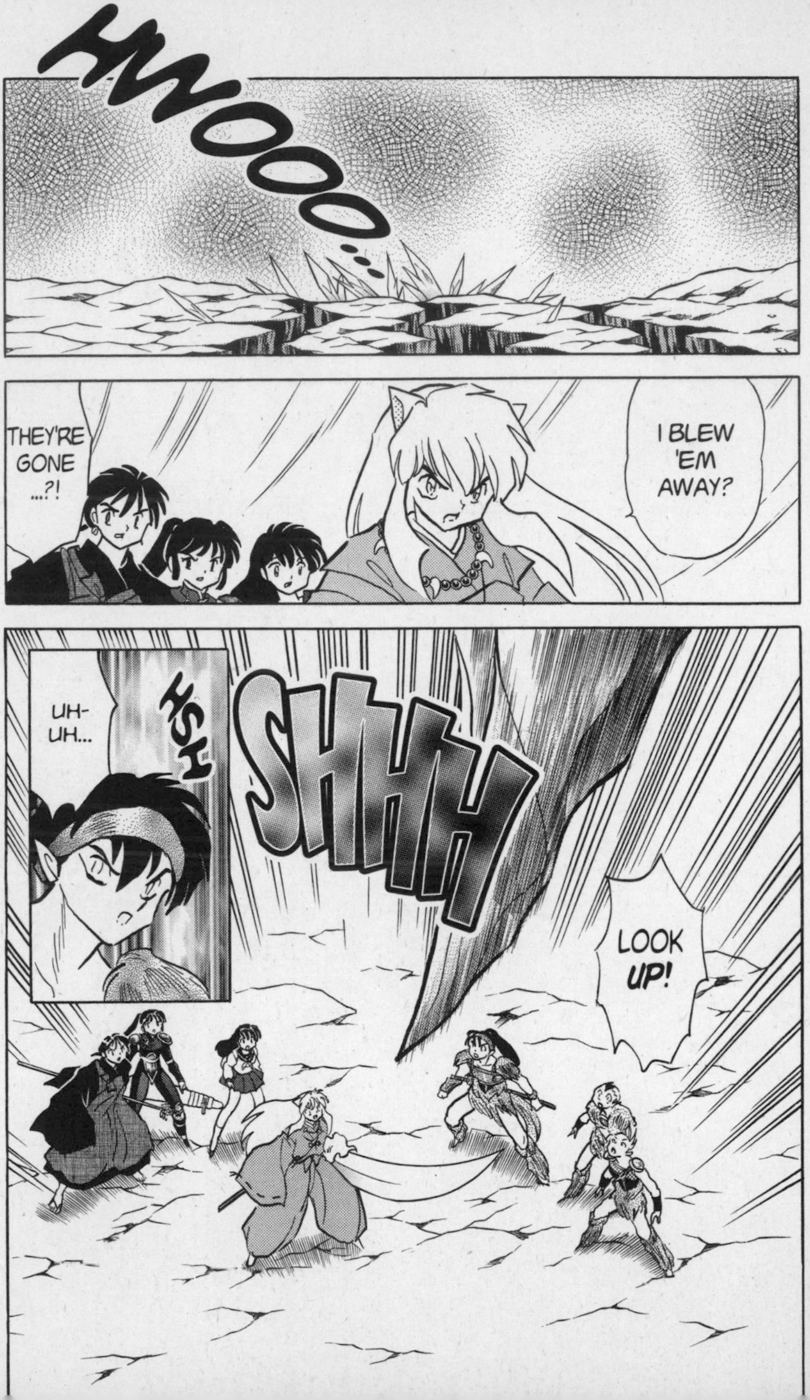
HWOOO...
THEY'RE GONE ...?!
I BLEW 'EM AWAY?
UH-UH...
HSH
SHHH
LOOK UP!

SCROLL 3
CORPSES

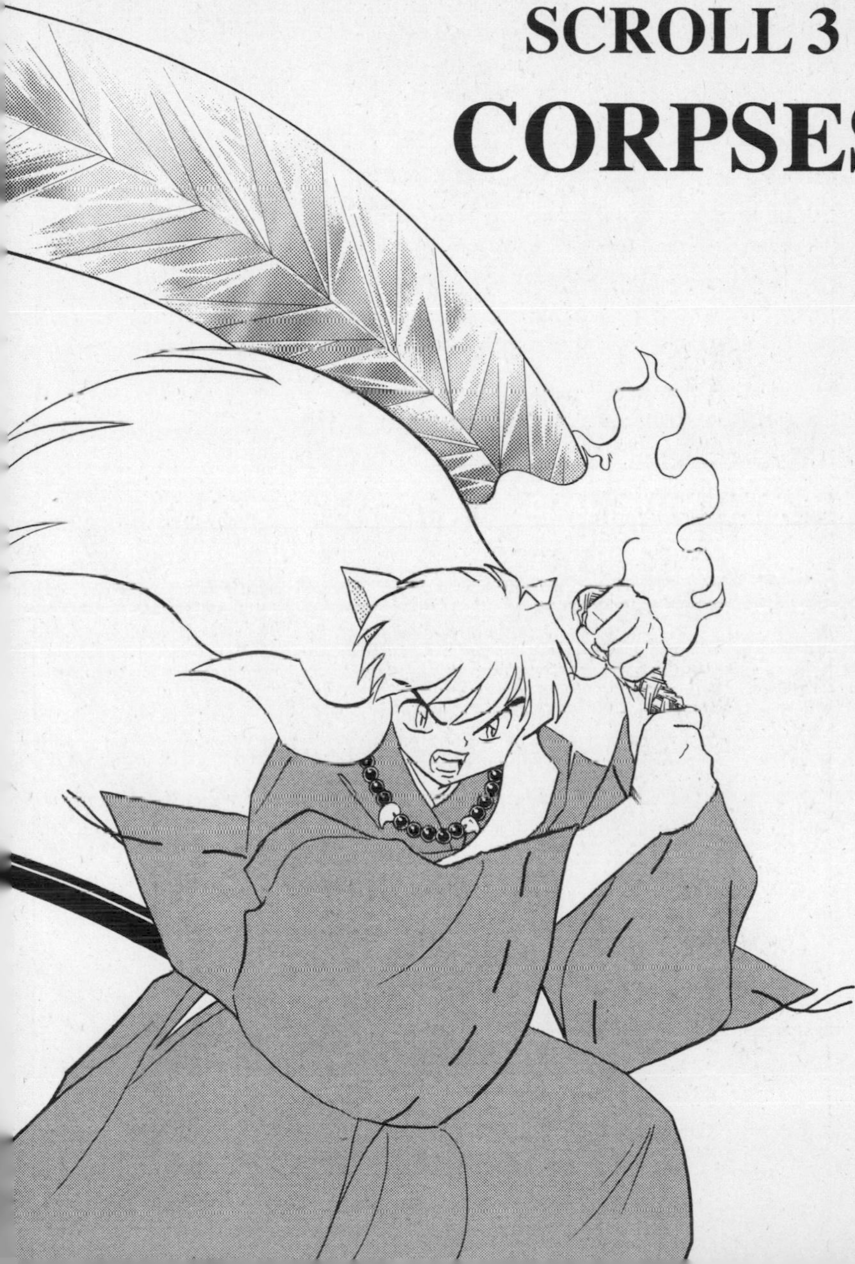

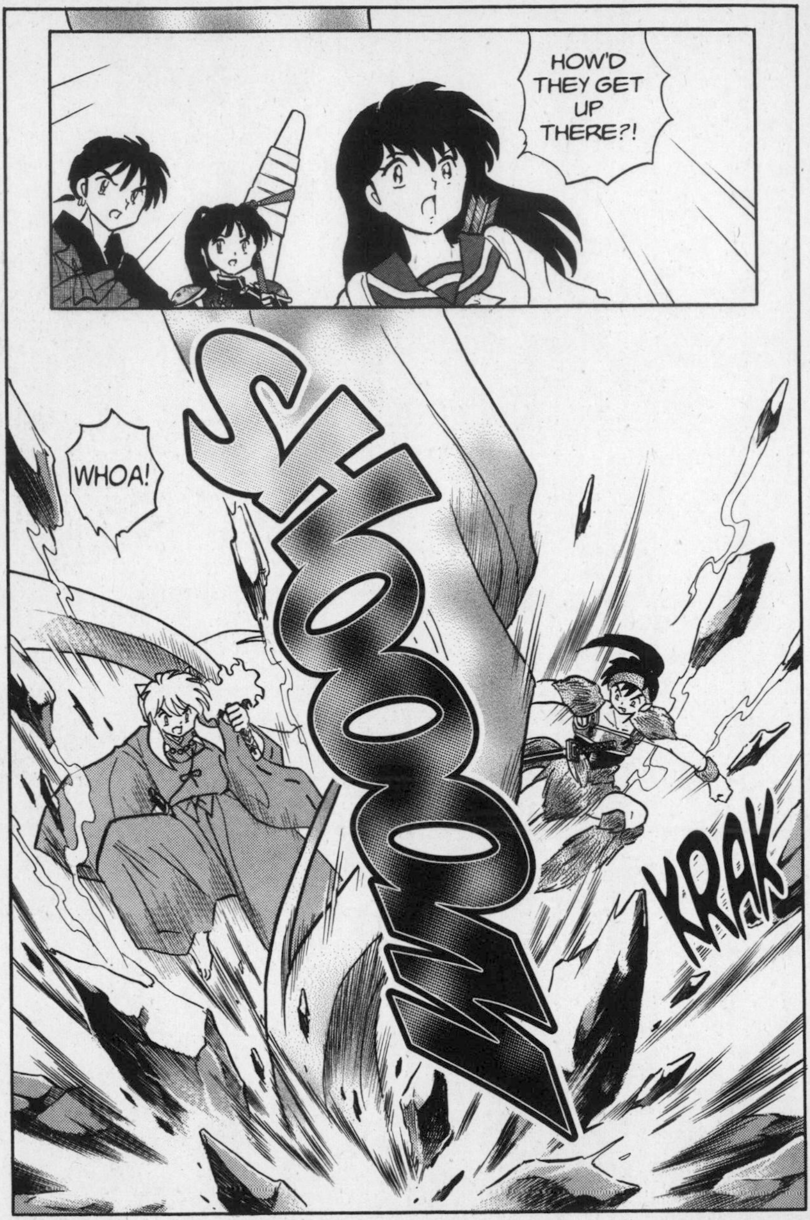
HOW'D THEY GET UP THERE?!
WHOA!
SHOOOM
KRAK

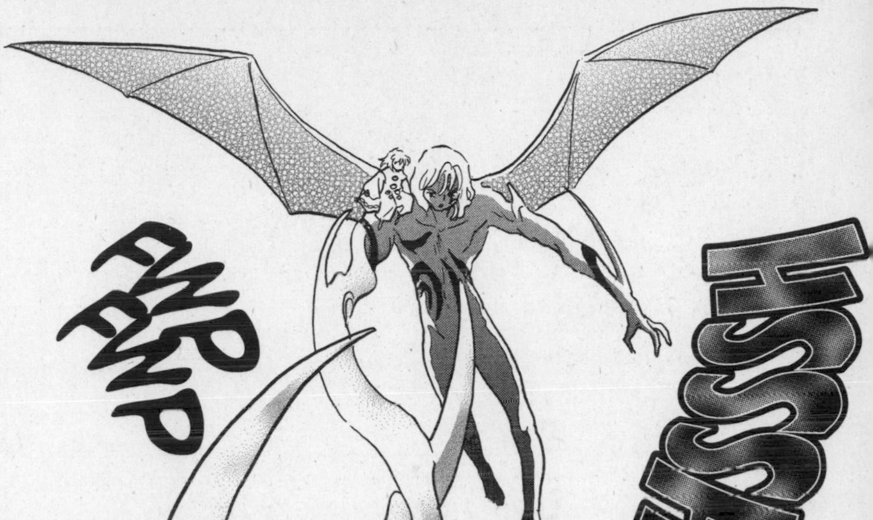
FWP FWP
HSSSH
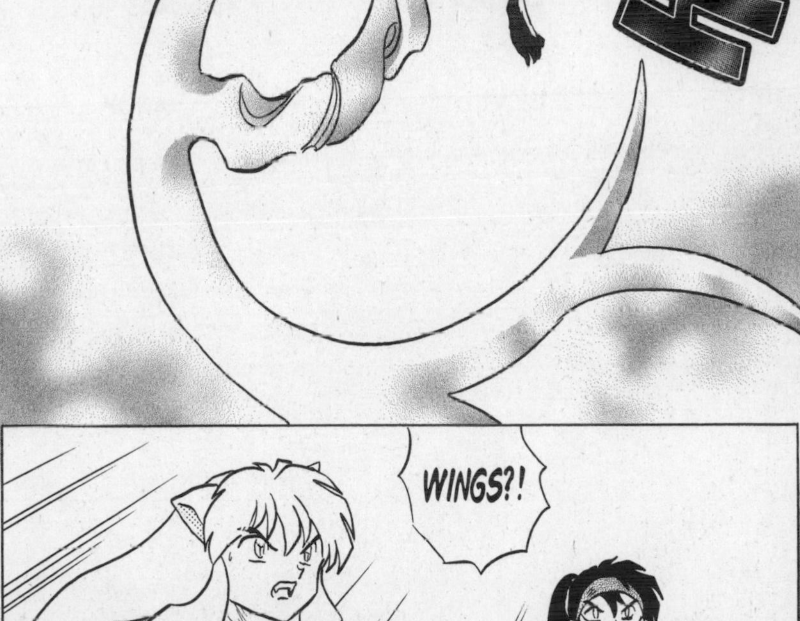
WINGS?!

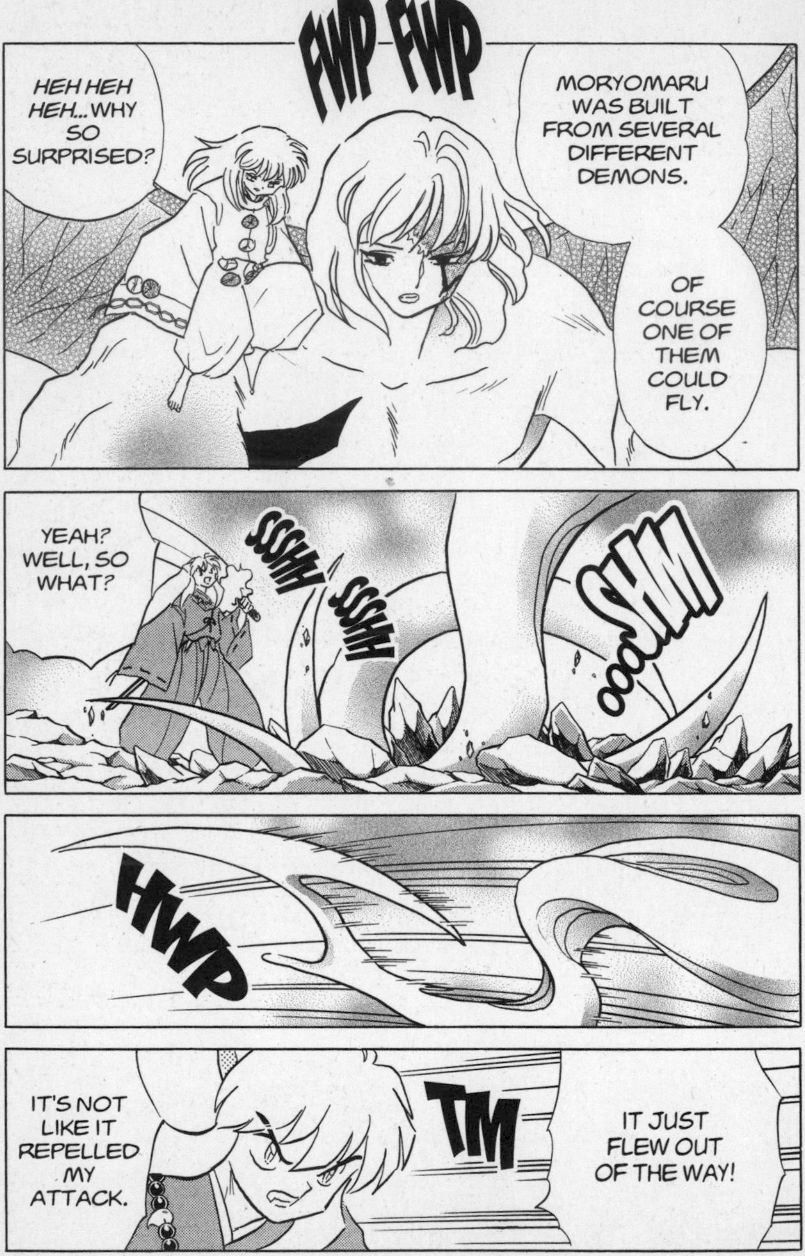
FWP FWP
HEH HEH HEH...WHY SO SURPRISED?
MORYOMARU WAS BUILT FROM SEVERAL DIFFERENT DEMONS.
OF COURSE ONE OF THEM COULD FLY.
YEAH? WELL, SO WHAT?
SSSHH
SSSHH
OOOSHM
HWP
IT'S NOT LIKE IT REPELLED MY ATTACK.
TM
IT JUST FLEW OUT OF THE WAY!

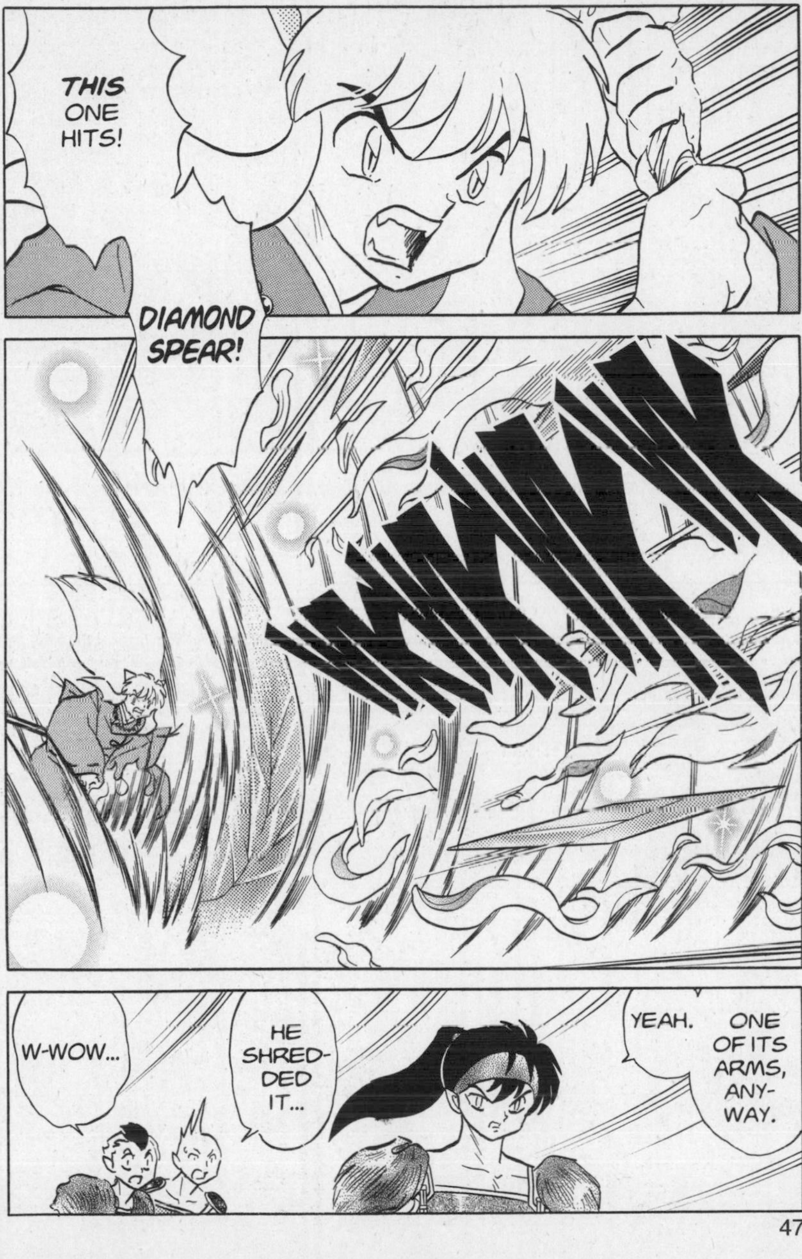
THIS ONE HITS!
DIAMOND SPEAR!
W-WOW...
HE SHRED-DED IT...
YEAH.
ONE OF ITS ARMS, ANY-WAY.

HE FLEW AWAY AGAIN?!

SSSHHH !

YOU! GET DOWN HERE!!

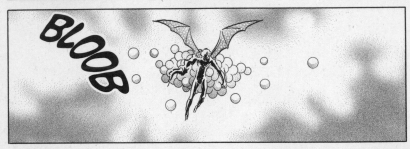

BLOOB

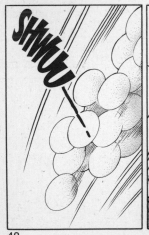

SHWUU

HAKU?!

UUUG

48

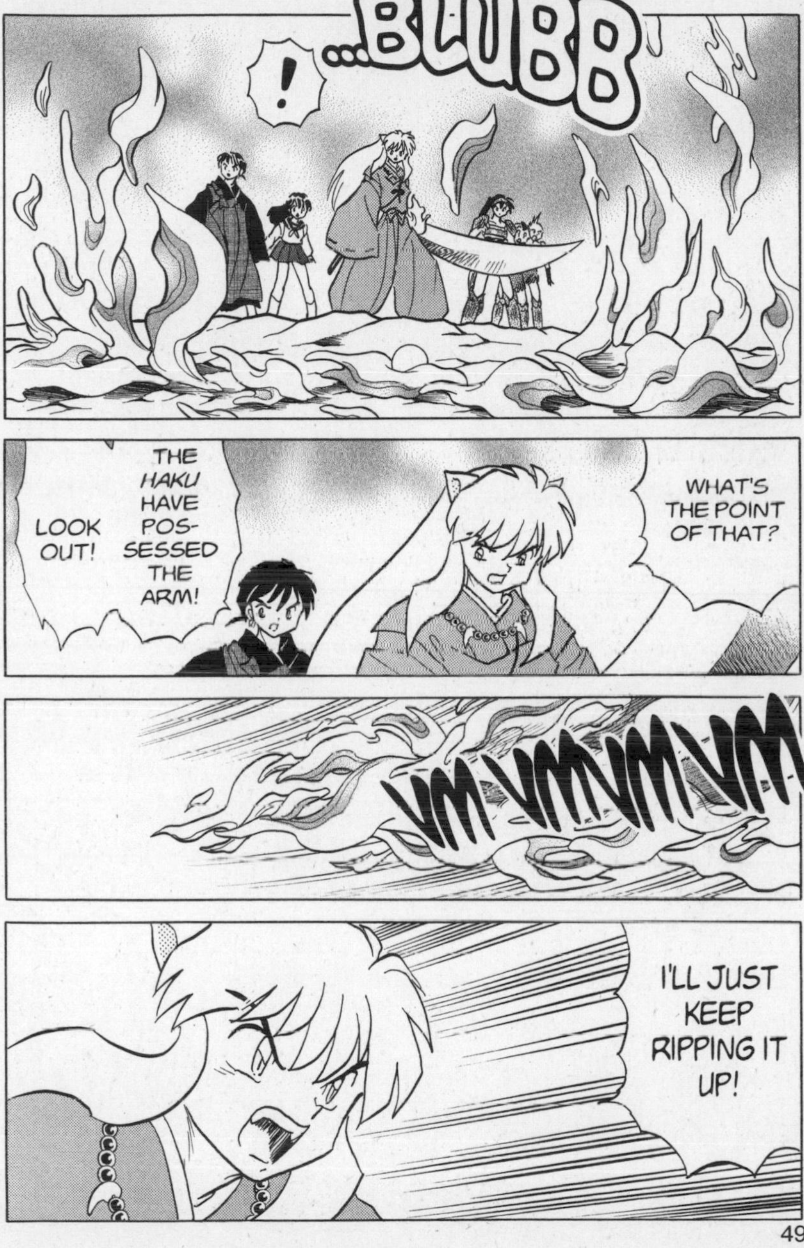
!
...BLUBB
LOOK OUT!
THE *HAKU* HAVE POS-SESSED THE ARM!
WHAT'S THE POINT OF THAT?
VM VM VM VM VM
I'LL JUST KEEP RIPPING IT UP!

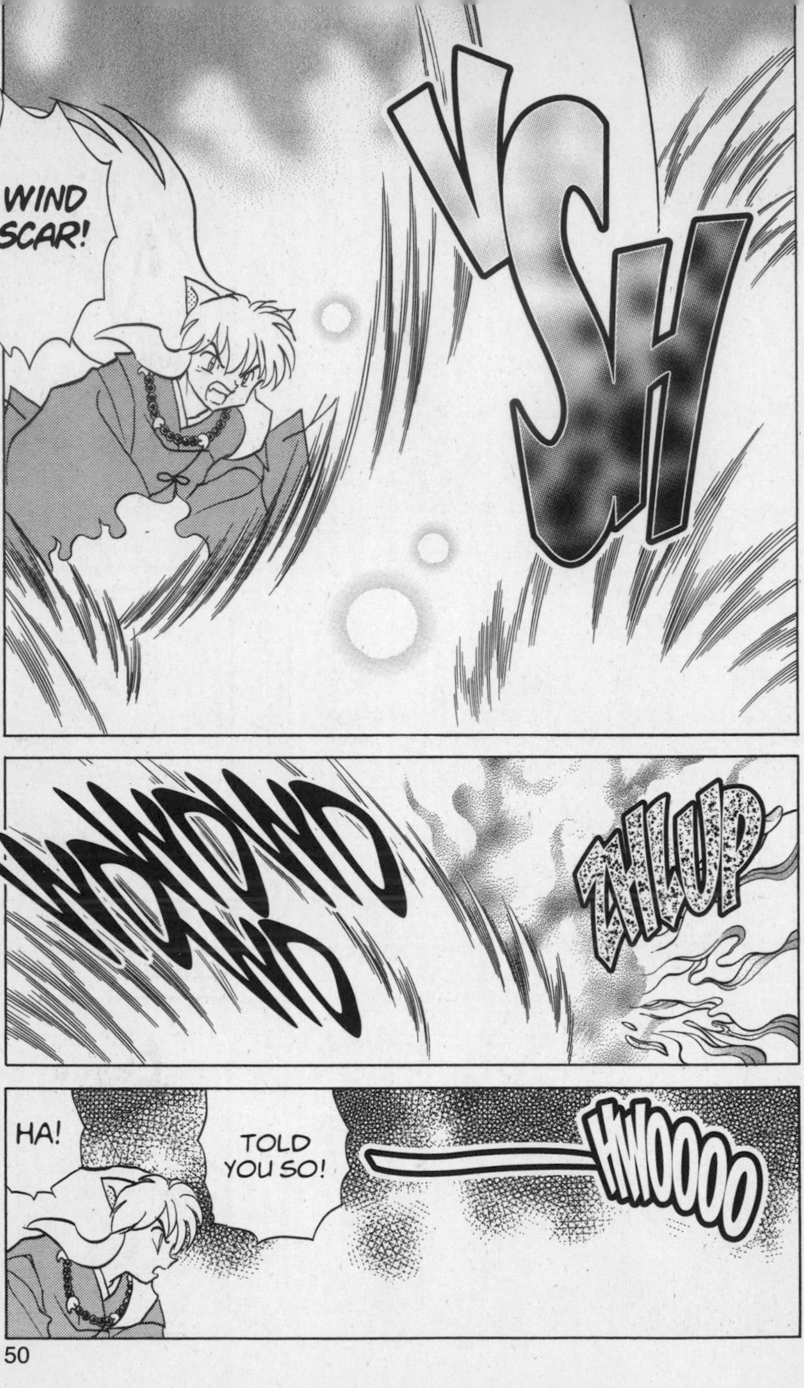
WIND SCAR!
VSCH
ZHLUP
HA!
TOLD YOU SO!
HWOOOO

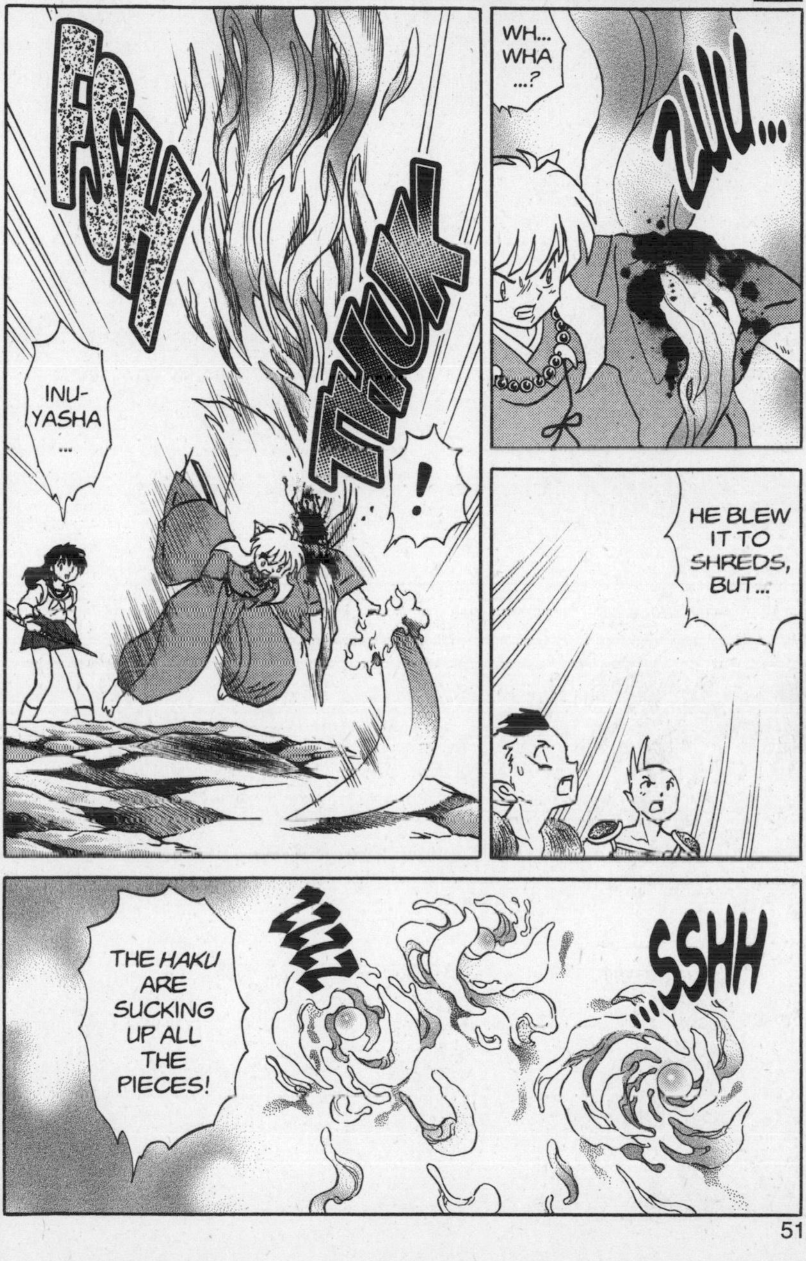
FSH
INU-YASHA...
THUK
!
WH... WHA...?
ZUU...
HE BLEW IT TO SHREDS, BUT...
THE *HAKU* ARE SUCKING UP ALL THE PIECES!
SSHH

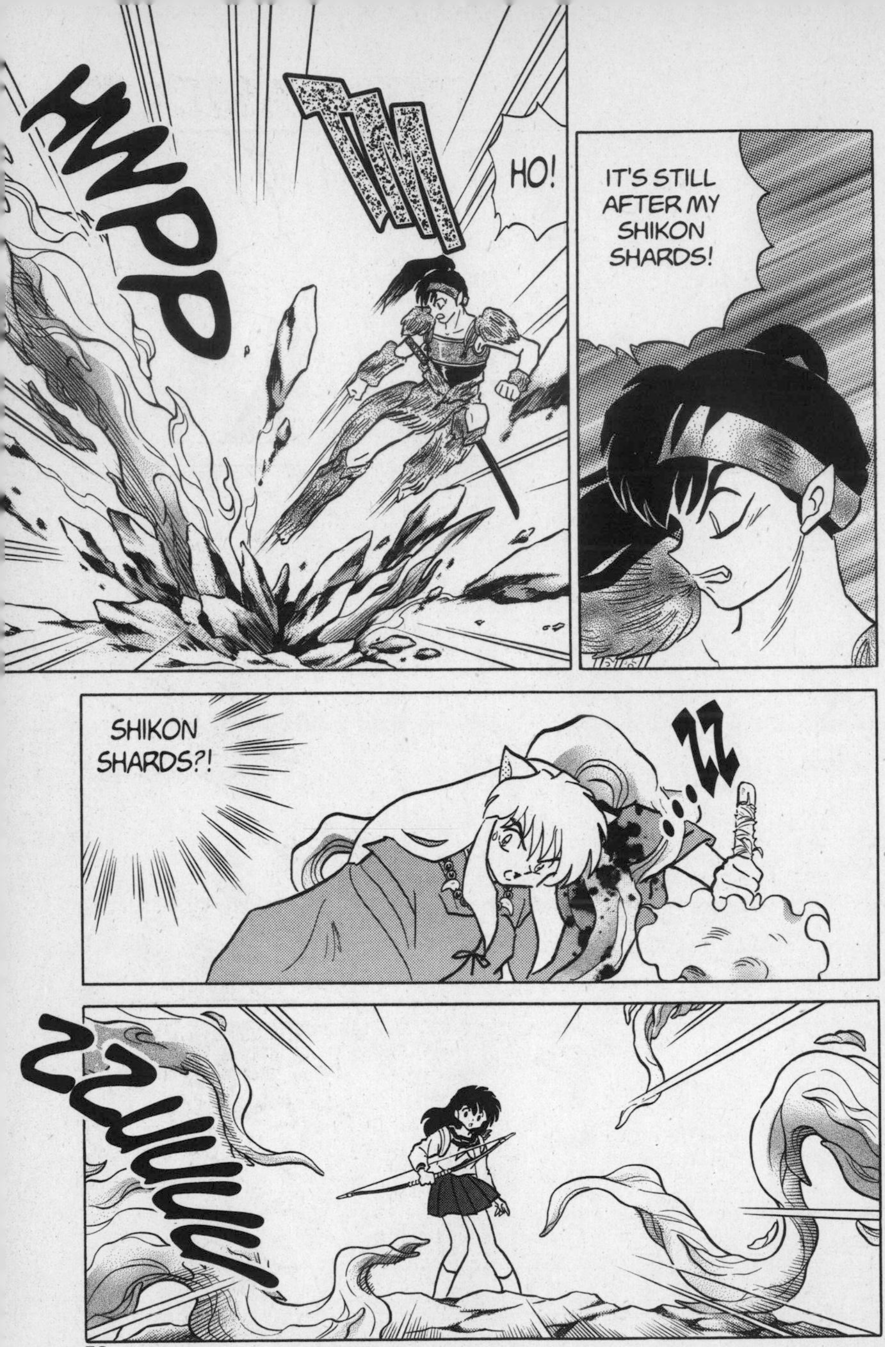
HMPP
TM
HO!
IT'S STILL AFTER MY SHIKON SHARDS!
SHIKON SHARDS?!

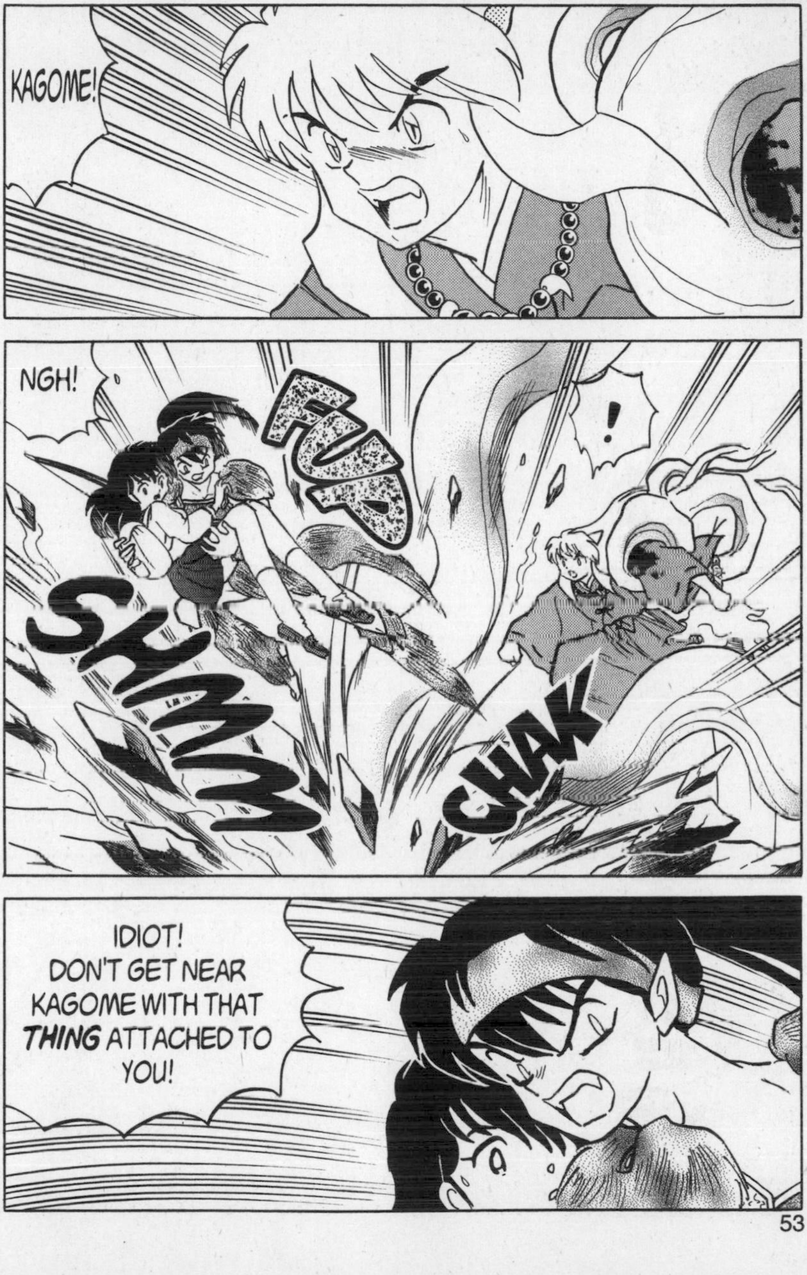
KAGOME!
NGH!
FUP
!
SHMMM
CHAK
IDIOT! DON'T GET NEAR KAGOME WITH THAT *THING* ATTACHED TO YOU!

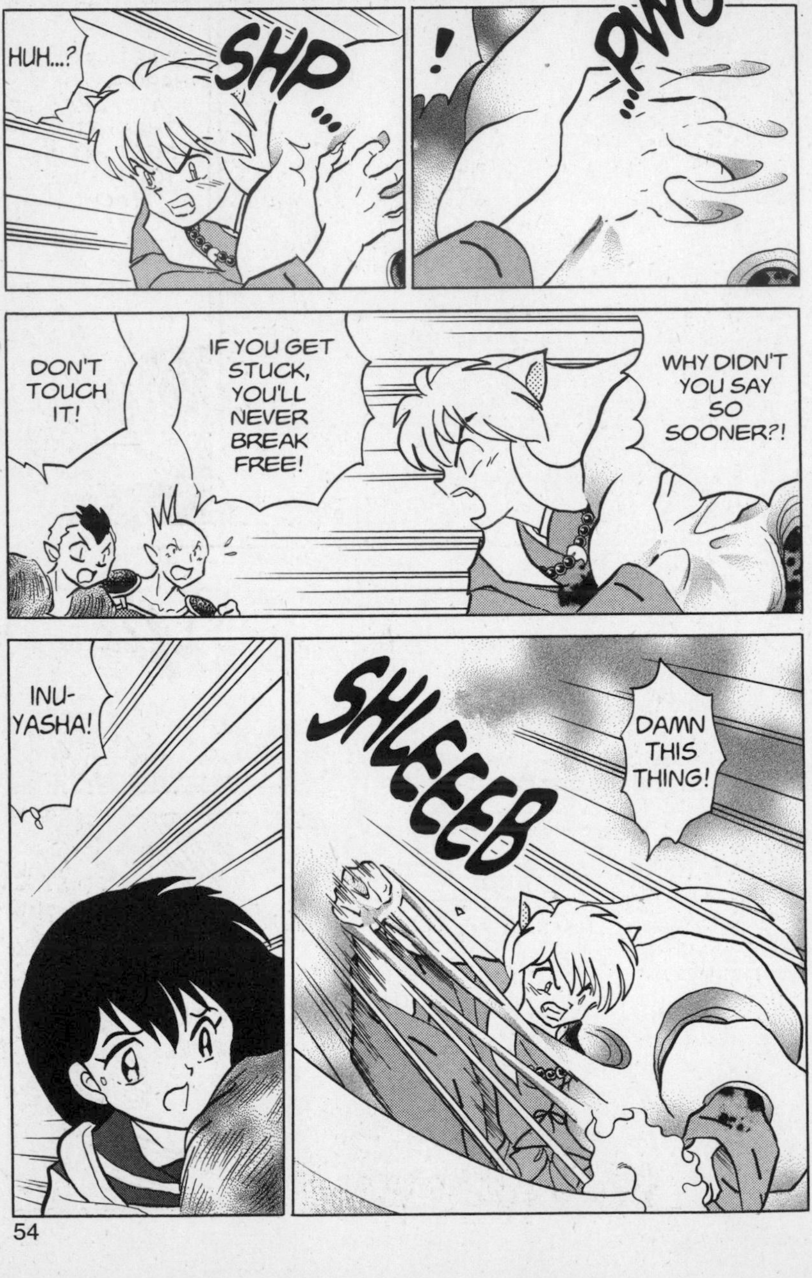
HUH...?
SHP...
!
PWG...
DON'T TOUCH IT!
IF YOU GET STUCK, YOU'LL NEVER BREAK FREE!
WHY DIDN'T YOU SAY SO SOONER?!
INU-YASHA!
SHWEEEB
DAMN THIS THING!

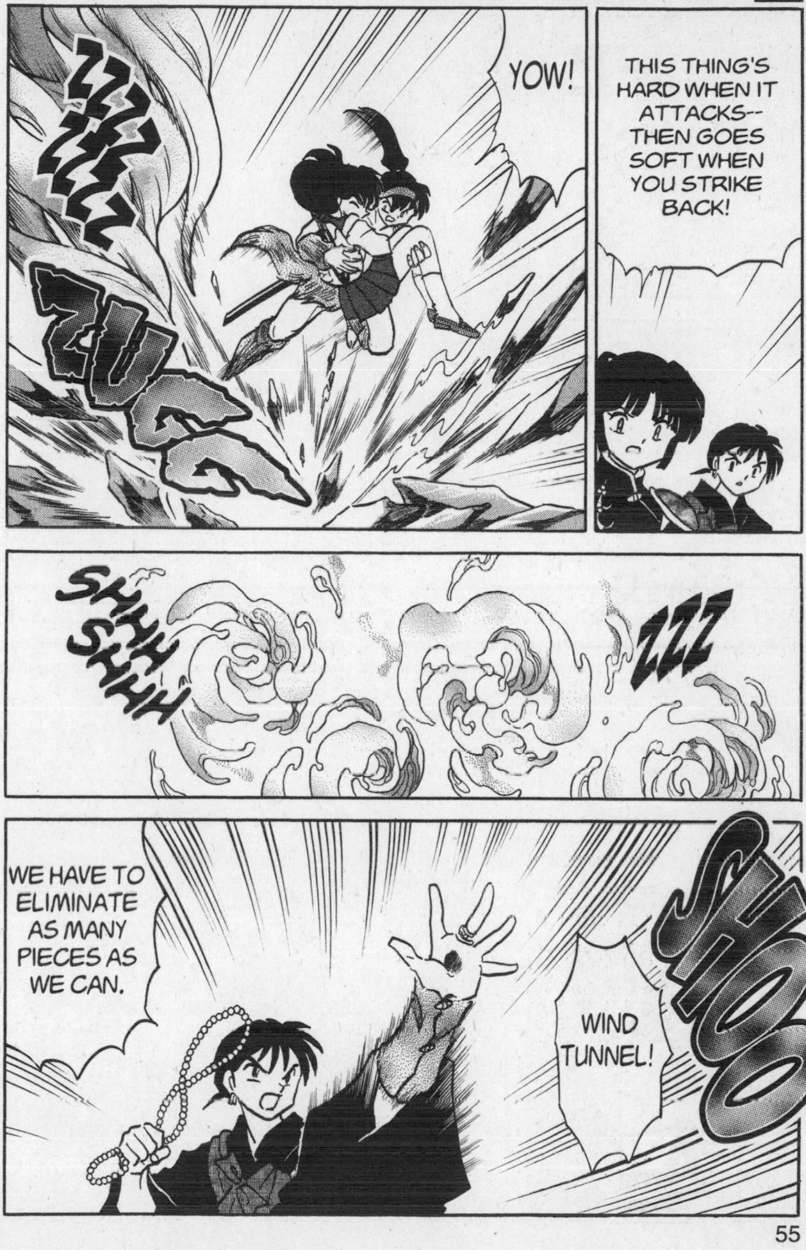
ZUGG
YOW!
THIS THING'S HARD WHEN IT ATTACKS-- THEN GOES SOFT WHEN YOU STRIKE BACK!
SHHH SHHH
ZZZ
WE HAVE TO ELIMINATE AS MANY PIECES AS WE CAN.
WIND TUNNEL!
SHOOO

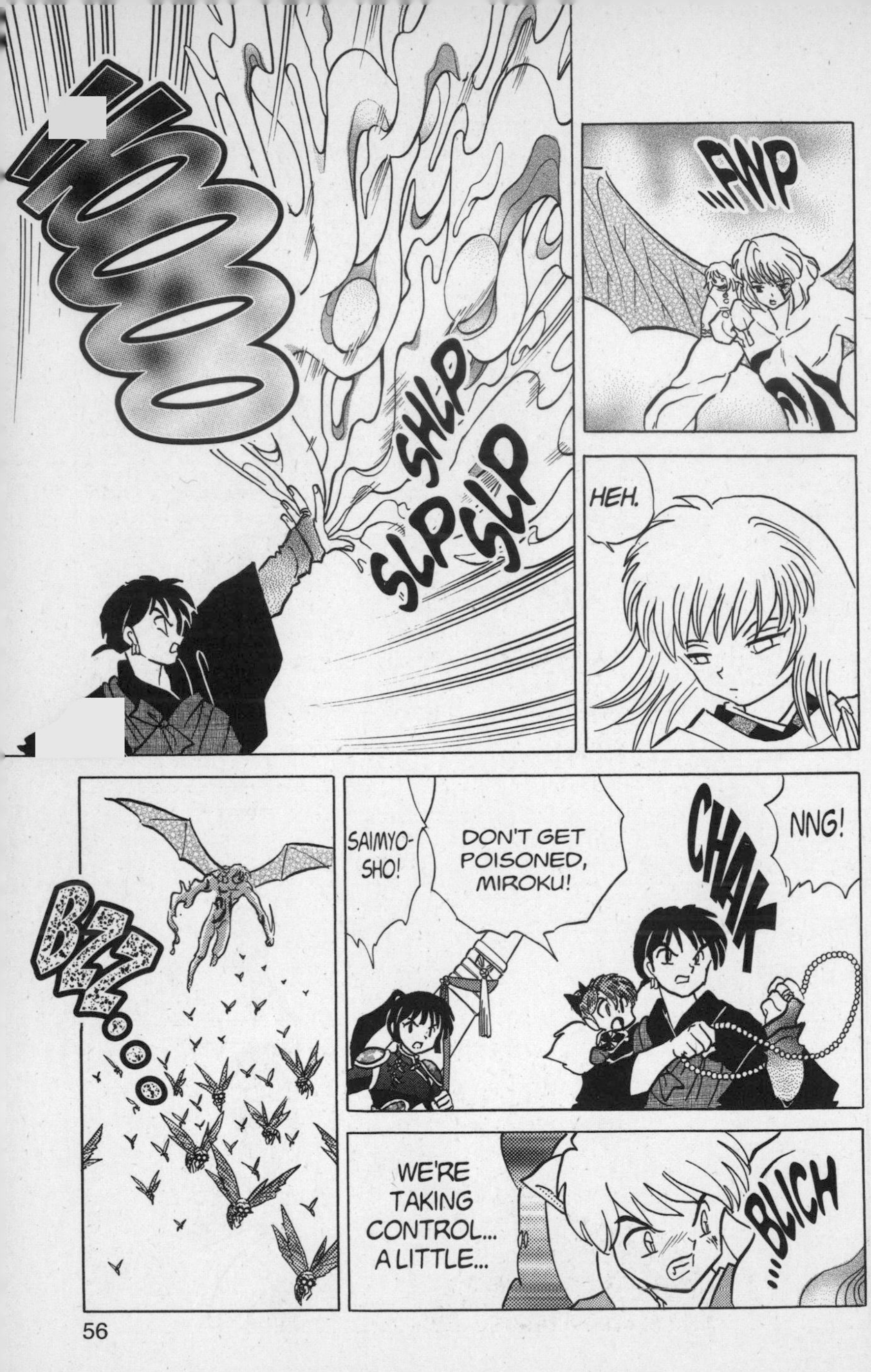
SHLP
SLP SLP
...FWP
HEH.
BZZ...
SAIMYO-SHO!
DON'T GET POISONED, MIROKU!
CHAK
NNG!
WE'RE TAKING CONTROL... A LITTLE...
...BLICH

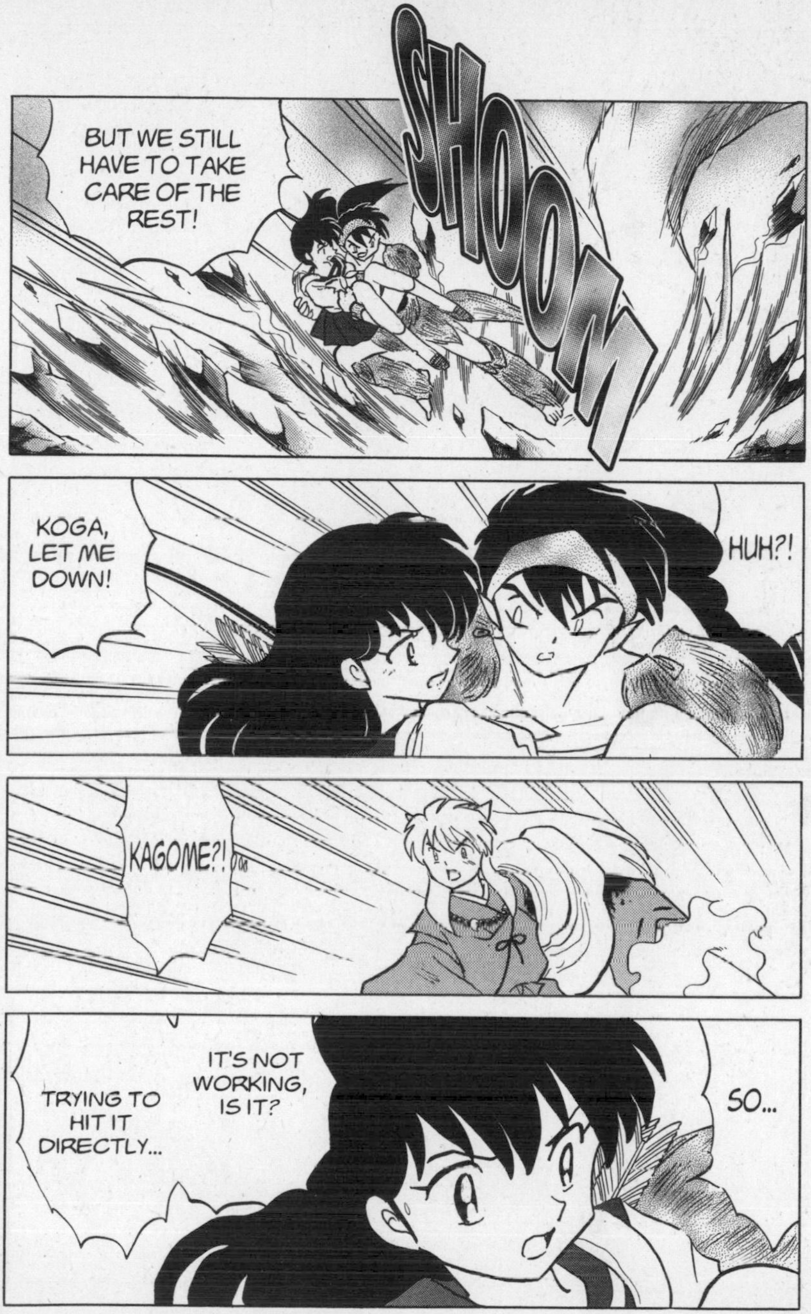

SHOOOM
BUT WE STILL HAVE TO TAKE CARE OF THE REST!
KOGA, LET ME DOWN!
HUH?!
KAGOME?!
TRYING TO HIT IT DIRECTLY...
IT'S NOT WORKING, IS IT?
SO...

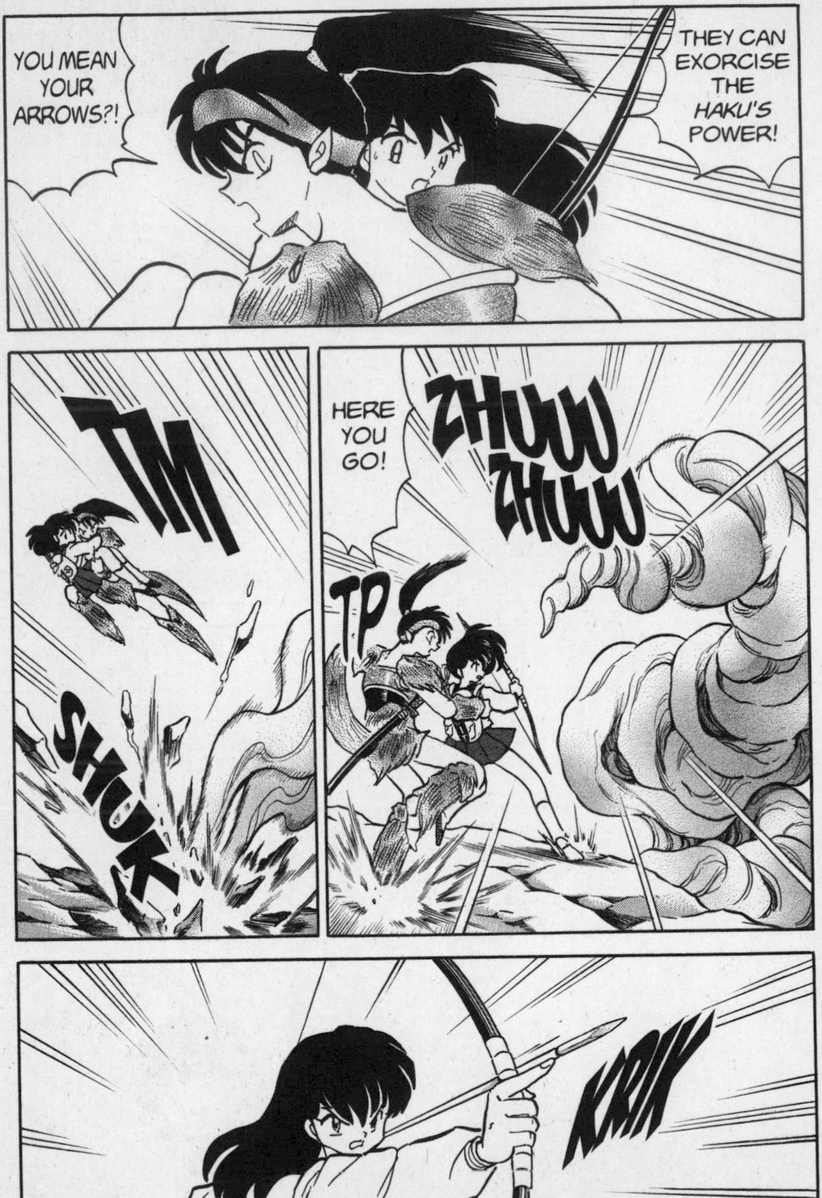
YOU MEAN YOUR ARROWS?!
THEY CAN EXORCISE THE HAKU'S POWER!
TM
SHUK
HERE YOU GO!
ZHUUU ZHUUU
TP
KRIK

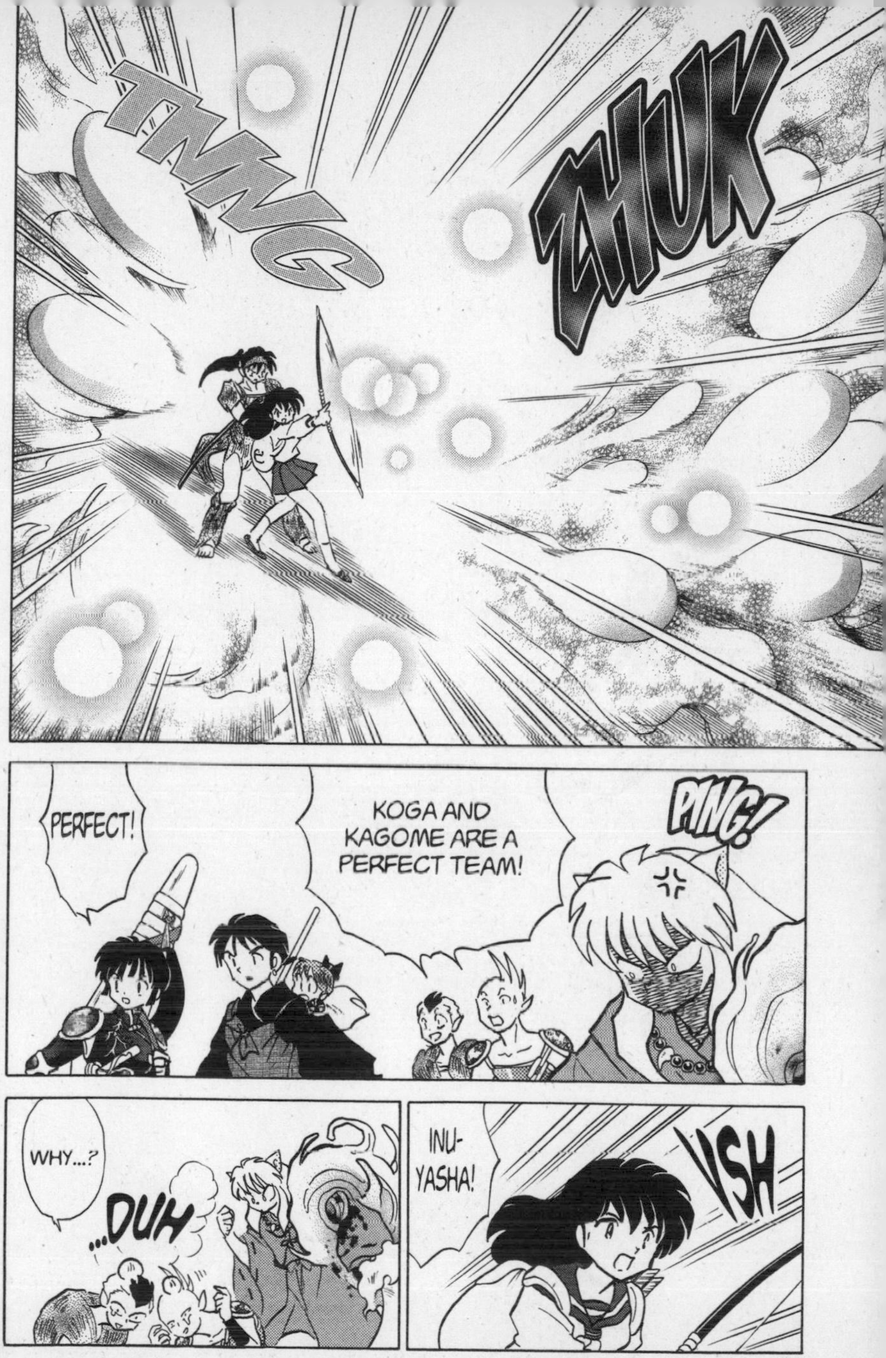
TWNG
ZHUK
PERFECT!
KOGA AND KAGOME ARE A PERFECT TEAM!
PING!
WHY...?
...DUH
INU-YASHA!
VSH

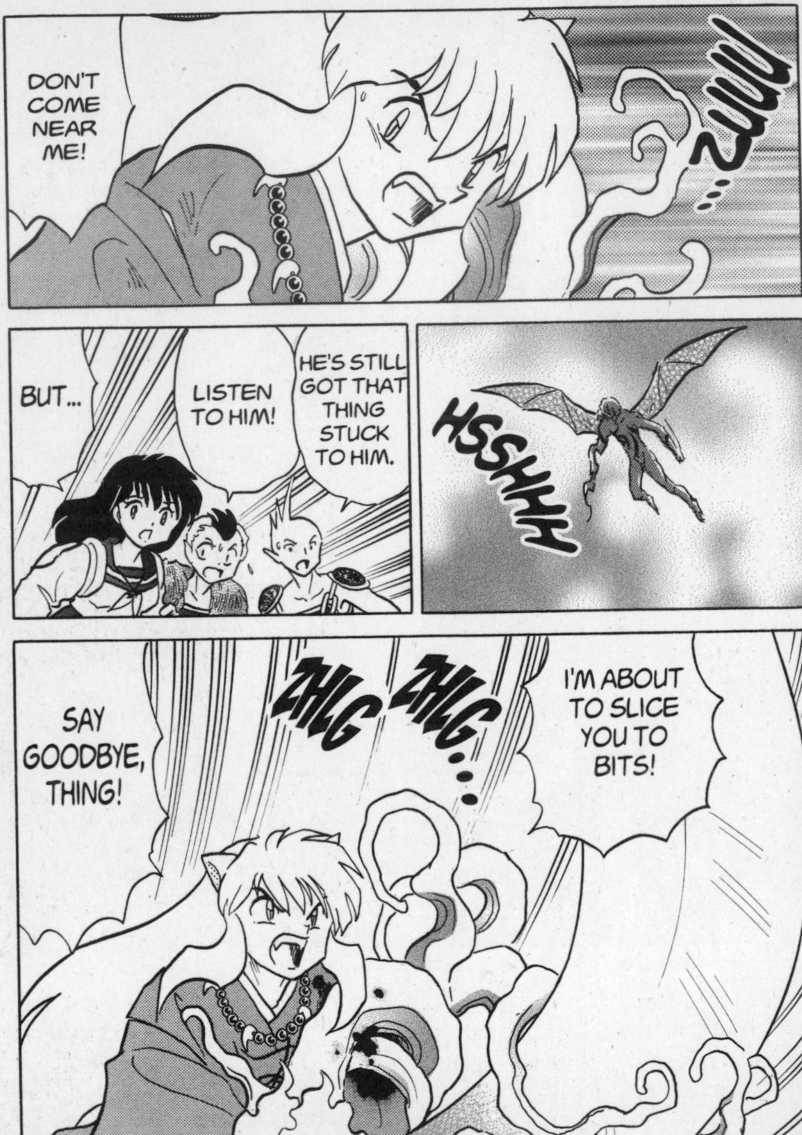
DON'T COME NEAR ME!
ZUUUU...
BUT...
LISTEN TO HIM!
HE'S STILL GOT THAT THING STUCK TO HIM.
HSSHHH
SAY GOODBYE, THING!
ZHLG ZHLG...
I'M ABOUT TO SLICE YOU TO BITS!

SCROLL 4
STOLEN OBJECTS

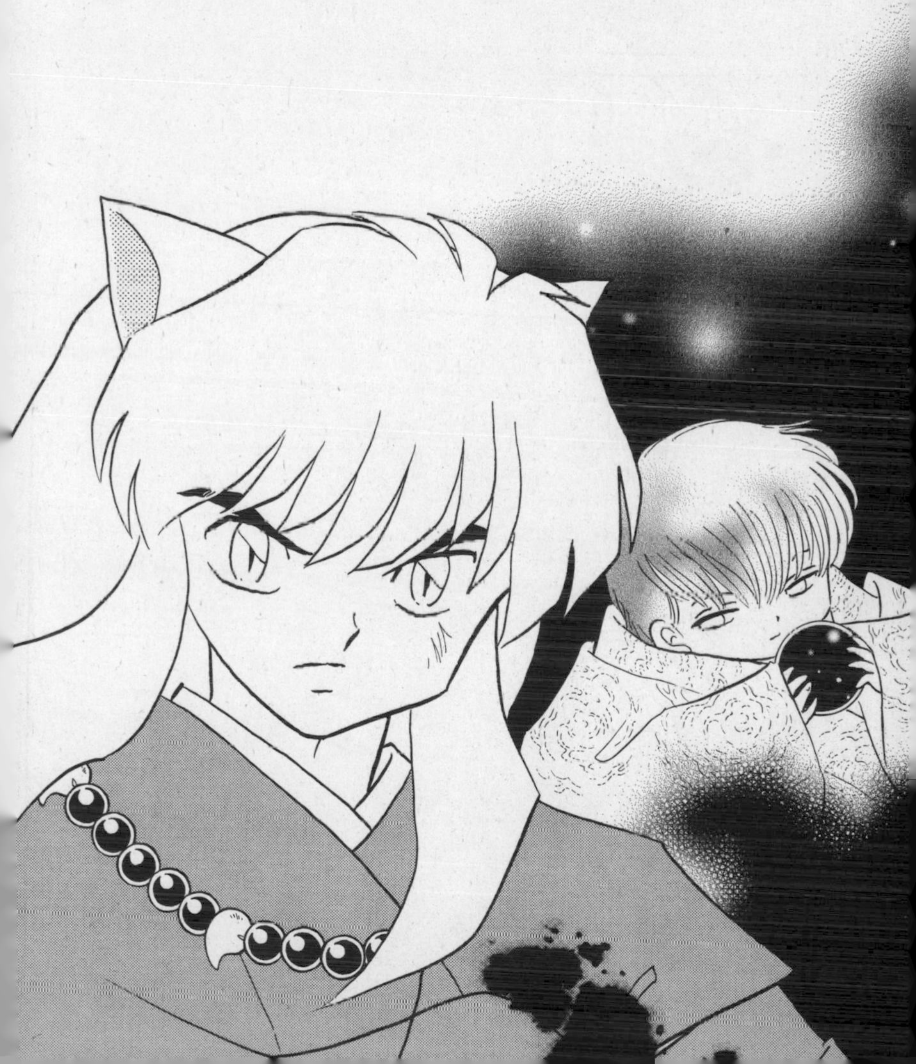

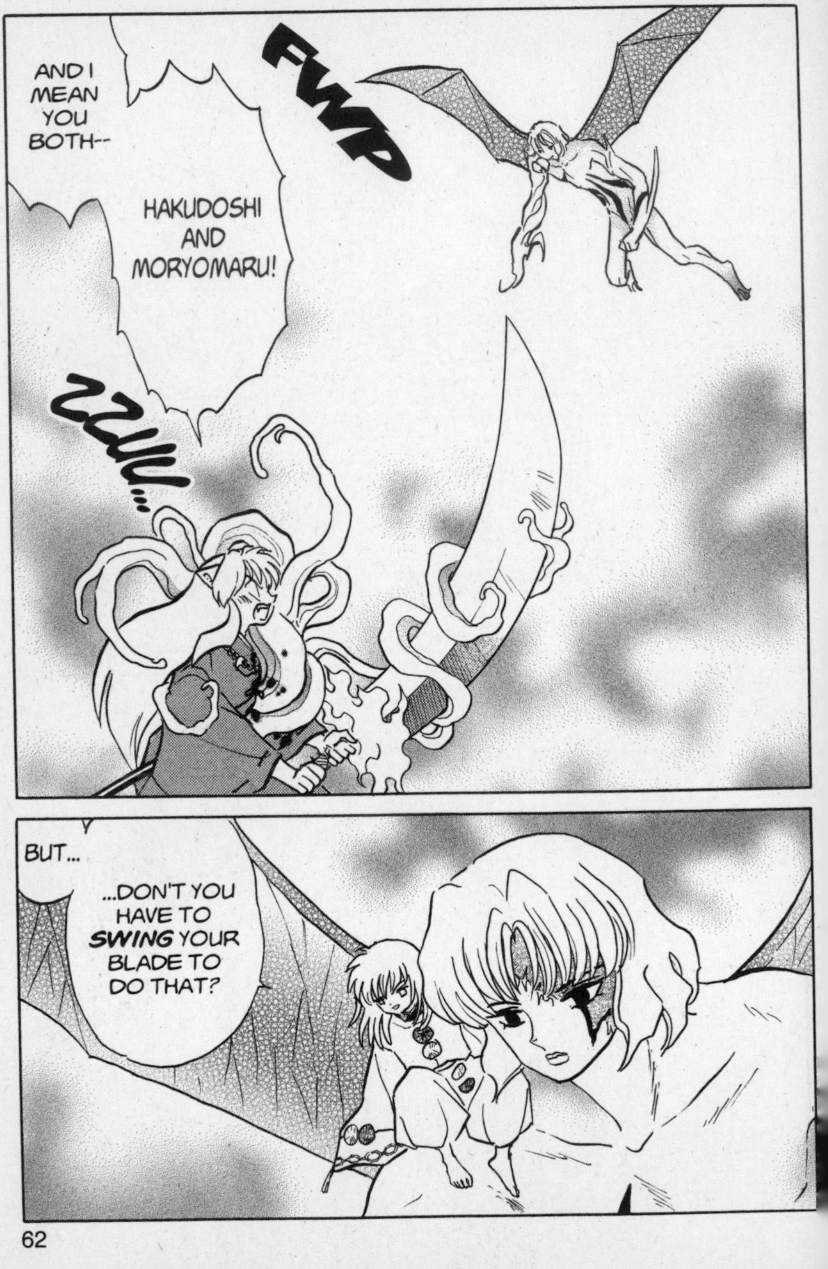
AND I MEAN YOU BOTH--
FWP
HAKUDOSHI AND MORYOMARU!
ZZUU...
BUT...
...DON'T YOU HAVE TO SWING YOUR BLADE TO DO THAT?

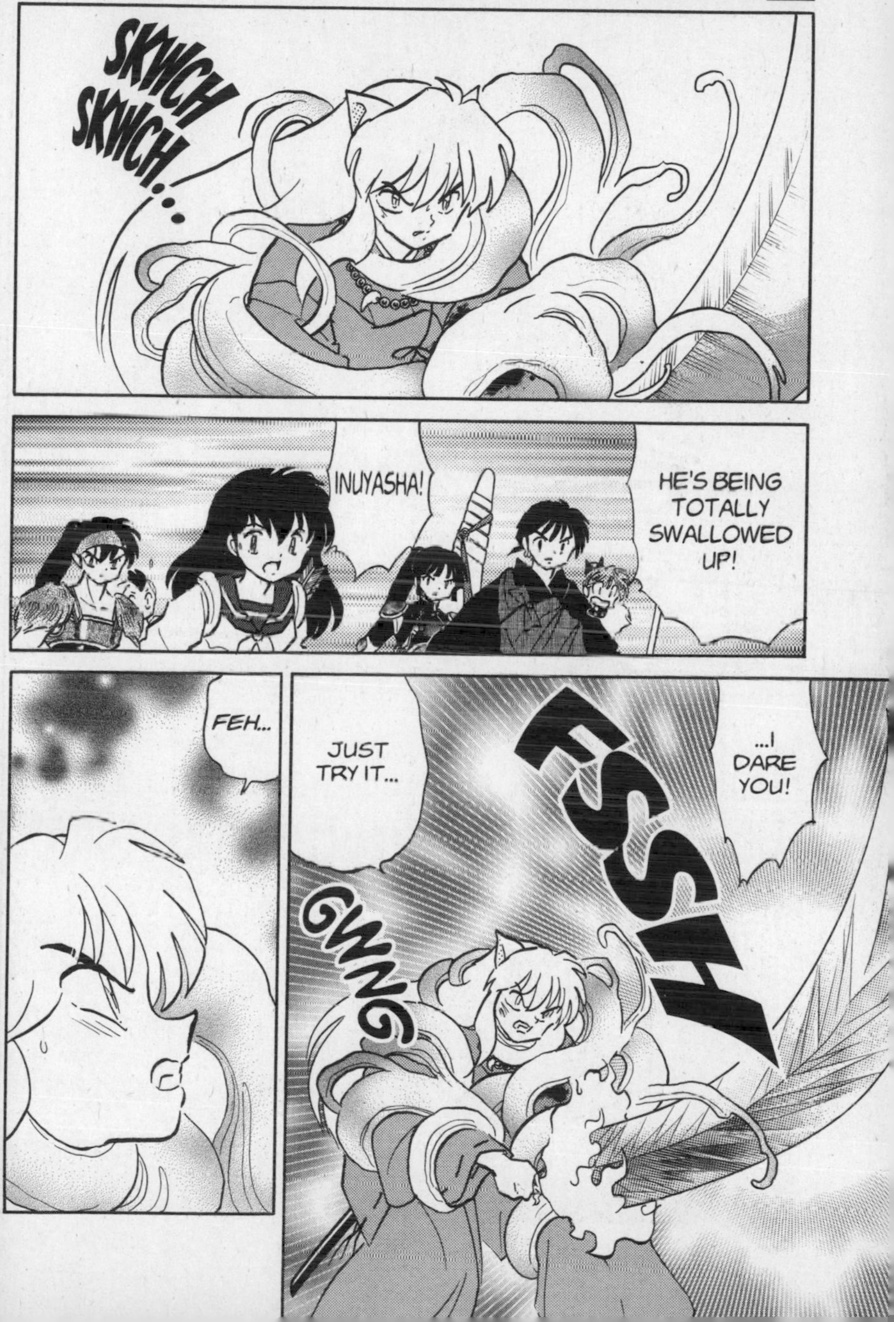
SKWCH SKWCH...
INUYASHA!
HE'S BEING TOTALLY SWALLOWED UP!
FEH...
JUST TRY IT...
FSSH
...I DARE YOU!
GWNG

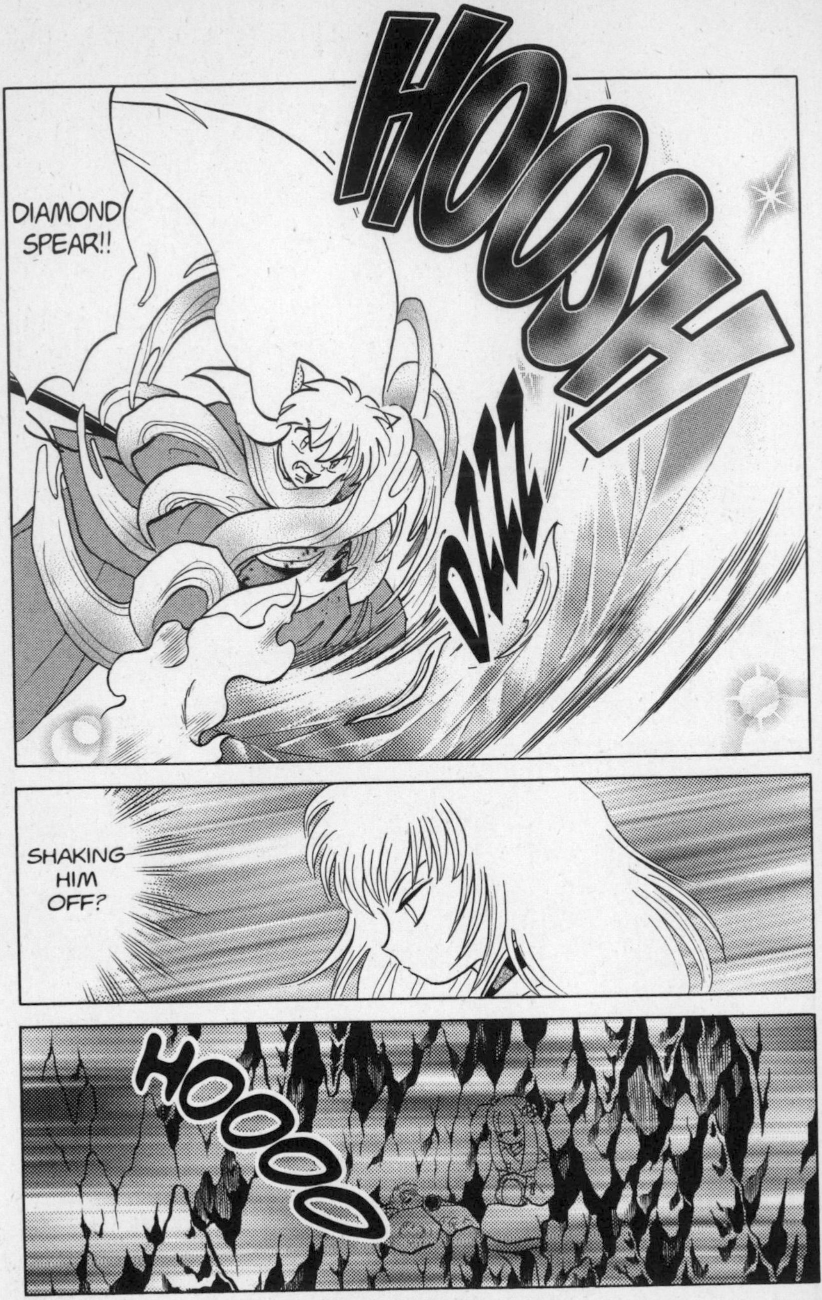
HOOSH
DIAMOND SPEAR!!
SHAKING HIM OFF?
HOOOOO

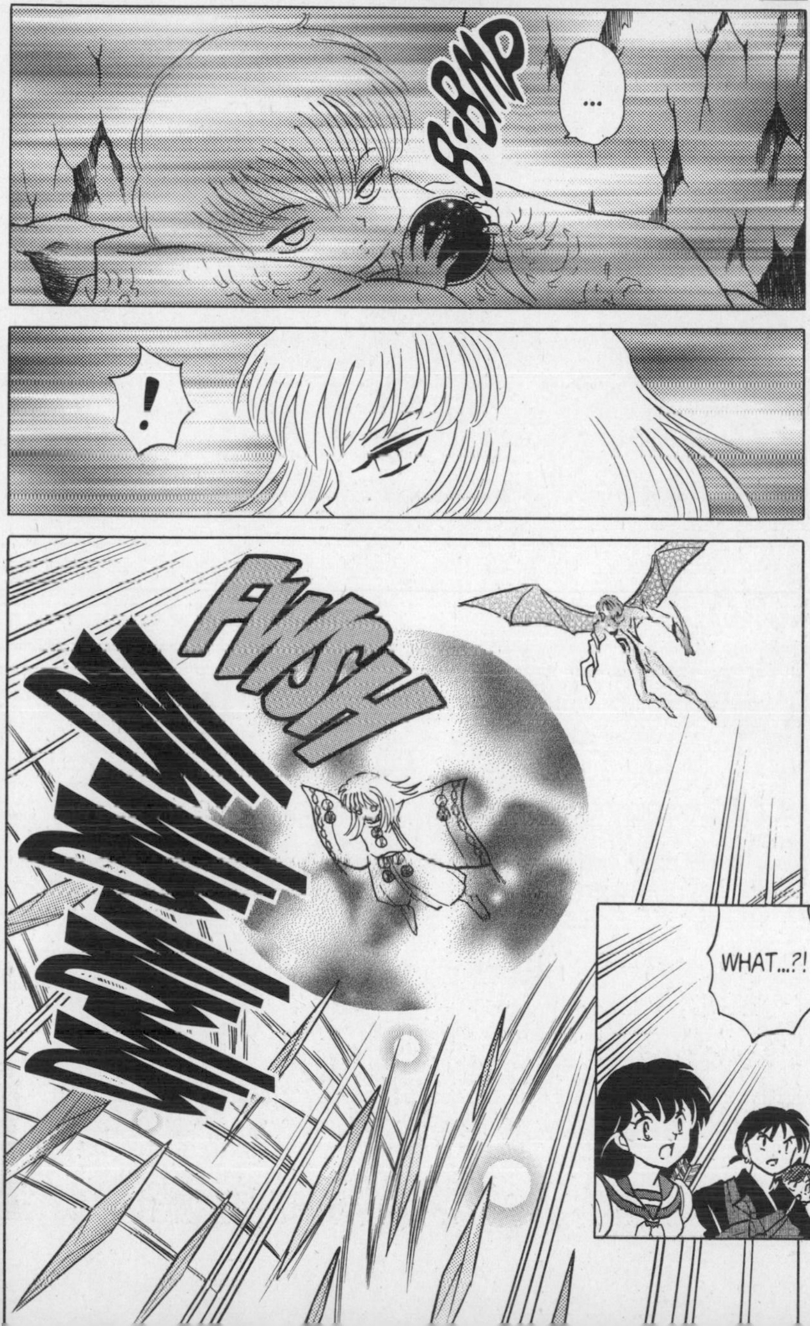
B-BMP
...
!
FWSH
WHAT...?!

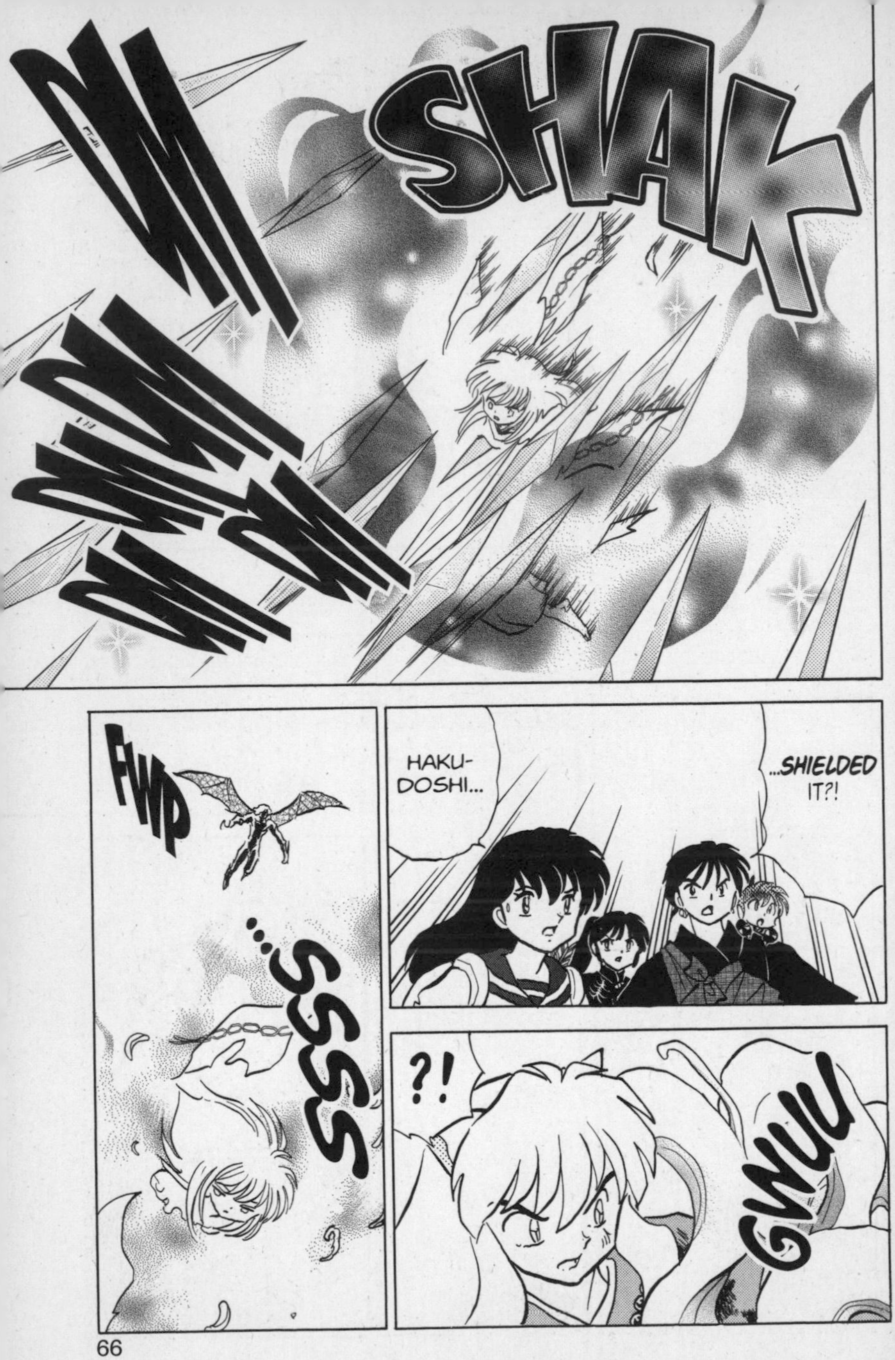
SHAK
FWP
...SSSS
HAKU-DOSHI...
...SHIELDED IT?!
?!
GWUU

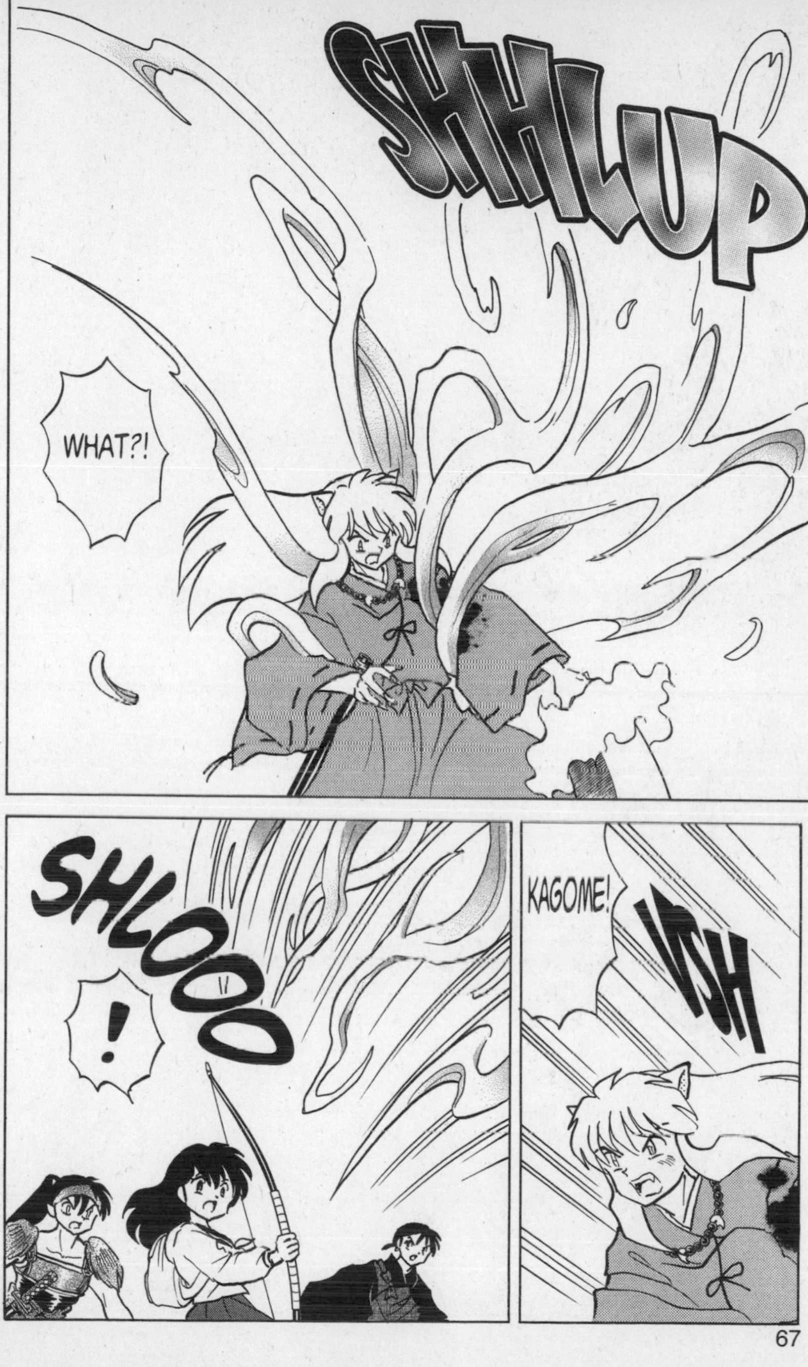
SHHLUP
WHAT?!
SHLOOO
!
KAGOME!
VSH

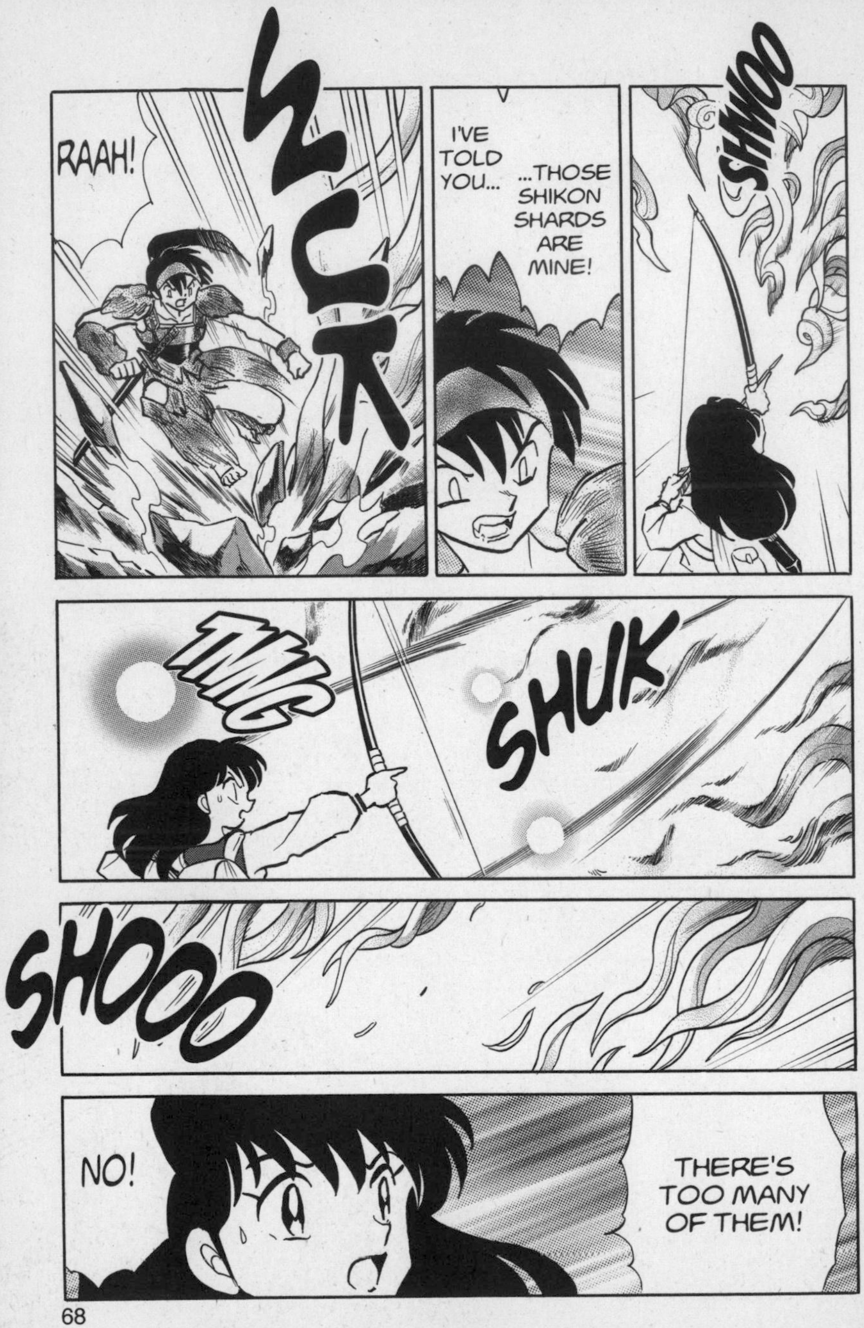
RAAH!
I'VE TOLD YOU...
...THOSE SHIKON SHARDS ARE MINE!
SHWOO
TWING
SHUK
SHOOO
NO!
THERE'S TOO MANY OF THEM!

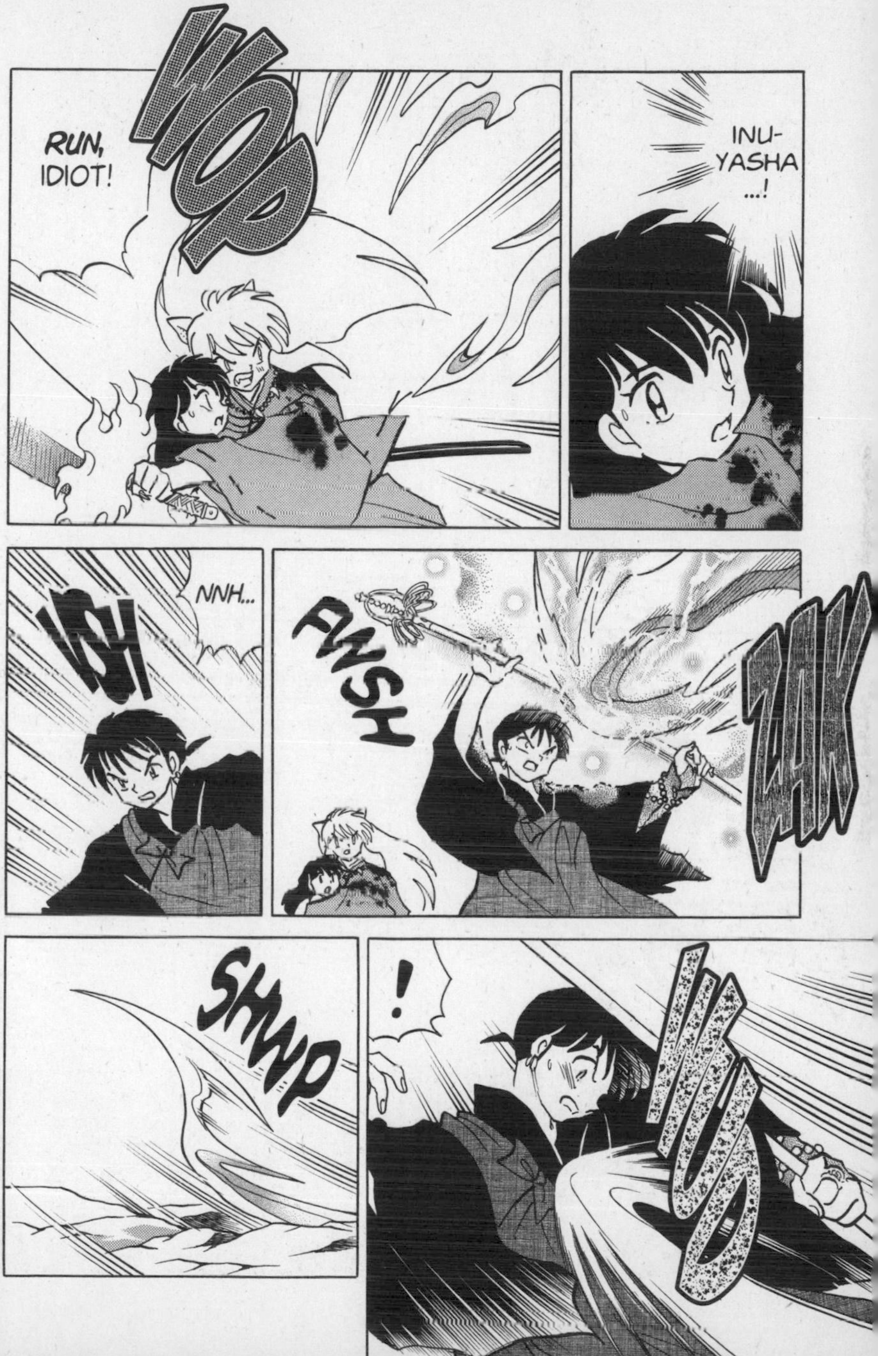
WOP
RUN, IDIOT!
INU-YASHA ...!
VOO
NNH...
FWSH
ZAK
SHWP
!
WHS

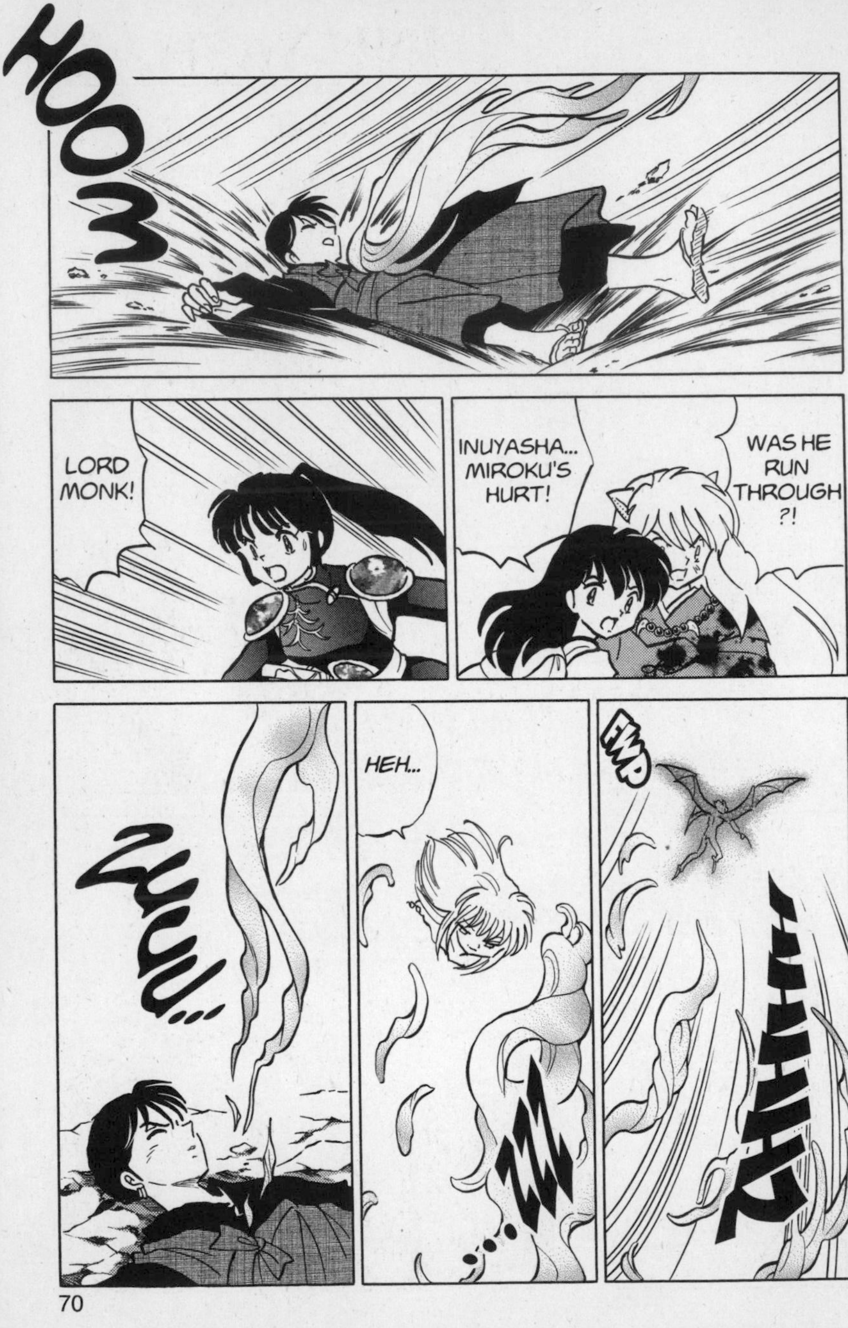
HOOM
LORD MONK!
INUYASHA... MIROKU'S HURT!
WAS HE RUN THROUGH ?!
HEH...

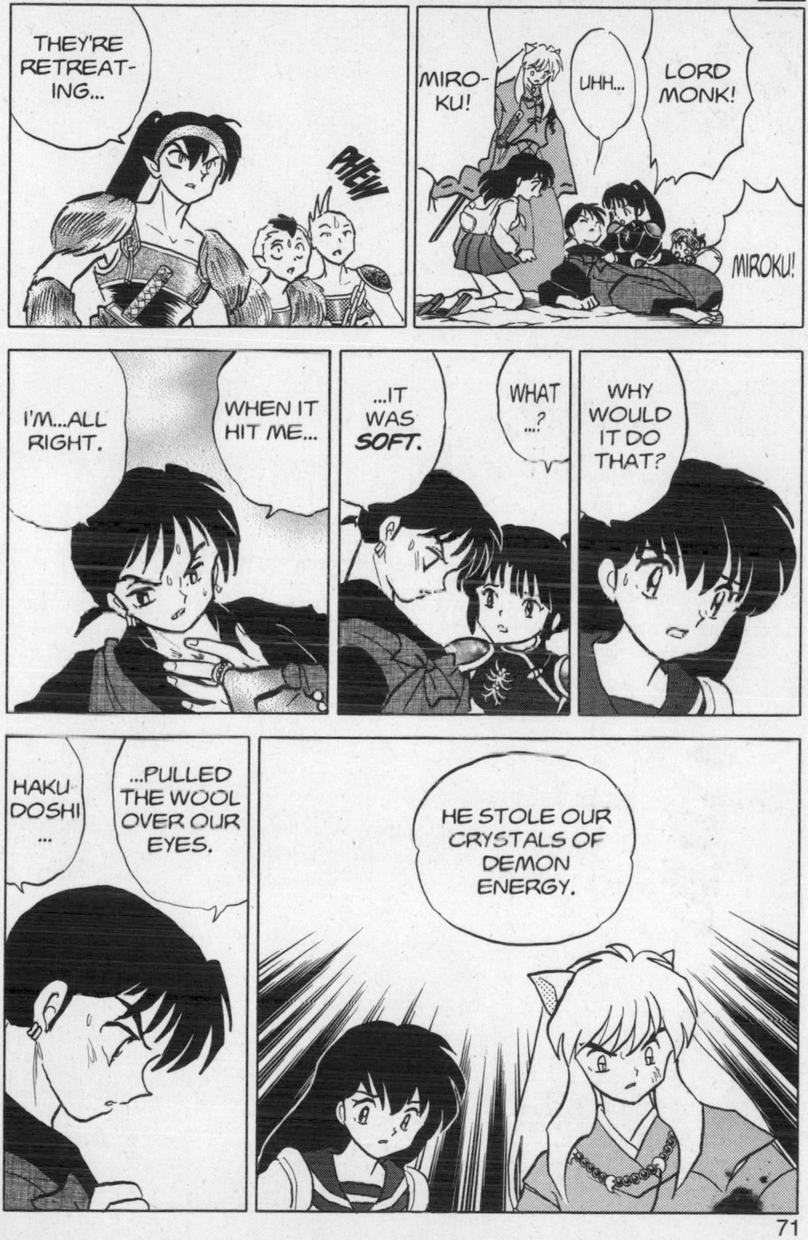
THEY'RE RETREAT-ING...
PHEW
MIRO-KU!
UHH...
LORD MONK!
MIROKU!
I'M...ALL RIGHT.
WHEN IT HIT ME...
...IT WAS SOFT.
WHAT ...?
WHY WOULD IT DO THAT?
HAKU-DOSHI ...
...PULLED THE WOOL OVER OUR EYES.
HE STOLE OUR CRYSTALS OF DEMON ENERGY.

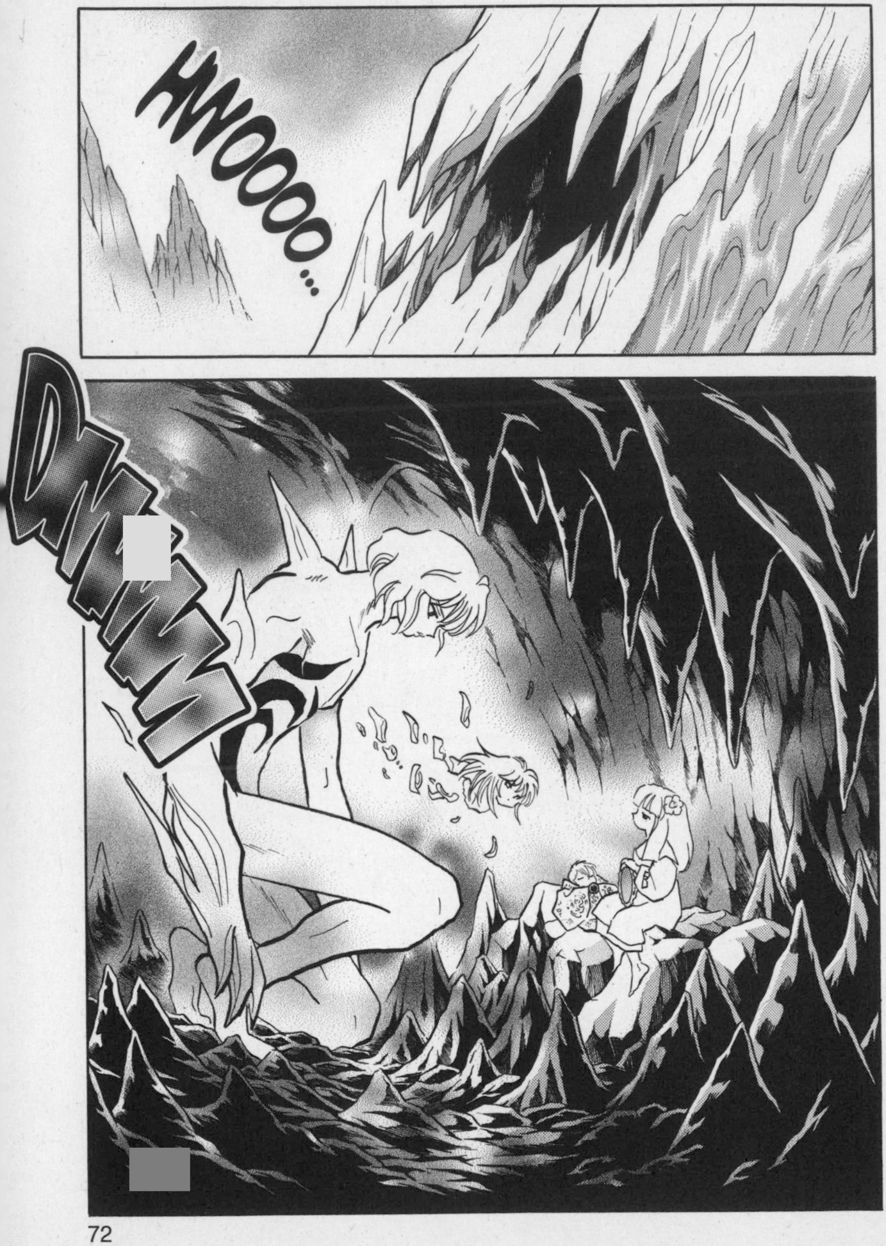
HWOOOO...
DMMMM

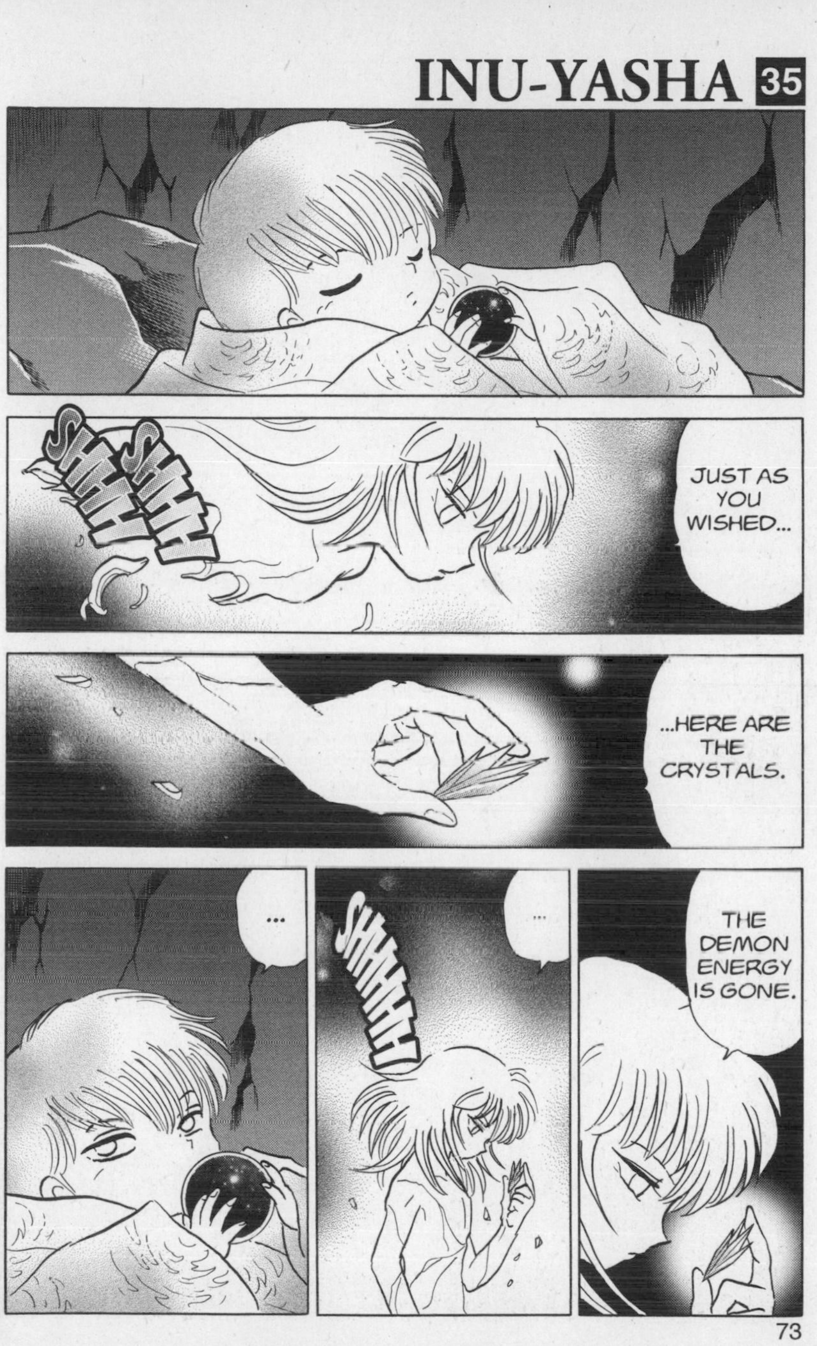
JUST AS YOU WISHED...
...HERE ARE THE CRYSTALS.
...
...
THE DEMON ENERGY IS GONE.

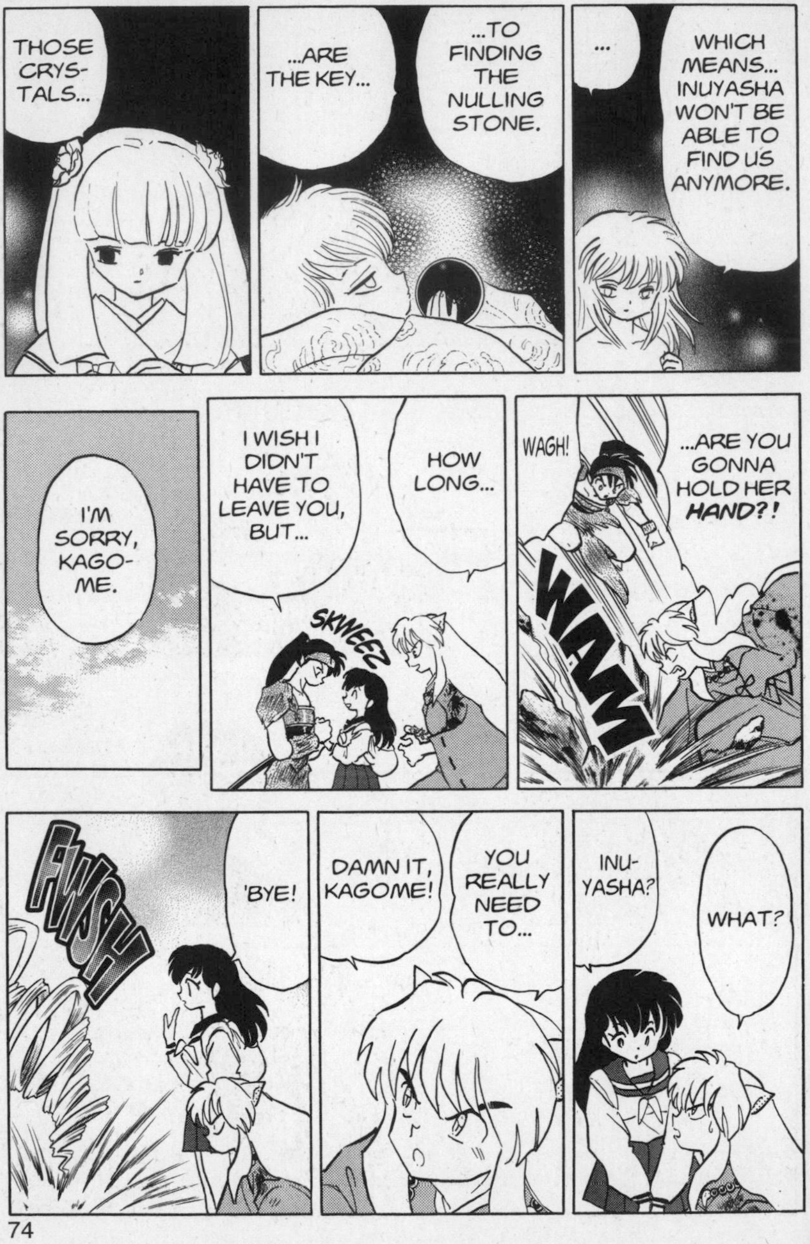
THOSE CRYSTALS...
...ARE THE KEY...
...TO FINDING THE NULLING STONE.
...
WHICH MEANS... INUYASHA WON'T BE ABLE TO FIND US ANYMORE.
I'M SORRY, KAGOME.
I WISH I DIDN'T HAVE TO LEAVE YOU, BUT...
HOW LONG...
SKWEEZ
WAGH!
...ARE YOU GONNA HOLD HER **HAND?!**
WAM
FWISH
'BYE!
DAMN IT, KAGOME!
YOU REALLY NEED TO...
INUYASHA?
WHAT?

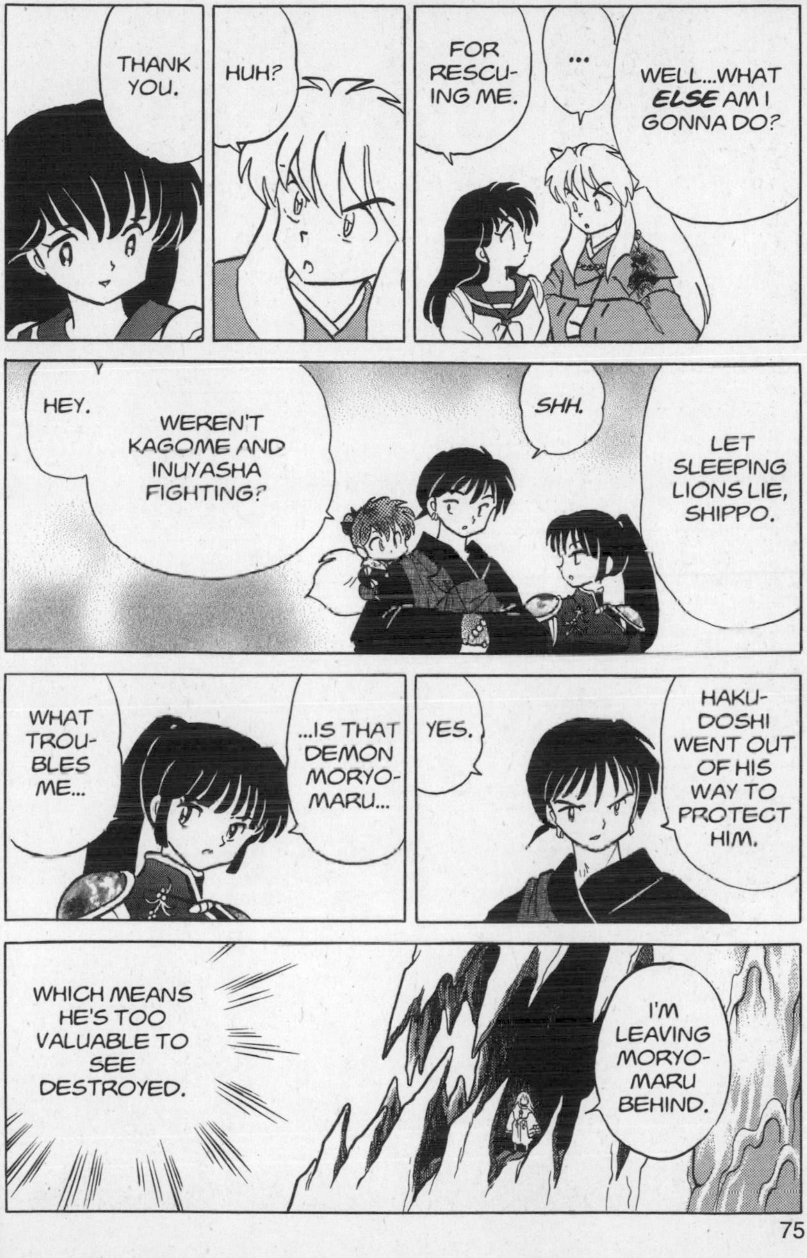
THANK YOU.
HUH?
FOR RESCUING ME.
...
WELL...WHAT *ELSE* AM I GONNA DO?
HEY.
WEREN'T KAGOME AND INUYASHA FIGHTING?
SHH.
LET SLEEPING LIONS LIE, SHIPPO.
WHAT TROUBLES ME...
...IS THAT DEMON MORYOMARU...
YES.
HAKUDOSHI WENT OUT OF HIS WAY TO PROTECT HIM.
WHICH MEANS HE'S TOO VALUABLE TO SEE DESTROYED.
I'M LEAVING MORYOMARU BEHIND.

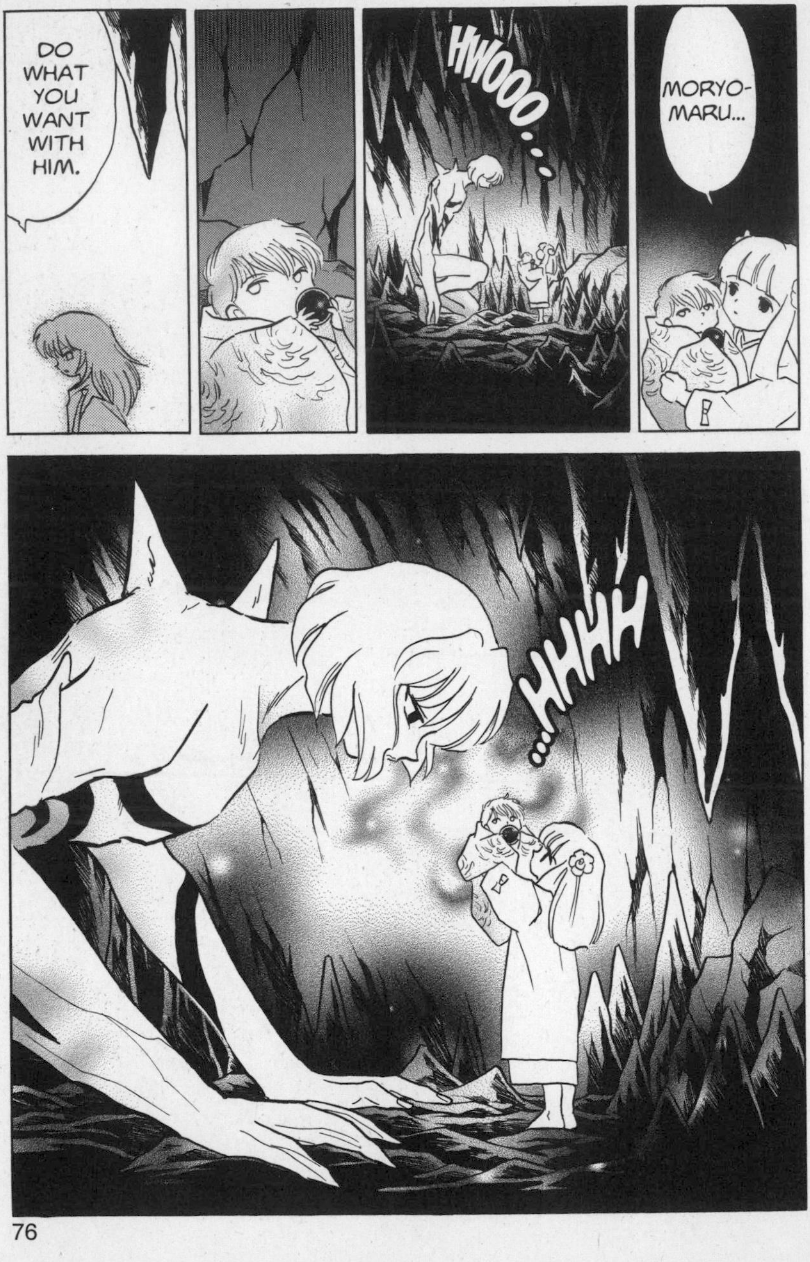
DO WHAT YOU WANT WITH HIM.
HWOOO...
MORYO-MARU...
HHHH...

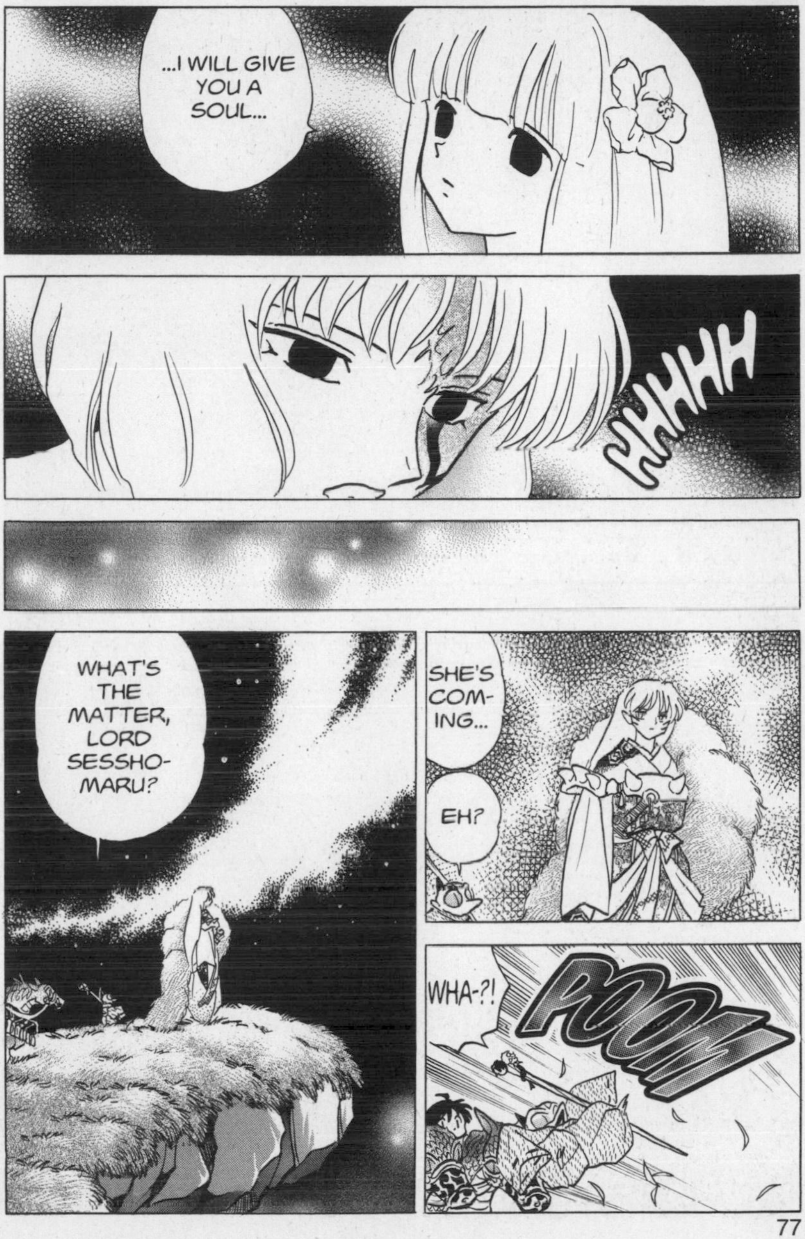
...I WILL GIVE YOU A SOUL...
HHHHH
WHAT'S THE MATTER, LORD SESSHOMARU?
SHE'S COMING...
EH?
WHA-?!
POOM

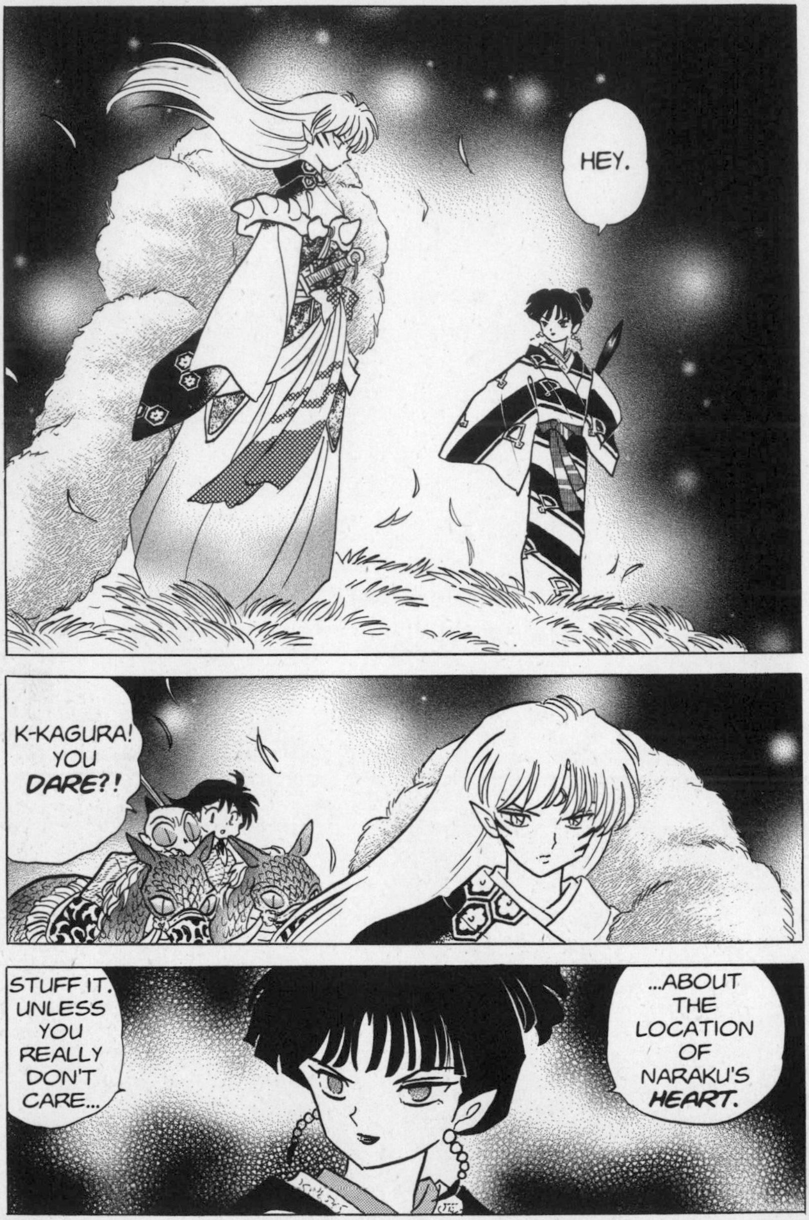
HEY.
K-KAGURA! YOU DARE?!
STUFF IT. UNLESS YOU REALLY DON'T CARE...
...ABOUT THE LOCATION OF NARAKU'S HEART.

SCROLL 5
THE FORGOTTEN FIANCÉE

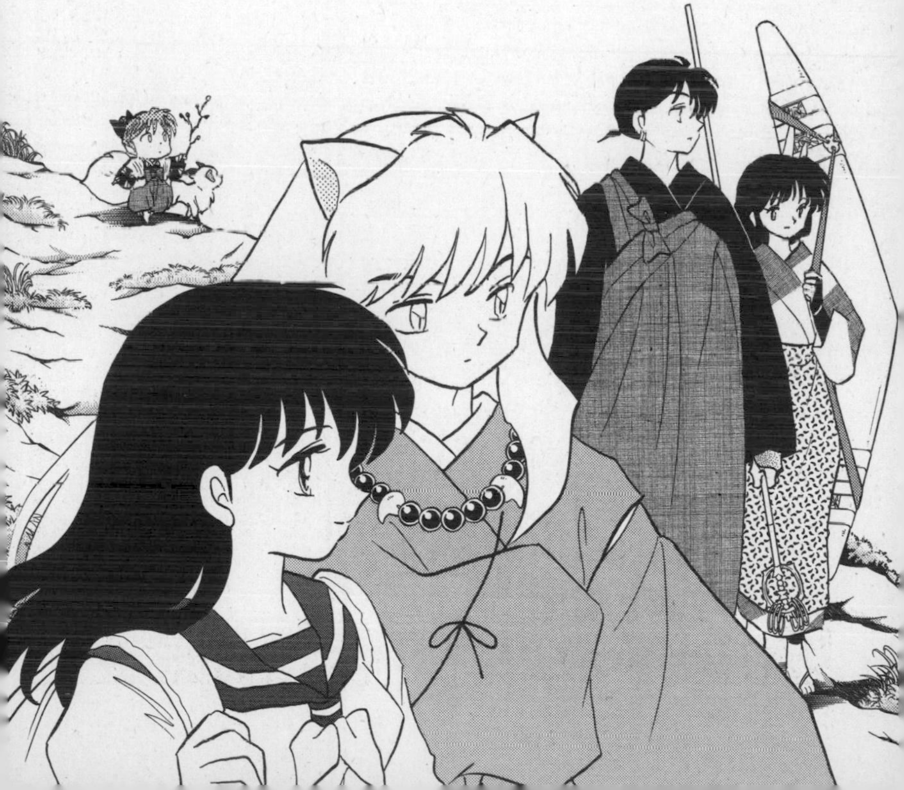

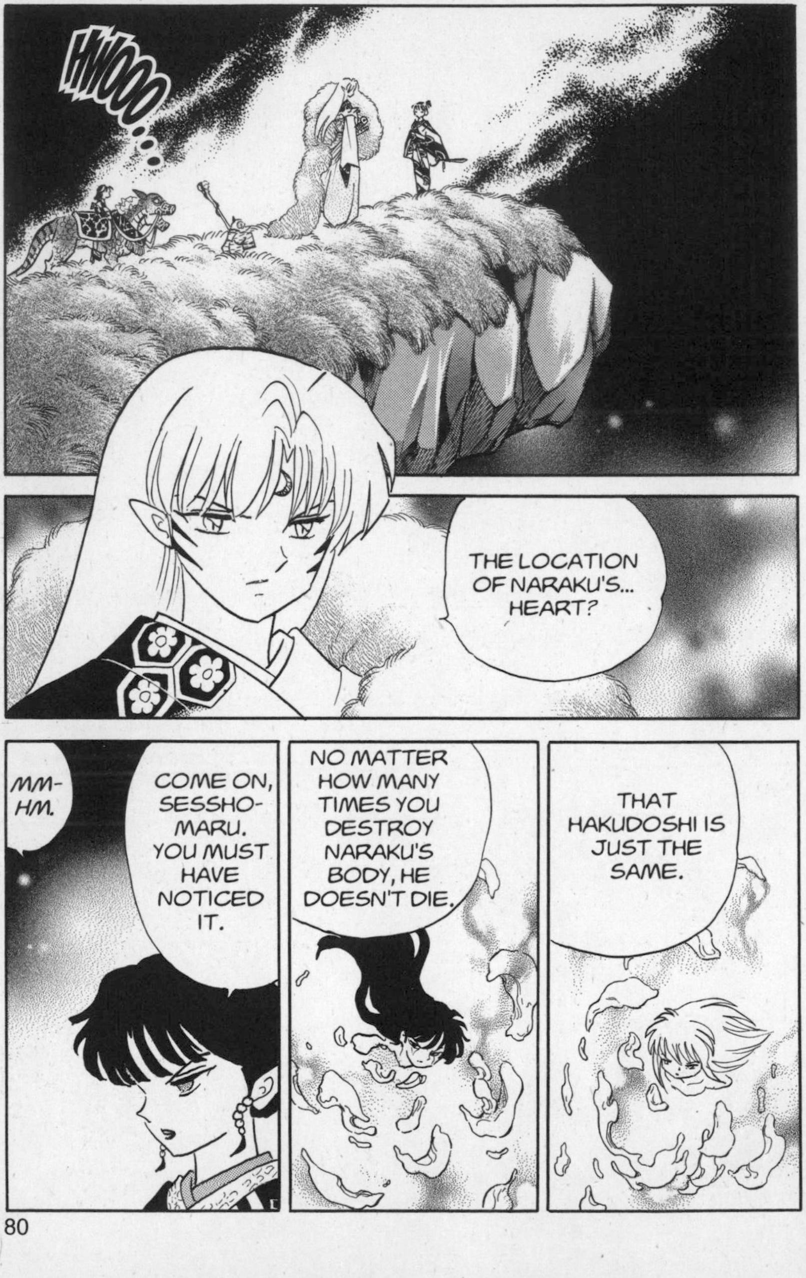
HWOOO....
THE LOCATION OF NARAKU'S... HEART?
MM-HM.
COME ON, SESSHO-MARU. YOU MUST HAVE NOTICED IT.
NO MATTER HOW MANY TIMES YOU DESTROY NARAKU'S BODY, HE DOESN'T DIE.
THAT HAKUDOSHI IS JUST THE SAME.

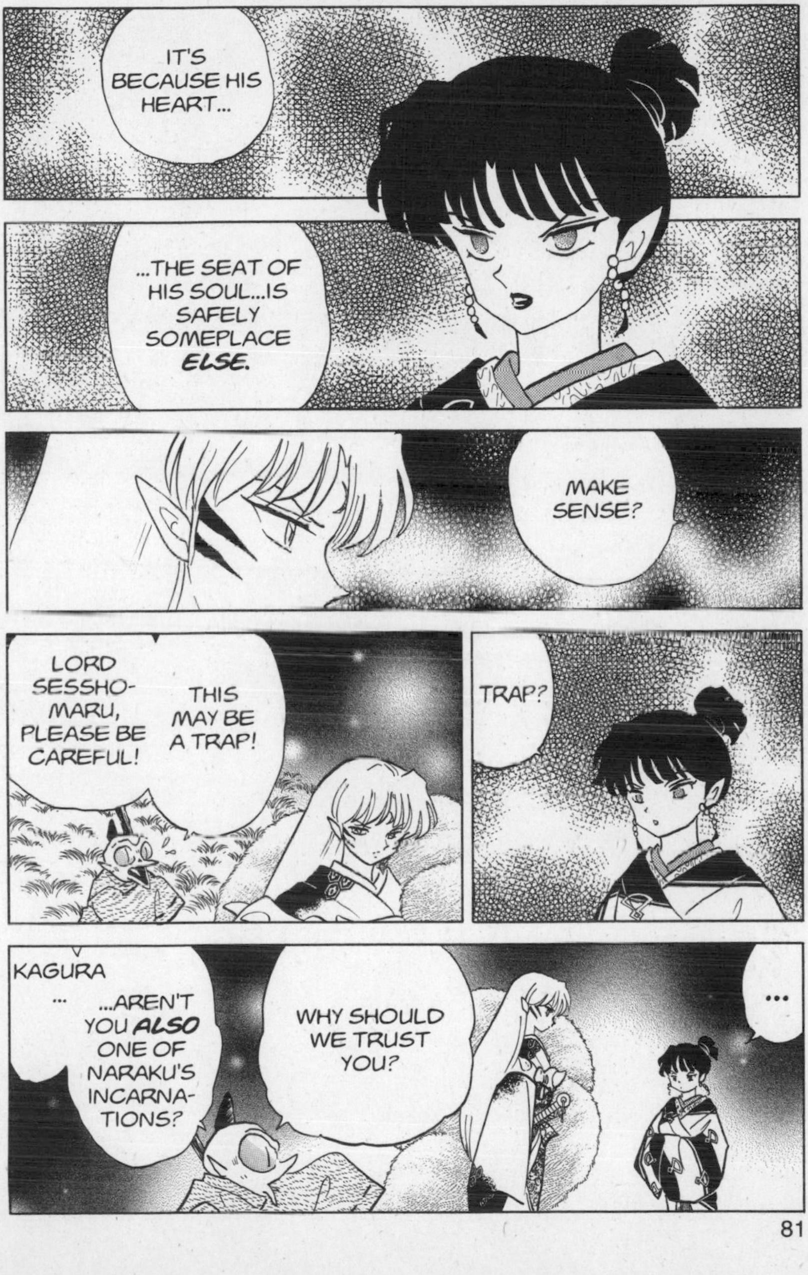
IT'S BECAUSE HIS HEART...
...THE SEAT OF HIS SOUL...IS SAFELY SOMEPLACE ELSE.
MAKE SENSE?
LORD SESSHO-MARU, PLEASE BE CAREFUL!
THIS MAY BE A TRAP!
TRAP?
KAGURA ...
...AREN'T YOU ALSO ONE OF NARAKU'S INCARNA-TIONS?
WHY SHOULD WE TRUST YOU?
...

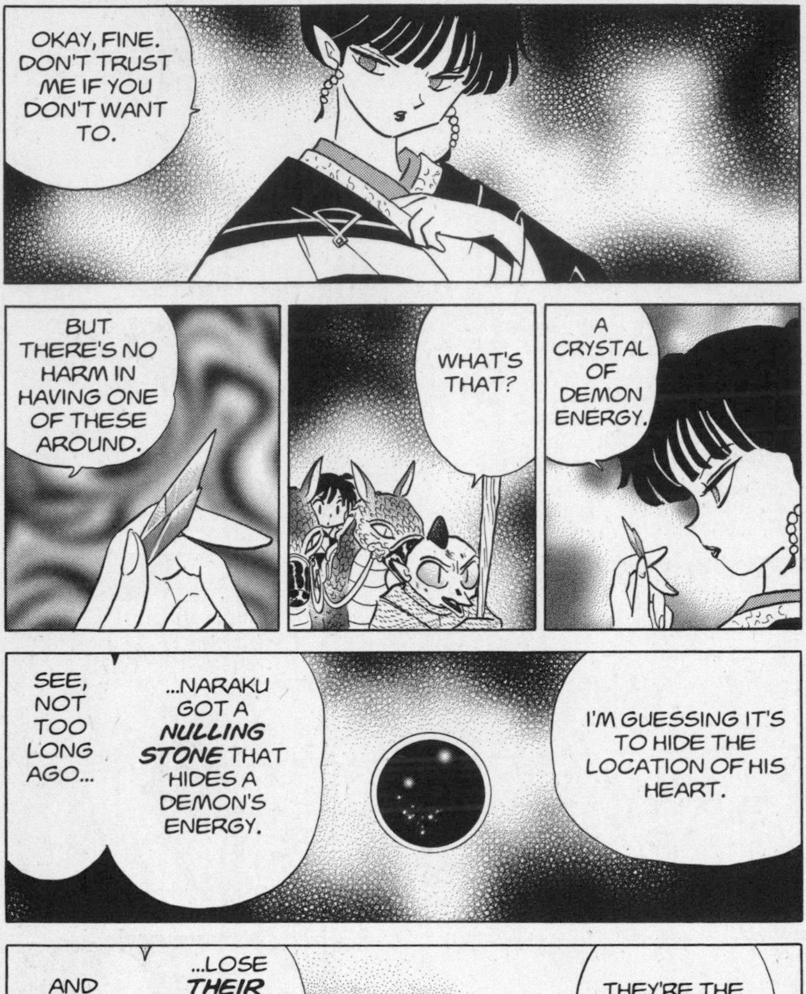
OKAY, FINE. DON'T TRUST ME IF YOU DON'T WANT TO.
BUT THERE'S NO HARM IN HAVING ONE OF THESE AROUND.
WHAT'S THAT?
A CRYSTAL OF DEMON ENERGY.
SEE, NOT TOO LONG AGO...
...NARAKU GOT A ***NULLING STONE*** THAT HIDES A DEMON'S ENERGY.
I'M GUESSING IT'S TO HIDE THE LOCATION OF HIS HEART.
AND THESE CRYSTALS ...
...LOSE ***THEIR*** ENERGY WHEN THEY'RE NEAR THAT STONE.
THEY'RE THE KEY TO FINDING NARAKU'S HEART.

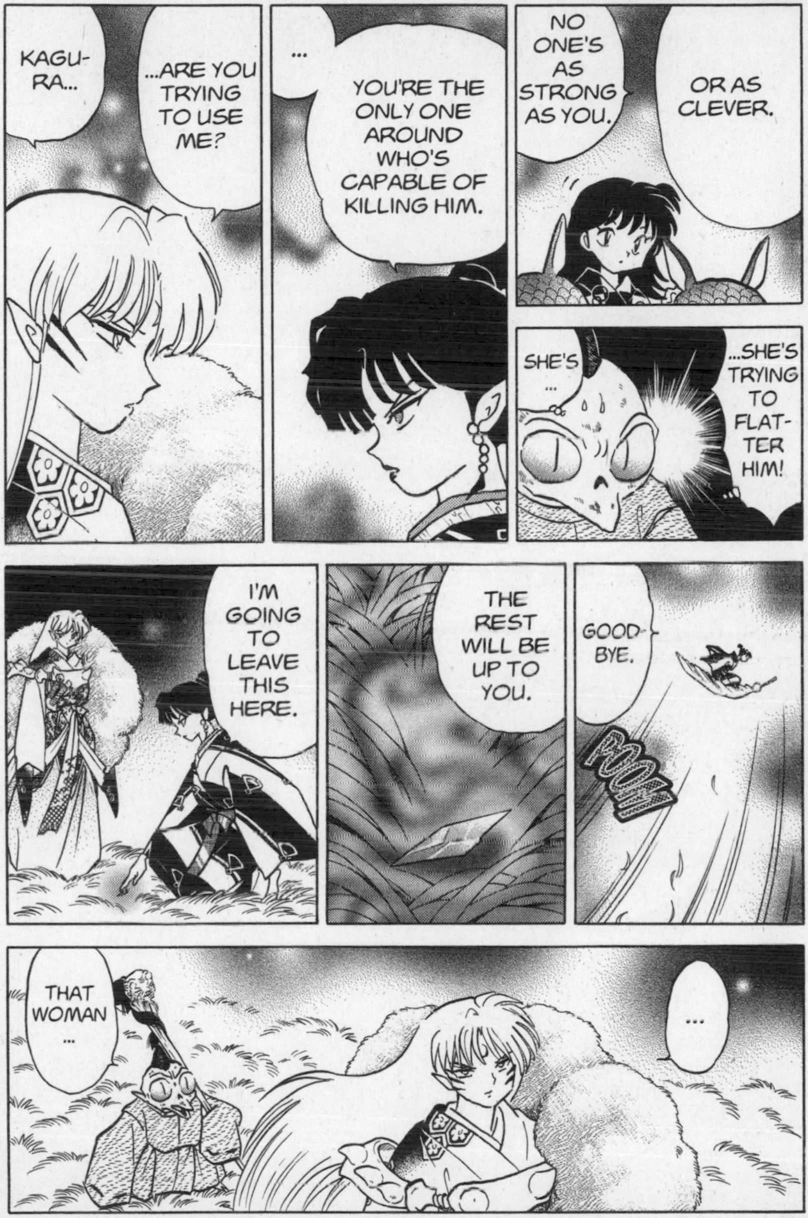
KAGURA...
...ARE YOU TRYING TO USE ME?
...
YOU'RE THE ONLY ONE AROUND WHO'S CAPABLE OF KILLING HIM.
NO ONE'S AS STRONG AS YOU.
OR AS CLEVER.
SHE'S ...
...SHE'S TRYING TO FLATTER HIM!
I'M GOING TO LEAVE THIS HERE.
THE REST WILL BE UP TO YOU.
GOODBYE.
BOOM
THAT WOMAN ...
...

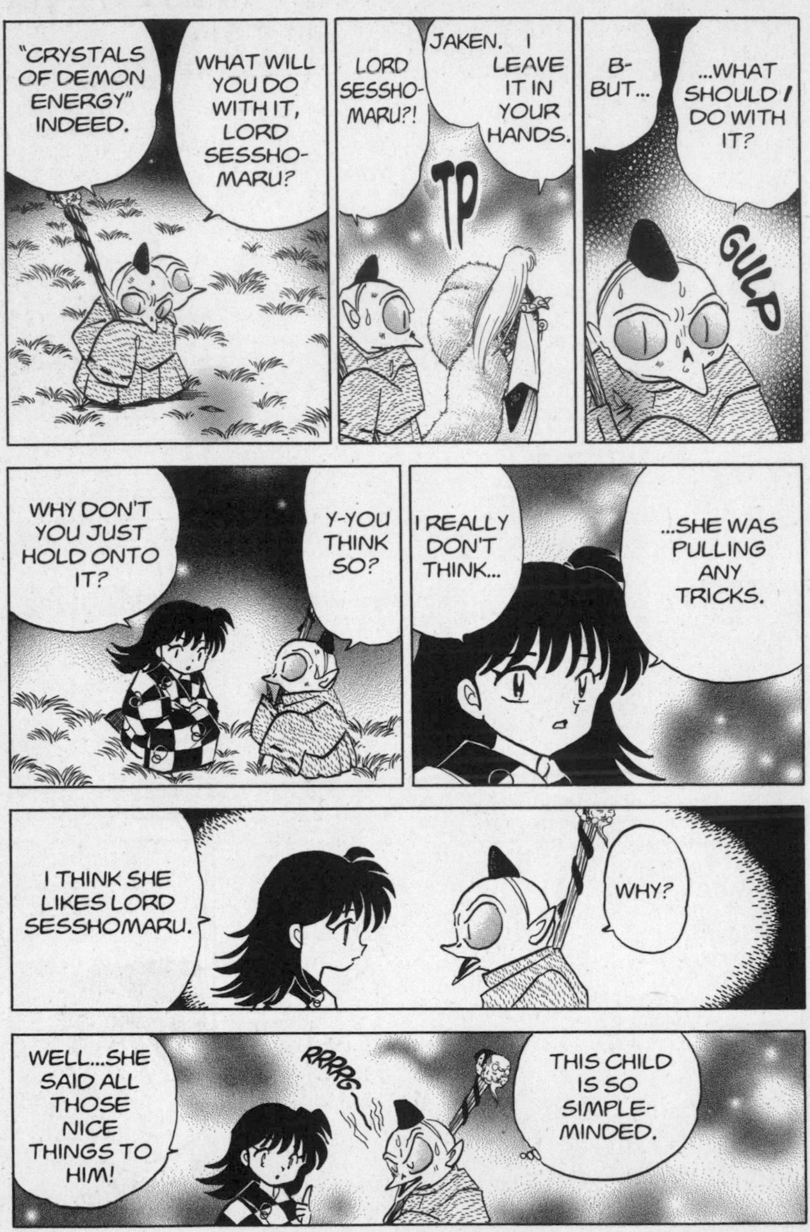
"CRYSTALS OF DEMON ENERGY" INDEED.
WHAT WILL YOU DO WITH IT, LORD SESSHO-MARU?
LORD SESSHO-MARU?!
JAKEN. I LEAVE IT IN YOUR HANDS.
TP
B-BUT...
...WHAT SHOULD I DO WITH IT?
GULP
WHY DON'T YOU JUST HOLD ONTO IT?
Y-YOU THINK SO?
I REALLY DON'T THINK...
...SHE WAS PULLING ANY TRICKS.
I THINK SHE LIKES LORD SESSHOMARU.
WHY?
WELL...SHE SAID ALL THOSE NICE THINGS TO HIM!
RRRRG
THIS CHILD IS SO SIMPLE-MINDED.

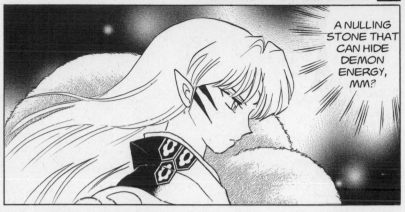

A NULLING STONE THAT CAN HIDE DEMON ENERGY, MM?

...SIGH...

LORD MIROKU IS STILL UPSET AT HIMSELF.

THAT THE CRYSTALS OF DEMON ENERGY GOT STOLEN?

HOW CAN I HAVE LET THAT HAPPEN?

IT'S NOT YOUR FAULT. BESIDES ...

...I'M JUST HAPPY YOU WEREN'T HURT.

SANGO ...

GULP

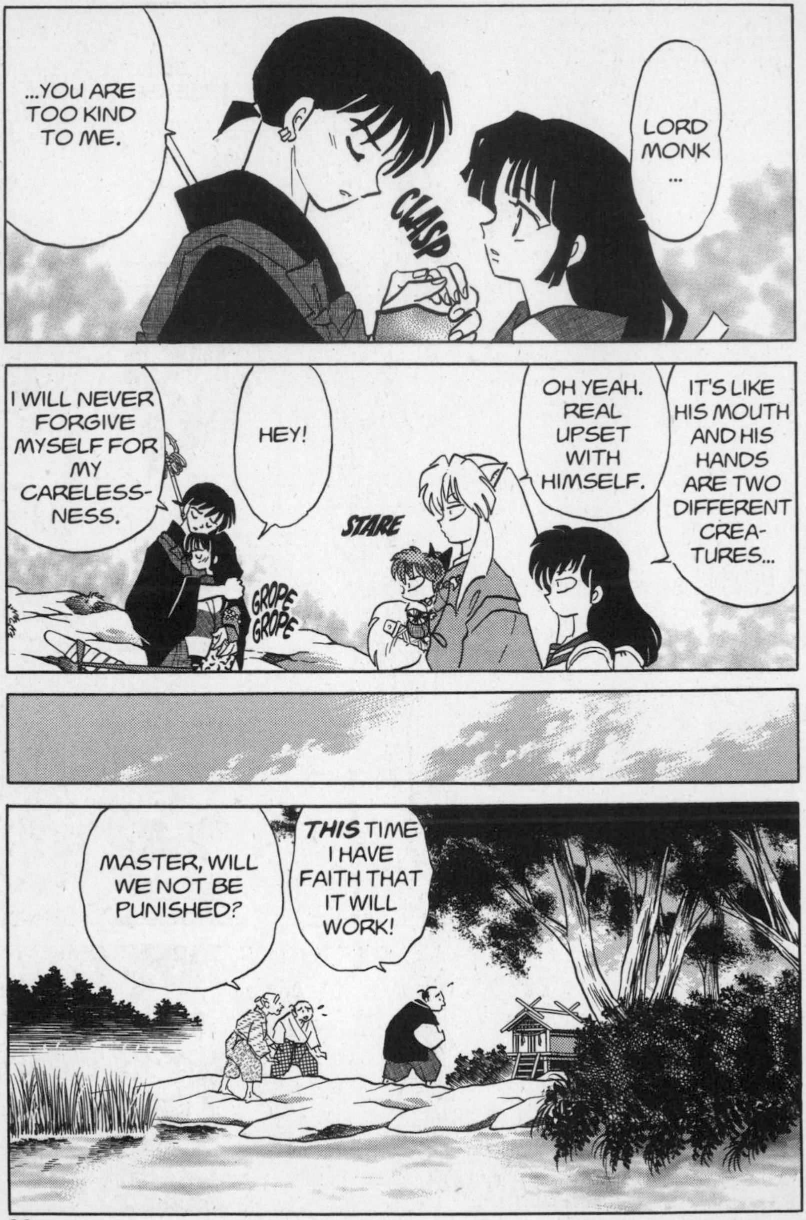
...YOU ARE TOO KIND TO ME.
CLASP
LORD MONK ...
I WILL NEVER FORGIVE MYSELF FOR MY CARELESS-NESS.
HEY!
GROPE GROPE
STARE
OH YEAH. REAL UPSET WITH HIMSELF.
IT'S LIKE HIS MOUTH AND HIS HANDS ARE TWO DIFFERENT CREA-TURES...
MASTER, WILL WE NOT BE PUNISHED?
THIS TIME I HAVE FAITH THAT IT WILL WORK!

I RECEIVED THIS PRAYER NOTE FROM A MOST RESPECTABLE MONK.

SO PLEASE...

...BE AT PEACE.

PAP

FFF

SHKA SHKA SHKA

RRRUMBL

YAAAA!

SHKA SHKA

...EARTH-QUAKE?

SHHH SHHH

AND...

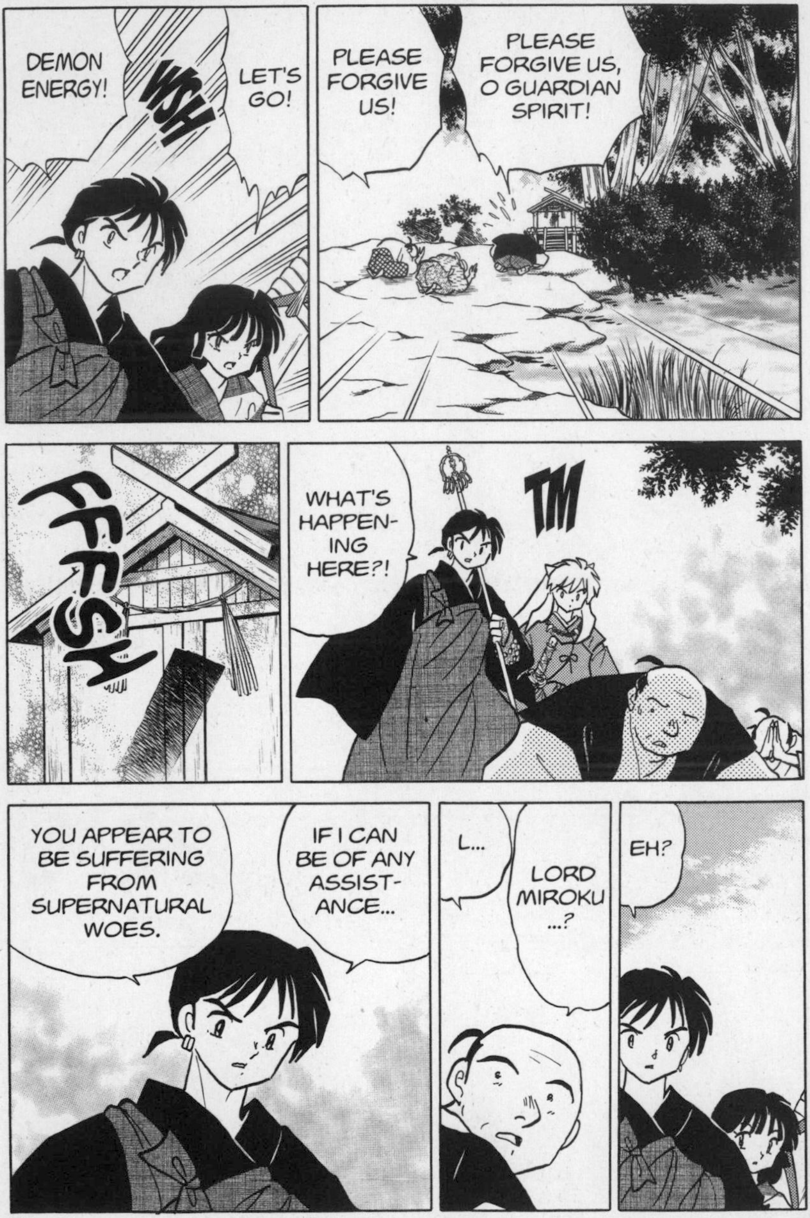
DEMON ENERGY!
WSH
LET'S GO!
PLEASE FORGIVE US!
PLEASE FORGIVE US, O GUARDIAN SPIRIT!
FFFSH
WHAT'S HAPPEN-ING HERE?!
TM
YOU APPEAR TO BE SUFFERING FROM SUPERNATURAL WOES.
IF I CAN BE OF ANY ASSIST-ANCE...
L...
LORD MIROKU ...?
EH?

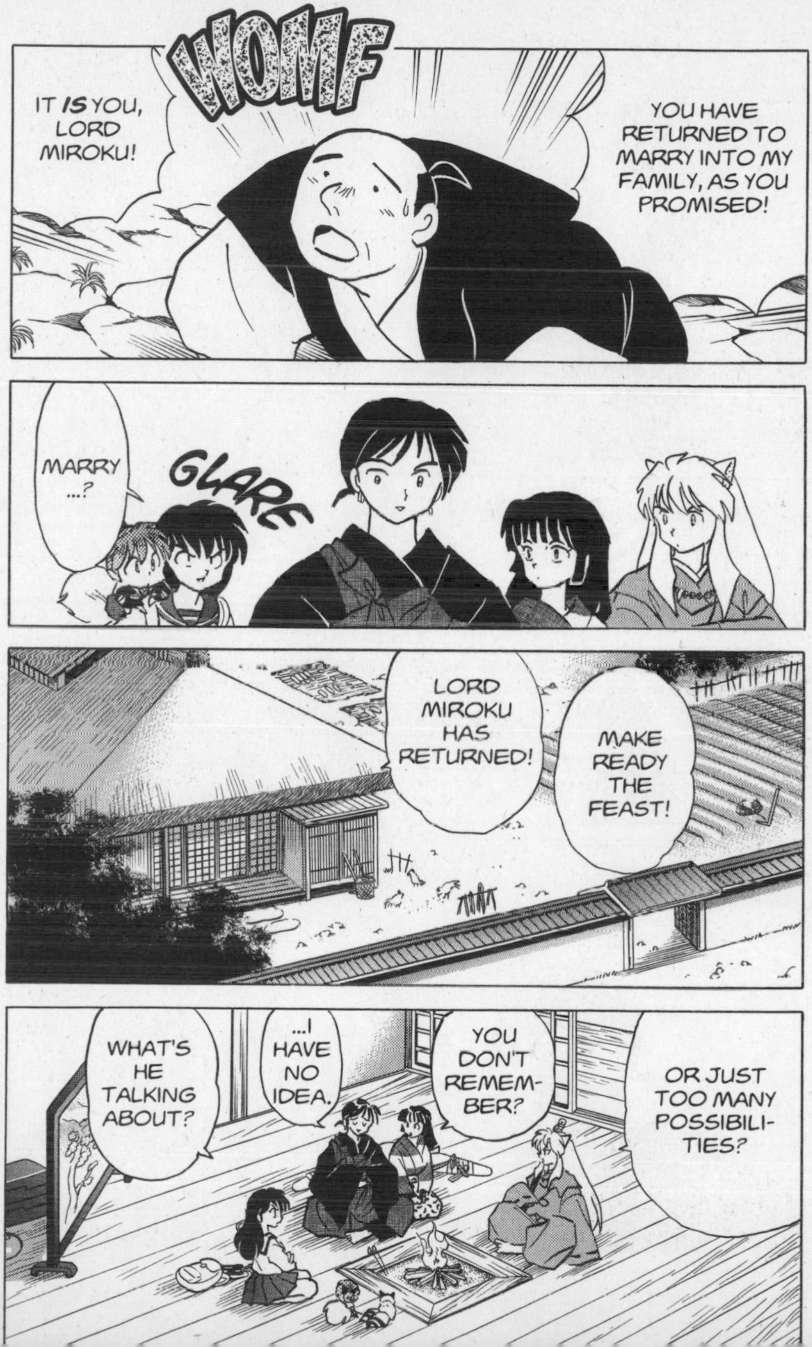
WOMF
IT IS YOU, LORD MIROKU!
YOU HAVE RETURNED TO MARRY INTO MY FAMILY, AS YOU PROMISED!
MARRY ...?
GLARE
LORD MIROKU HAS RETURNED!
MAKE READY THE FEAST!
WHAT'S HE TALKING ABOUT?
...I HAVE NO IDEA.
YOU DON'T REMEM-BER?
OR JUST TOO MANY POSSIBILI-TIES?

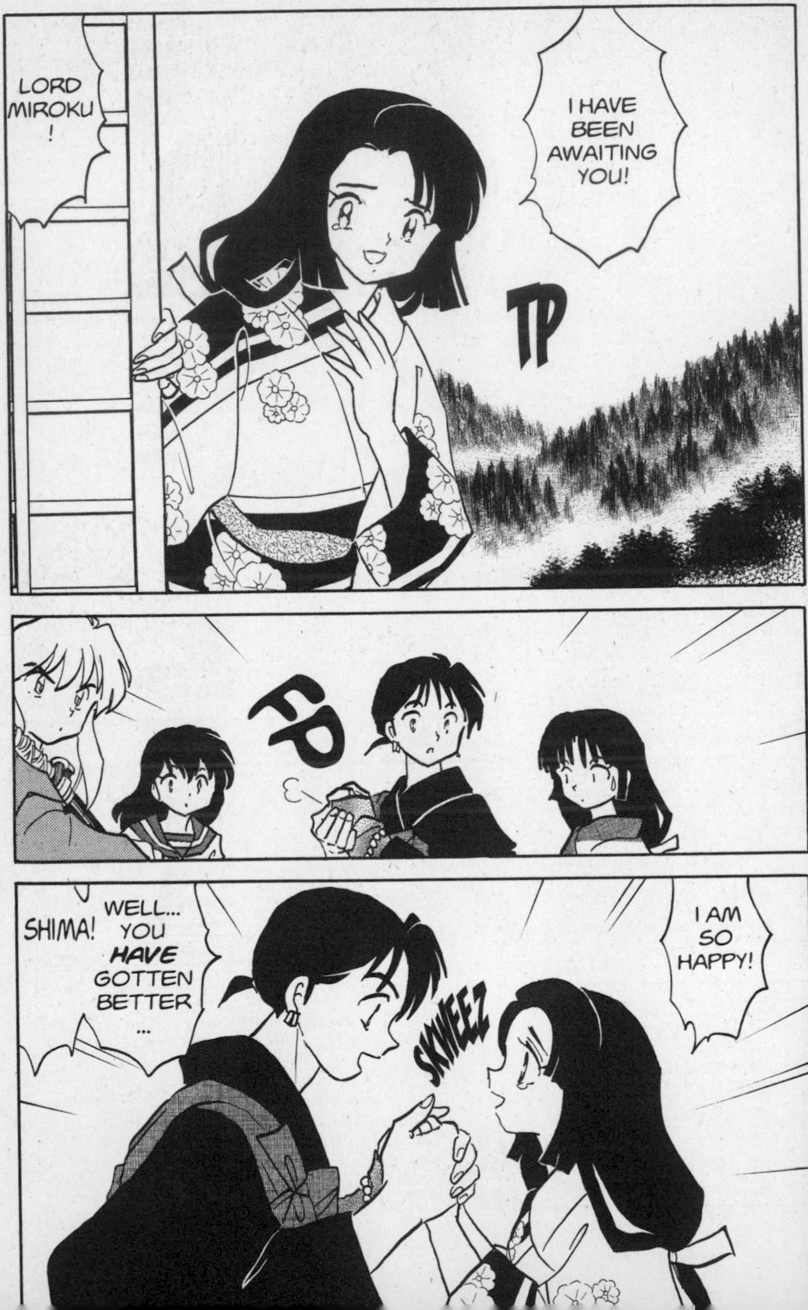
LORD MIROKU!
I HAVE BEEN AWAITING YOU!
TP
FP
SHIMA!
WELL... YOU *HAVE* GOTTEN BETTER...
I AM SO HAPPY!
SKWEEZ

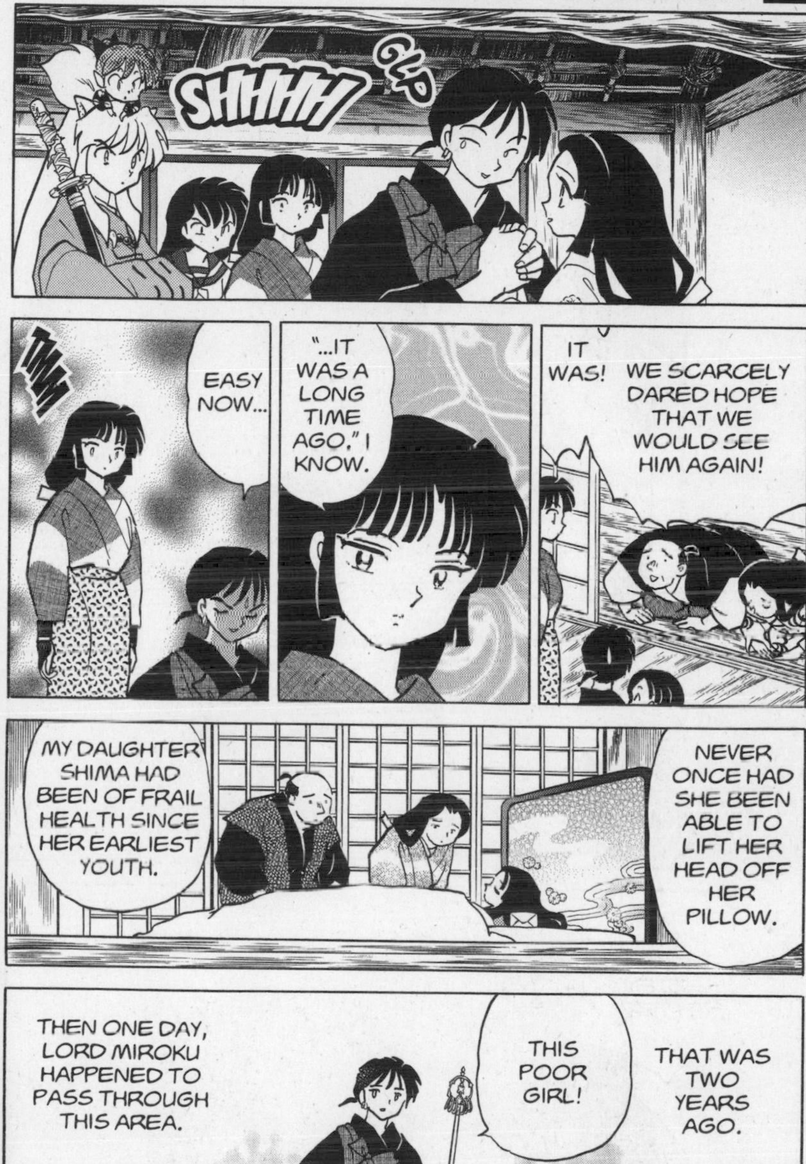
SHHHHH!
GLP
EASY NOW...
"...IT WAS A LONG TIME AGO," I KNOW.
IT WAS!
WE SCARCELY DARED HOPE THAT WE WOULD SEE HIM AGAIN!
MY DAUGHTER SHIMA HAD BEEN OF FRAIL HEALTH SINCE HER EARLIEST YOUTH.
NEVER ONCE HAD SHE BEEN ABLE TO LIFT HER HEAD OFF HER PILLOW.
THEN ONE DAY, LORD MIROKU HAPPENED TO PASS THROUGH THIS AREA.
THIS POOR GIRL!
THAT WAS TWO YEARS AGO.

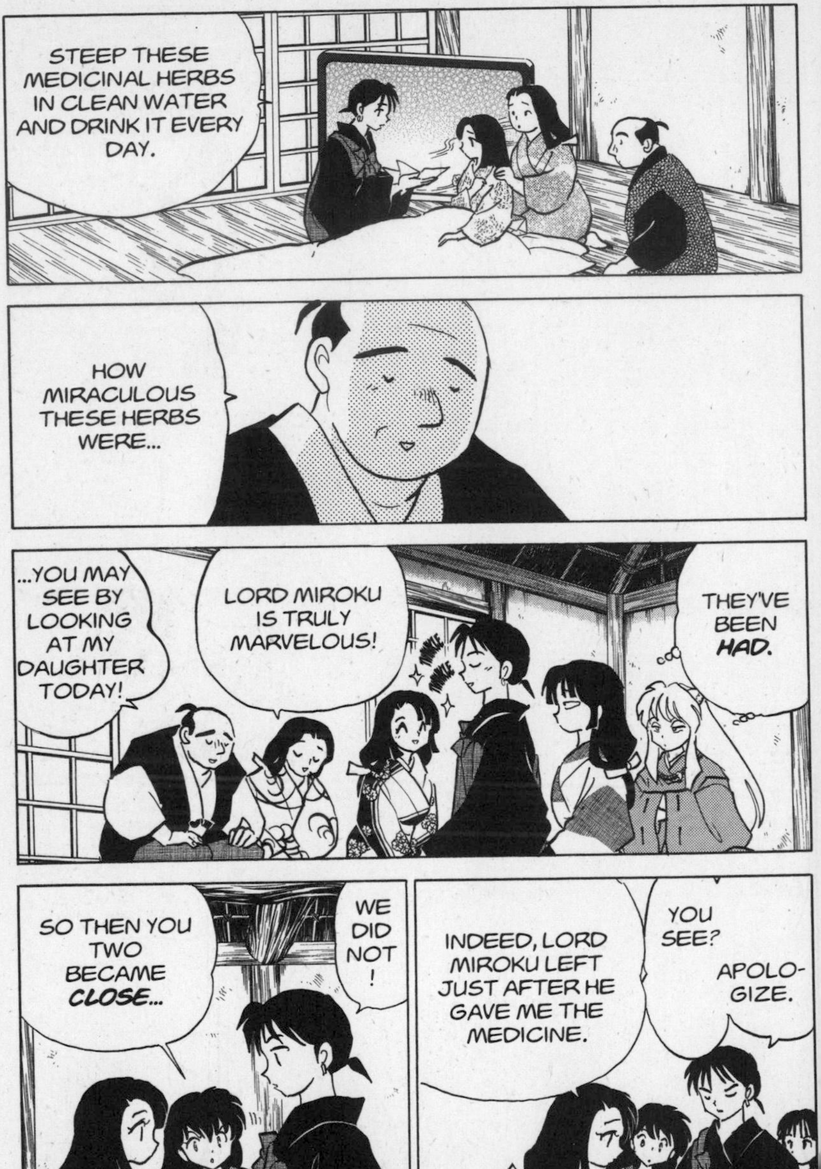
STEEP THESE MEDICINAL HERBS IN CLEAN WATER AND DRINK IT EVERY DAY.
HOW MIRACULOUS THESE HERBS WERE...
...YOU MAY SEE BY LOOKING AT MY DAUGHTER TODAY!
LORD MIROKU IS TRULY MARVELOUS!
THEY'VE BEEN HAD.
SO THEN YOU TWO BECAME CLOSE...
WE DID NOT!
INDEED, LORD MIROKU LEFT JUST AFTER HE GAVE ME THE MEDICINE.
YOU SEE?
APOLOGIZE.

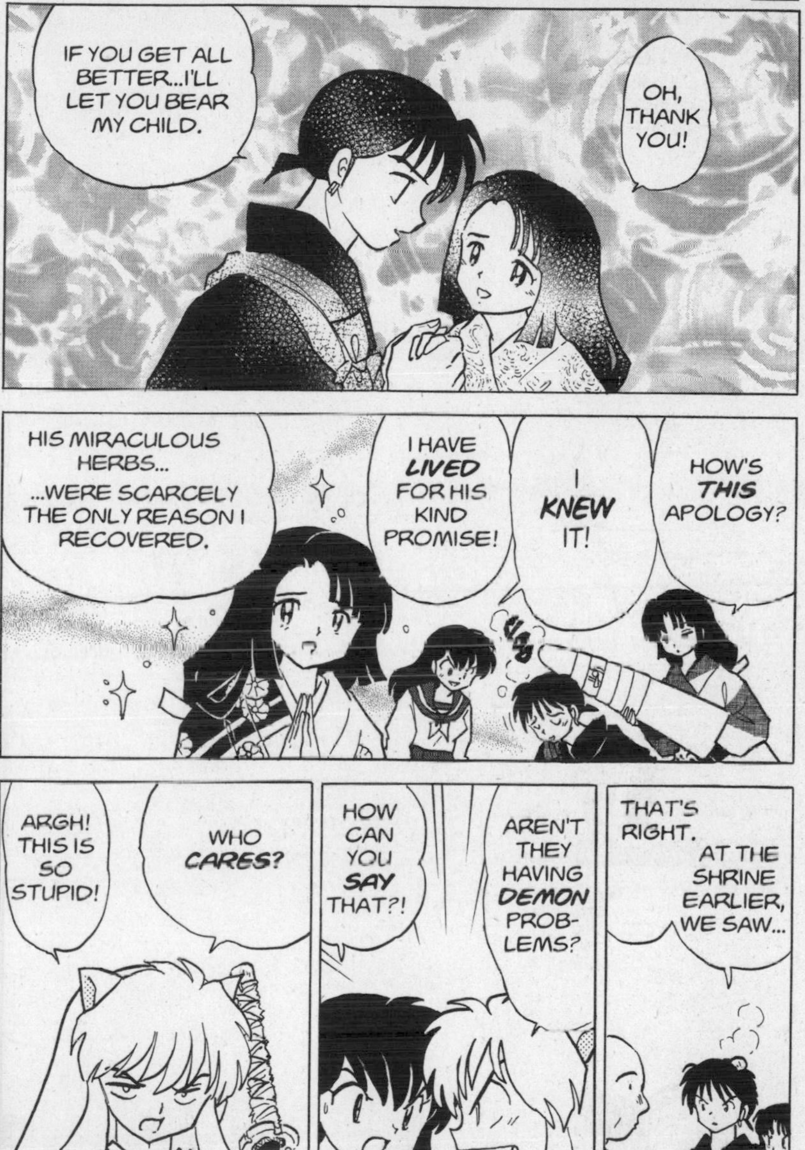
IF YOU GET ALL BETTER...I'LL LET YOU BEAR MY CHILD.
OH, THANK YOU!
HIS MIRACULOUS HERBS...
...WERE SCARCELY THE ONLY REASON I RECOVERED.
I HAVE LIVED FOR HIS KIND PROMISE!
I KNEW IT!
HOW'S THIS APOLOGY?
ARGH! THIS IS SO STUPID!
WHO CARES?
HOW CAN YOU SAY THAT?!
AREN'T THEY HAVING DEMON PROB-LEMS?
THAT'S RIGHT.
AT THE SHRINE EARLIER, WE SAW...

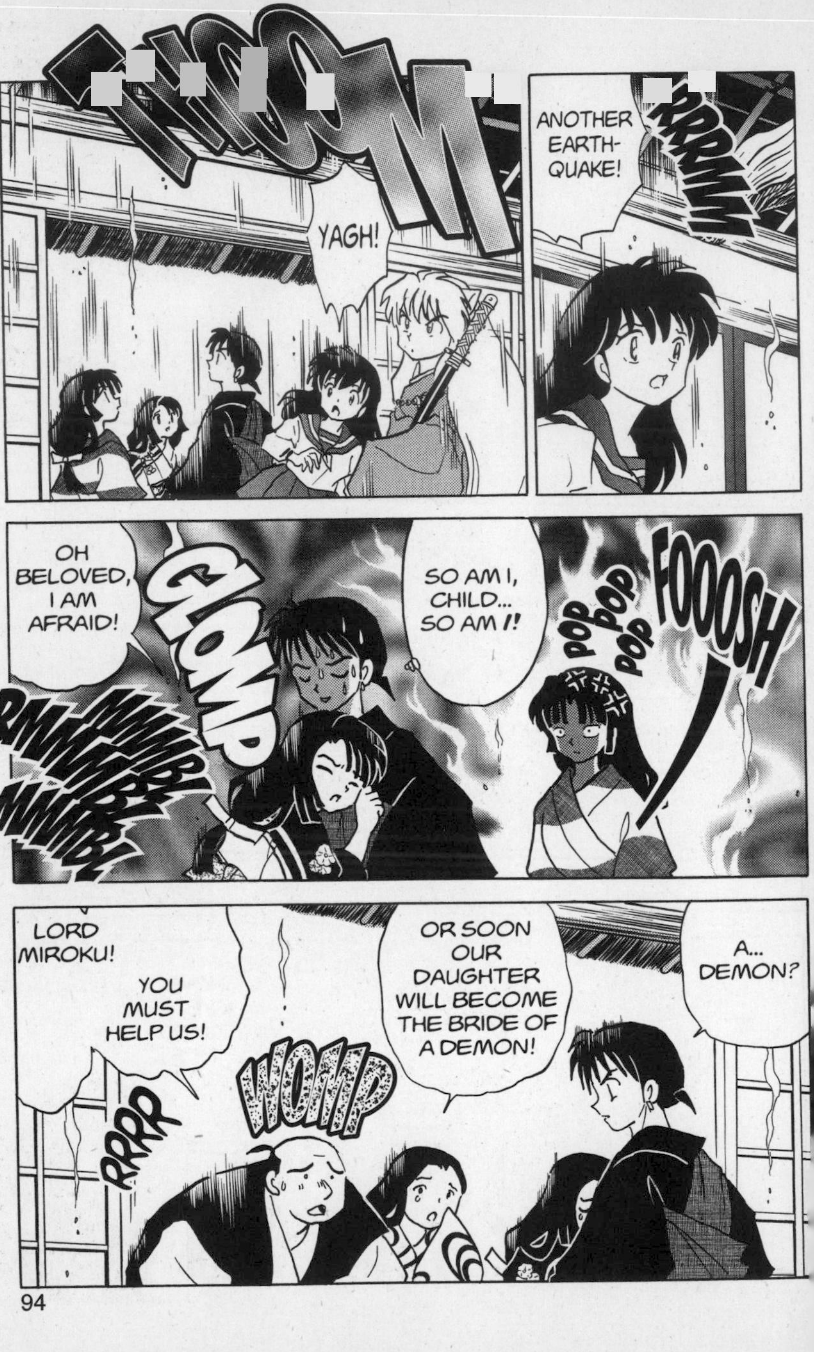
THOOM
YAGH!
ANOTHER EARTH-QUAKE!
OH BELOVED, I AM AFRAID!
GLOMP
SO AM I, CHILD... SO AM I!
FOOOSH
LORD MIROKU!
YOU MUST HELP US!
RRRR
WOMP
OR SOON OUR DAUGHTER WILL BECOME THE BRIDE OF A DEMON!
A... DEMON?

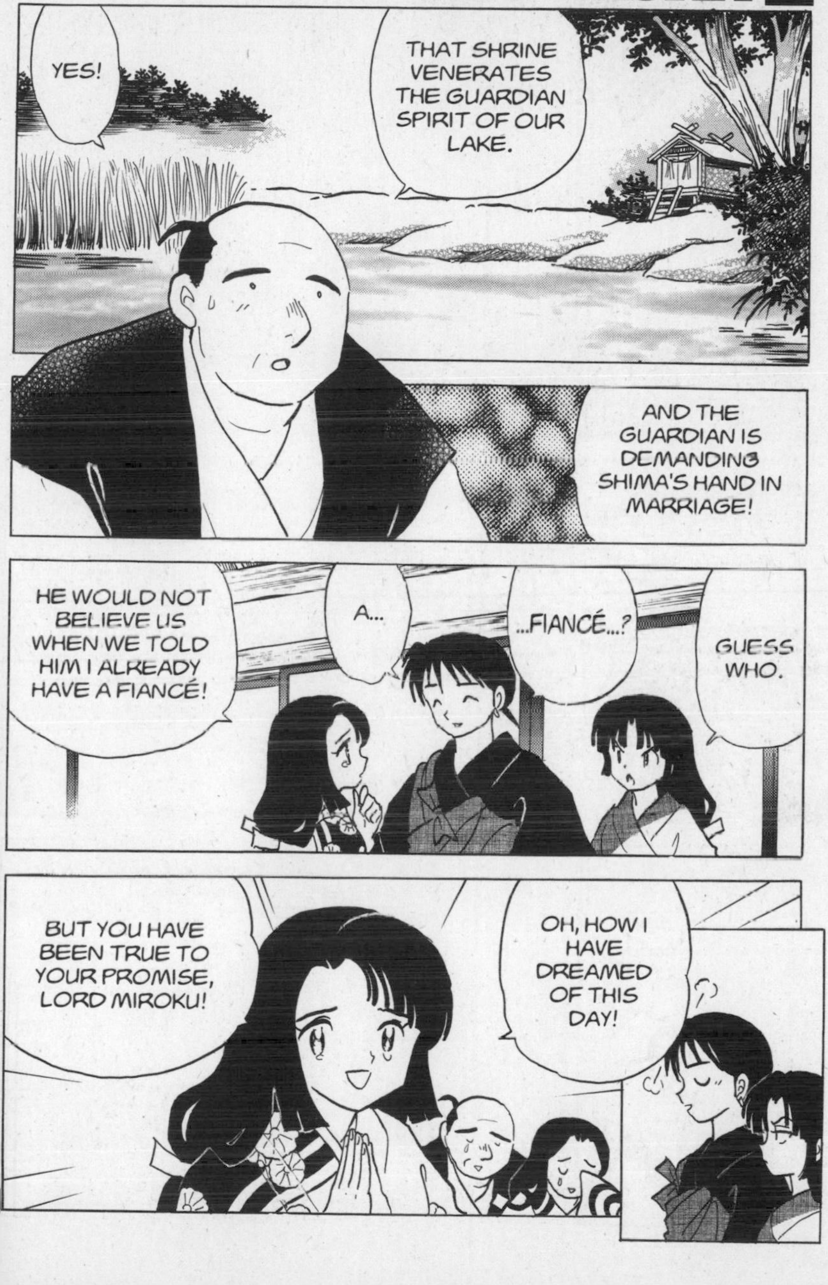
YES!
THAT SHRINE VENERATES THE GUARDIAN SPIRIT OF OUR LAKE.
AND THE GUARDIAN IS DEMANDING SHIMA'S HAND IN MARRIAGE!
HE WOULD NOT BELIEVE US WHEN WE TOLD HIM I ALREADY HAVE A FIANCÉ!
A...
...FIANCÉ...?
GUESS WHO.
BUT YOU HAVE BEEN TRUE TO YOUR PROMISE, LORD MIROKU!
OH, HOW I HAVE DREAMED OF THIS DAY!

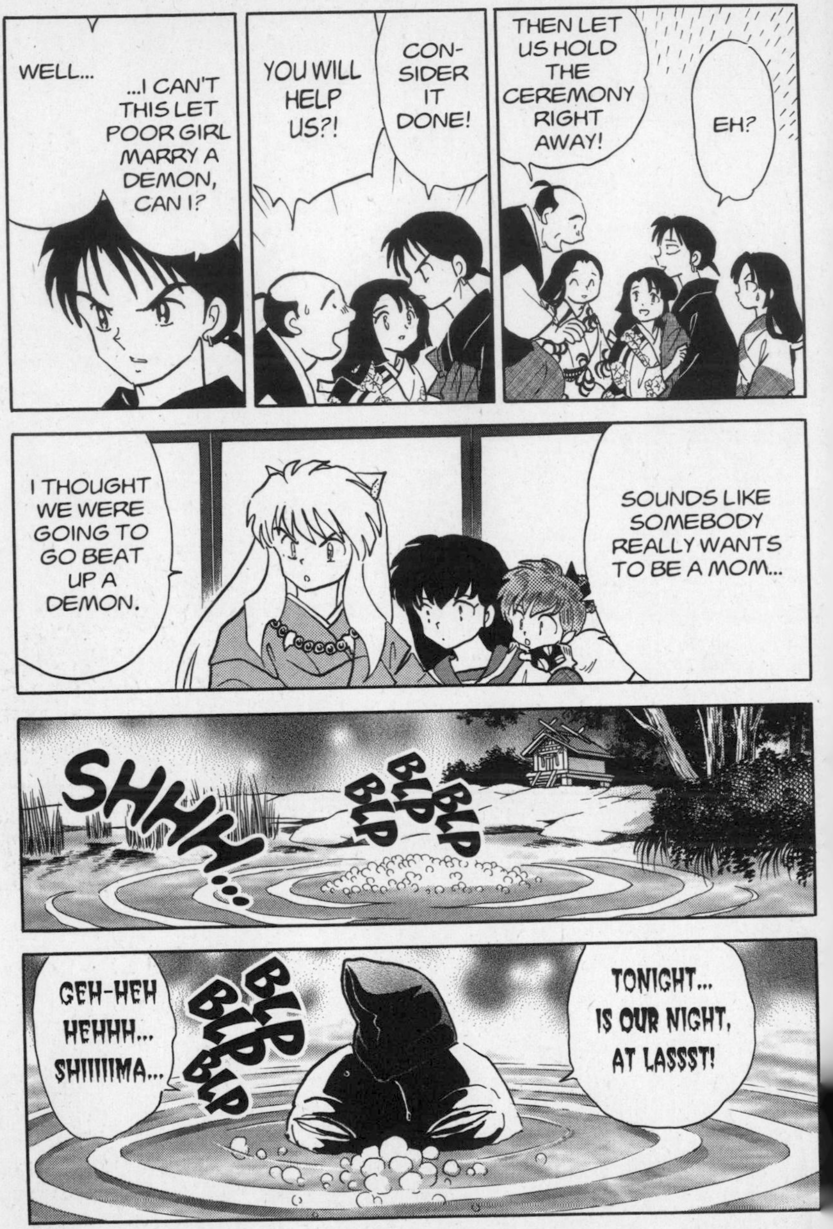
WELL...
...I CAN'T THIS LET POOR GIRL MARRY A DEMON, CAN I?
YOU WILL HELP US?!
CON-SIDER IT DONE!
THEN LET US HOLD THE CEREMONY RIGHT AWAY!
EH?
I THOUGHT WE WERE GOING TO GO BEAT UP A DEMON.
SOUNDS LIKE SOMEBODY REALLY WANTS TO BE A MOM...
SHHH...
BLP BLP BLP
GEH-HEH HEHHH... SHIIIIIMA...
BLP BLP BLP
TONIGHT... IS OUR NIGHT, AT LASSST!

SCROLL 6

PAST INDISCRETIONS

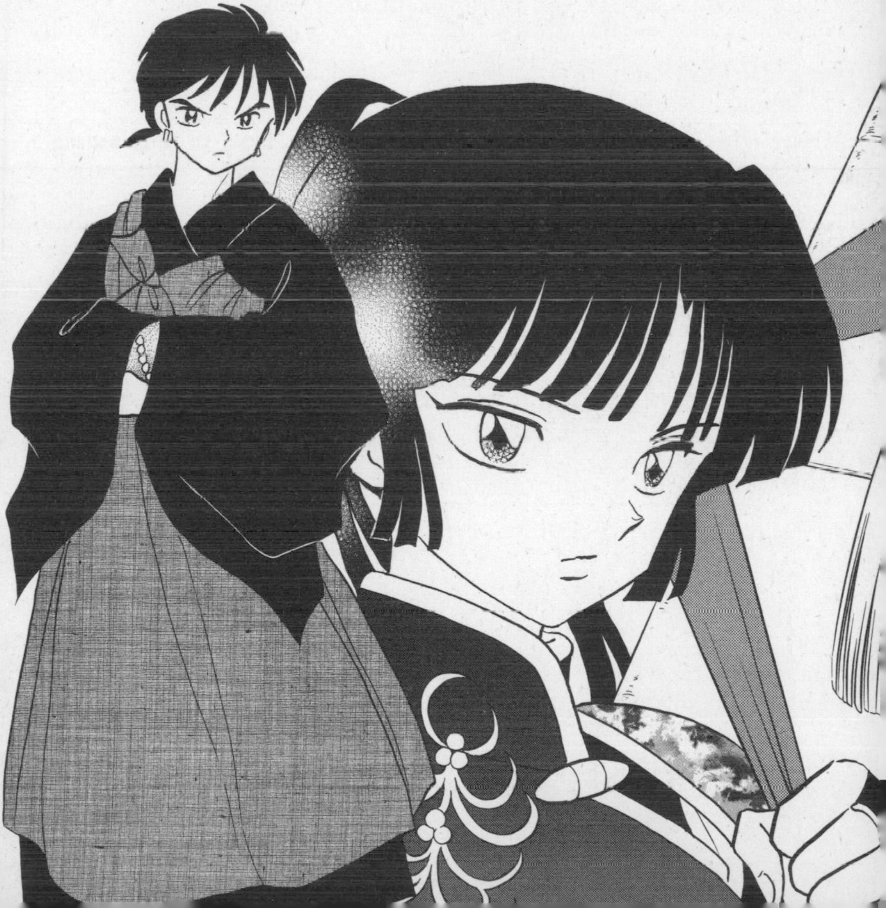

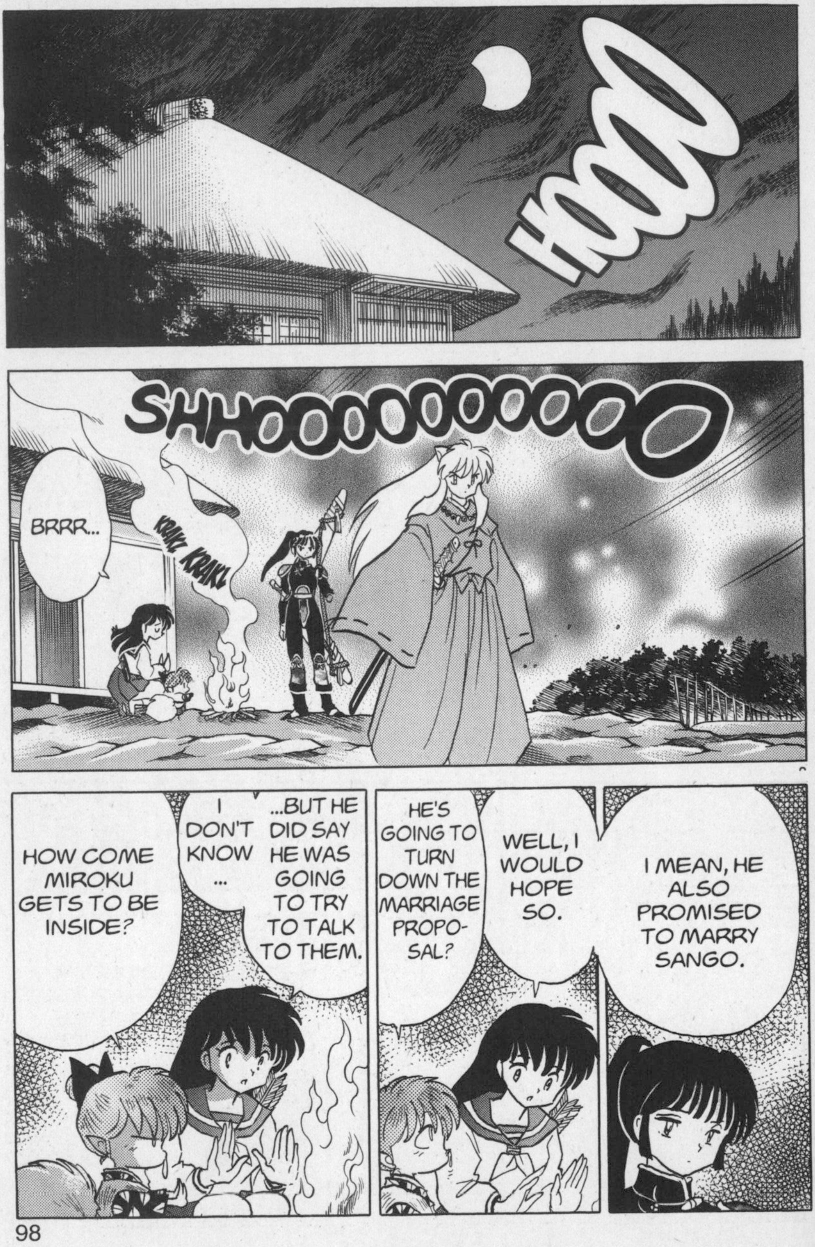
HOOOO
SHOOOOOOOOOO
BRRR...
KRAKL KRAKL
HOW COME MIROKU GETS TO BE INSIDE?
I DON'T KNOW ...
...BUT HE DID SAY HE WAS GOING TO TRY TO TALK TO THEM.
HE'S GOING TO TURN DOWN THE MARRIAGE PROPO-SAL?
WELL, I WOULD HOPE SO.
I MEAN, HE ALSO PROMISED TO MARRY SANGO.

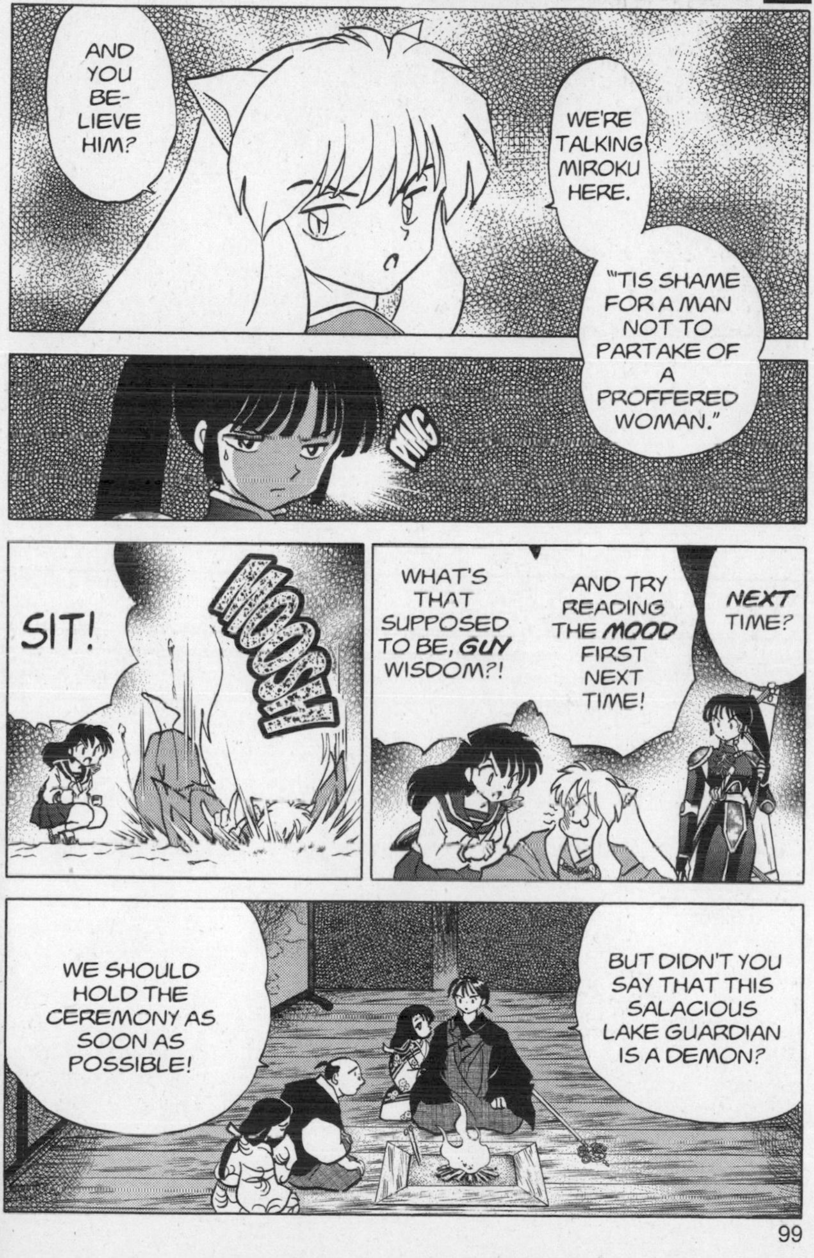
AND YOU BE- LIEVE HIM?
WE'RE TALKING MIROKU HERE.
"TIS SHAME FOR A MAN NOT TO PARTAKE OF A PROFFERED WOMAN."
PING
SIT!
WOOSH!
WHAT'S THAT SUPPOSED TO BE, *GUY* WISDOM?!
AND TRY READING THE *MOOD* FIRST NEXT TIME!
NEXT TIME?
WE SHOULD HOLD THE CEREMONY AS SOON AS POSSIBLE!
BUT DIDN'T YOU SAY THAT THIS SALACIOUS LAKE GUARDIAN IS A DEMON?

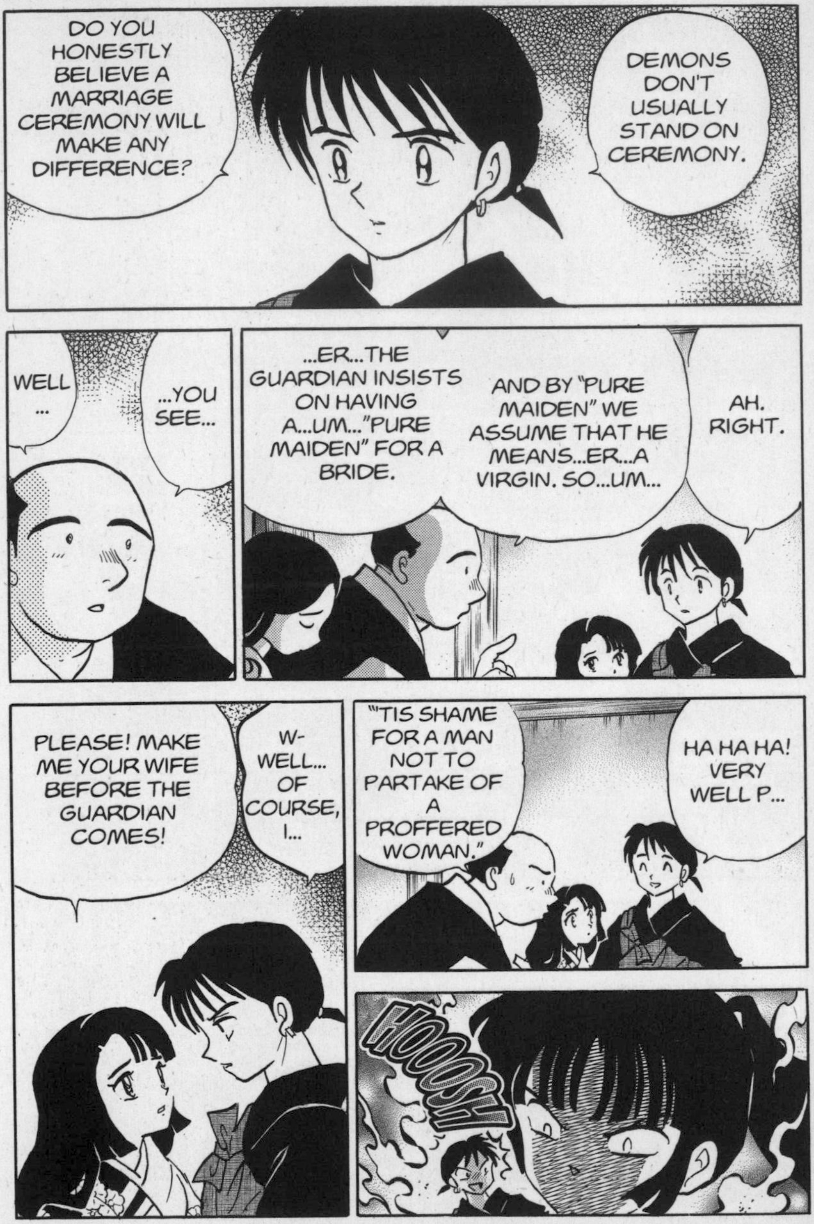

DO YOU HONESTLY BELIEVE A MARRIAGE CEREMONY WILL MAKE ANY DIFFERENCE?
DEMONS DON'T USUALLY STAND ON CEREMONY.
WELL ...
...YOU SEE...
...ER...THE GUARDIAN INSISTS ON HAVING A...UM..."PURE MAIDEN" FOR A BRIDE.
AND BY "PURE MAIDEN" WE ASSUME THAT HE MEANS...ER...A VIRGIN. SO...UM...
AH. RIGHT.
PLEASE! MAKE ME YOUR WIFE BEFORE THE GUARDIAN COMES!
W-WELL... OF COURSE, I...
"TIS SHAME FOR A MAN NOT TO PARTAKE OF A PROFFERED WOMAN."
HA HA HA! VERY WELL P...
HOOOSH!!

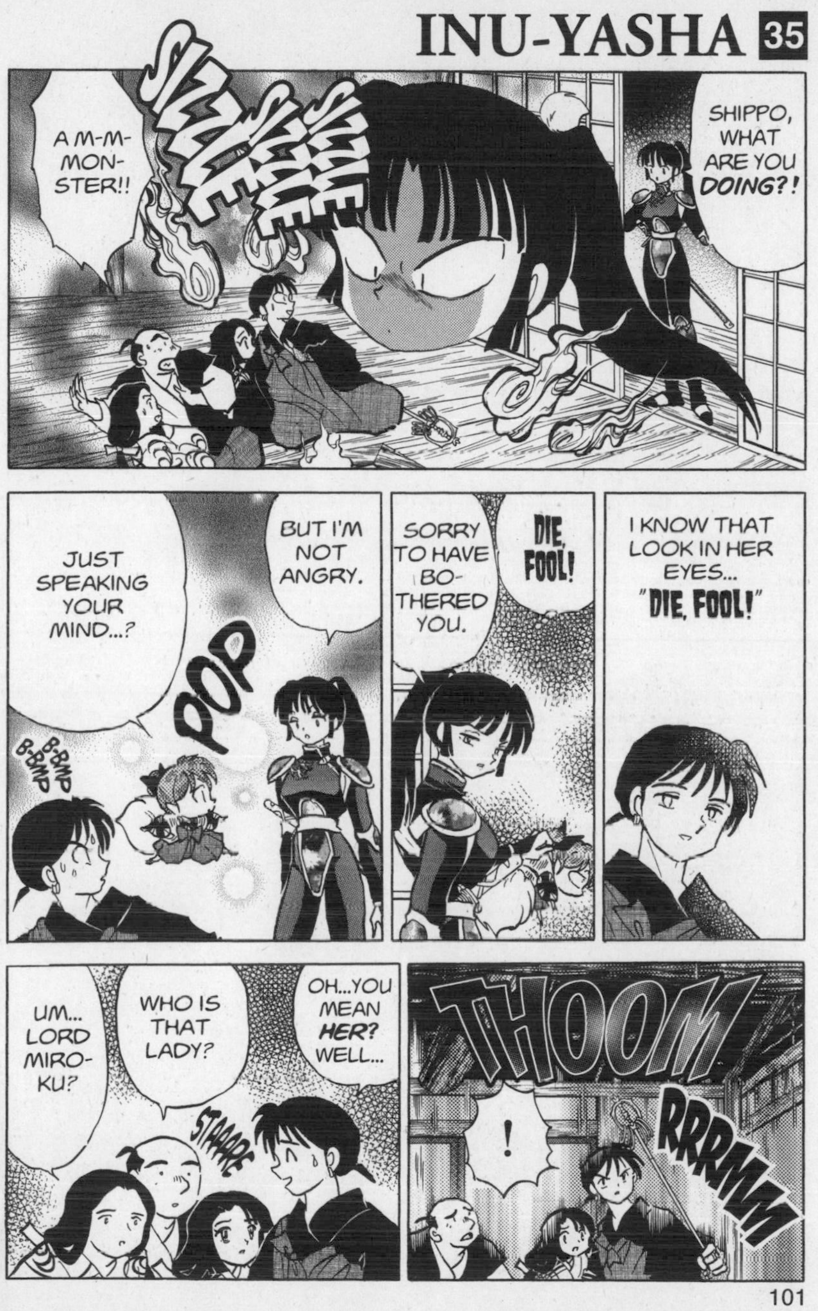
A M-M-MONSTER!!
SIZZLE
SIZZLE
SHIPPO, WHAT ARE YOU *DOING?!*
JUST SPEAKING YOUR MIND...?
B-BMP B-BMP
POP
BUT I'M NOT ANGRY.
SORRY TO HAVE BOTHERED YOU.
DIE, FOOL!
I KNOW THAT LOOK IN HER EYES... "DIE, FOOL!"
UM... LORD MIROKU?
WHO IS THAT LADY?
OH...YOU MEAN *HER?* WELL...
STAAARE
THOOM
!
RRRMM

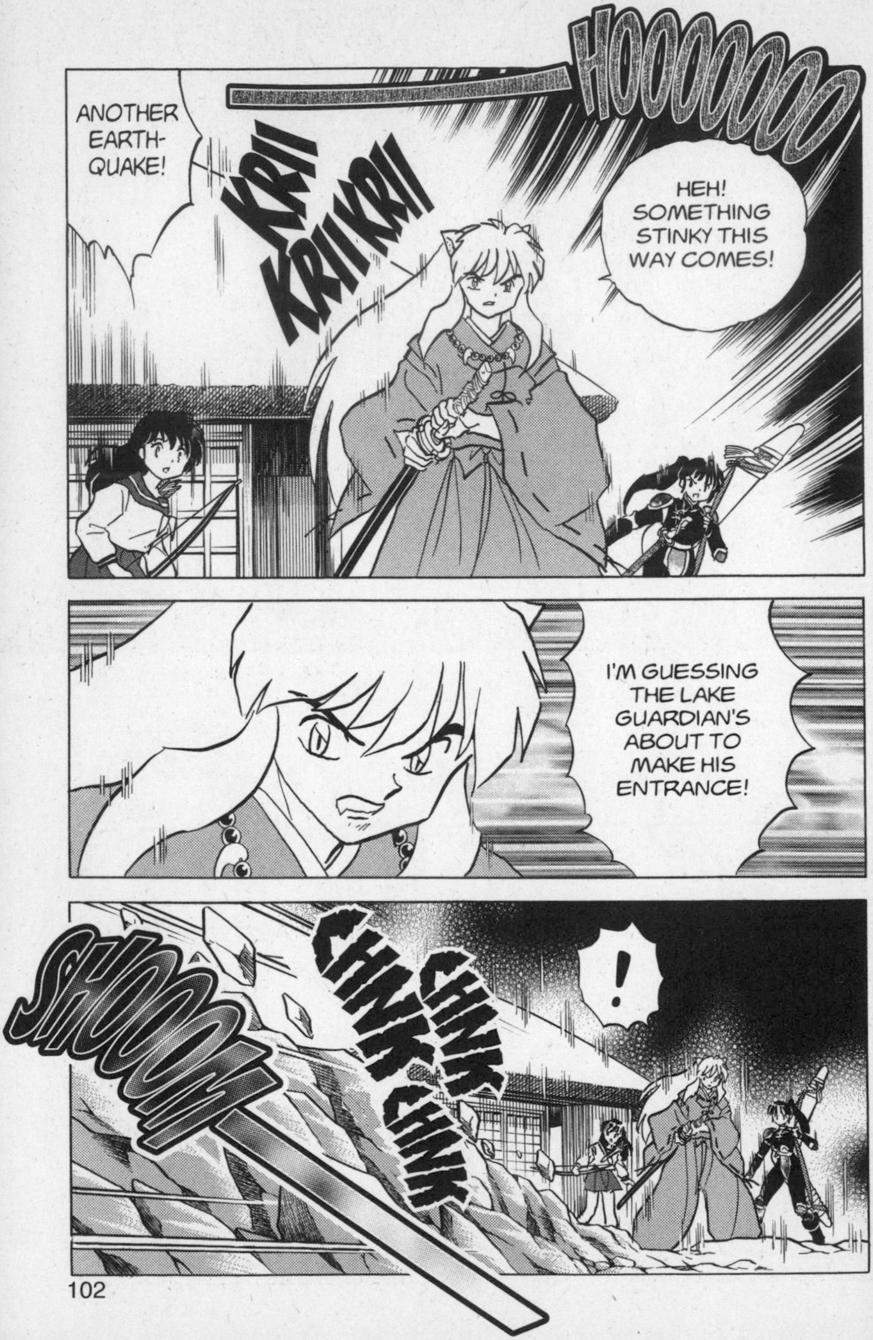
HOOOOOOO
ANOTHER EARTH-QUAKE!
KRII KRII KRII
HEH! SOMETHING STINKY THIS WAY COMES!
I'M GUESSING THE LAKE GUARDIAN'S ABOUT TO MAKE HIS ENTRANCE!
SHOOOM
CHINK CHINK CHINK
!

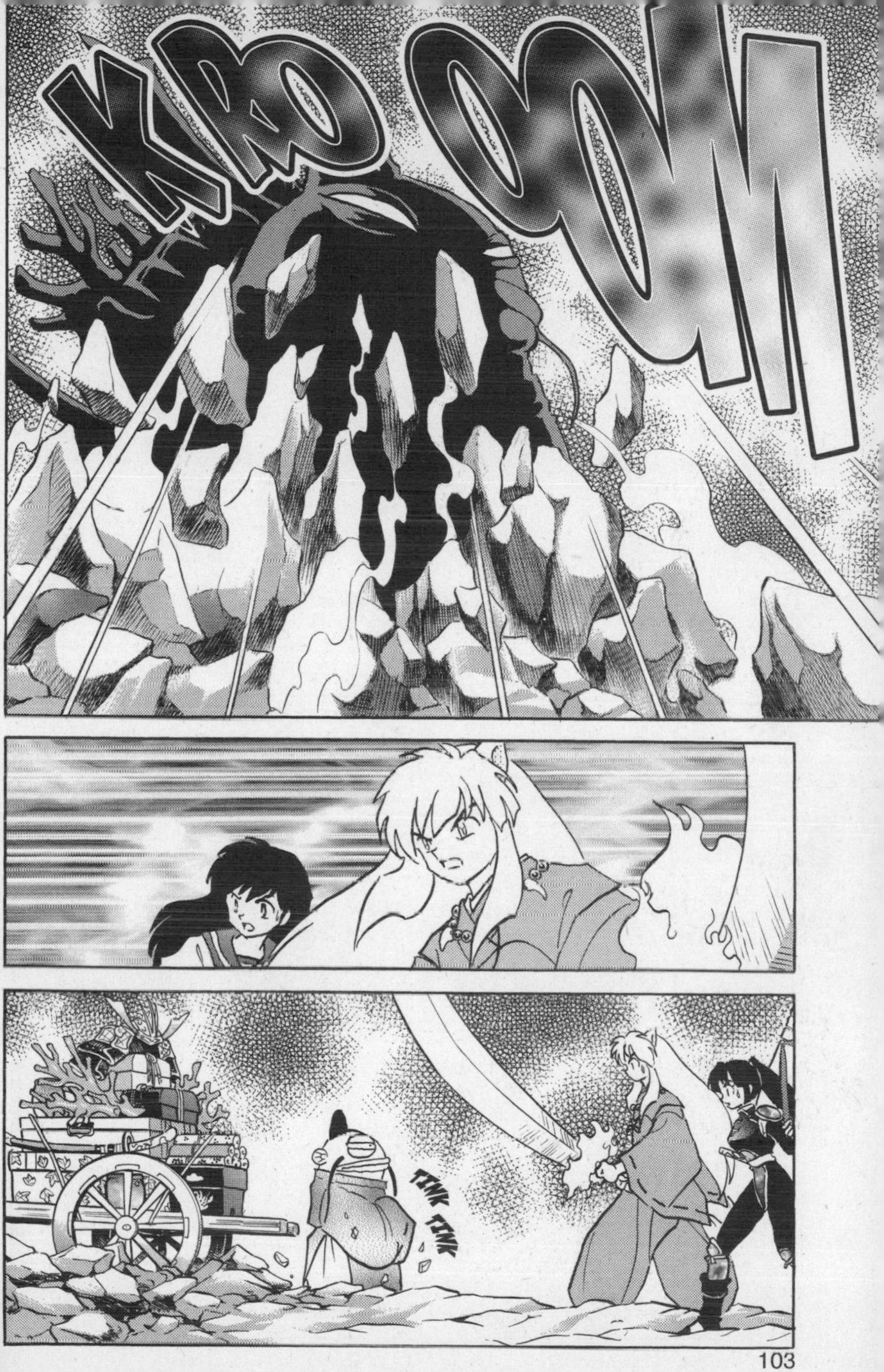
KRA-BOOM
TINK TINK

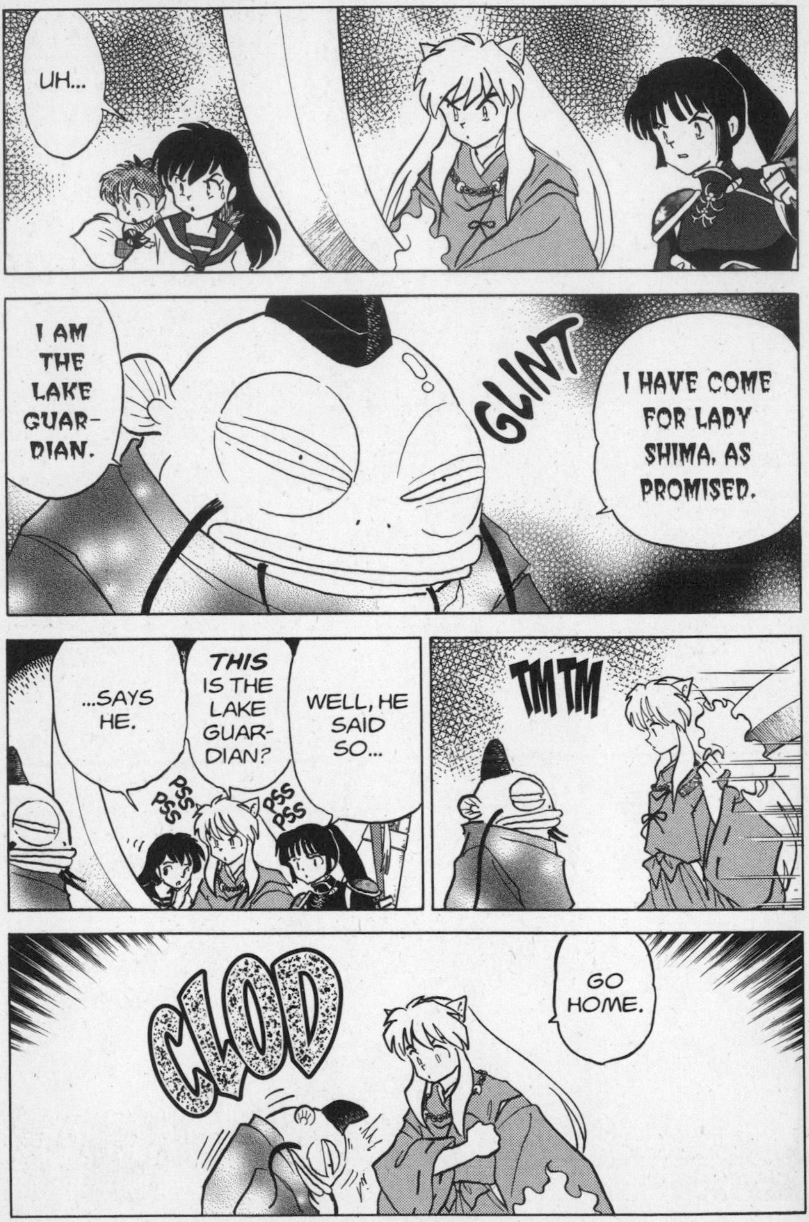
UH...
I AM THE LAKE GUARDIAN.
GLINT
I HAVE COME FOR LADY SHIMA, AS PROMISED.
...SAYS HE.
THIS IS THE LAKE GUARDIAN?
WELL, HE SAID SO...
PSS PSS
PSS PSS
TMTM
CLOD
GO HOME.

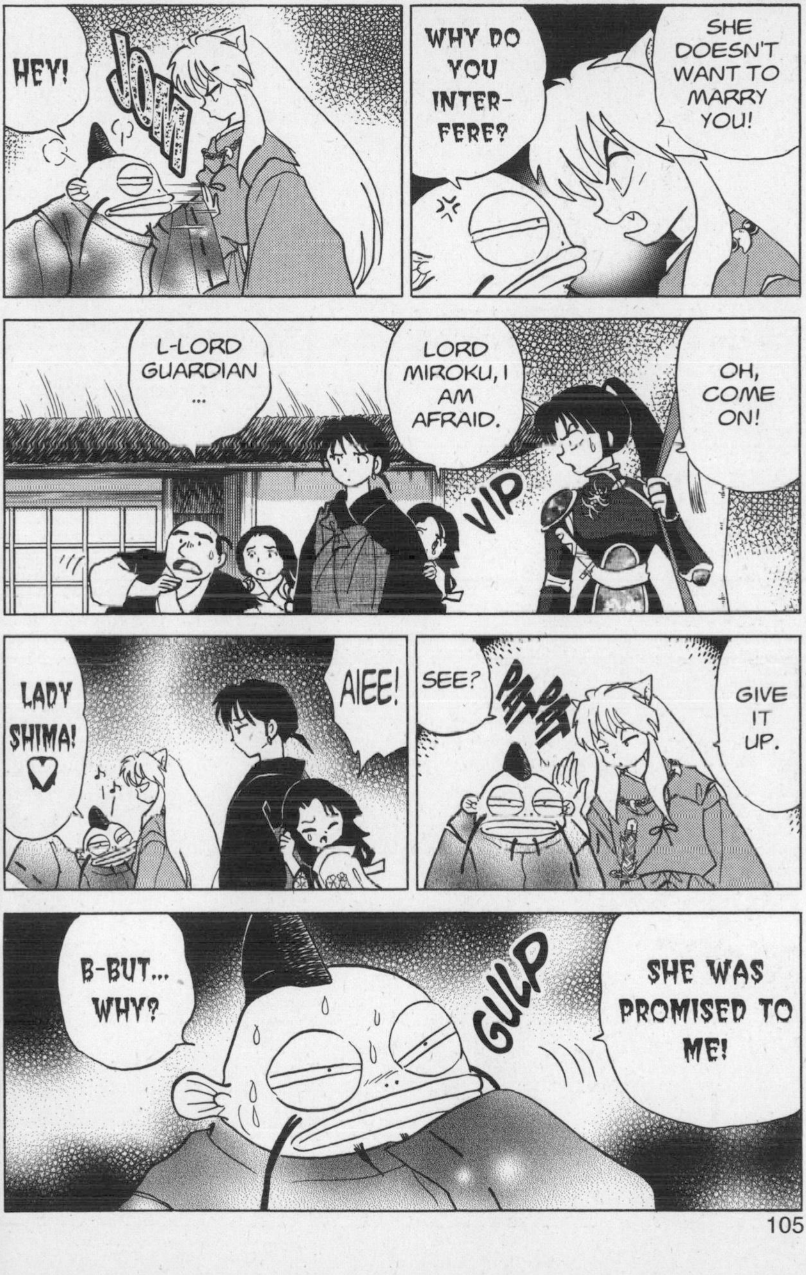
HEY!
JOM
WHY DO YOU INTER-FERE?
SHE DOESN'T WANT TO MARRY YOU!
L-LORD GUARDIAN ...
LORD MIROKU, I AM AFRAID.
VIP
OH, COME ON!
LADY SHIMA! ♥
AIEE!
SEE?
PAT PAT
GIVE IT UP.
B-BUT... WHY?
GULP
SHE WAS PROMISED TO ME!

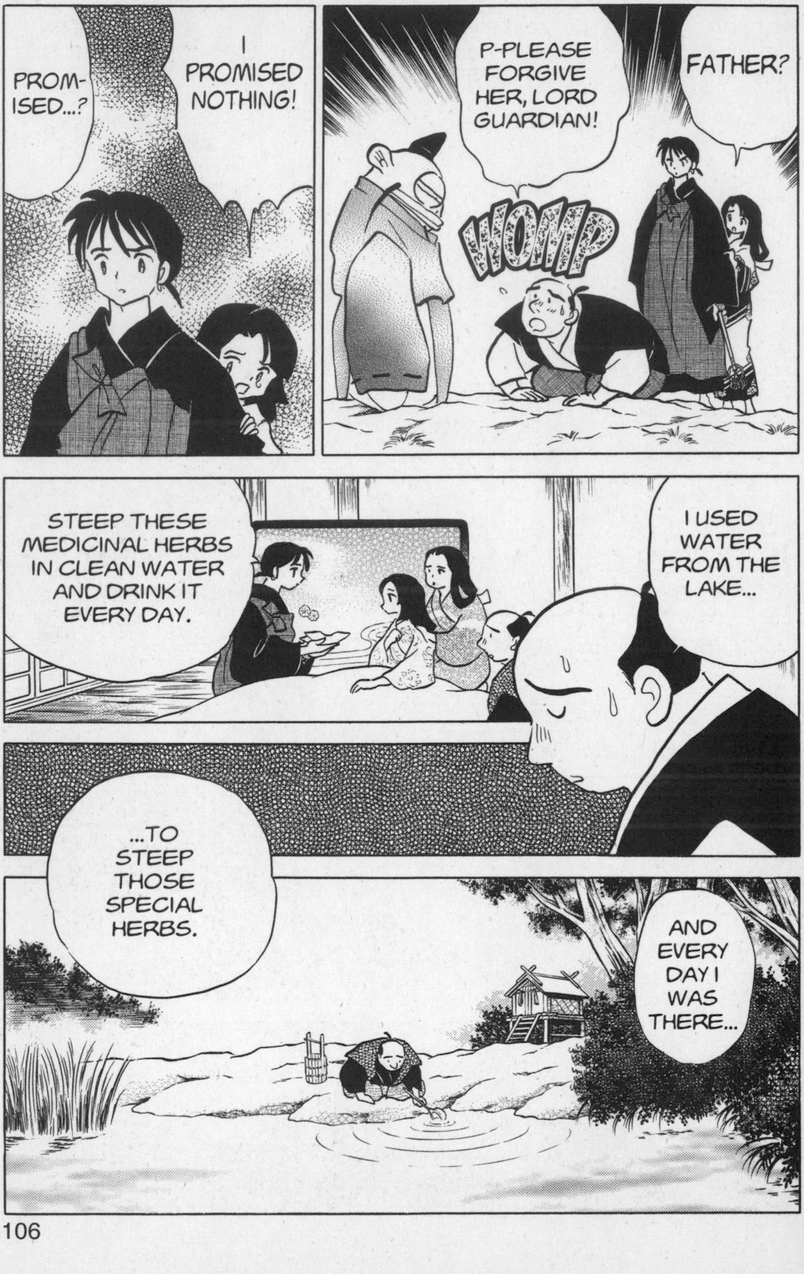
PROM-ISED...?
I PROMISED NOTHING!
P-PLEASE FORGIVE HER, LORD GUARDIAN!
WOMP
FATHER?
STEEP THESE MEDICINAL HERBS IN CLEAN WATER AND DRINK IT EVERY DAY.
I USED WATER FROM THE LAKE...
...TO STEEP THOSE SPECIAL HERBS.
AND EVERY DAY I WAS THERE...

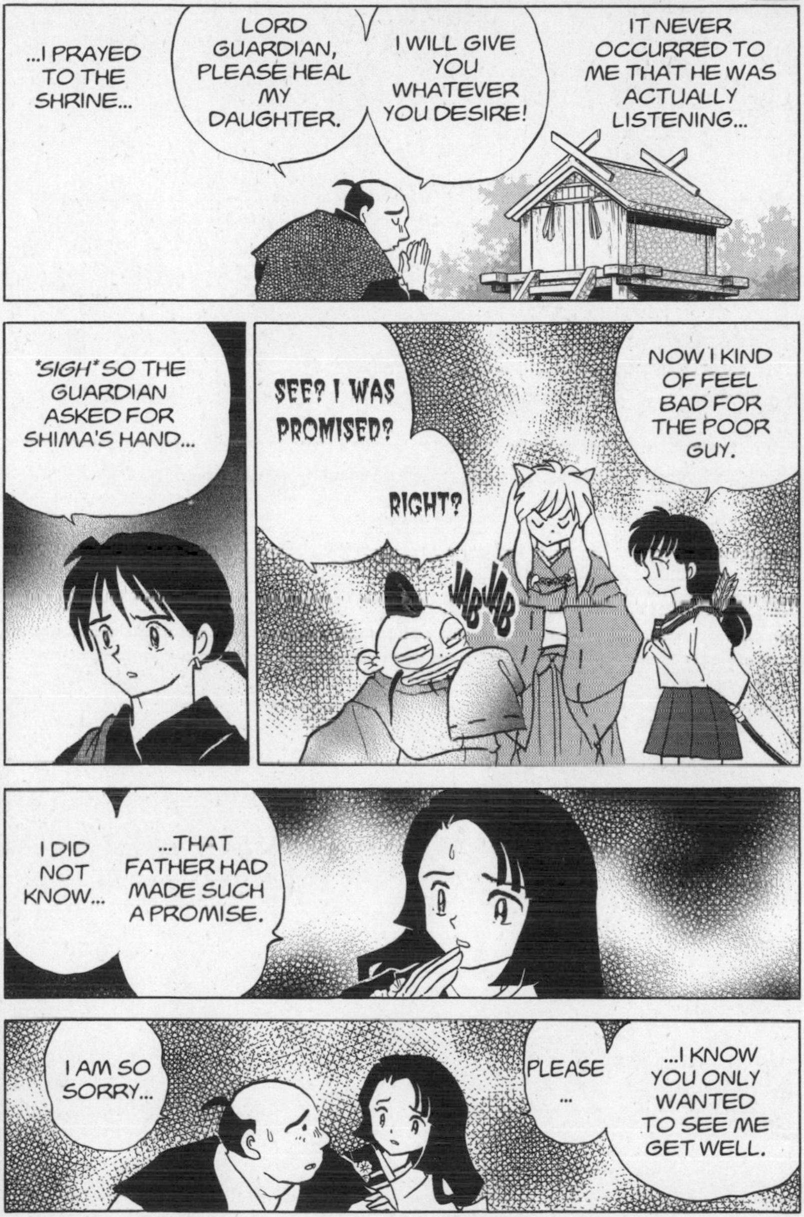
...I PRAYED TO THE SHRINE...
LORD GUARDIAN, PLEASE HEAL MY DAUGHTER.
I WILL GIVE YOU WHATEVER YOU DESIRE!
IT NEVER OCCURRED TO ME THAT HE WAS ACTUALLY LISTENING...
SIGH SO THE GUARDIAN ASKED FOR SHIMA'S HAND...
SEE? I WAS PROMISED?
RIGHT?
JAB JAB
NOW I KIND OF FEEL BAD FOR THE POOR GUY.
I DID NOT KNOW...
...THAT FATHER HAD MADE SUCH A PROMISE.
I AM SO SORRY...
PLEASE ...
...I KNOW YOU ONLY WANTED TO SEE ME GET WELL.

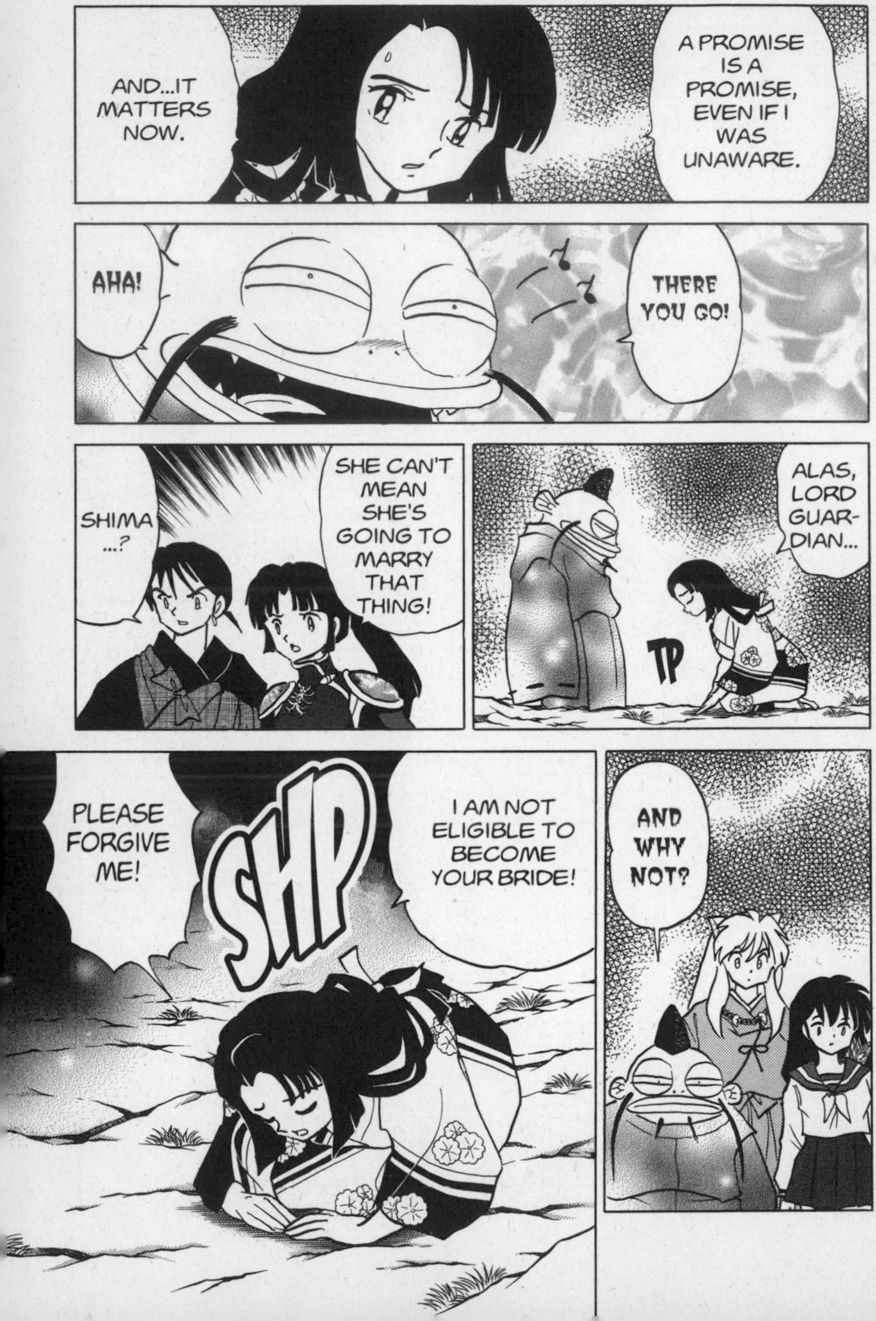
AND...IT MATTERS NOW.
A PROMISE IS A PROMISE, EVEN IF I WAS UNAWARE.
AHA!
THERE YOU GO!
SHIMA ...?
SHE CAN'T MEAN SHE'S GOING TO MARRY THAT THING!
ALAS, LORD GUARDIAN...
TP
PLEASE FORGIVE ME!
SHP
I AM NOT ELIGIBLE TO BECOME YOUR BRIDE!
AND WHY NOT?

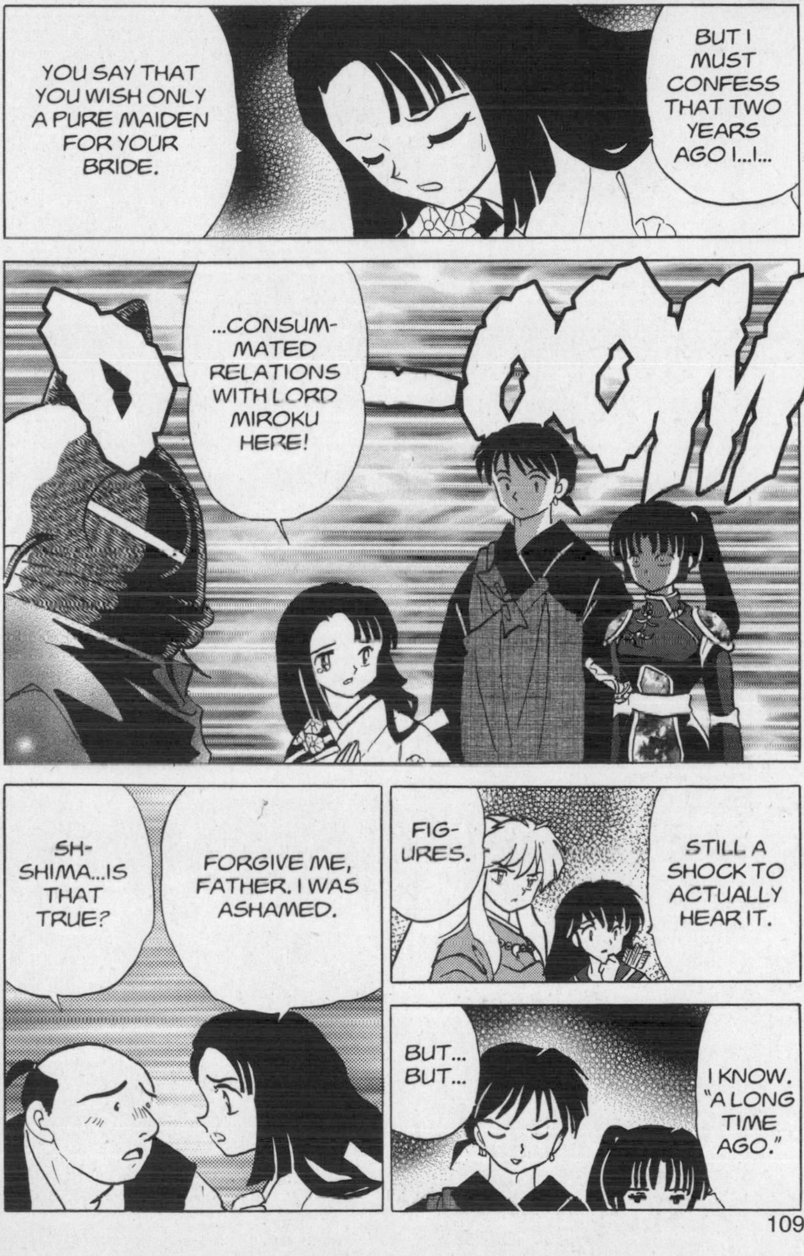
YOU SAY THAT YOU WISH ONLY A PURE MAIDEN FOR YOUR BRIDE.
BUT I MUST CONFESS THAT TWO YEARS AGO I...I...
D
...CONSUM-MATED RELATIONS WITH LORD MIROKU HERE!
OOM
SH-SHIMA...IS THAT TRUE?
FORGIVE ME, FATHER. I WAS ASHAMED.
FIG-URES.
STILL A SHOCK TO ACTUALLY HEAR IT.
BUT... BUT...
I KNOW. "A LONG TIME AGO."

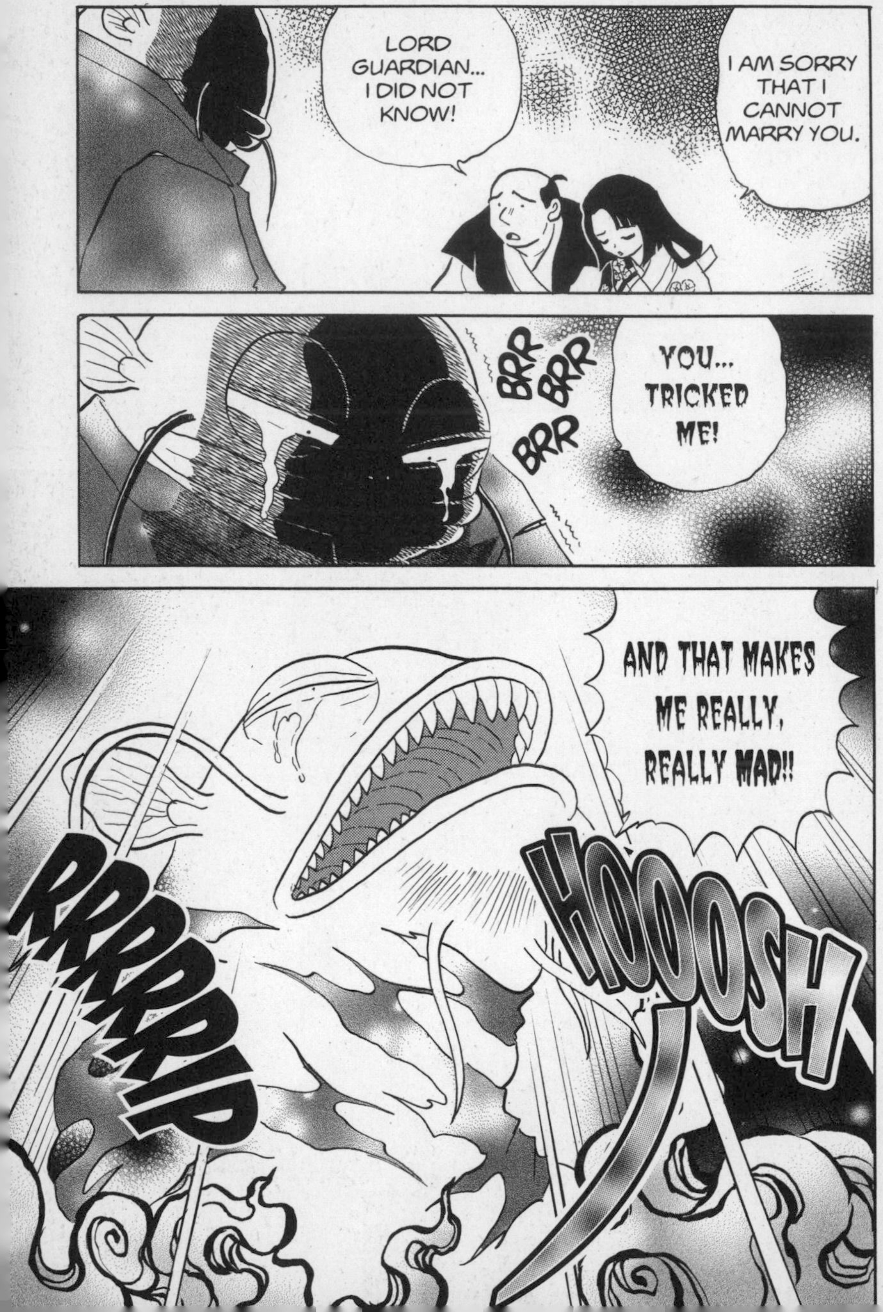
I AM SORRY THAT I CANNOT MARRY YOU.
LORD GUARDIAN... I DID NOT KNOW!
YOU... TRICKED ME!
BRR BRR BRR
AND THAT MAKES ME REALLY, REALLY MAD!!
WHOOOSH
RRRRRIP

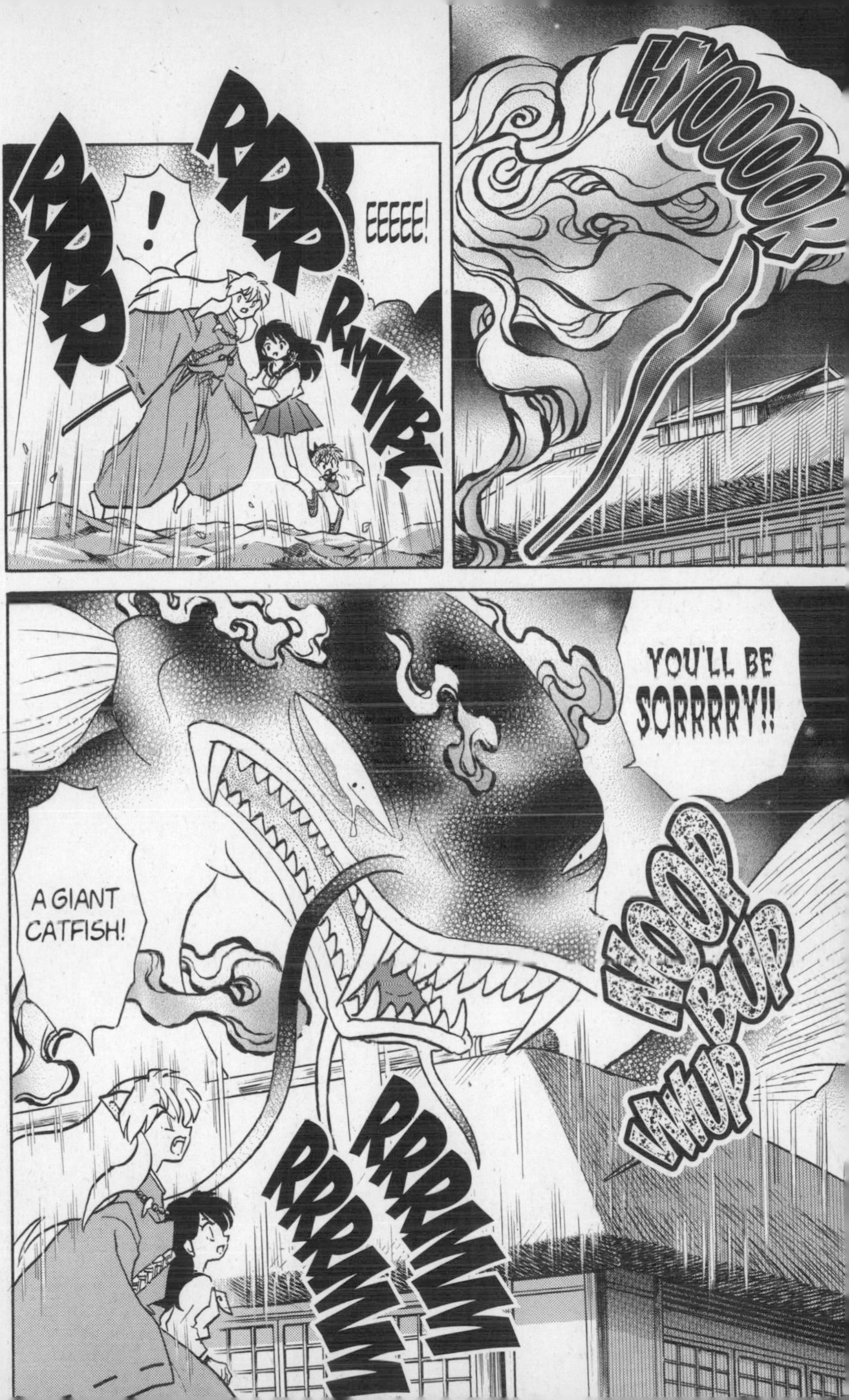
!
EEEEE!
YOU'LL BE SORRRRY!!
A GIANT CATFISH!

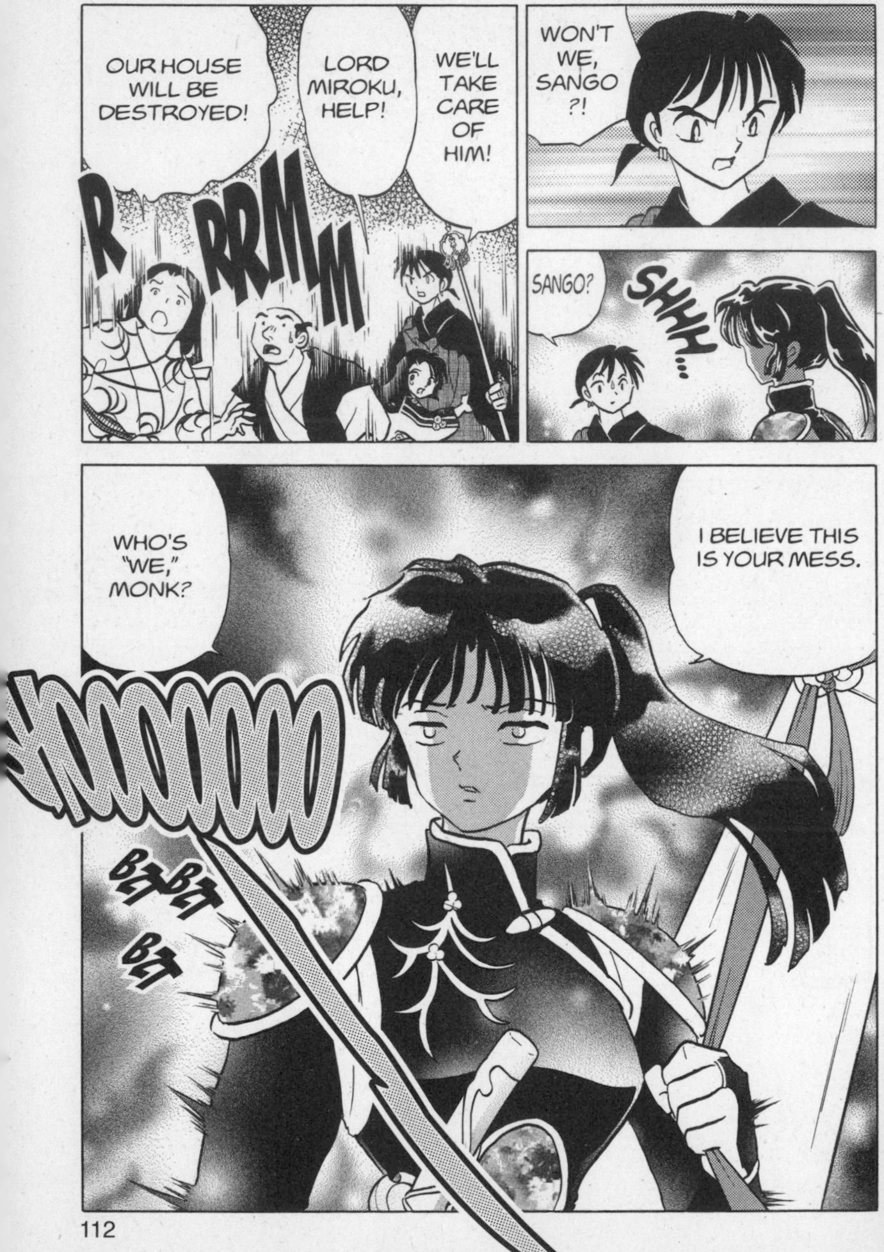
OUR HOUSE WILL BE DESTROYED!
LORD MIROKU, HELP!
WE'LL TAKE CARE OF HIM!
RRRMMM
WON'T WE, SANGO ?!
SANGO?
SHHHH...
WHO'S "WE," MONK?
I BELIEVE THIS IS YOUR MESS.
BZT BZT
BZT

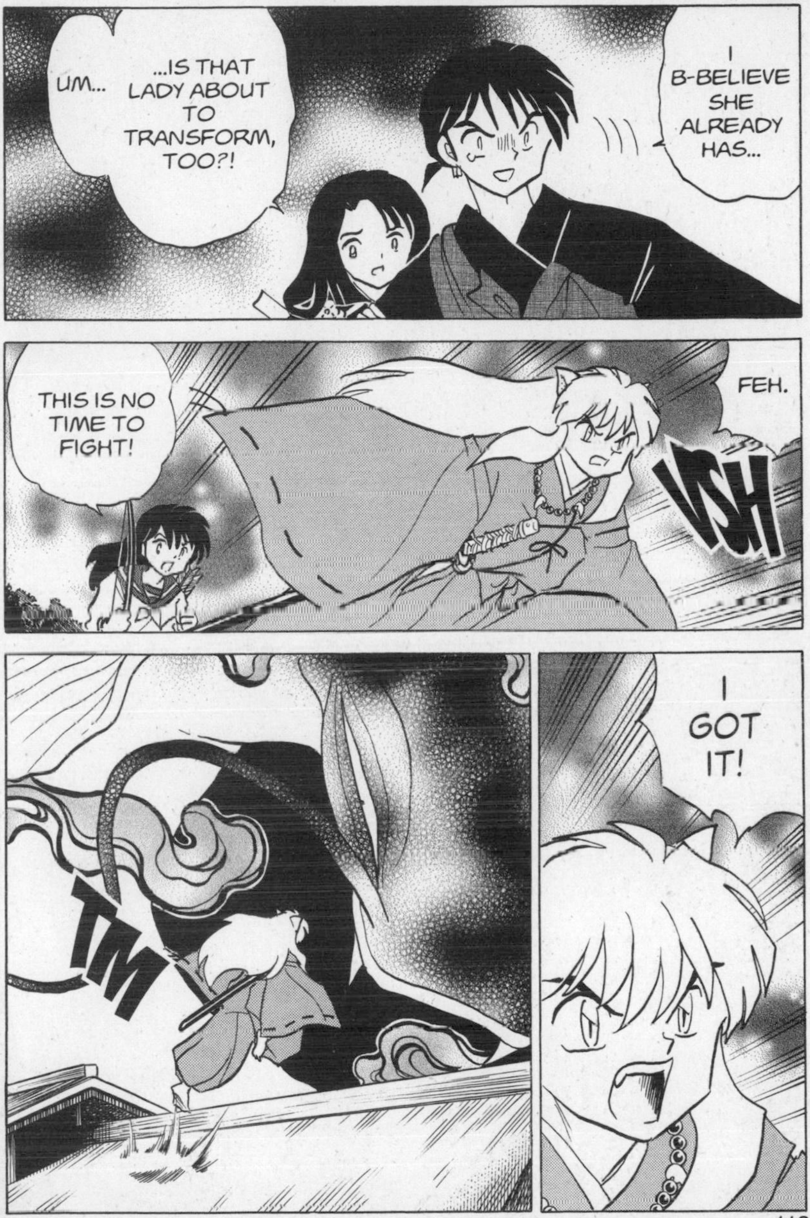
UM...
...IS THAT LADY ABOUT TO TRANSFORM, TOO?!
I B-BELIEVE SHE ALREADY HAS...
THIS IS NO TIME TO FIGHT!
FEH.
VSH
TM
I GOT IT!

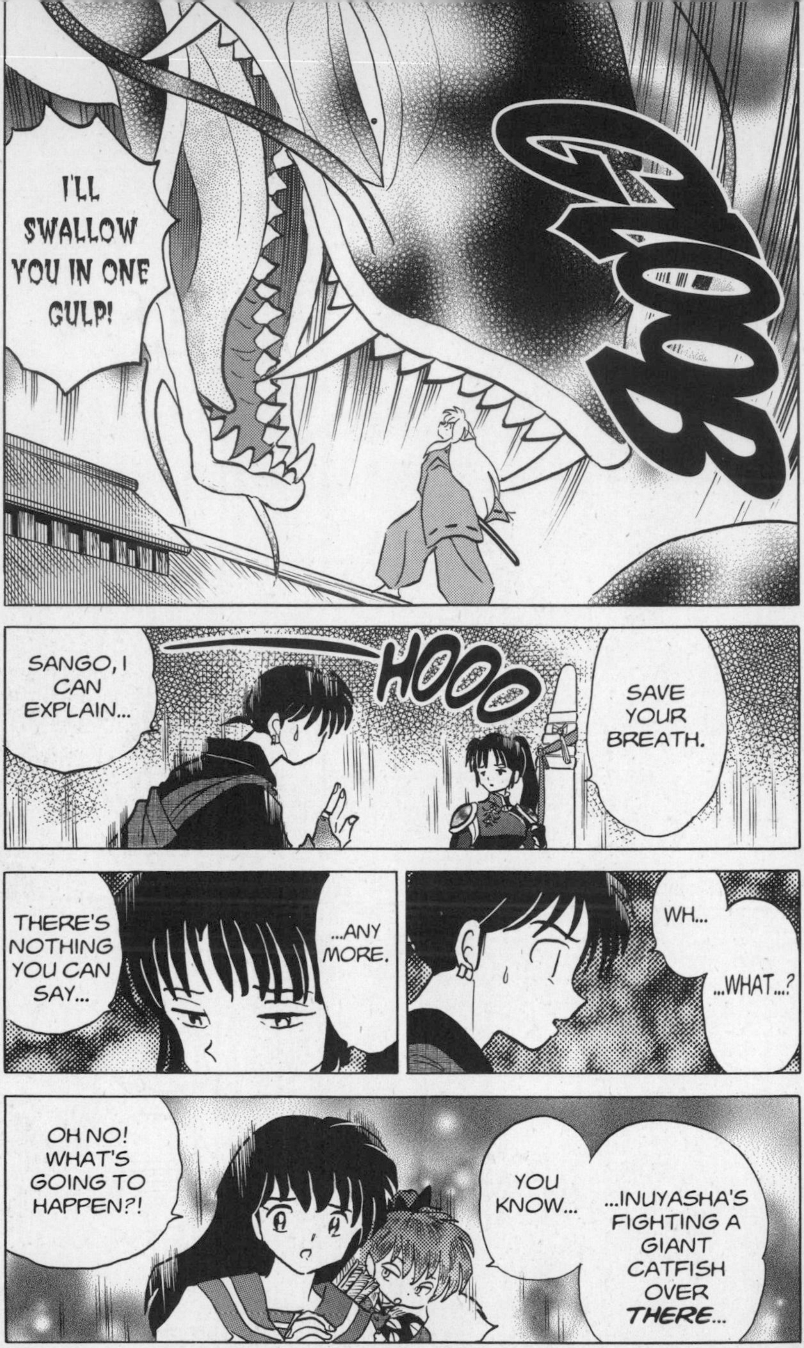
I'LL SWALLOW YOU IN ONE GULP!
GABOOB
SANGO, I CAN EXPLAIN...
HOOO
SAVE YOUR BREATH.
THERE'S NOTHING YOU CAN SAY...
...ANY MORE.
WH...
...WHAT...?
OH NO! WHAT'S GOING TO HAPPEN?!
YOU KNOW...
...INUYASHA'S FIGHTING A GIANT CATFISH OVER THERE...

SCROLL 7
FORGIVENESS

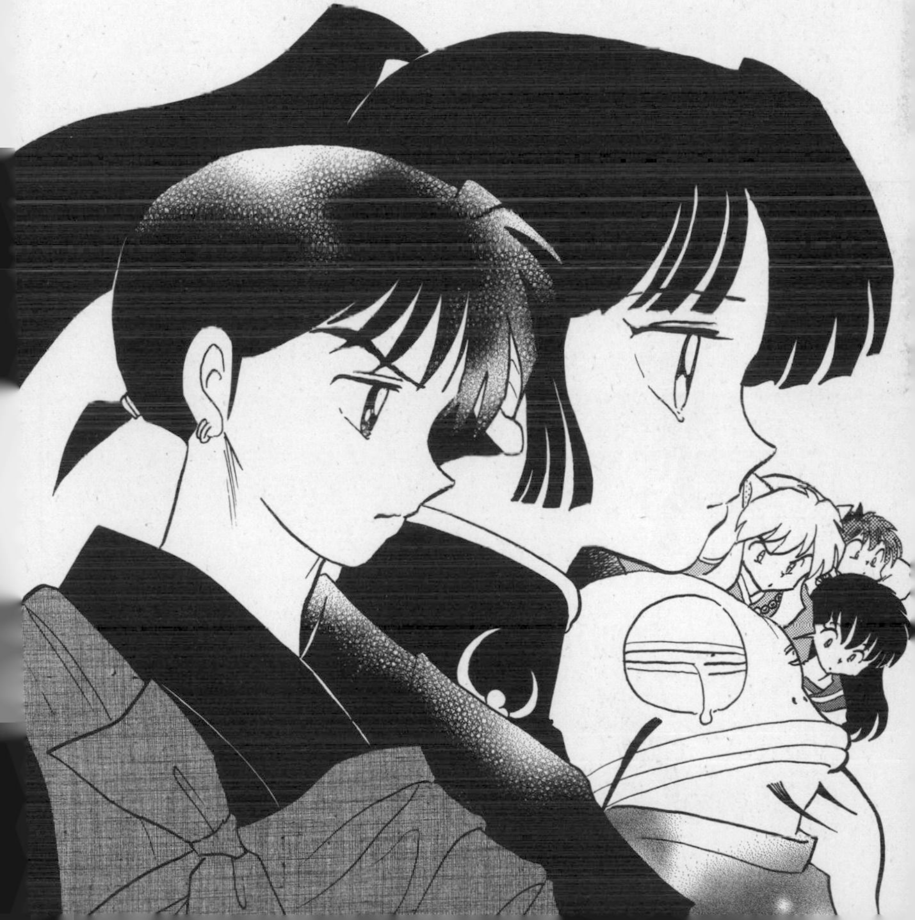

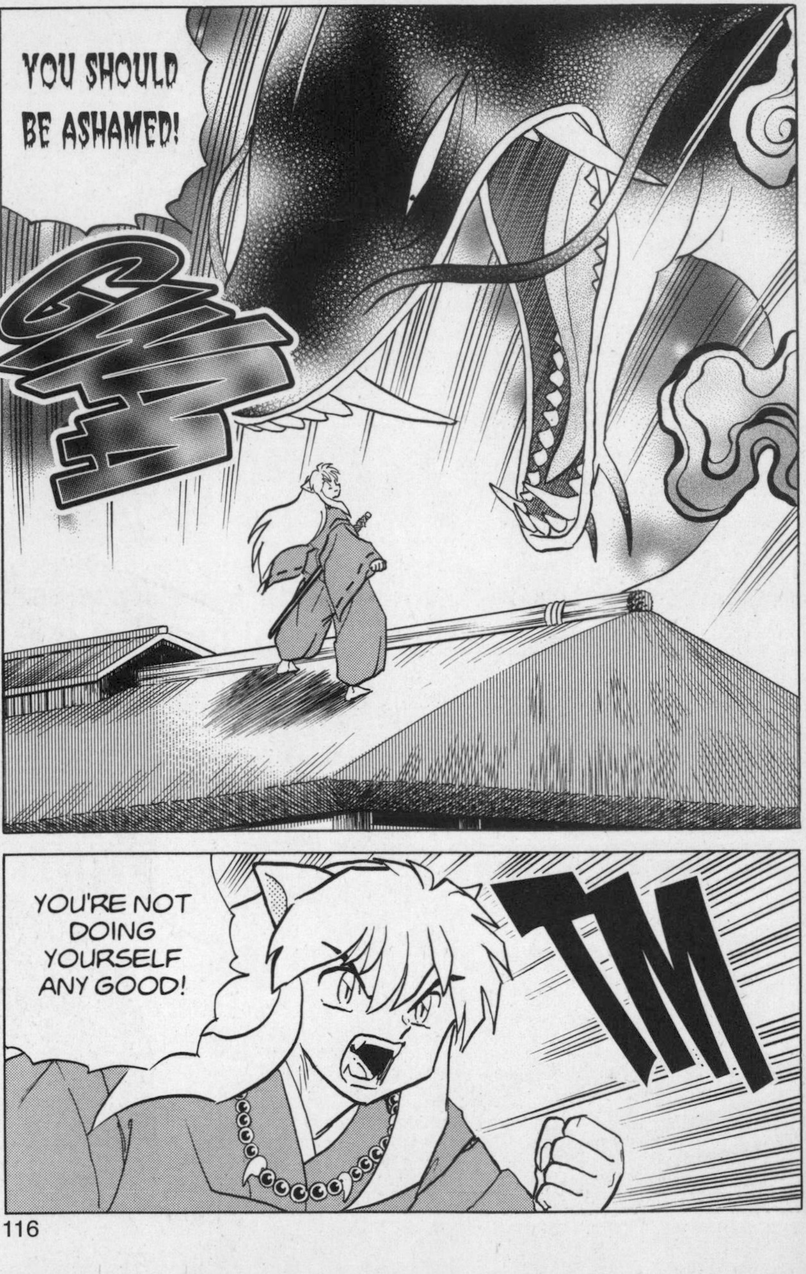
YOU SHOULD BE ASHAMED!
YOU'RE NOT DOING YOURSELF ANY GOOD!
TM

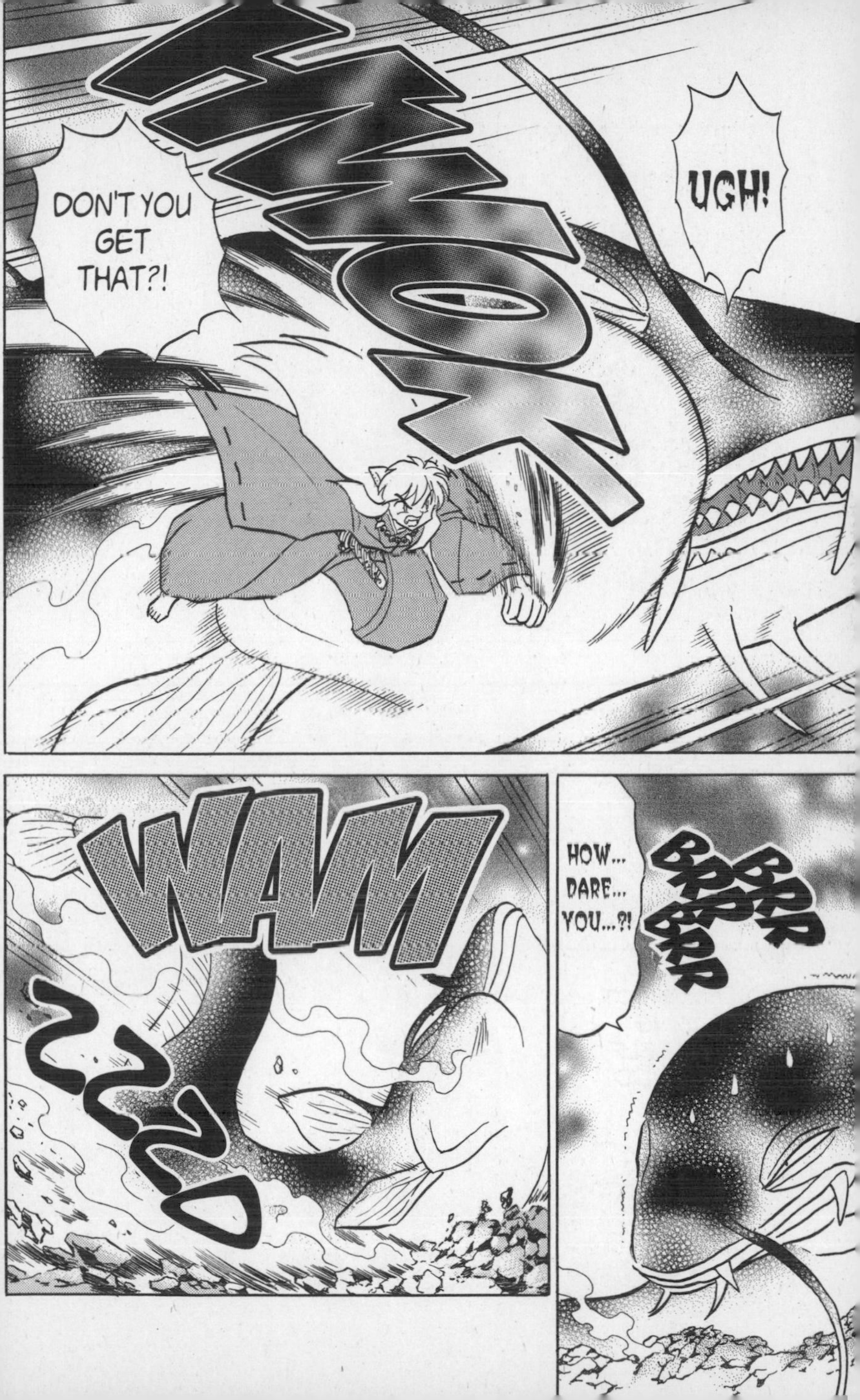
DON'T YOU GET THAT?!
UGH!
WAM
HOW... DARE... YOU...?!
BRRR
BRRR

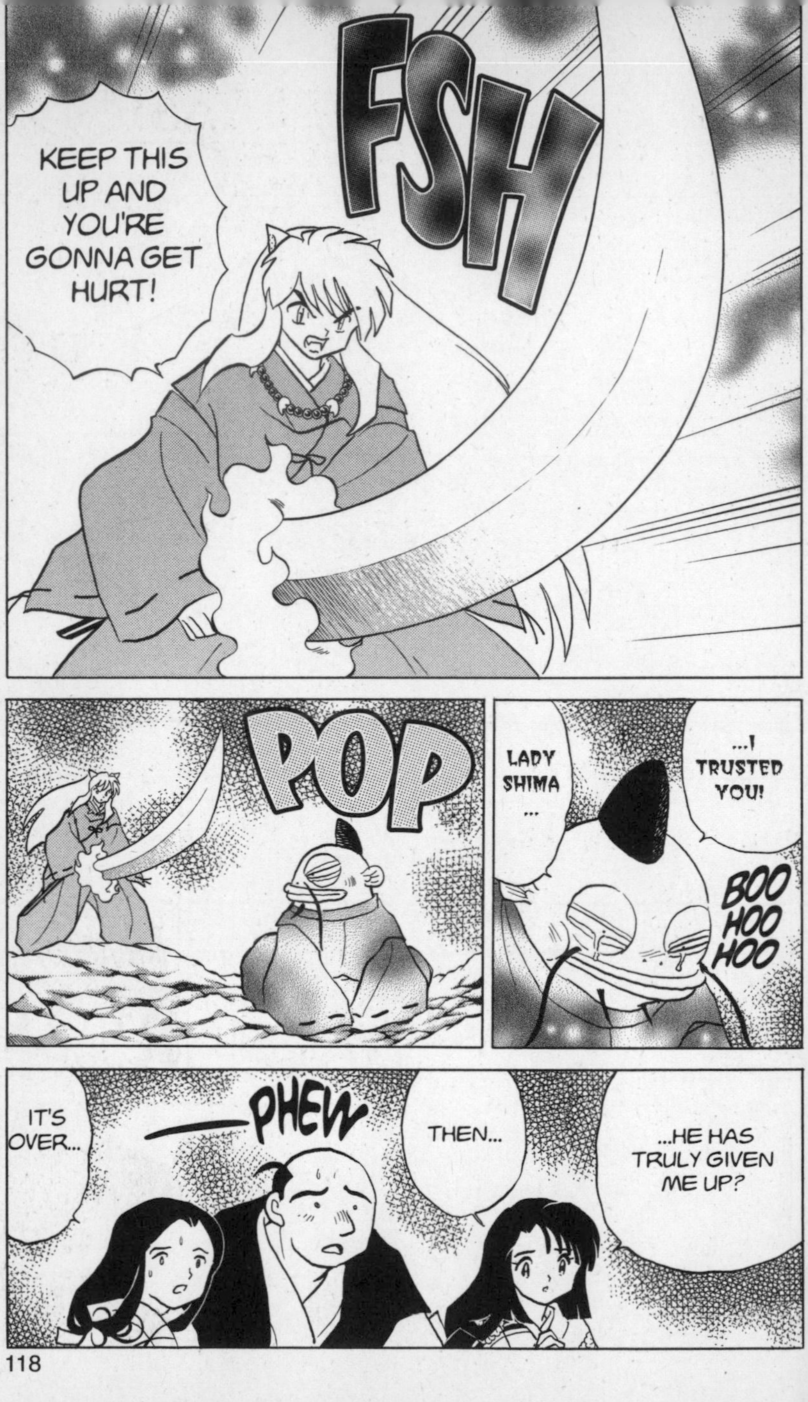
FSH
KEEP THIS UP AND YOU'RE GONNA GET HURT!
POP
LADY SHIMA...
...I TRUSTED YOU!
BOO HOO HOO
IT'S OVER...
PHEW
THEN...
...HE HAS TRULY GIVEN ME UP?

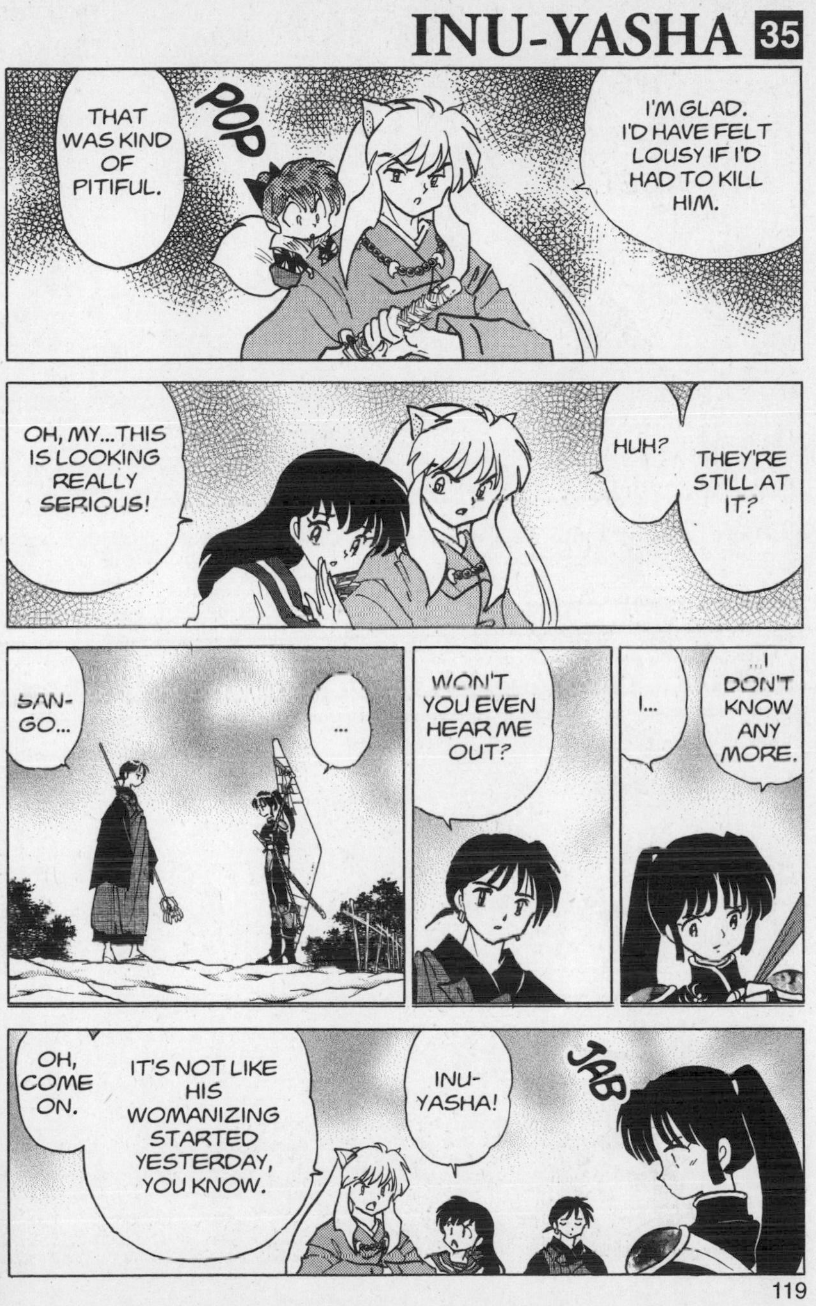
THAT WAS KIND OF PITIFUL.
POP
I'M GLAD. I'D HAVE FELT LOUSY IF I'D HAD TO KILL HIM.
OH, MY...THIS IS LOOKING REALLY SERIOUS!
HUH?
THEY'RE STILL AT IT?
SAN-GO...
...
WON'T YOU EVEN HEAR ME OUT?
I...
...I DON'T KNOW ANY MORE.
OH, COME ON.
IT'S NOT LIKE HIS WOMANIZING STARTED YESTERDAY, YOU KNOW.
INU-YASHA!
JAB

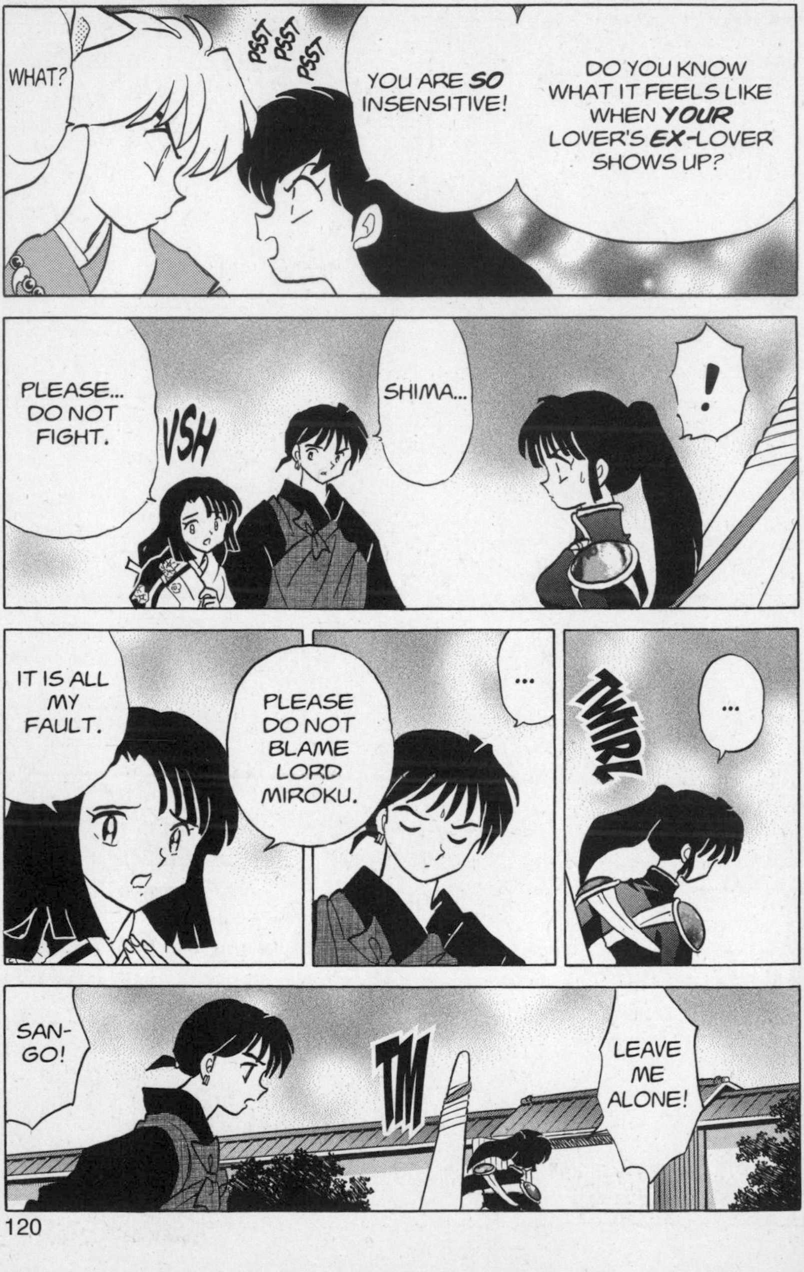
WHAT?
PSST PSST PSST
YOU ARE SO INSENSITIVE!
DO YOU KNOW WHAT IT FEELS LIKE WHEN YOUR LOVER'S EX-LOVER SHOWS UP?
PLEASE... DO NOT FIGHT.
VSH
SHIMA...
!
IT IS ALL MY FAULT.
PLEASE DO NOT BLAME LORD MIROKU.
...
TWIRL
...
SAN-GO!
TM
LEAVE ME ALONE!

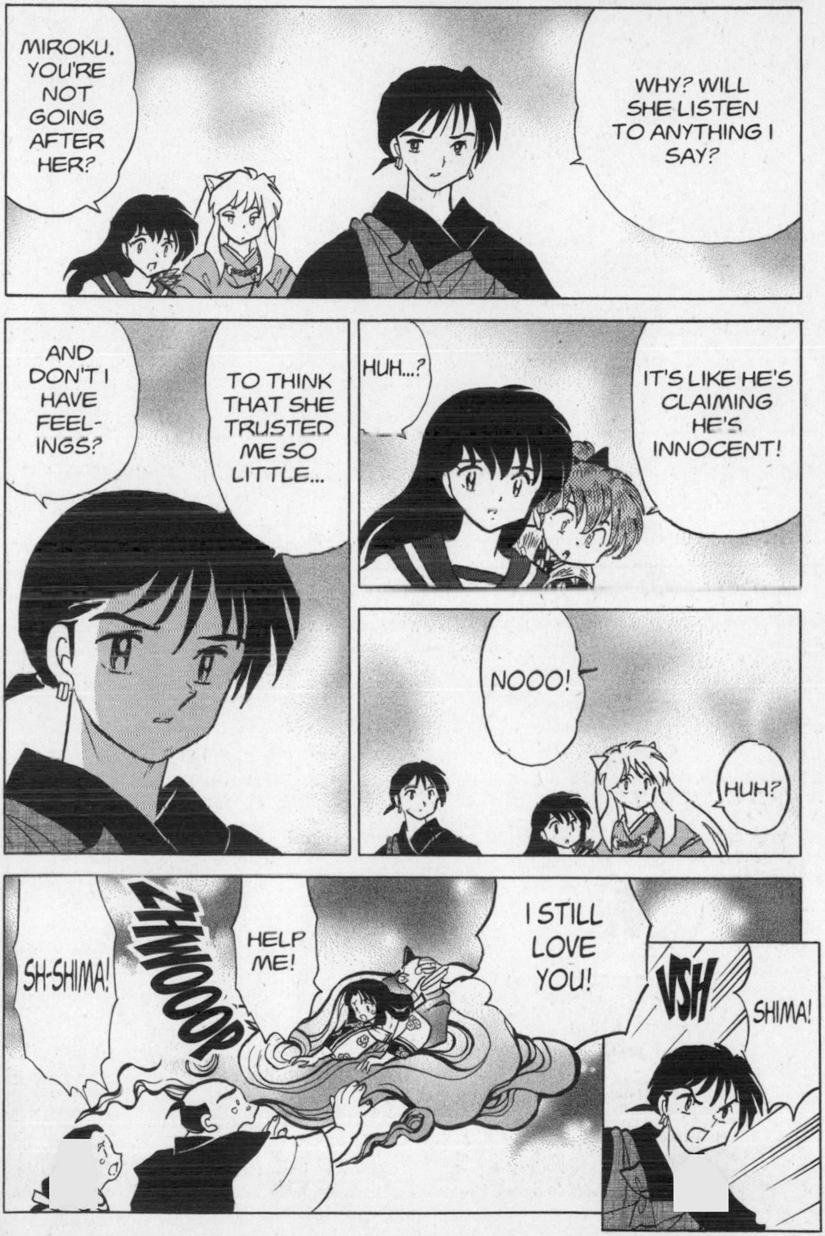

MIROKU. YOU'RE NOT GOING AFTER HER?
WHY? WILL SHE LISTEN TO ANYTHING I SAY?
AND DON'T I HAVE FEEL-INGS?
TO THINK THAT SHE TRUSTED ME SO LITTLE...
HUH...?
IT'S LIKE HE'S CLAIMING HE'S INNOCENT!
NOOO!
HUH?
SH-SHIMA!
ZHWOOOOP
HELP ME!
I STILL LOVE YOU!
VSH
SHIMA!

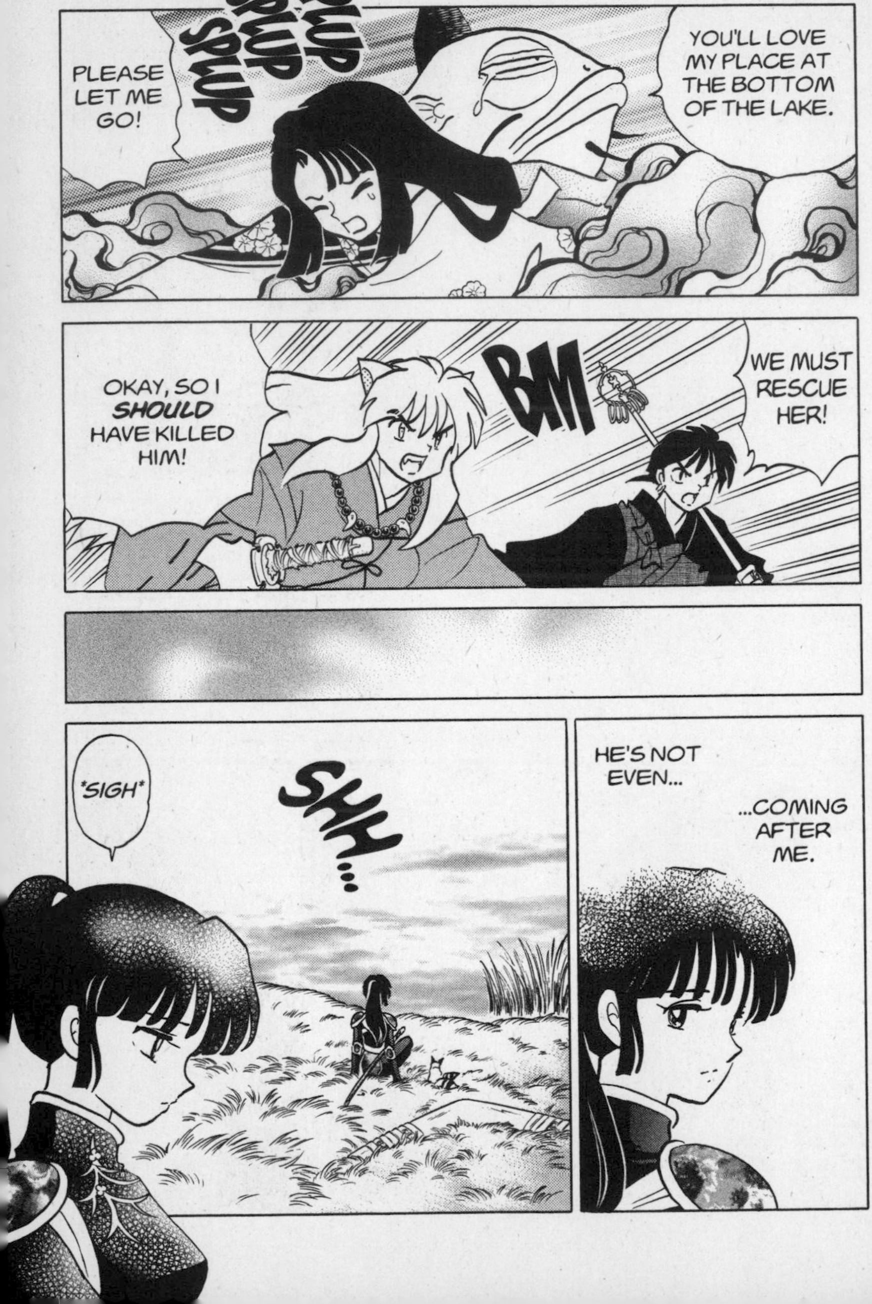
PLEASE LET ME GO!
SPLUP SPLUP SPLUP
YOU'LL LOVE MY PLACE AT THE BOTTOM OF THE LAKE.
OKAY, SO I SHOULD HAVE KILLED HIM!
BM
WE MUST RESCUE HER!
SIGH
SHH...
HE'S NOT EVEN...
...COMING AFTER ME.

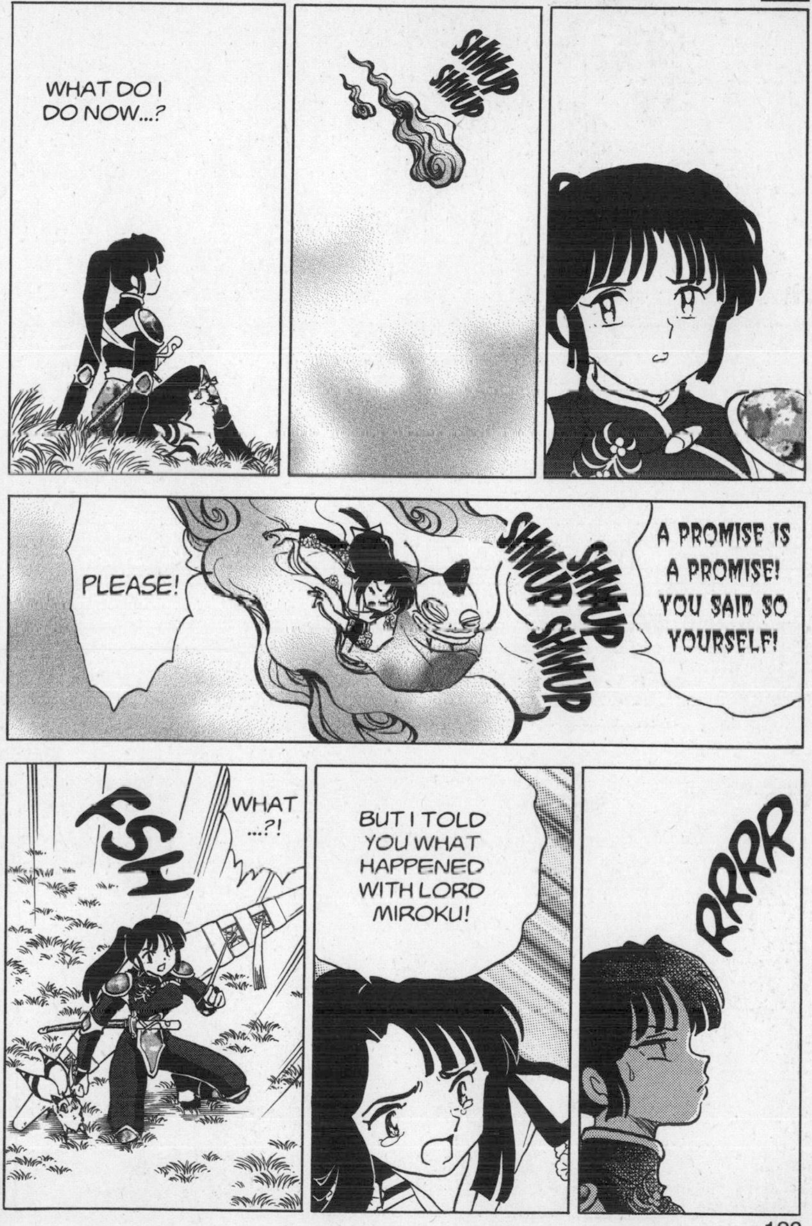
WHAT DO I DO NOW...?
SHWUP SHWUP
PLEASE!
SHWUP SHWUP SHWUP
A PROMISE IS A PROMISE! YOU SAID SO YOURSELF!
FSH
WHAT ...?!
BUT I TOLD YOU WHAT HAPPENED WITH LORD MIROKU!
RRRR

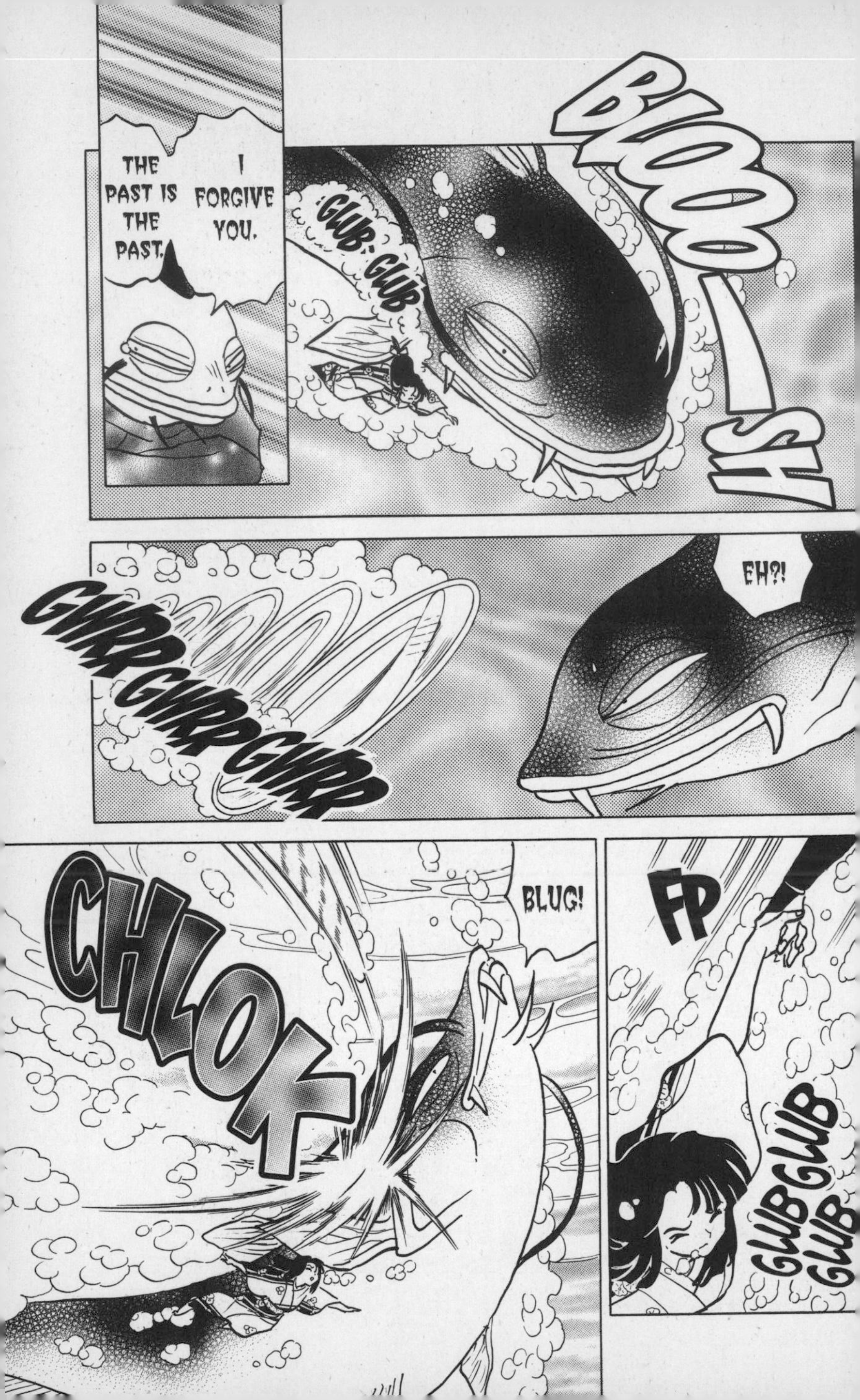
THE PAST IS THE PAST.
I FORGIVE YOU.
GLUB GLUB
BLOOOOOSH
GWRP GWRP GWRP
EH?!
CHLOK
BLUG!
FP
GLUB GLUB GLUB

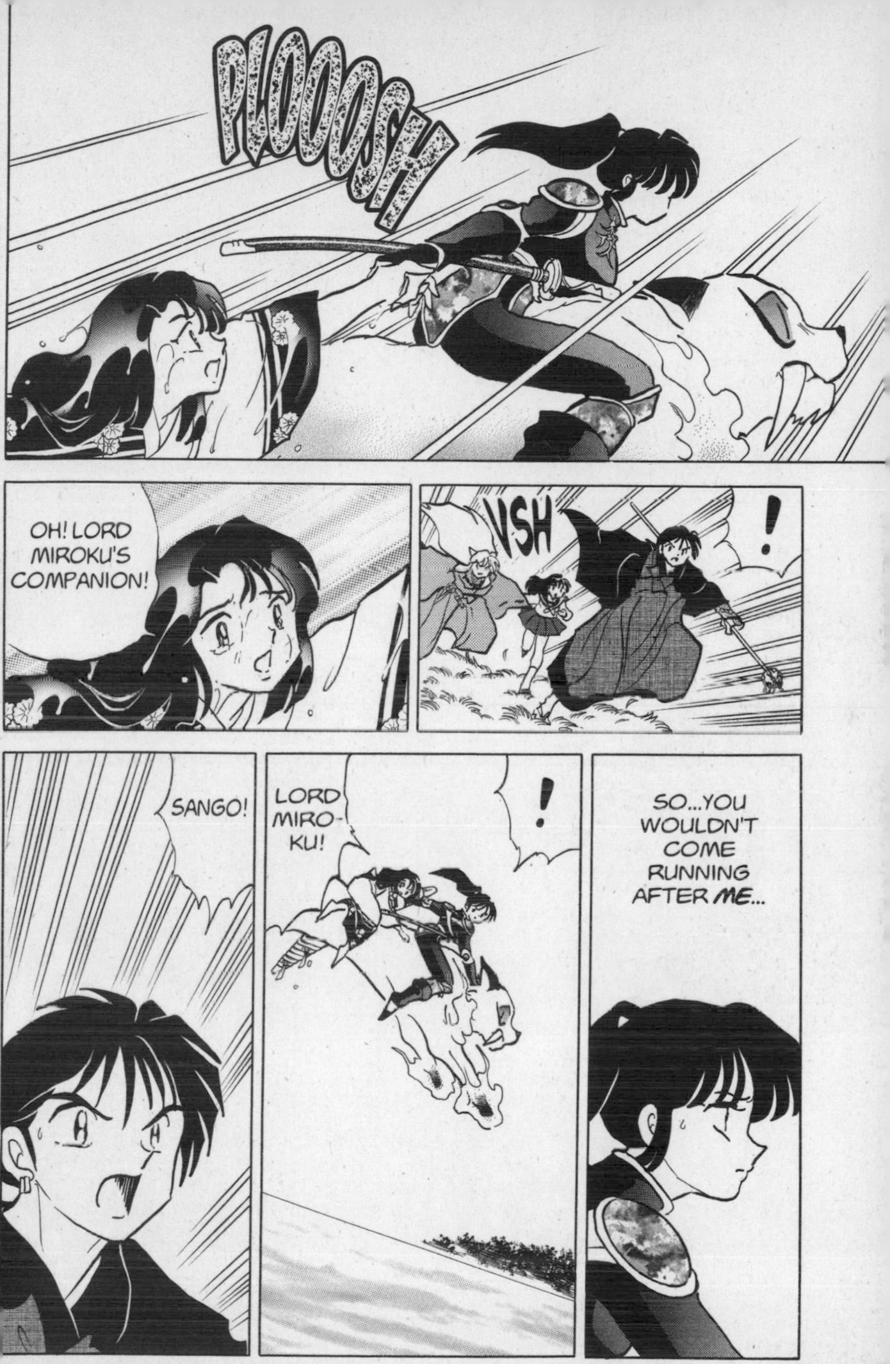
PLOOOSH
OH! LORD MIROKU'S COMPANION!
VSH
!
SANGO!
LORD MIRO-KU!
!
SO...YOU WOULDN'T COME RUNNING AFTER *ME*...

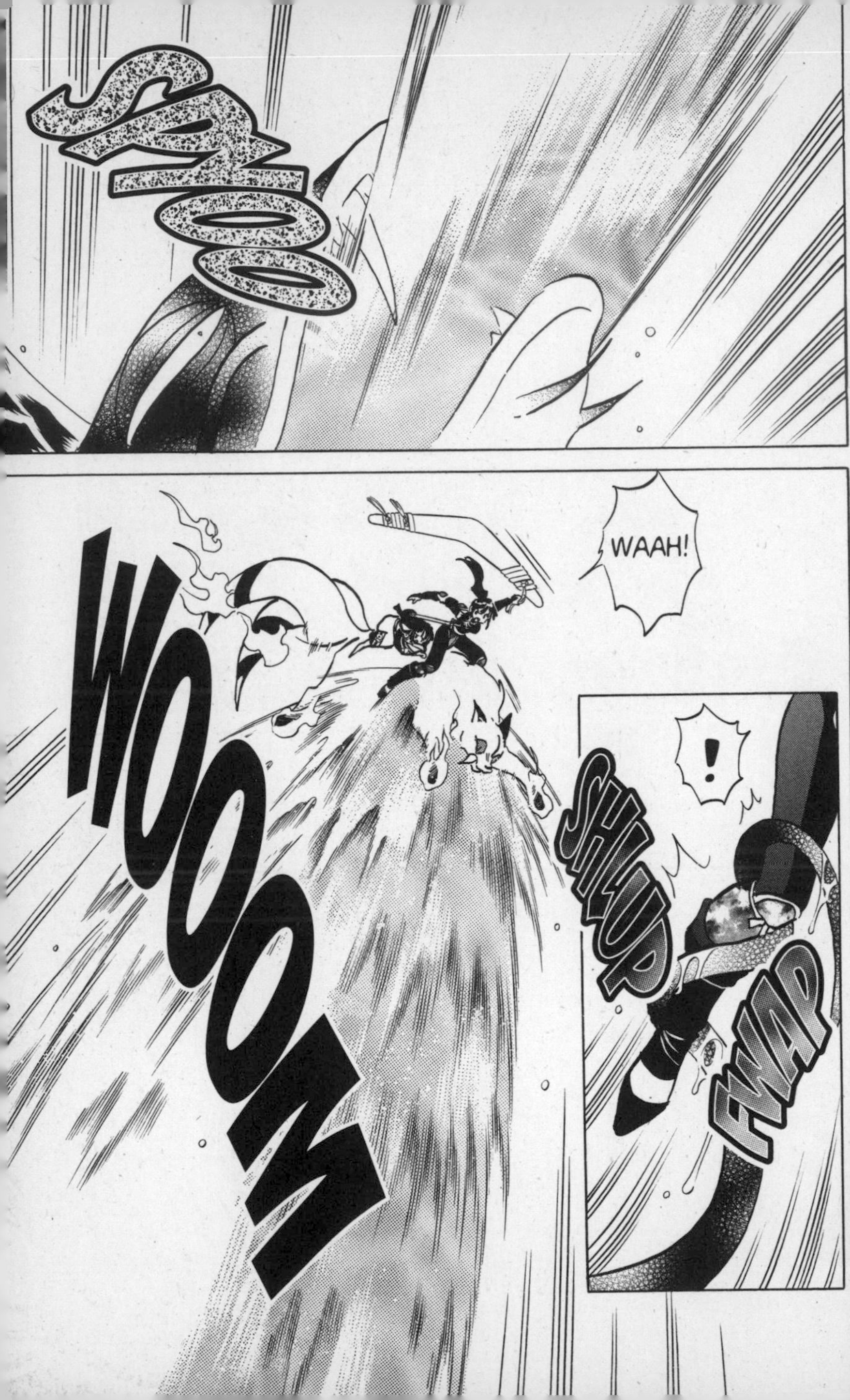
SPLOOOOO
WOOOOOM
WAAH!
!
SHLUP
FWAP

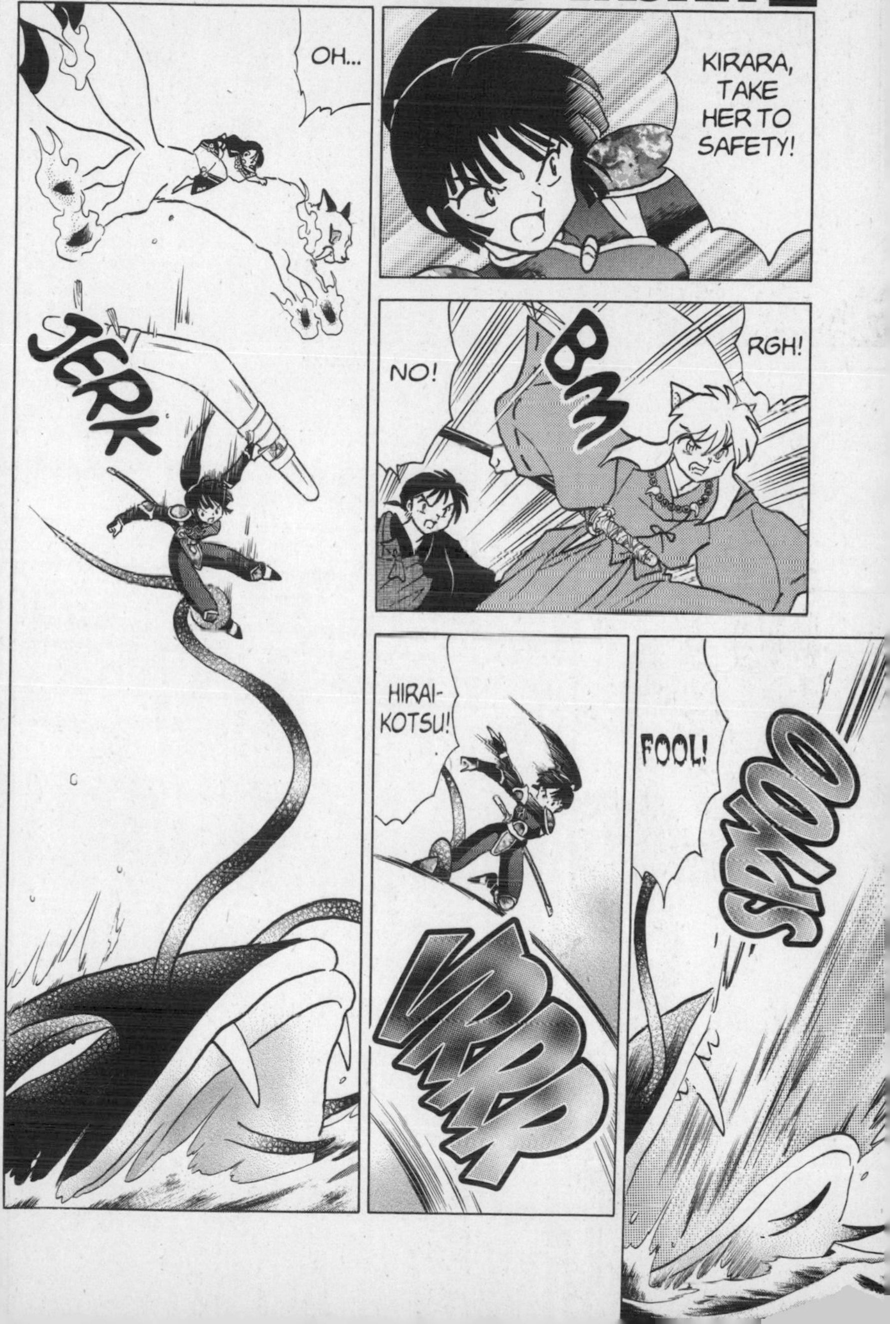
OH...
JERK
KIRARA, TAKE HER TO SAFETY!
NO!
BM
RGH!
HIRAI-KOTSU!
VRRP
FOOL!
SPLOO

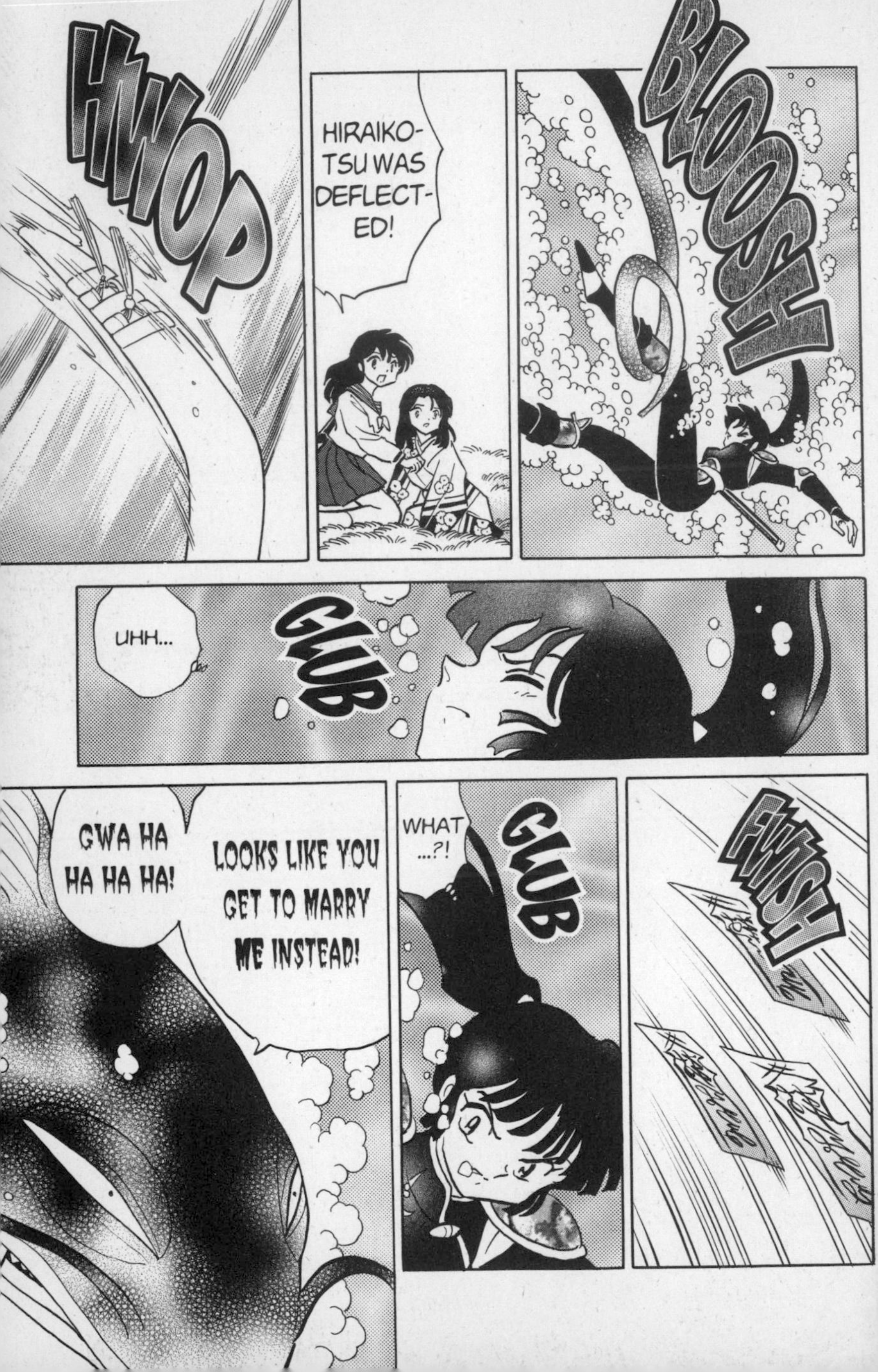
HWWOP
HIRAIKO-TSU WAS DEFLECT-ED!
BLOOOSH!
UHH...
GLUB
GWA HA HA HA HA!
LOOKS LIKE YOU GET TO MARRY ME INSTEAD!
WHAT ...?!
GLUB
FWISH!

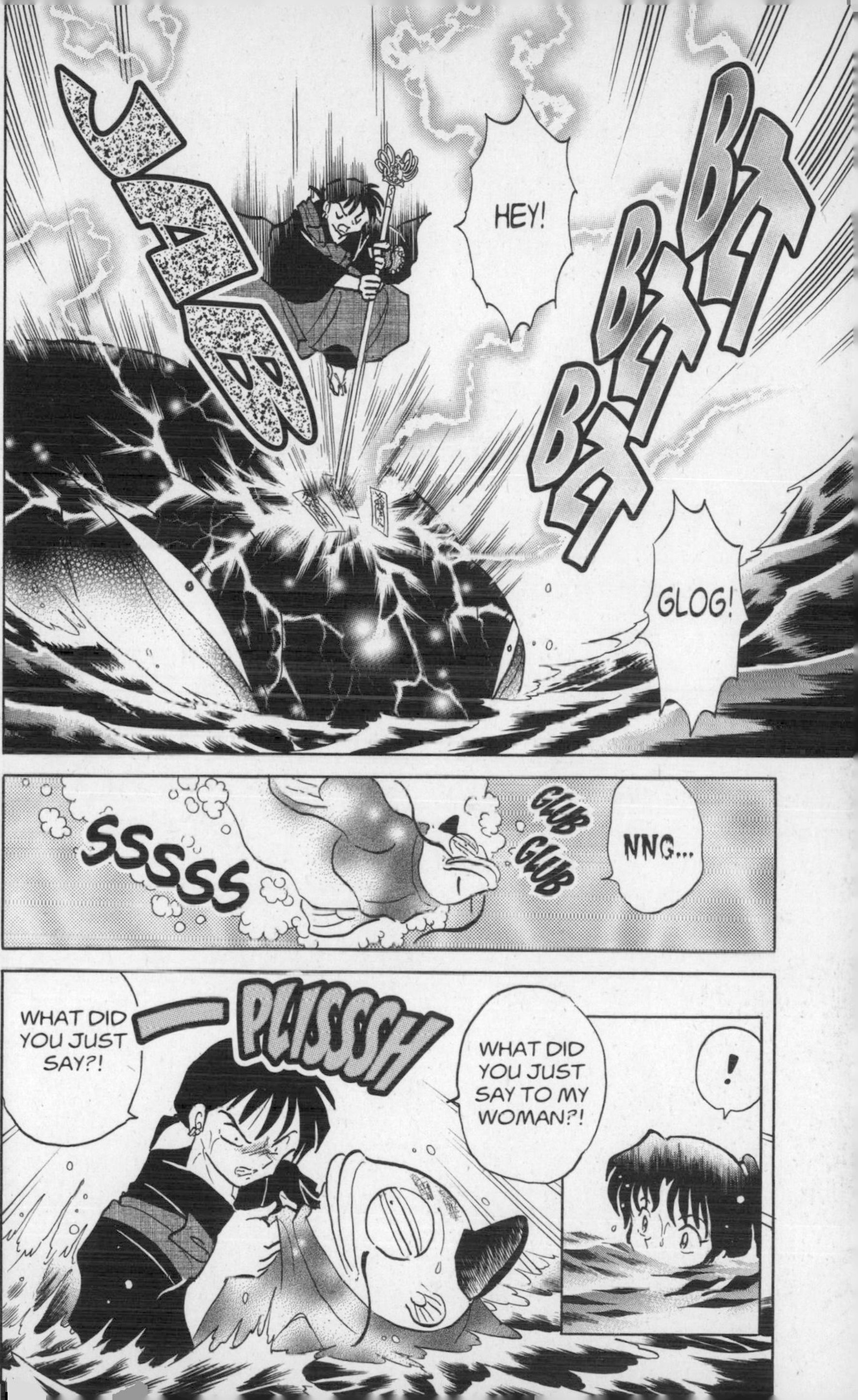
JABB
HEY!
BZT BZT BZT
GLOG!
SSSSS
GLUB GLUB
NNG...
WHAT DID YOU JUST SAY?!
PLISSSH
WHAT DID YOU JUST SAY TO MY WOMAN?!
!

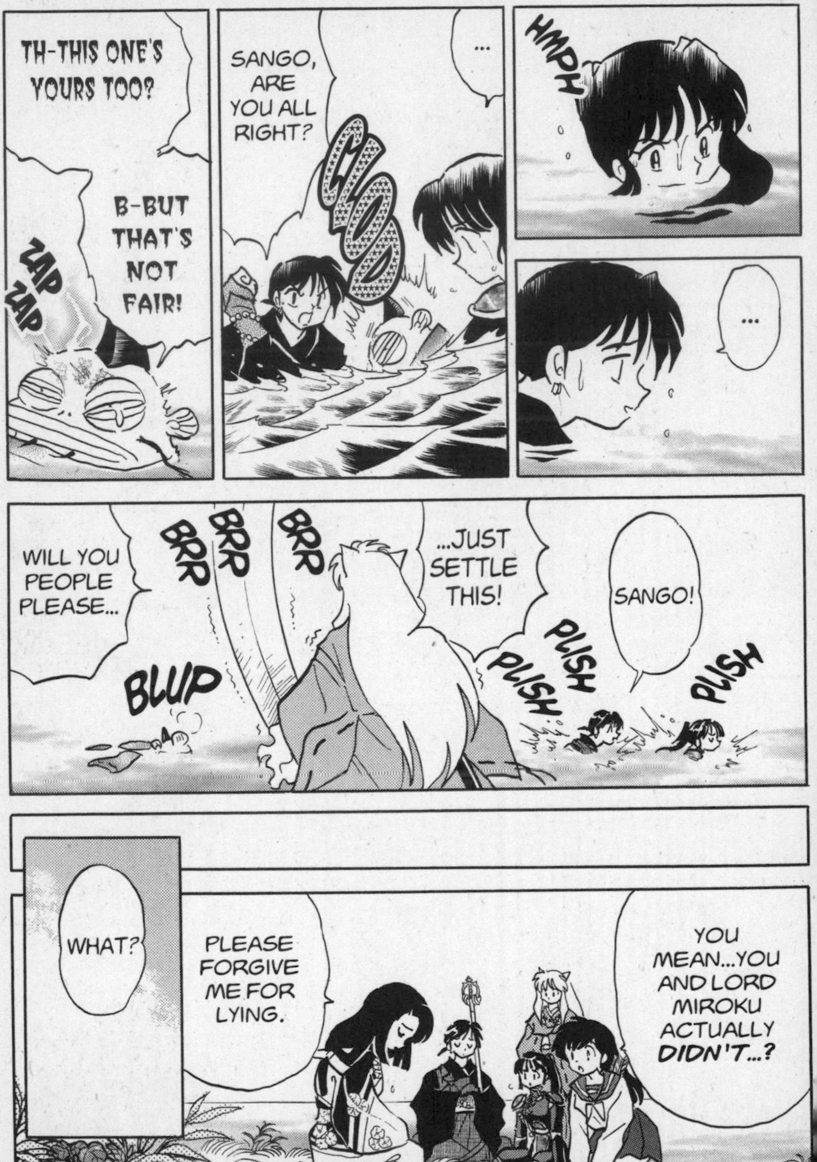
TH-THIS ONE'S YOURS TOO?
B-BUT THAT'S NOT FAIR!
ZAP ZAP
SANGO, ARE YOU ALL RIGHT?
...
CLOD
HMPH
...
WILL YOU PEOPLE PLEASE...
BRR BRR
BRR
BLUP
...JUST SETTLE THIS!
PLISH PLISH
SANGO!
PLISH
WHAT?
PLEASE FORGIVE ME FOR LYING.
YOU MEAN...YOU AND LORD MIROKU ACTUALLY DIDN'T...?

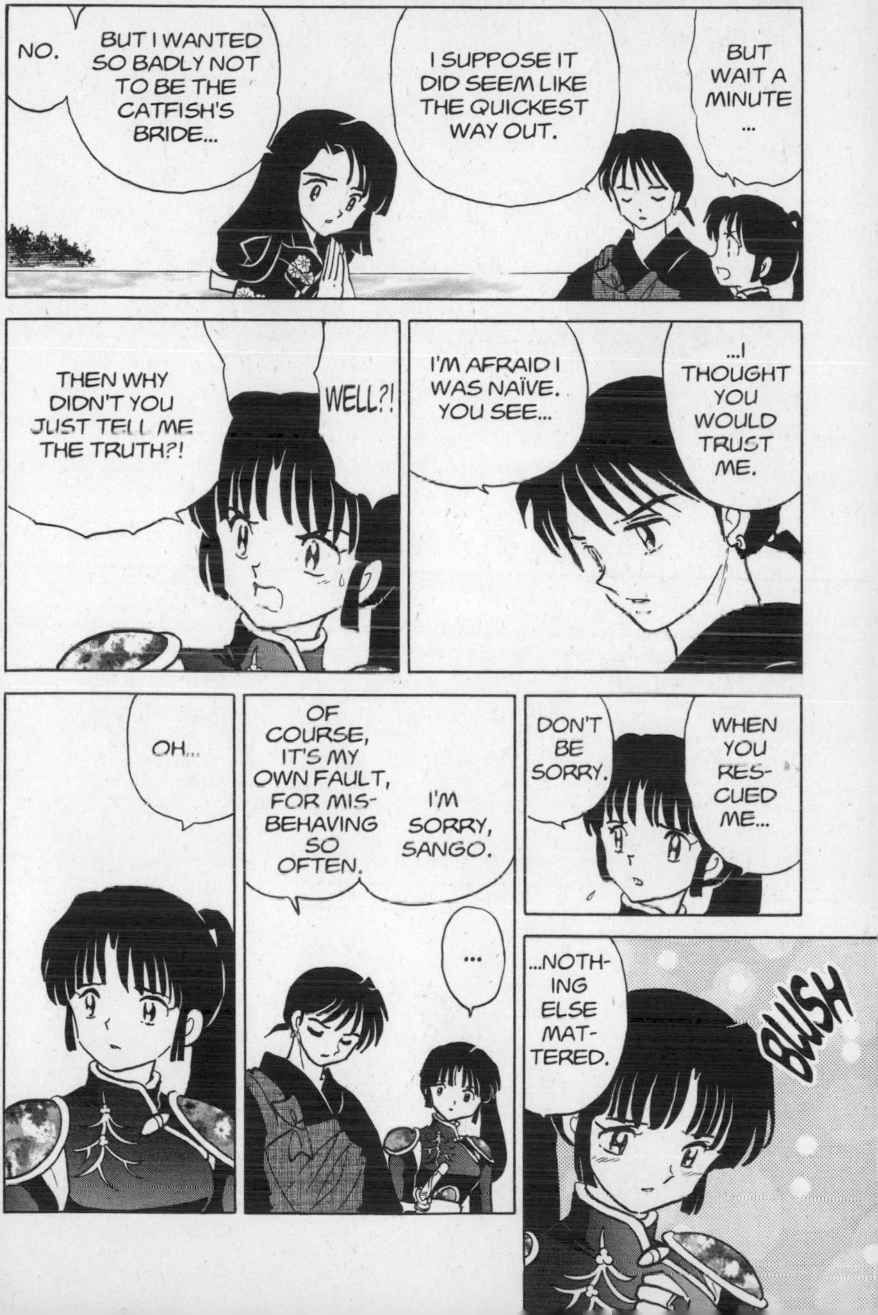
NO.
BUT I WANTED SO BADLY NOT TO BE THE CATFISH'S BRIDE...
I SUPPOSE IT DID SEEM LIKE THE QUICKEST WAY OUT.
BUT WAIT A MINUTE ...
THEN WHY DIDN'T YOU JUST TELL ME THE TRUTH?!
WELL?!
I'M AFRAID I WAS NAÏVE. YOU SEE...
...I THOUGHT YOU WOULD TRUST ME.
OH...
OF COURSE, IT'S MY OWN FAULT, FOR MIS-BEHAVING SO OFTEN.
I'M SORRY, SANGO.
...
DON'T BE SORRY.
WHEN YOU RES-CUED ME...
...NOTH-ING ELSE MAT-TERED.
BLUSH

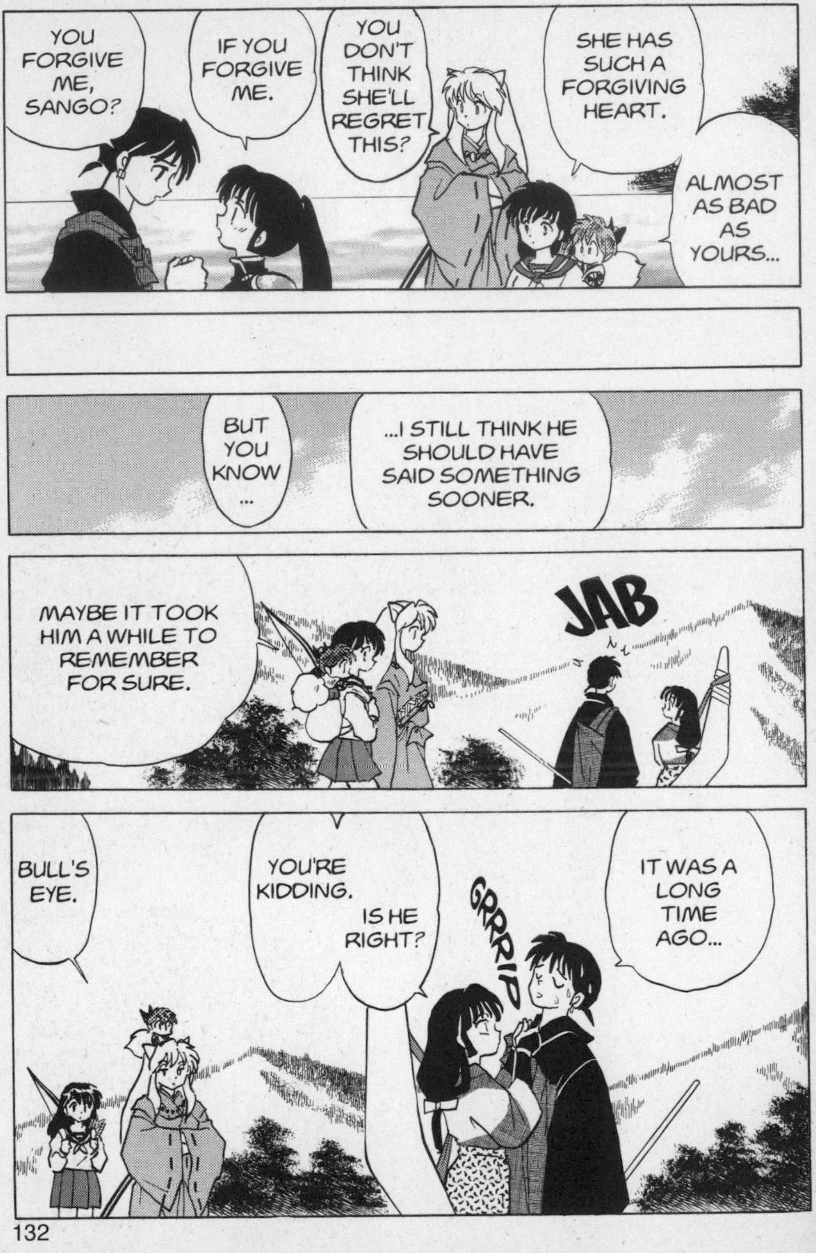
YOU FORGIVE ME, SANGO?
IF YOU FORGIVE ME.
YOU DON'T THINK SHE'LL REGRET THIS?
SHE HAS SUCH A FORGIVING HEART.
ALMOST AS BAD AS YOURS...
BUT YOU KNOW ...
...I STILL THINK HE SHOULD HAVE SAID SOMETHING SOONER.
MAYBE IT TOOK HIM A WHILE TO REMEMBER FOR SURE.
JAB
BULL'S EYE.
YOU'RE KIDDING.
IS HE RIGHT?
GRRRIP
IT WAS A LONG TIME AGO...

SCROLL 8

THE ACOLYTES

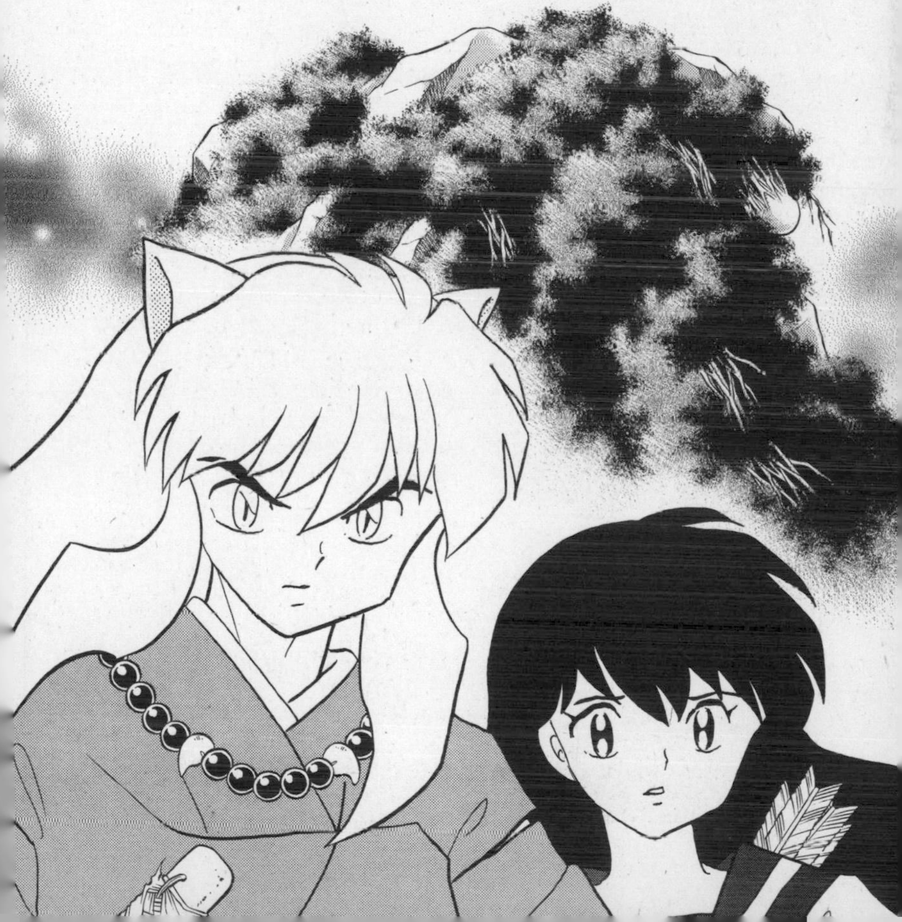

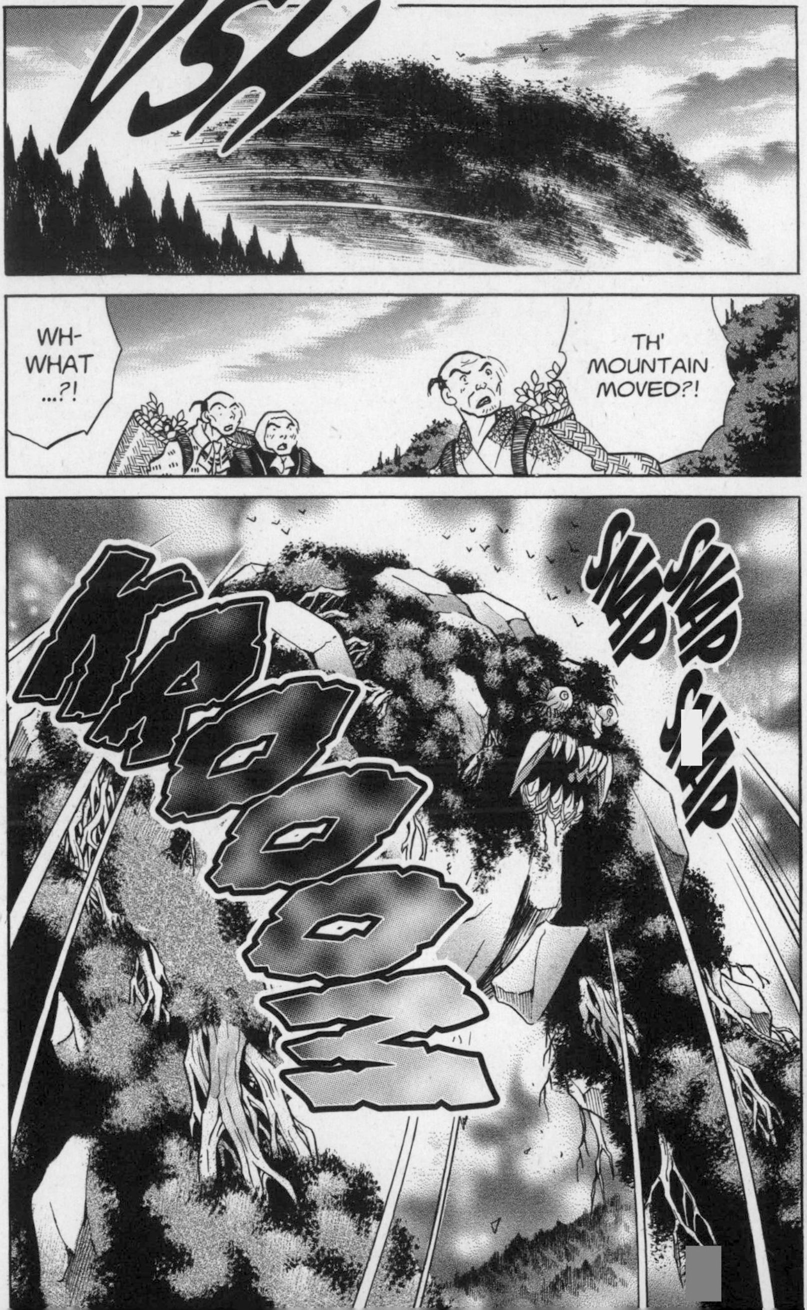
VSH
WH- WHAT ...?!
TH' MOUNTAIN MOVED?!
KAOOOM
SNAP SNAP
SNAP SNAP

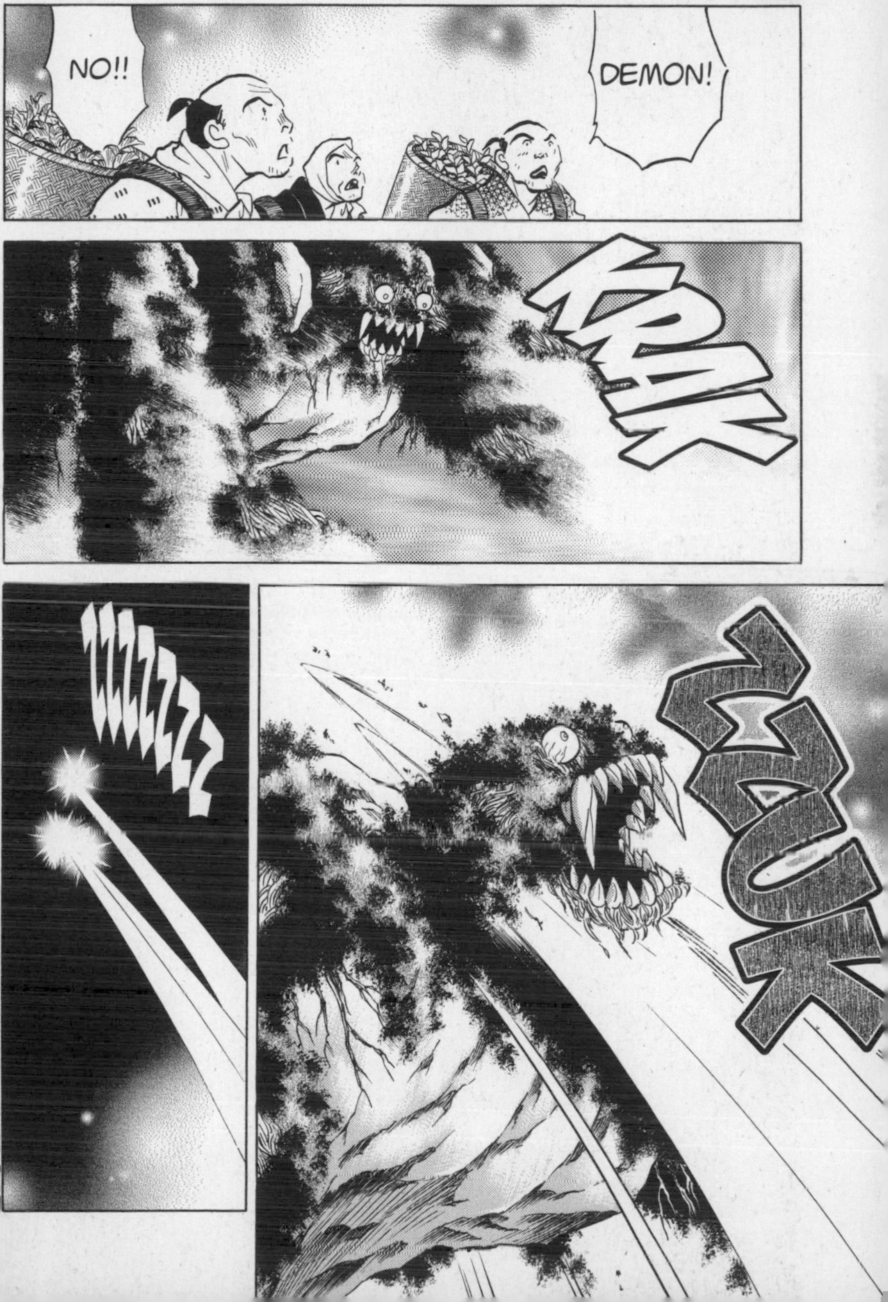
DEMON!
NO!!
KRAK

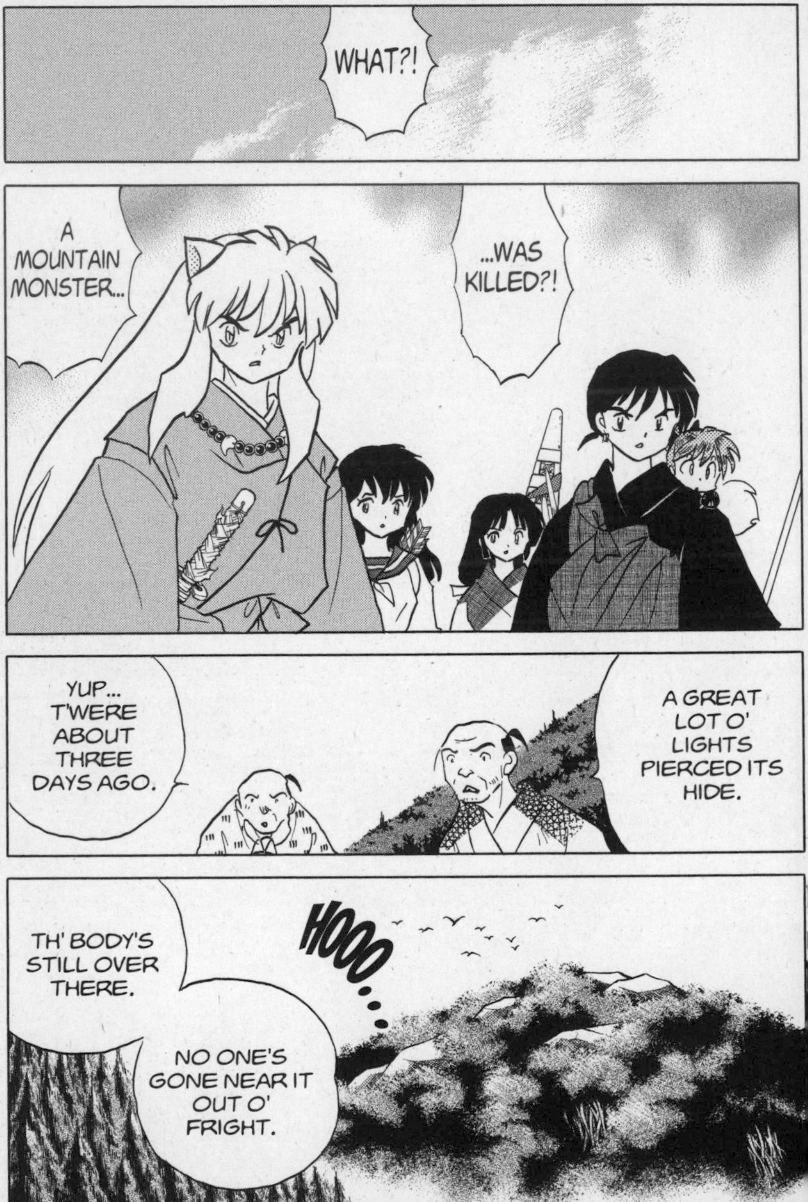
WHAT?!
A MOUNTAIN MONSTER...
...WAS KILLED?!
YUP... T'WERE ABOUT THREE DAYS AGO.
A GREAT LOT O' LIGHTS PIERCED ITS HIDE.
TH' BODY'S STILL OVER THERE.
HOOO...
NO ONE'S GONE NEAR IT OUT O' FRIGHT.

THE ONLY MOUNTAIN MONSTER I KNOW IS GAKUSANJIN...

DM

DM

...BUT I SENSE NO DEMONIC ENERGY HERE.

IT'S LIKE AN ORDINARY MOUNTAIN.

...

BUT...THERE ARE SMELLS LINGERING...

NO QUESTION, IT'S...

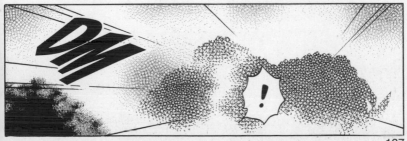

DM

!

OH...!

FLAP
FLAP

TP

...GAKU-SANJIN'S HEAD.

YEAH.

GAKUSANJIN TOLD US...

...THAT NARAKU HAD STOLEN HIS "NULLING STONE"...

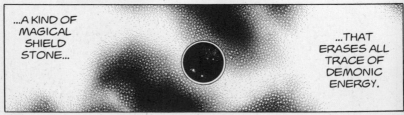

...A KIND OF MAGICAL SHIELD STONE...

...THAT ERASES ALL TRACE OF DEMONIC ENERGY.

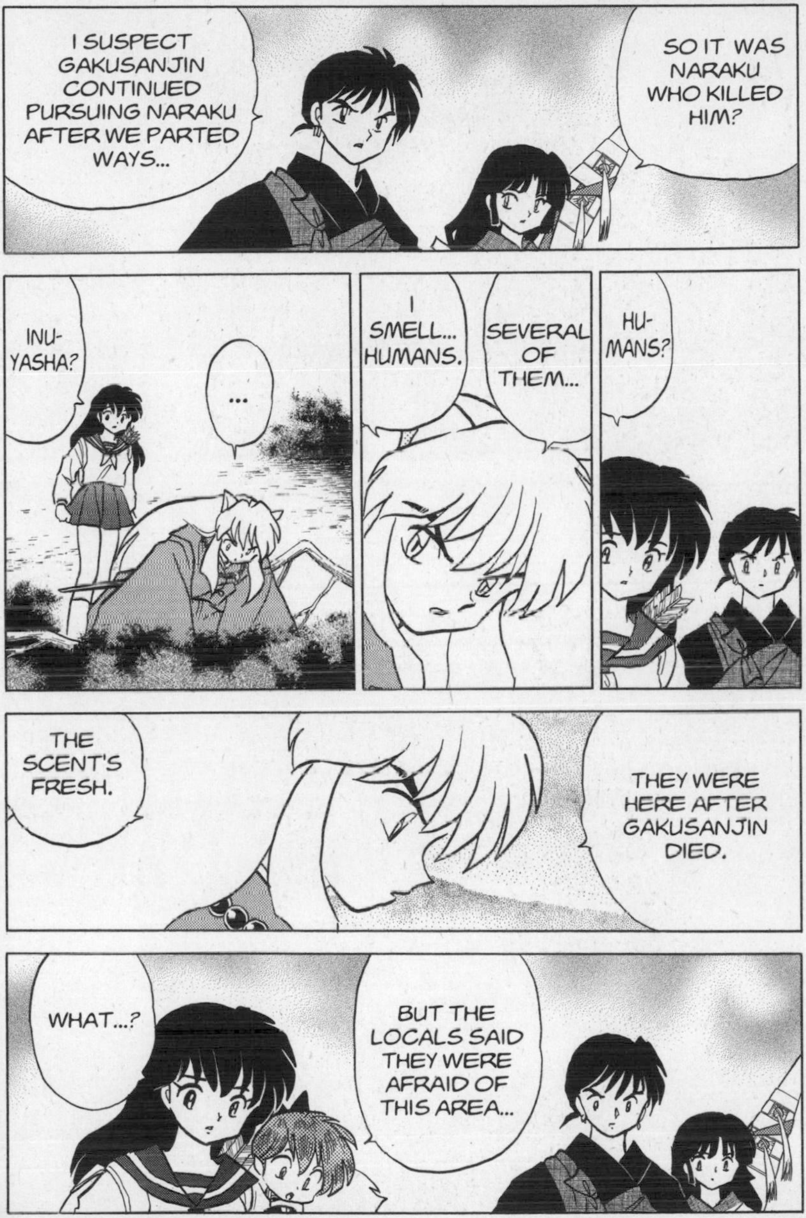
I SUSPECT GAKUSANJIN CONTINUED PURSUING NARAKU AFTER WE PARTED WAYS...
SO IT WAS NARAKU WHO KILLED HIM?
INU-YASHA?
...
I SMELL... HUMANS.
SEVERAL OF THEM...
HU-MANS?
THE SCENT'S FRESH.
THEY WERE HERE AFTER GAKUSANJIN DIED.
WHAT...?
BUT THE LOCALS SAID THEY WERE AFRAID OF THIS AREA...

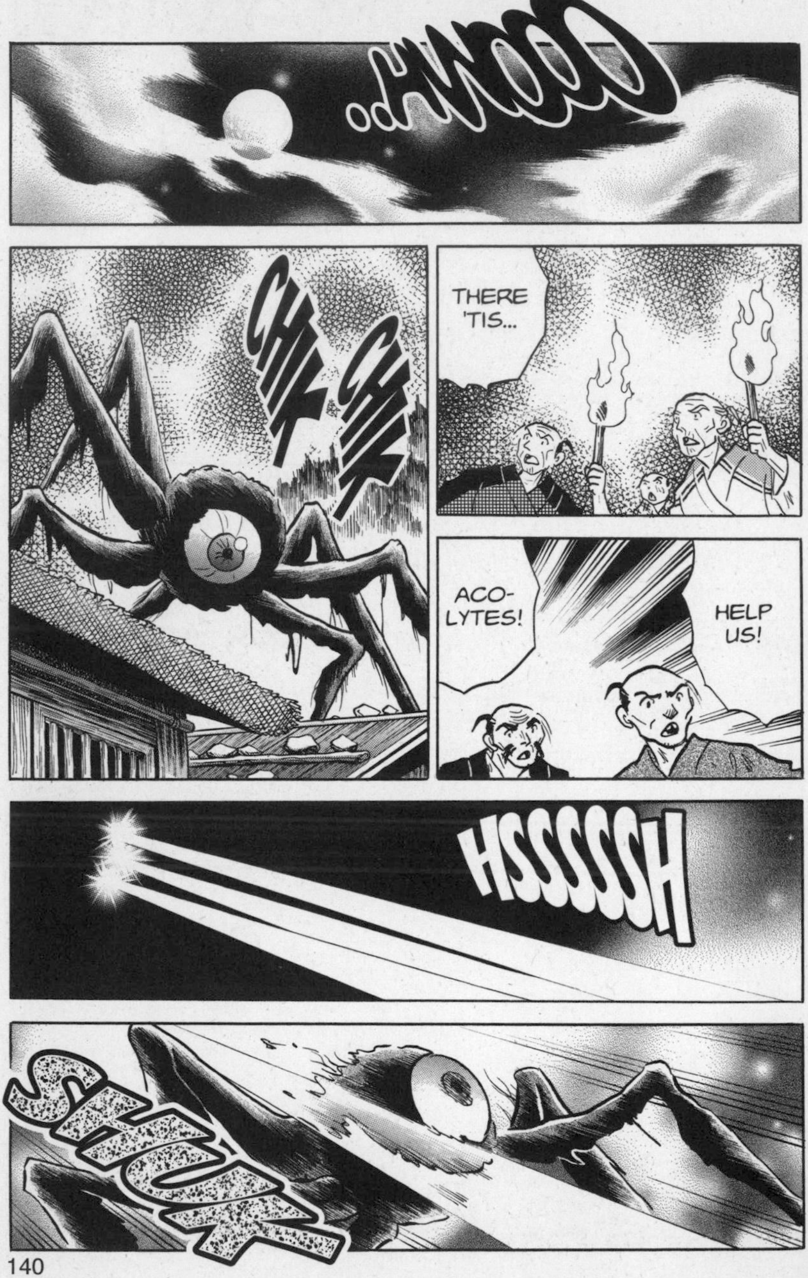
CHIK CHIK
THERE 'TIS...
ACO-LYTES!
HELP US!
HSSSSSH

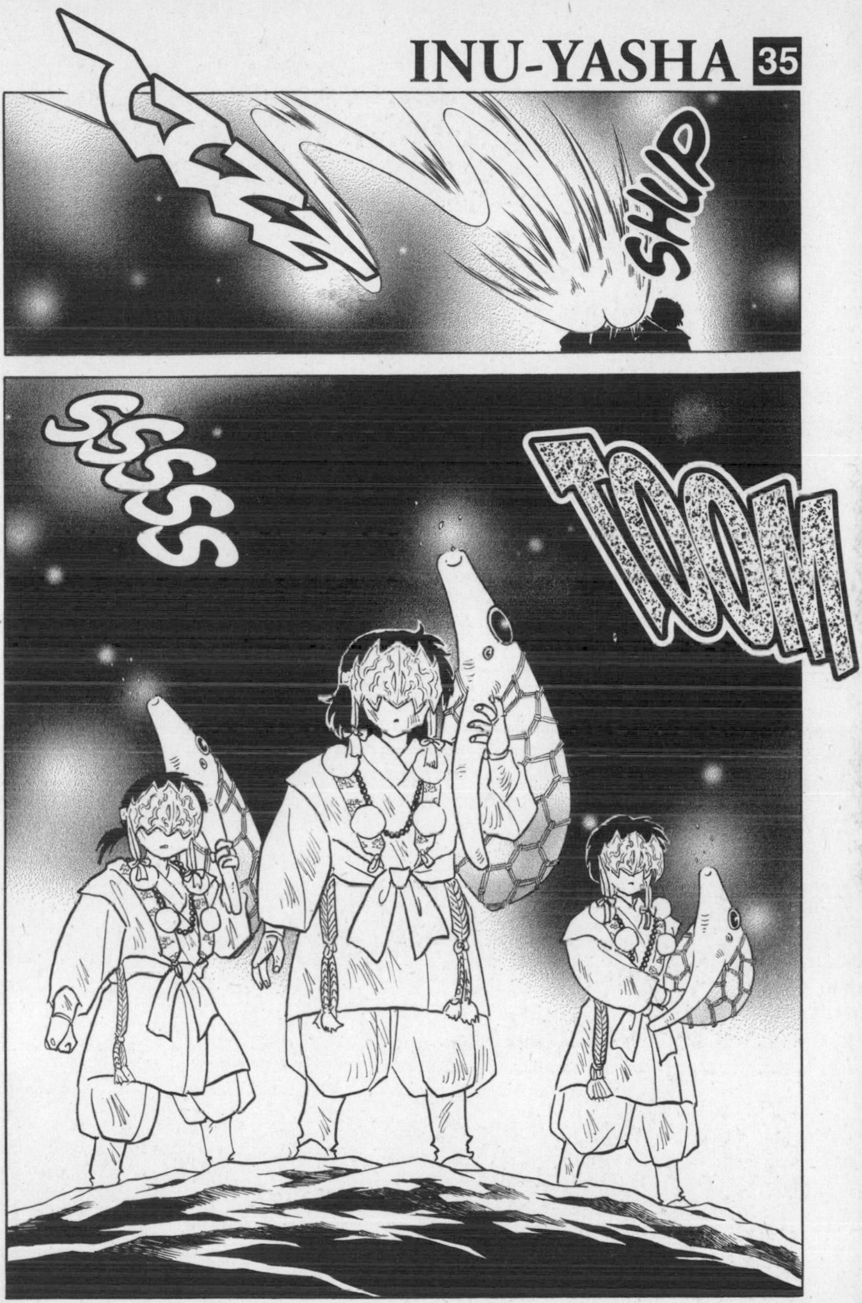
SHUP
SSSSS
TOOM

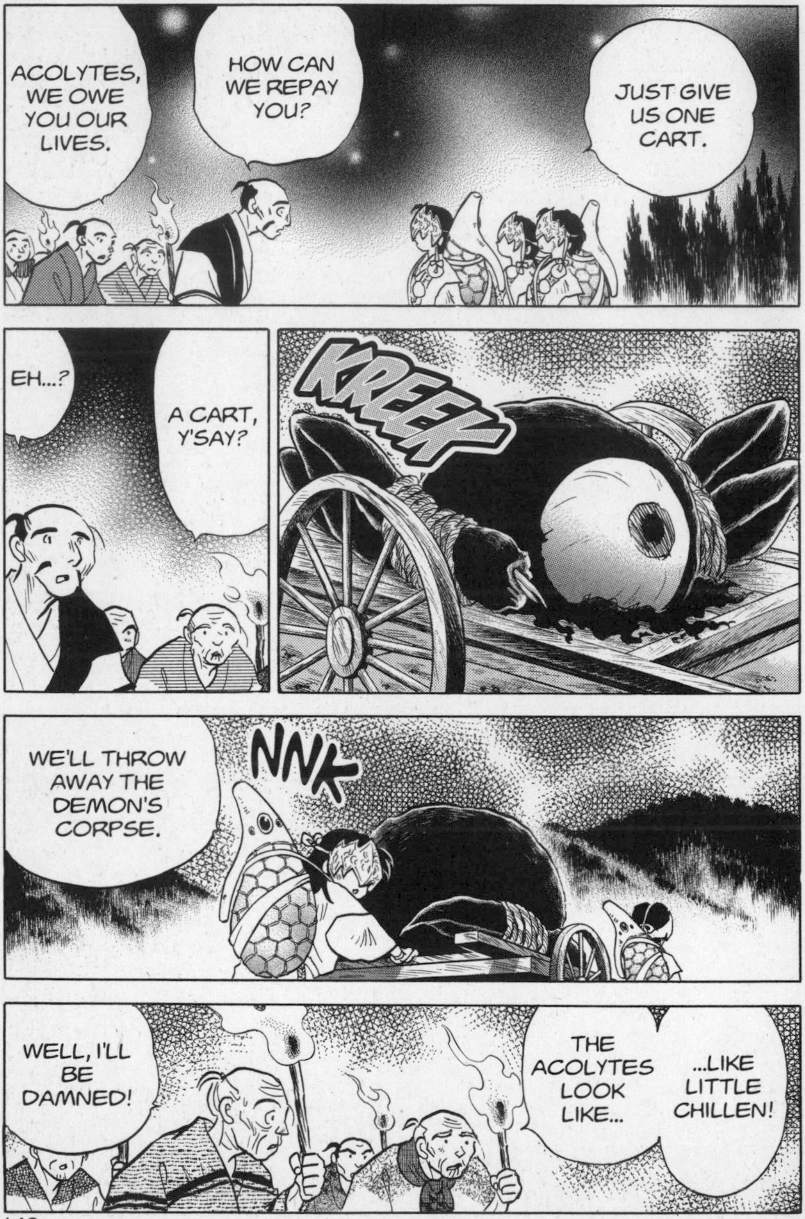
ACOLYTES, WE OWE YOU OUR LIVES.
HOW CAN WE REPAY YOU?
JUST GIVE US ONE CART.
EH...?
A CART, Y'SAY?
KREEK
WE'LL THROW AWAY THE DEMON'S CORPSE.
NNK
WELL, I'LL BE DAMNED!
THE ACOLYTES LOOK LIKE...
...LIKE LITTLE CHILLEN!

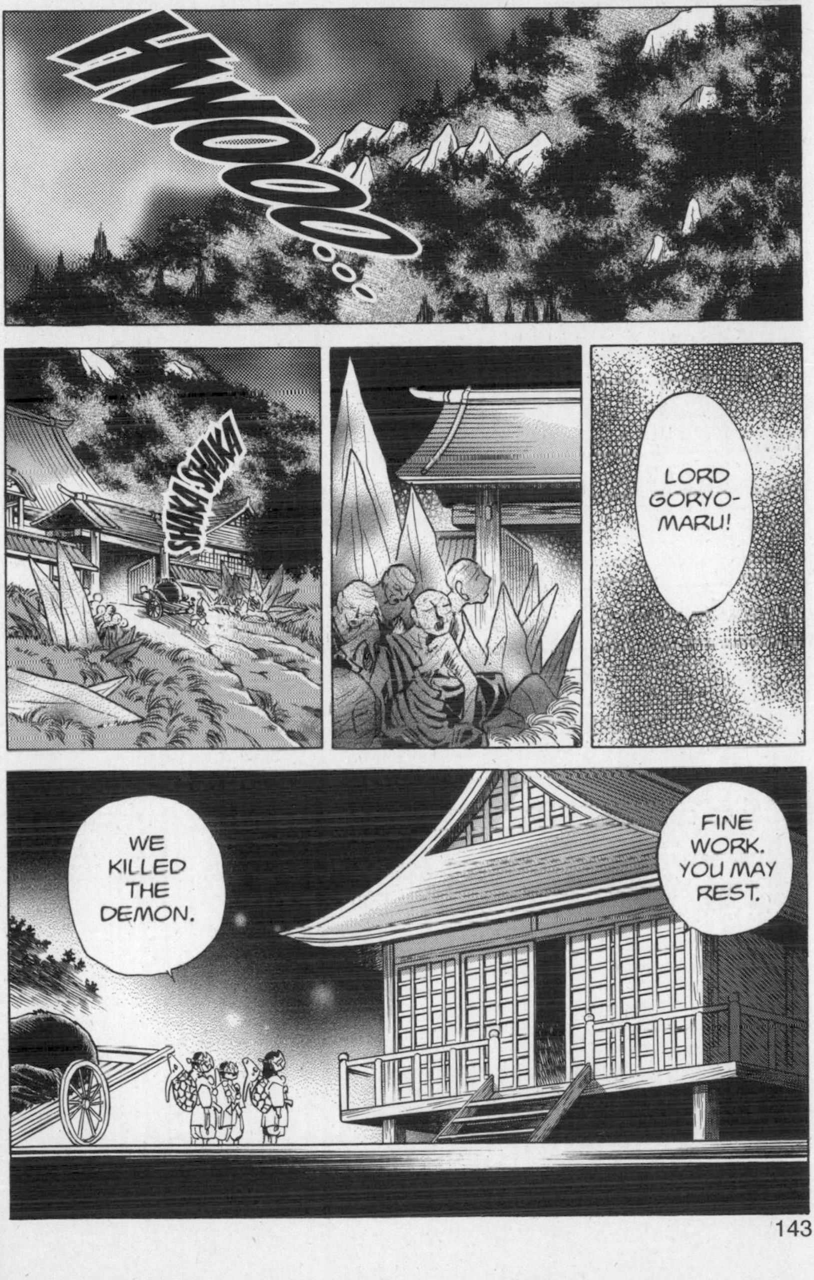
HWOOOO...
SHAKA SHAKA
LORD GORYO-MARU!
WE KILLED THE DEMON.
FINE WORK. YOU MAY REST.

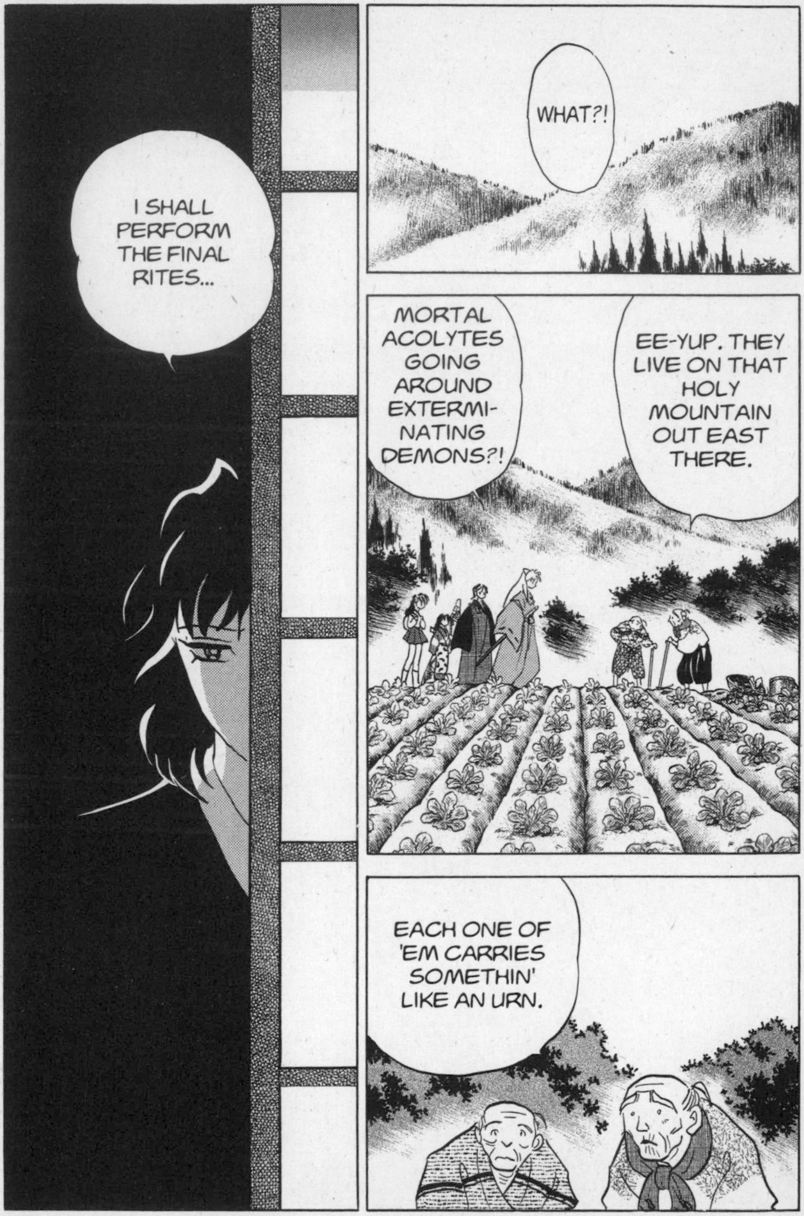
I SHALL PERFORM THE FINAL RITES...
WHAT?!
MORTAL ACOLYTES GOING AROUND EXTERMINATING DEMONS?!
EE-YUP. THEY LIVE ON THAT HOLY MOUNTAIN OUT EAST THERE.
EACH ONE OF 'EM CARRIES SOMETHIN' LIKE AN URN.

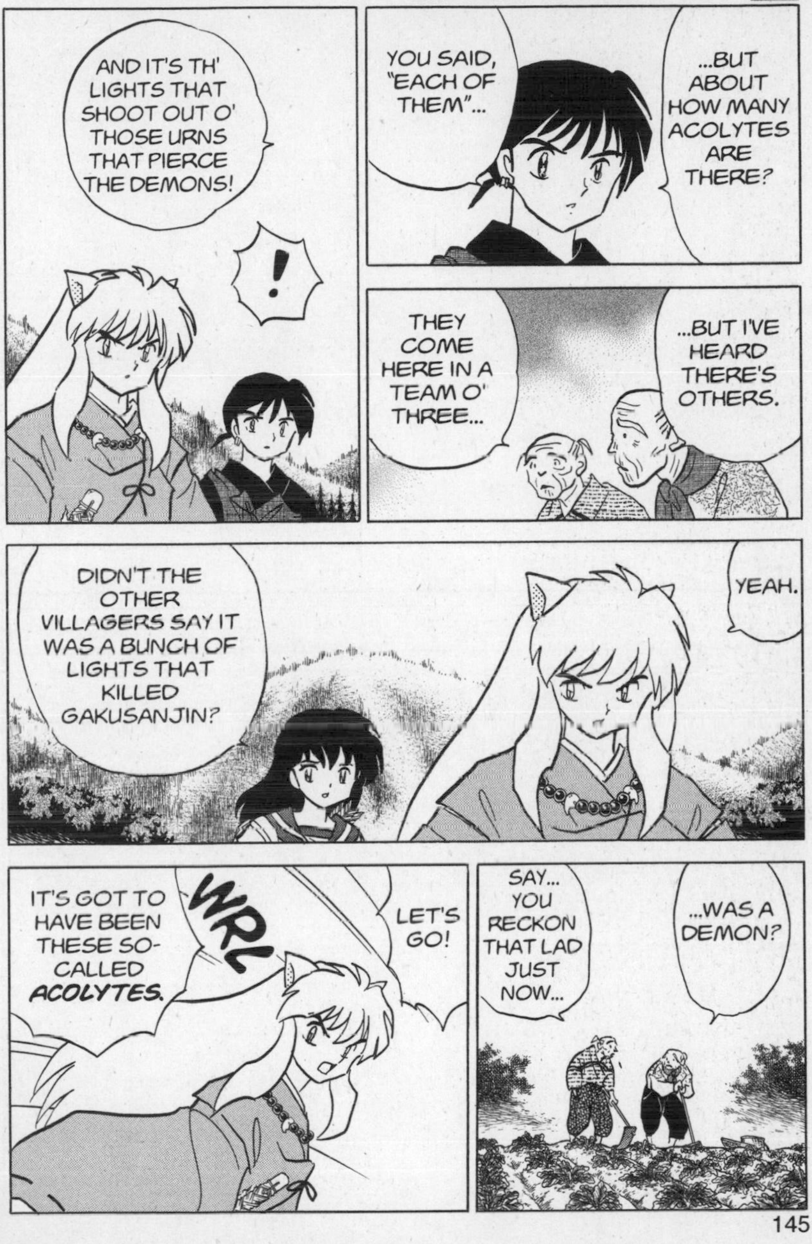
AND IT'S TH' LIGHTS THAT SHOOT OUT O' THOSE URNS THAT PIERCE THE DEMONS!
!
YOU SAID, "EACH OF THEM"...
...BUT ABOUT HOW MANY ACOLYTES ARE THERE?
THEY COME HERE IN A TEAM O' THREE...
...BUT I'VE HEARD THERE'S OTHERS.
DIDN'T THE OTHER VILLAGERS SAY IT WAS A BUNCH OF LIGHTS THAT KILLED GAKUSANJIN?
YEAH.
IT'S GOT TO HAVE BEEN THESE SO-CALLED ***ACOLYTES.***
WRL
LET'S GO!
SAY... YOU RECKON THAT LAD JUST NOW...
...WAS A DEMON?

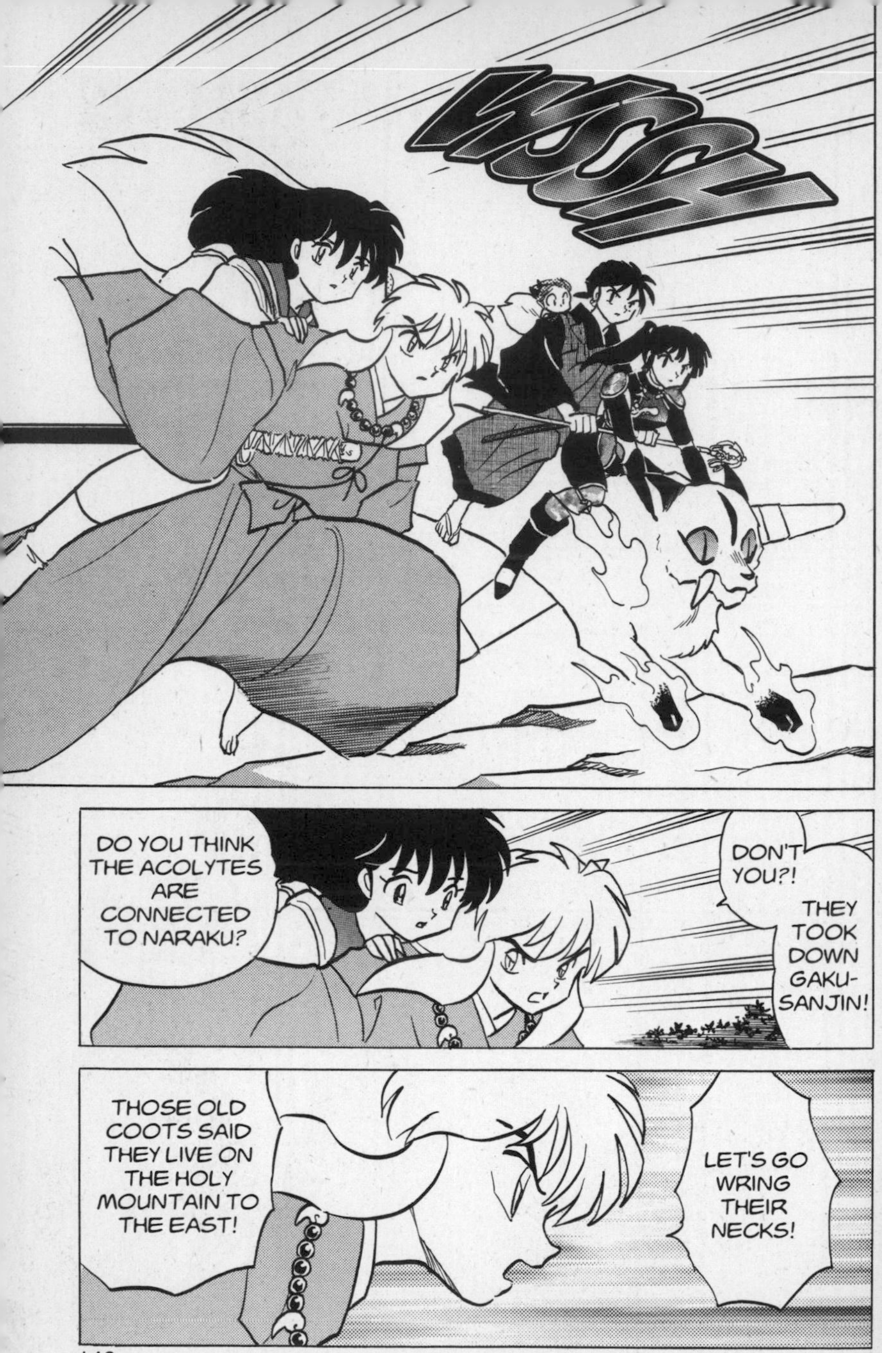
WSSH
DO YOU THINK THE ACOLYTES ARE CONNECTED TO NARAKU?
DON'T YOU?!
THEY TOOK DOWN GAKU-SANJIN!
THOSE OLD COOTS SAID THEY LIVE ON THE HOLY MOUNTAIN TO THE EAST!
LET'S GO WRING THEIR NECKS!

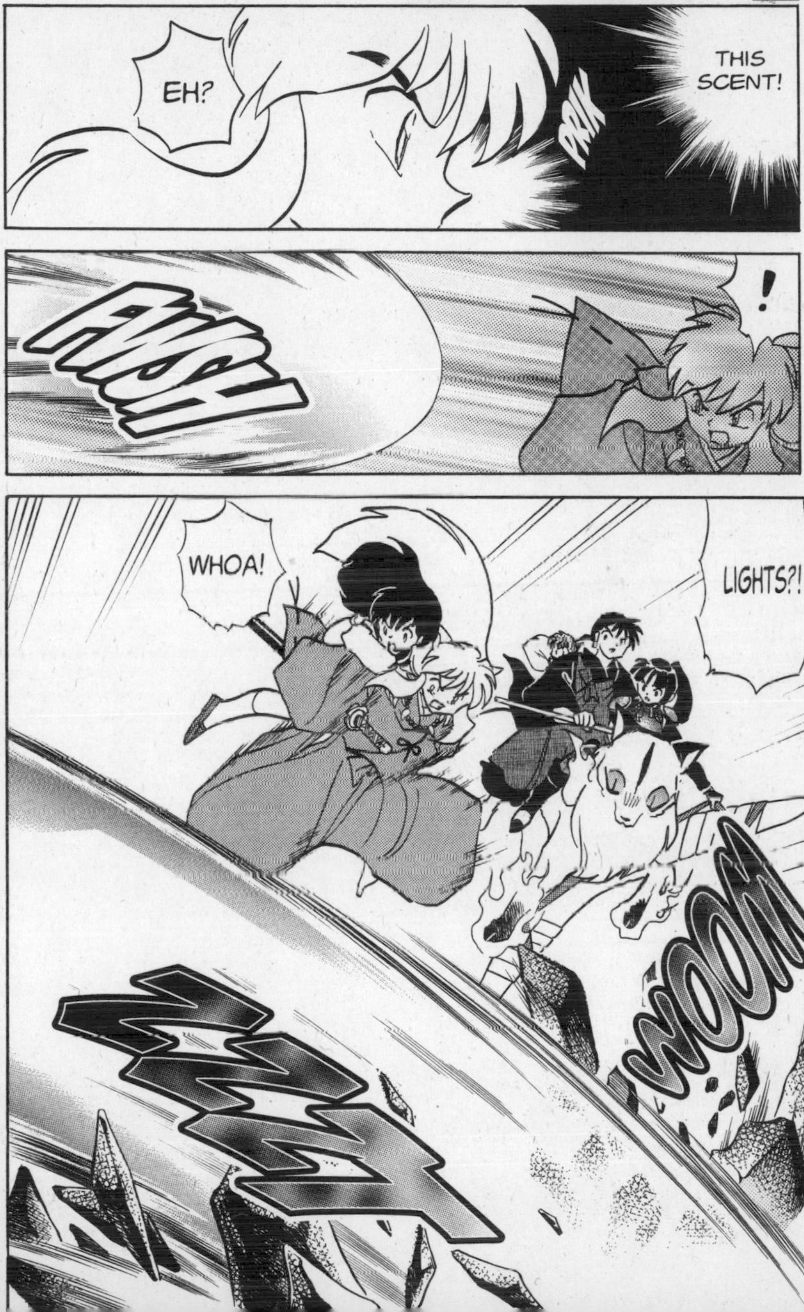
EH?
PRIK
THIS SCENT!
!
WHOA!
LIGHTS?!
WOOM

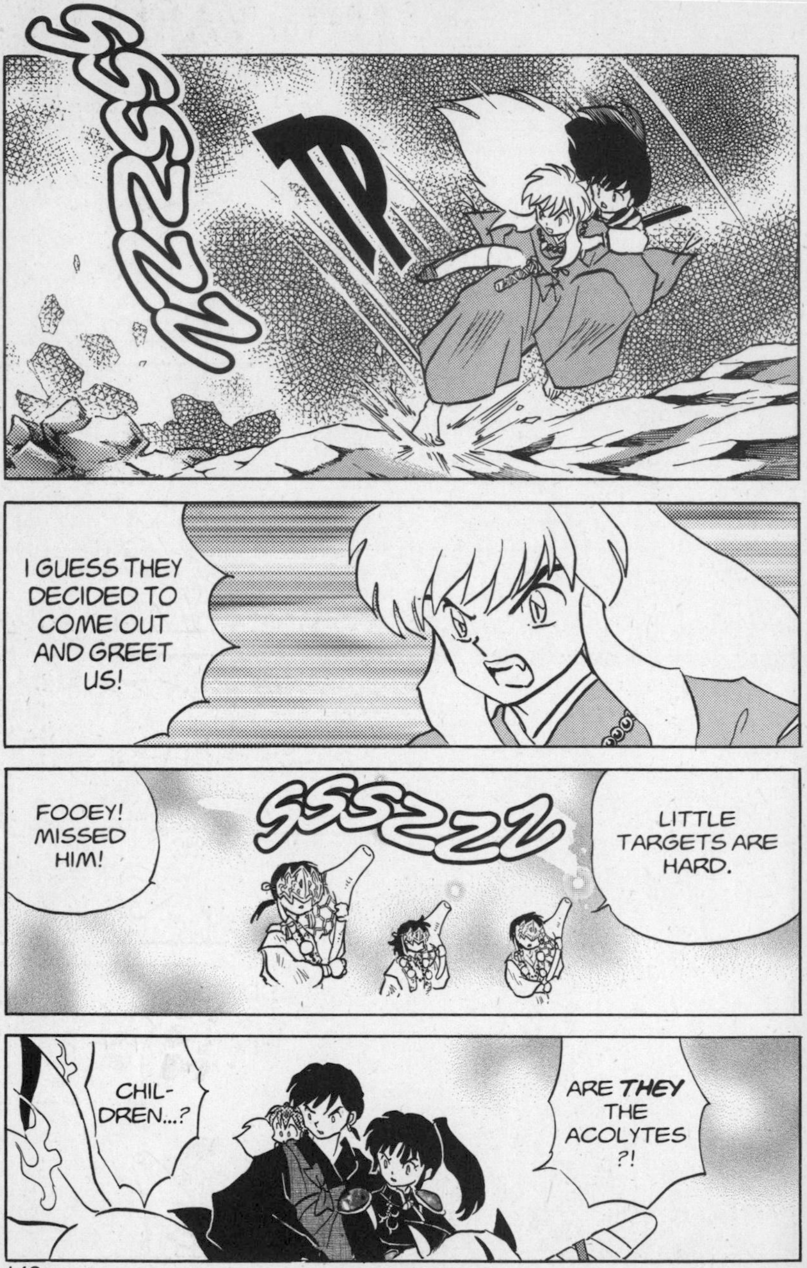
SSSZZZ
I GUESS THEY DECIDED TO COME OUT AND GREET US!
FOOEY! MISSED HIM!
SSSZZZ
LITTLE TARGETS ARE HARD.
CHIL-DREN...?
ARE *THEY* THE ACOLYTES ?!

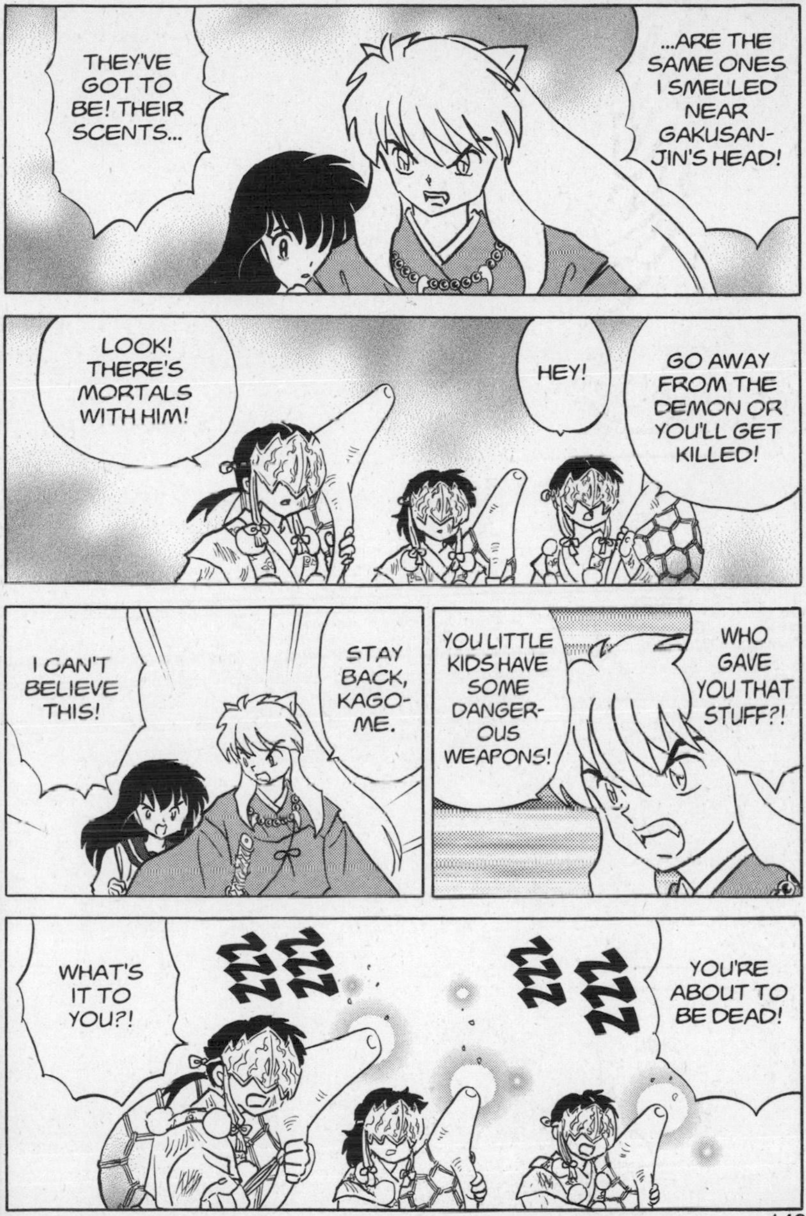
THEY'VE GOT TO BE! THEIR SCENTS...
...ARE THE SAME ONES I SMELLED NEAR GAKUSAN-JIN'S HEAD!
LOOK! THERE'S MORTALS WITH HIM!
HEY!
GO AWAY FROM THE DEMON OR YOU'LL GET KILLED!
I CAN'T BELIEVE THIS!
STAY BACK, KAGO-ME.
YOU LITTLE KIDS HAVE SOME DANGER-OUS WEAPONS!
WHO GAVE YOU THAT STUFF?!
WHAT'S IT TO YOU?!
ZZZ
ZZZ
ZZZ
ZZZ
YOU'RE ABOUT TO BE DEAD!

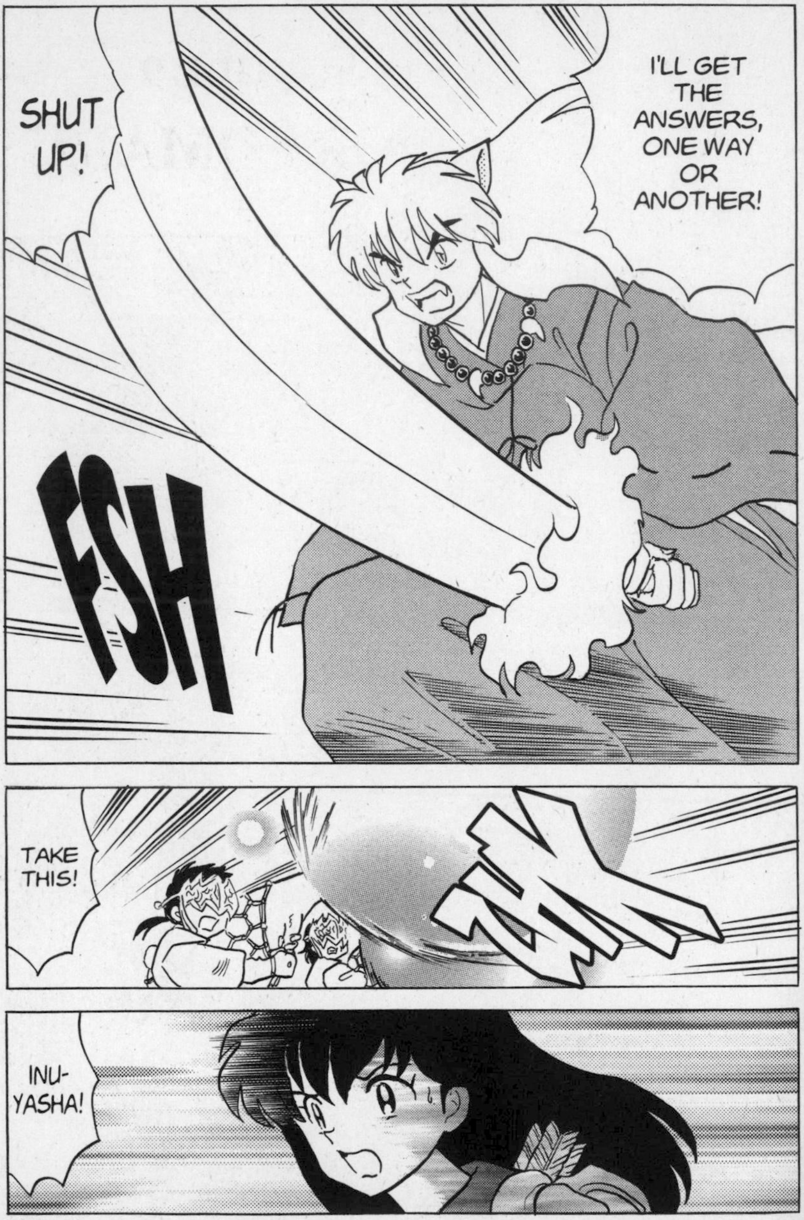
SHUT UP!
I'LL GET THE ANSWERS, ONE WAY OR ANOTHER!
FSH
TAKE THIS!
INU-YASHA!

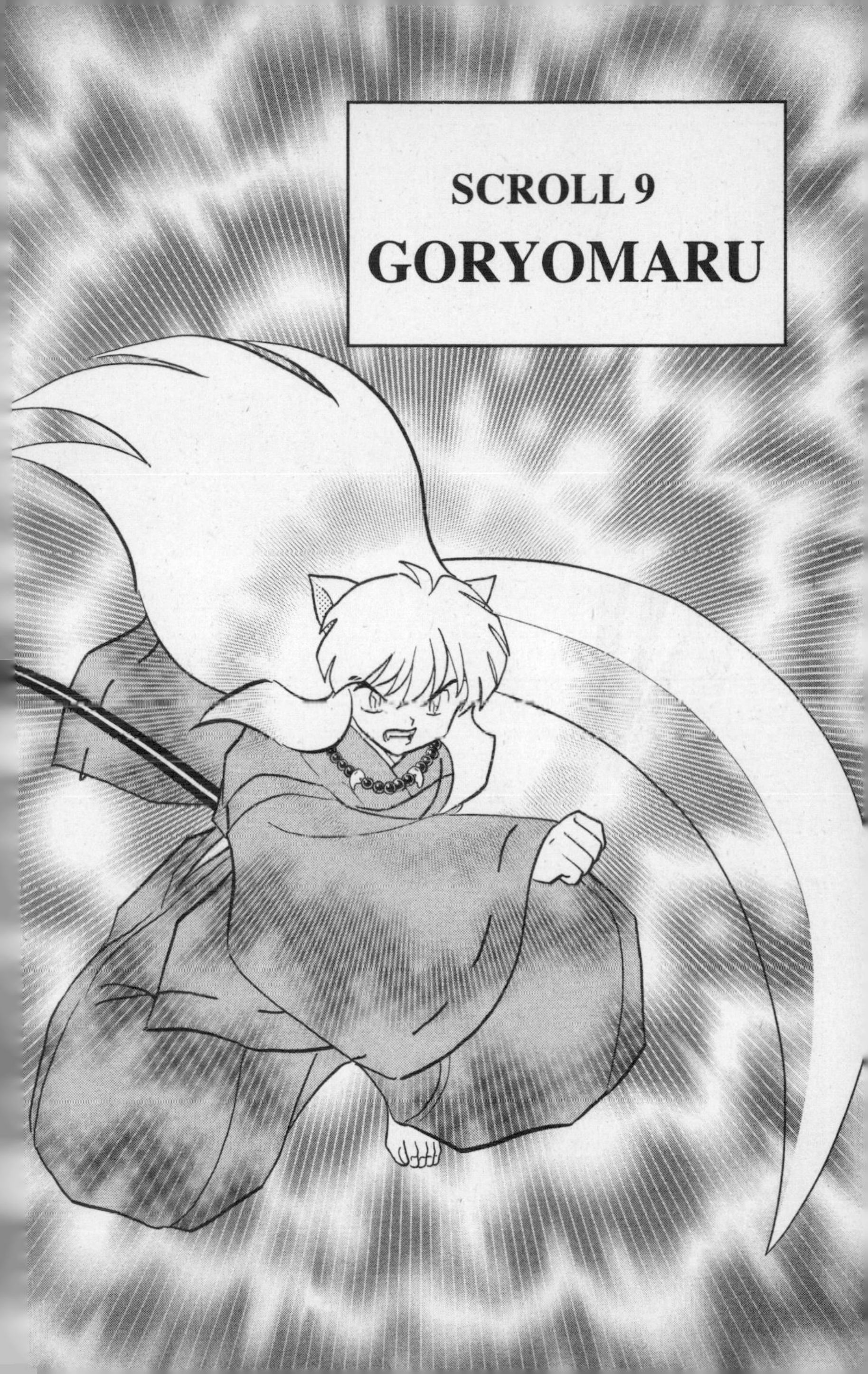
SCROLL 9
GORYOMARU

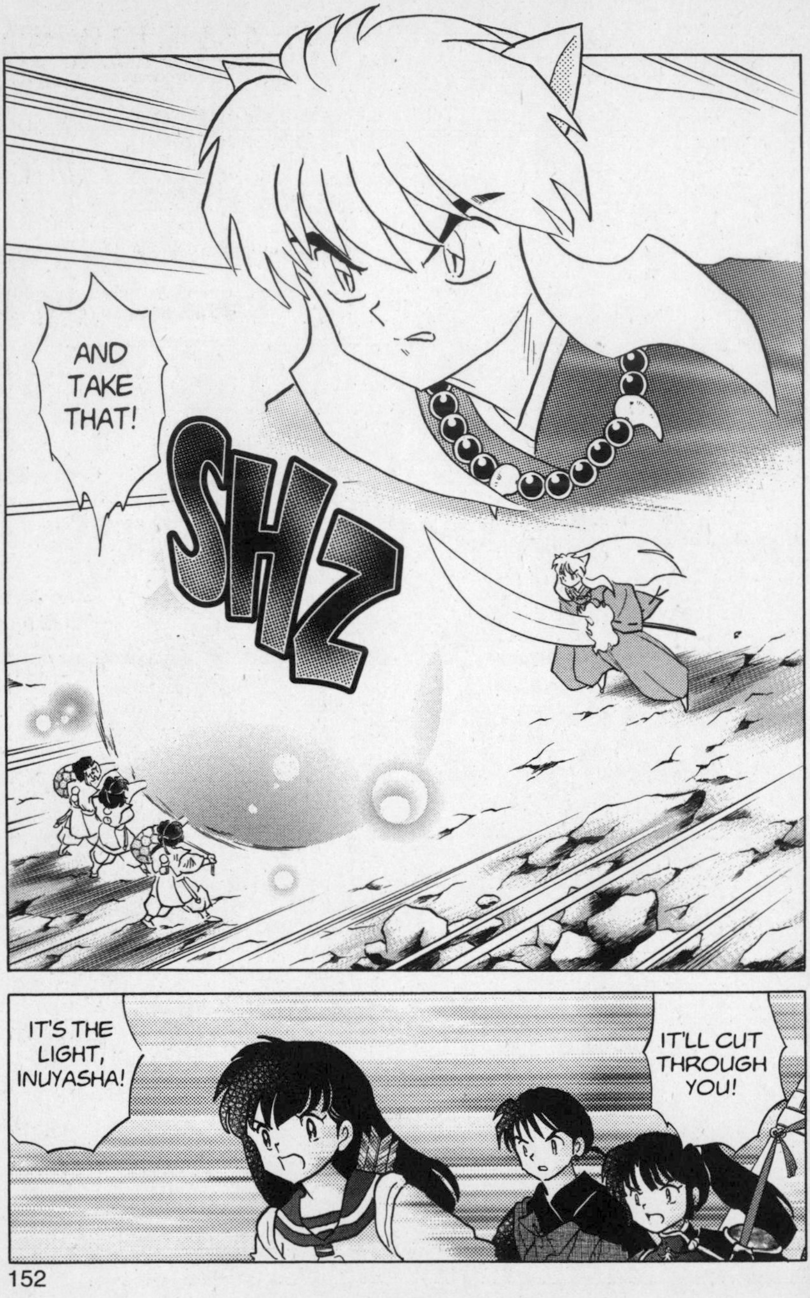
AND TAKE THAT!
SHZ
IT'S THE LIGHT, INUYASHA!
IT'LL CUT THROUGH YOU!

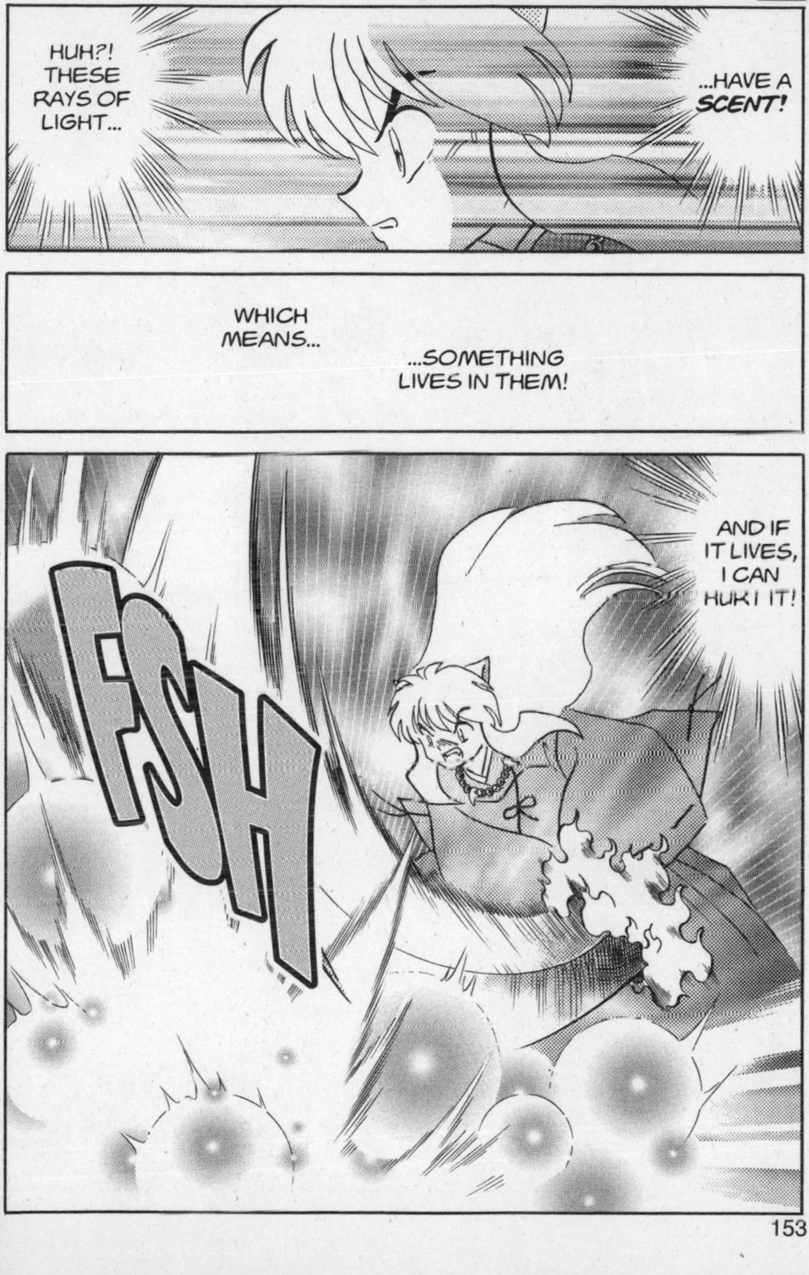
HUH?! THESE RAYS OF LIGHT...
...HAVE A SCENT!
WHICH MEANS...
...SOMETHING LIVES IN THEM!
FSH
AND IF IT LIVES, I CAN HURT IT!

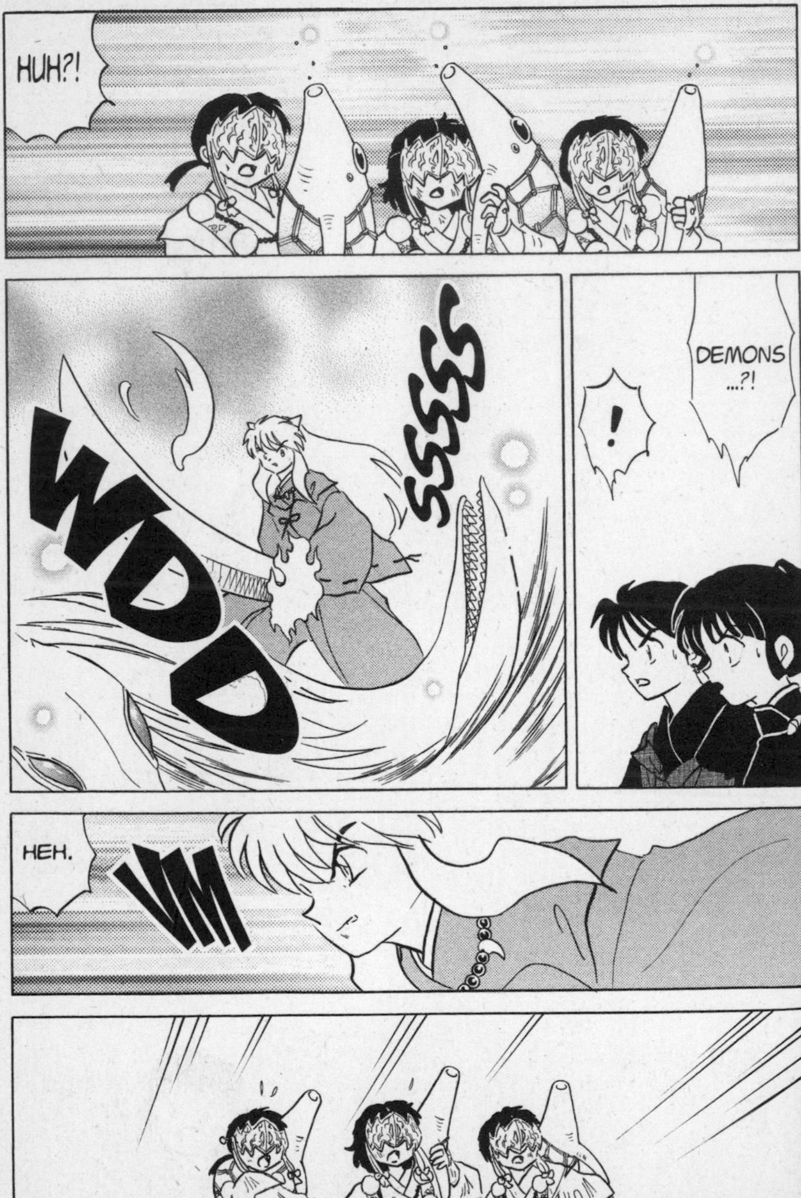
HUH?!
WDDD
SSSSS
!
DEMONS ...?!
HEH.
VM

EEEEEK!
WHAT ARE YOU DOING?!
IT SEEMS THEY REALLY ARE CHILDREN...
BUT WHAT'S HAPPENING HERE?!
NOW SPILL IT!
HOW DID YOU GET AHOLD OF THOSE URNS?!
SHUT UP, DEMON!
WE WOULDN'T TELL YOU EVEN IF WE WERE GONNA DIE!

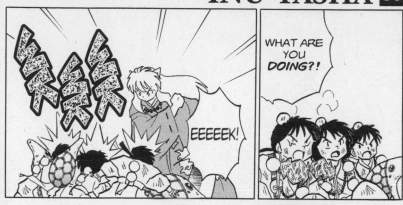

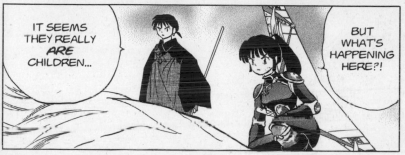

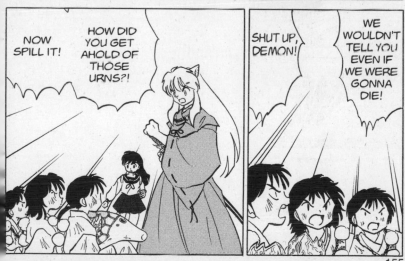

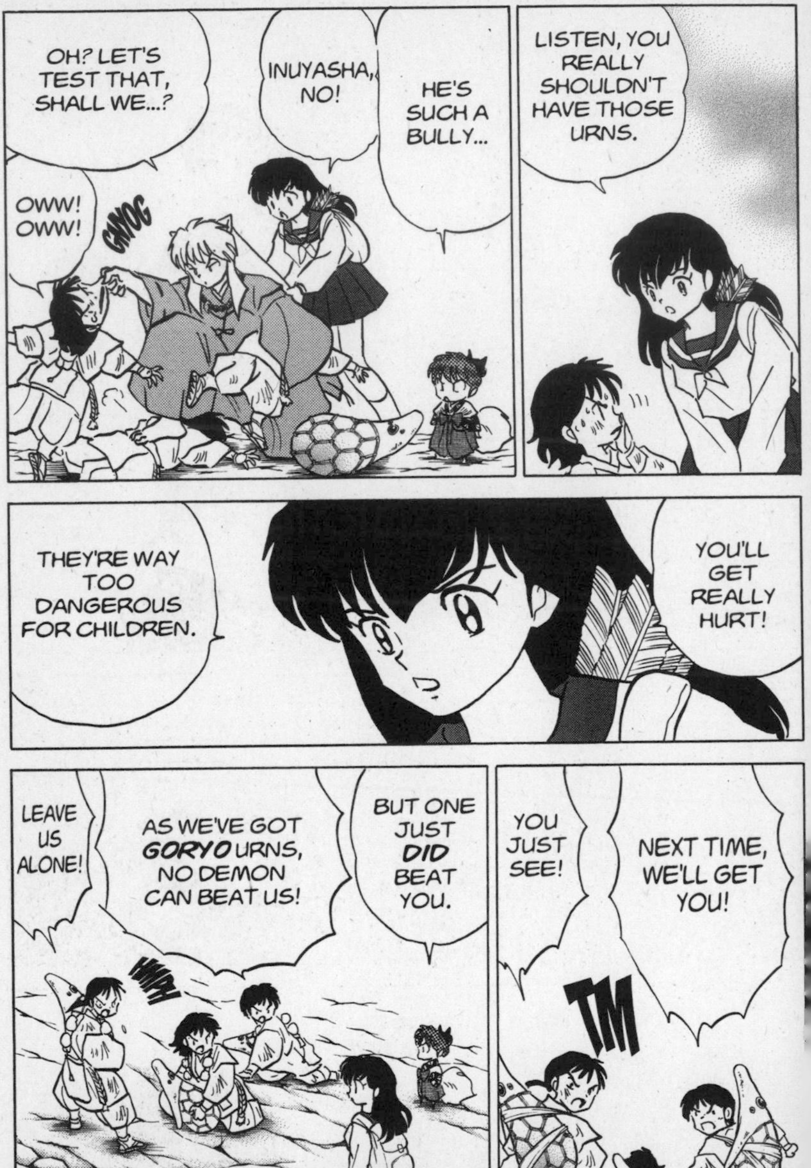
OH? LET'S TEST THAT, SHALL WE...?
INUYASHA, NO!
HE'S SUCH A BULLY...
OWW! OWW!
GNYOG
LISTEN, YOU REALLY SHOULDN'T HAVE THOSE URNS.
THEY'RE WAY TOO DANGEROUS FOR CHILDREN.
YOU'LL GET REALLY HURT!
LEAVE US ALONE!
AS WE'VE GOT GORYO URNS, NO DEMON CAN BEAT US!
BUT ONE JUST DID BEAT YOU.
HMPH
YOU JUST SEE!
NEXT TIME, WE'LL GET YOU!
TM

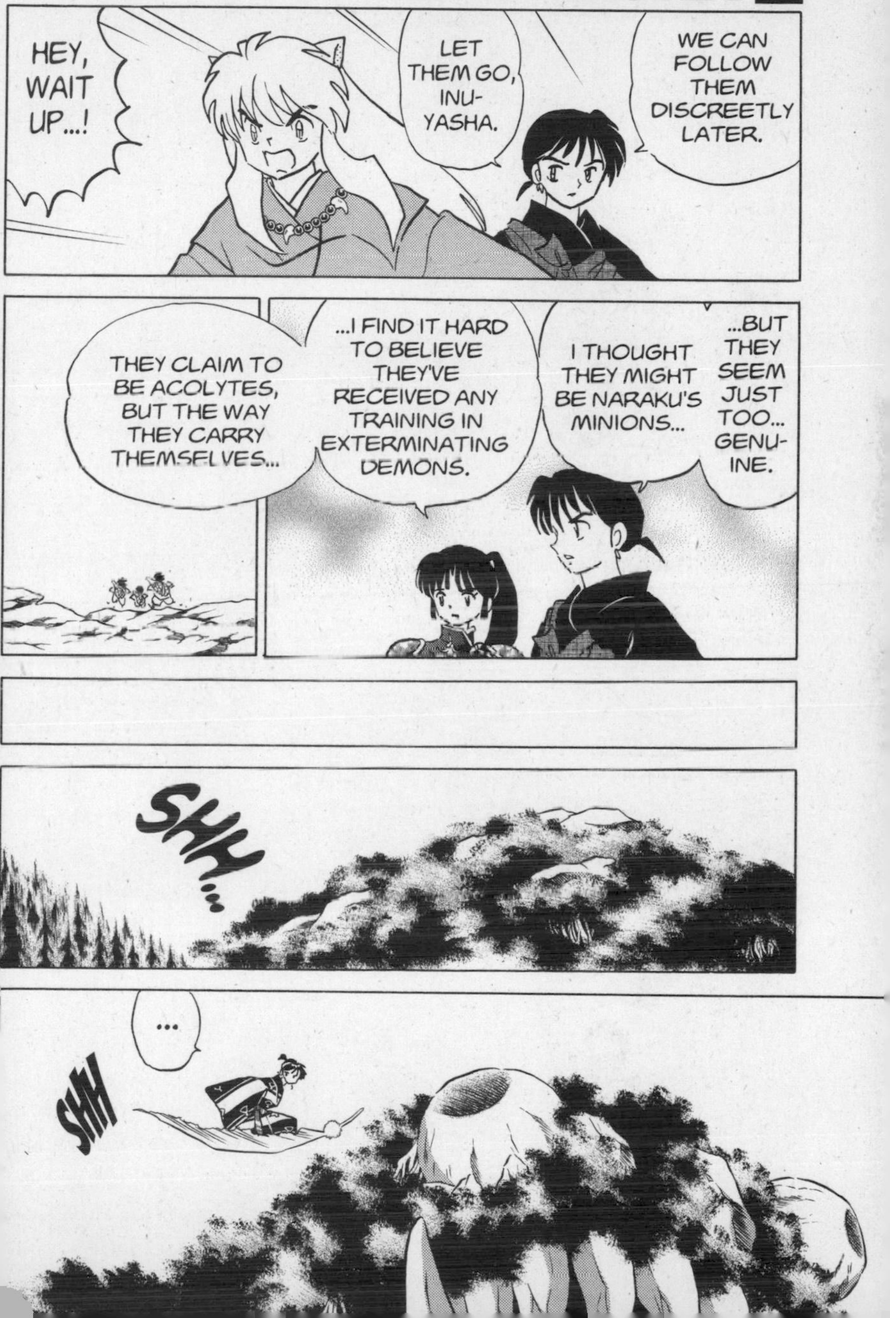
HEY, WAIT UP...!
LET THEM GO, INU-YASHA.
WE CAN FOLLOW THEM DISCREETLY LATER.
THEY CLAIM TO BE ACOLYTES, BUT THE WAY THEY CARRY THEMSELVES...
...I FIND IT HARD TO BELIEVE THEY'VE RECEIVED ANY TRAINING IN EXTERMINATING DEMONS.
I THOUGHT THEY MIGHT BE NARAKU'S MINIONS...
...BUT THEY SEEM JUST TOO... GENUINE.
SHH...
...
SHH

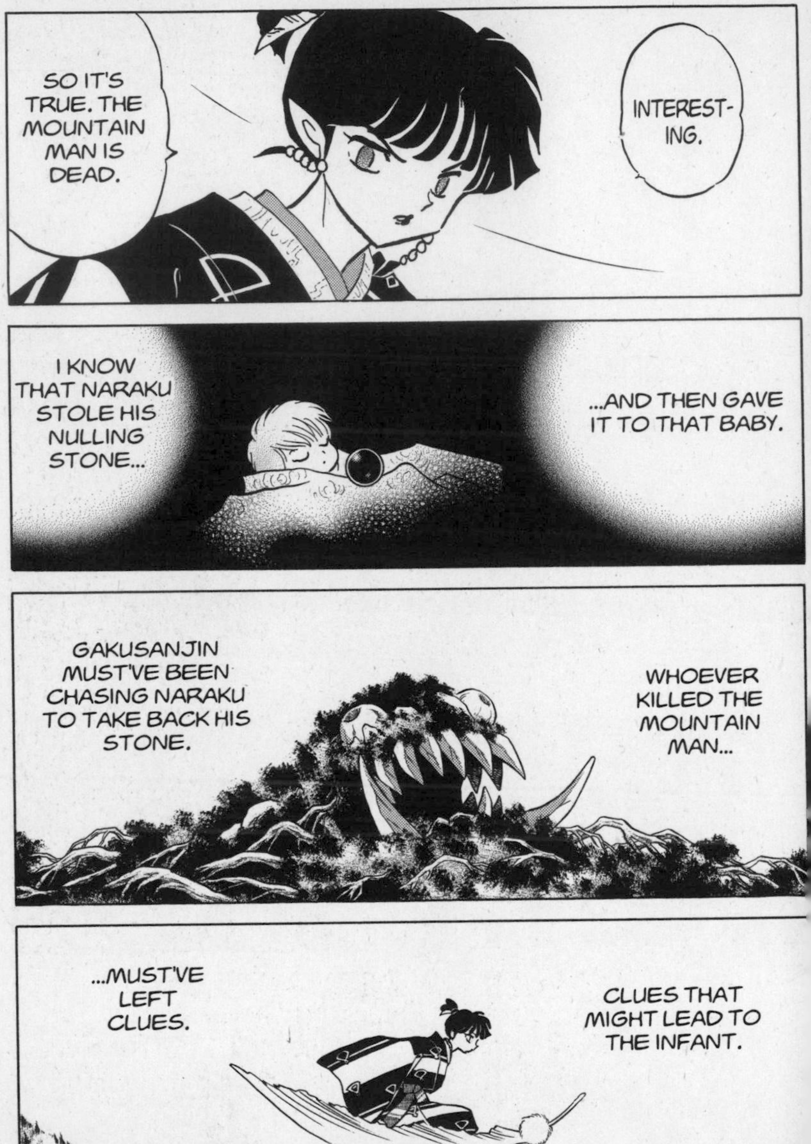
SO IT'S TRUE. THE MOUNTAIN MAN IS DEAD.
INTEREST-ING.
I KNOW THAT NARAKU STOLE HIS NULLING STONE...
...AND THEN GAVE IT TO THAT BABY.
GAKUSANJIN MUST'VE BEEN CHASING NARAKU TO TAKE BACK HIS STONE.
WHOEVER KILLED THE MOUNTAIN MAN...
...MUST'VE LEFT CLUES.
CLUES THAT MIGHT LEAD TO THE INFANT.

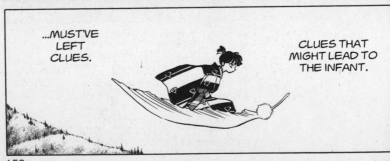

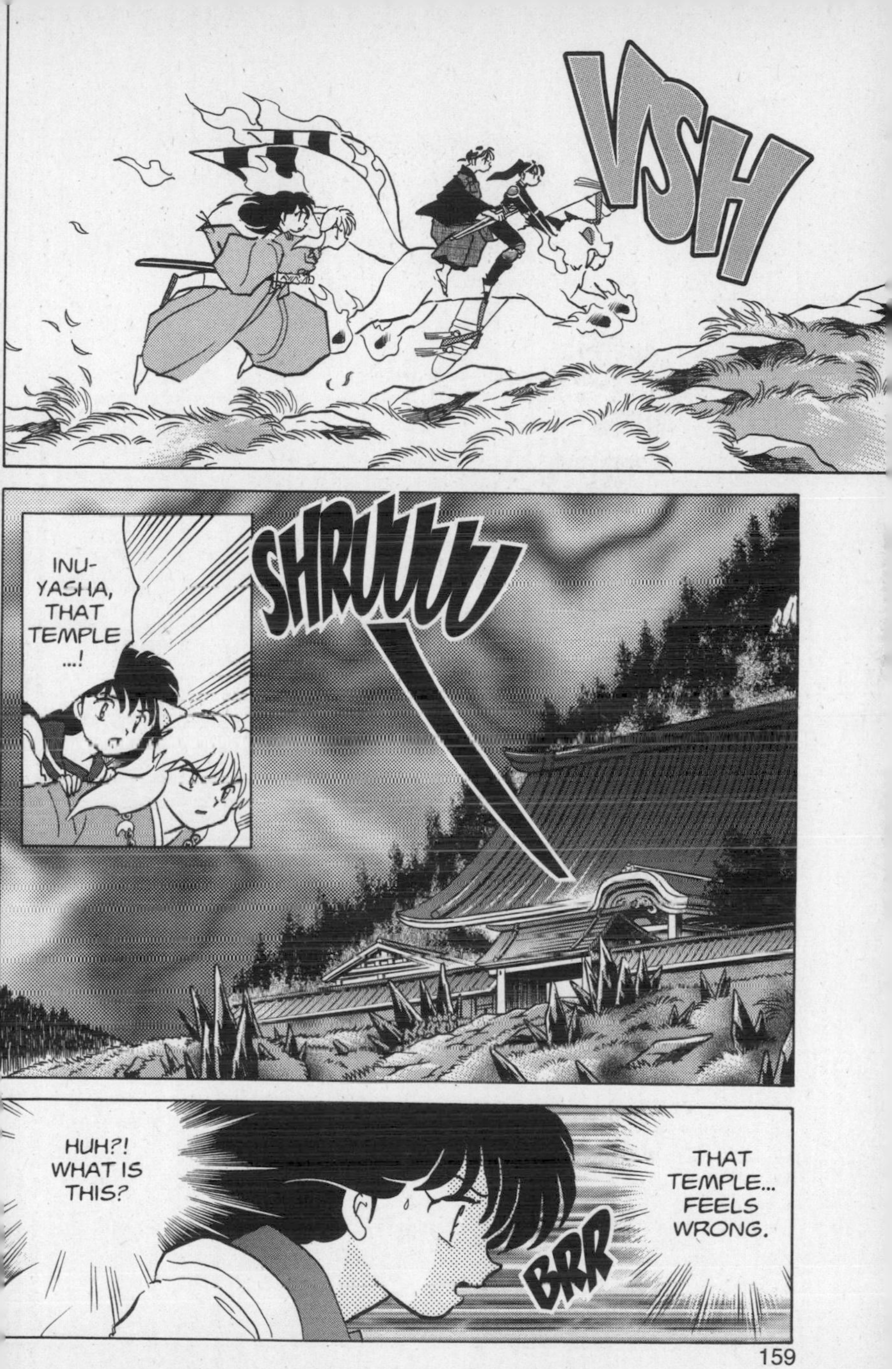
VSH
INU-YASHA, THAT TEMPLE ...!
SHRUUUU
HUH?! WHAT IS THIS?
THAT TEMPLE... FEELS WRONG.
BRR

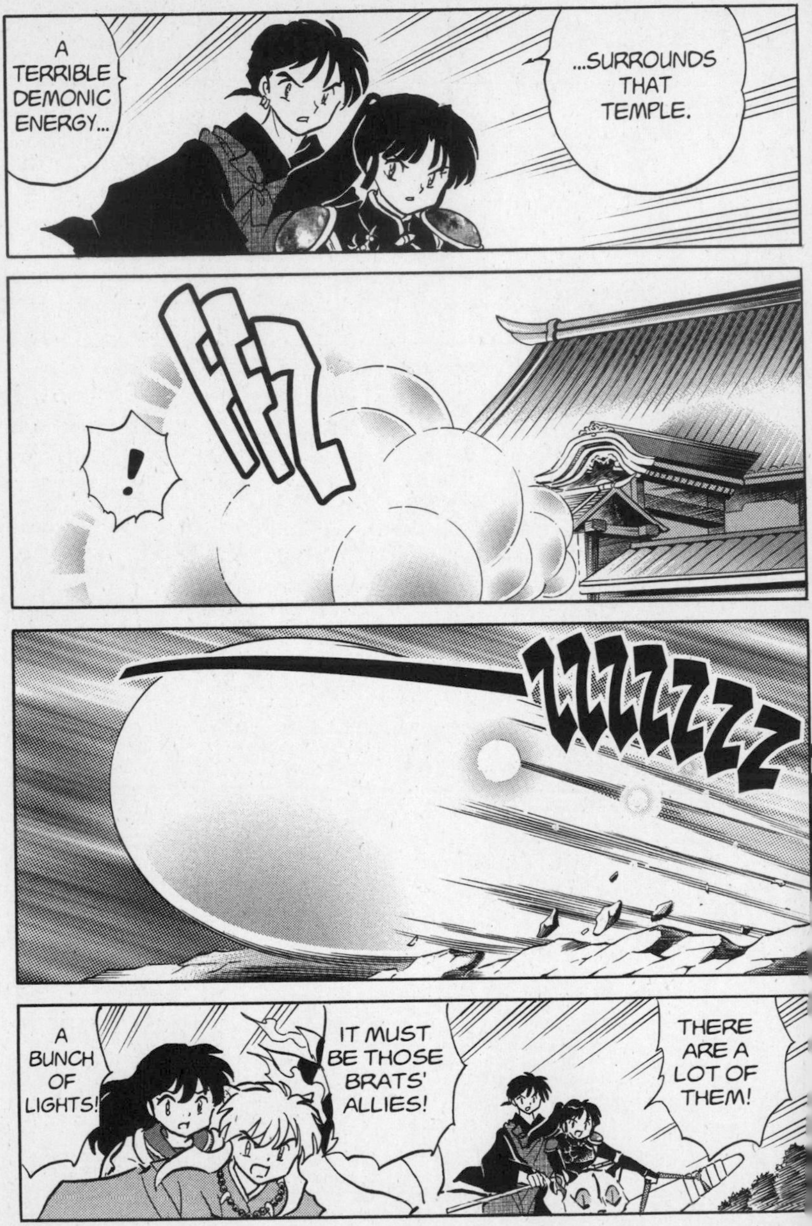
A TERRIBLE DEMONIC ENERGY...
...SURROUNDS THAT TEMPLE.
!
A BUNCH OF LIGHTS!
IT MUST BE THOSE BRATS' ALLIES!
THERE ARE A LOT OF THEM!

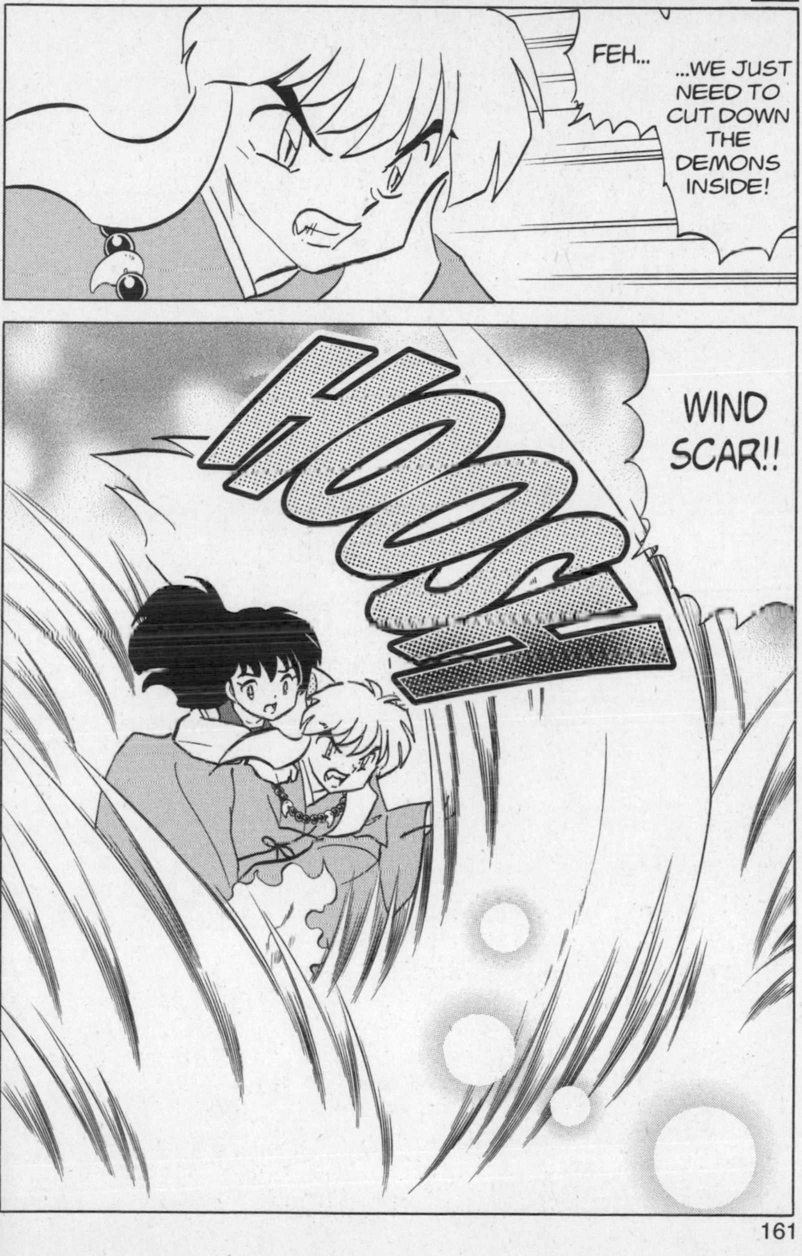
FEH...
...WE JUST NEED TO CUT DOWN THE DEMONS INSIDE!
HOOSH!
WIND SCAR!!

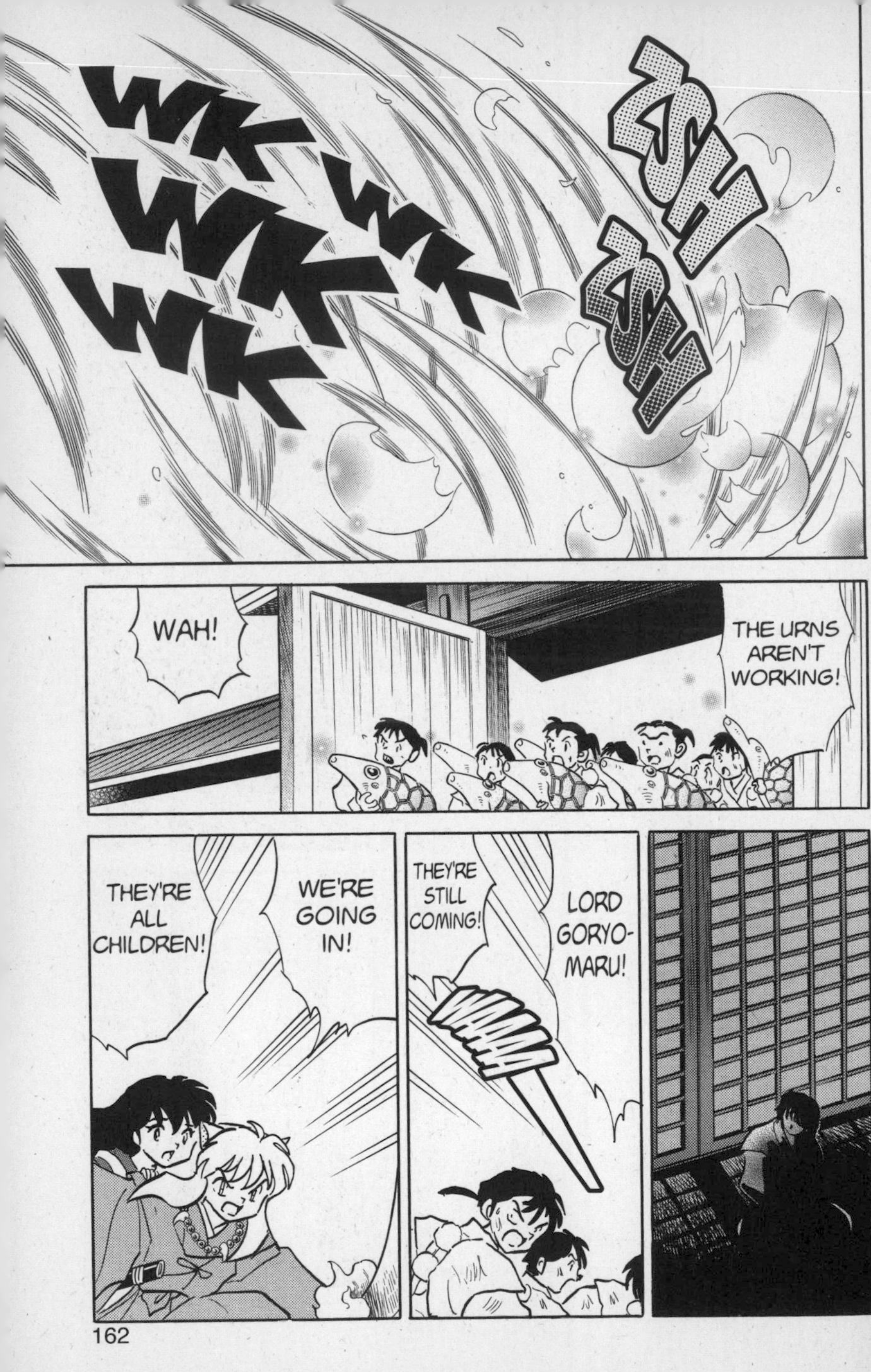
WK WK WK
WK WK
ZASH ZASH
WAH!
THE URNS AREN'T WORKING!
THEY'RE ALL CHILDREN!
WE'RE GOING IN!
THEY'RE STILL COMING!
LORD GORYO-MARU!

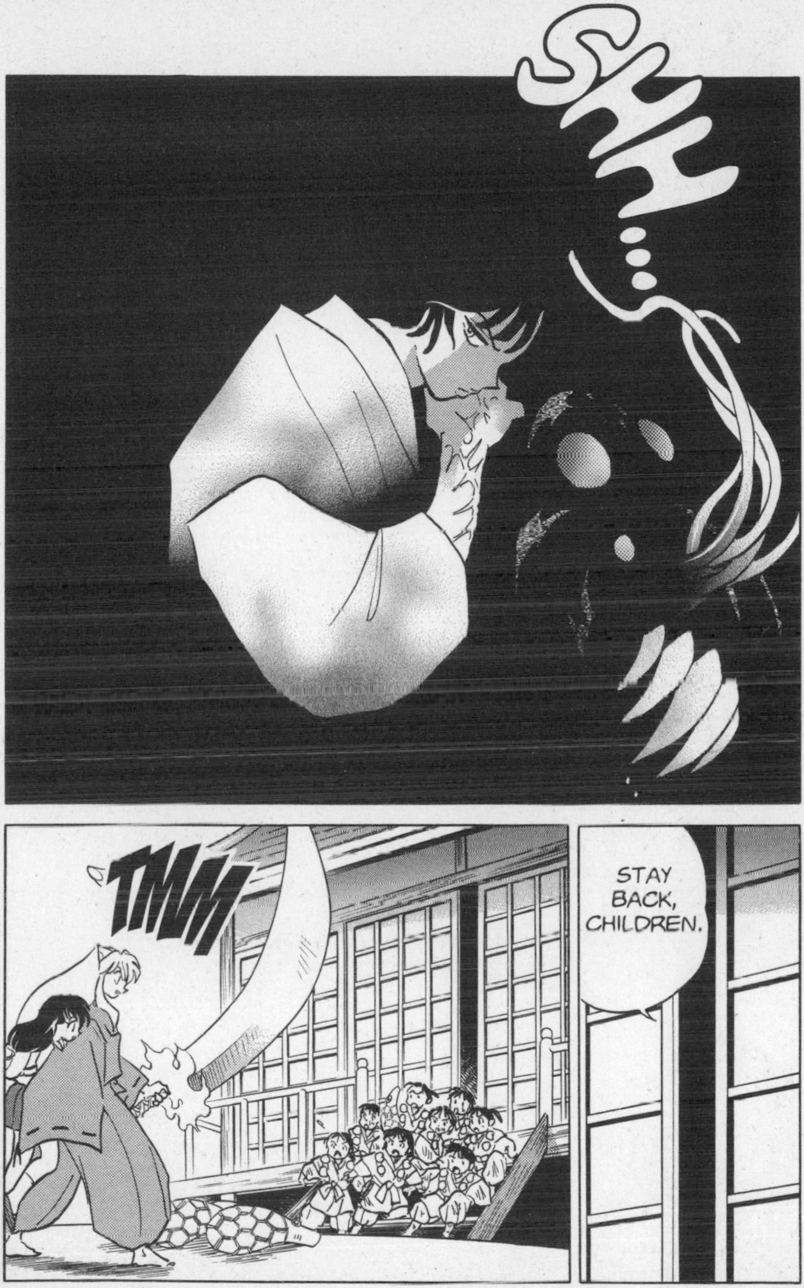
SHH...
TMM
STAY BACK, CHILDREN.

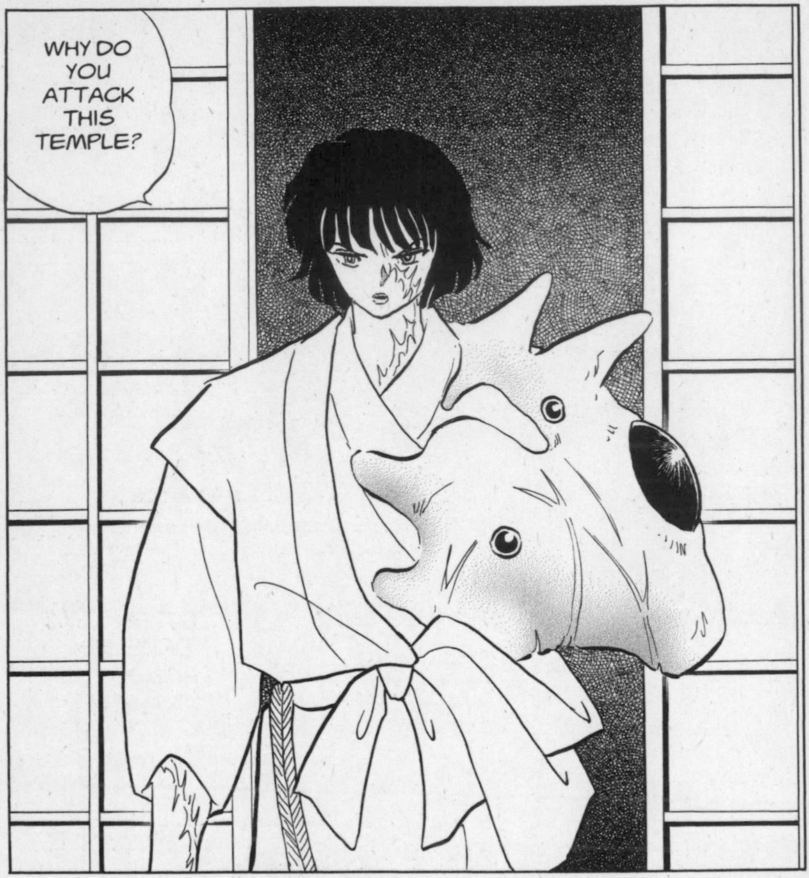
WHY DO YOU ATTACK THIS TEMPLE?

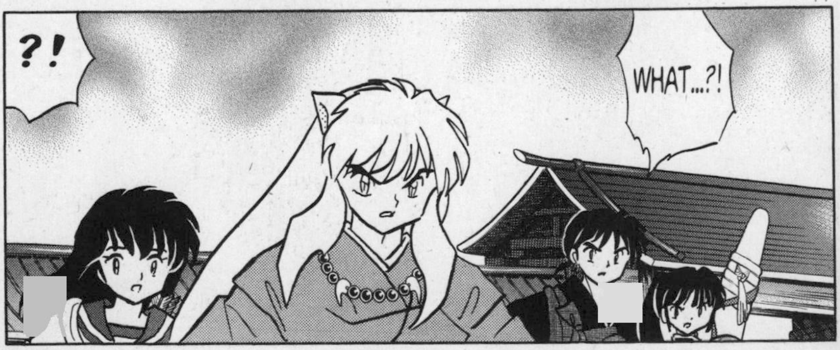
?!
WHAT...?!

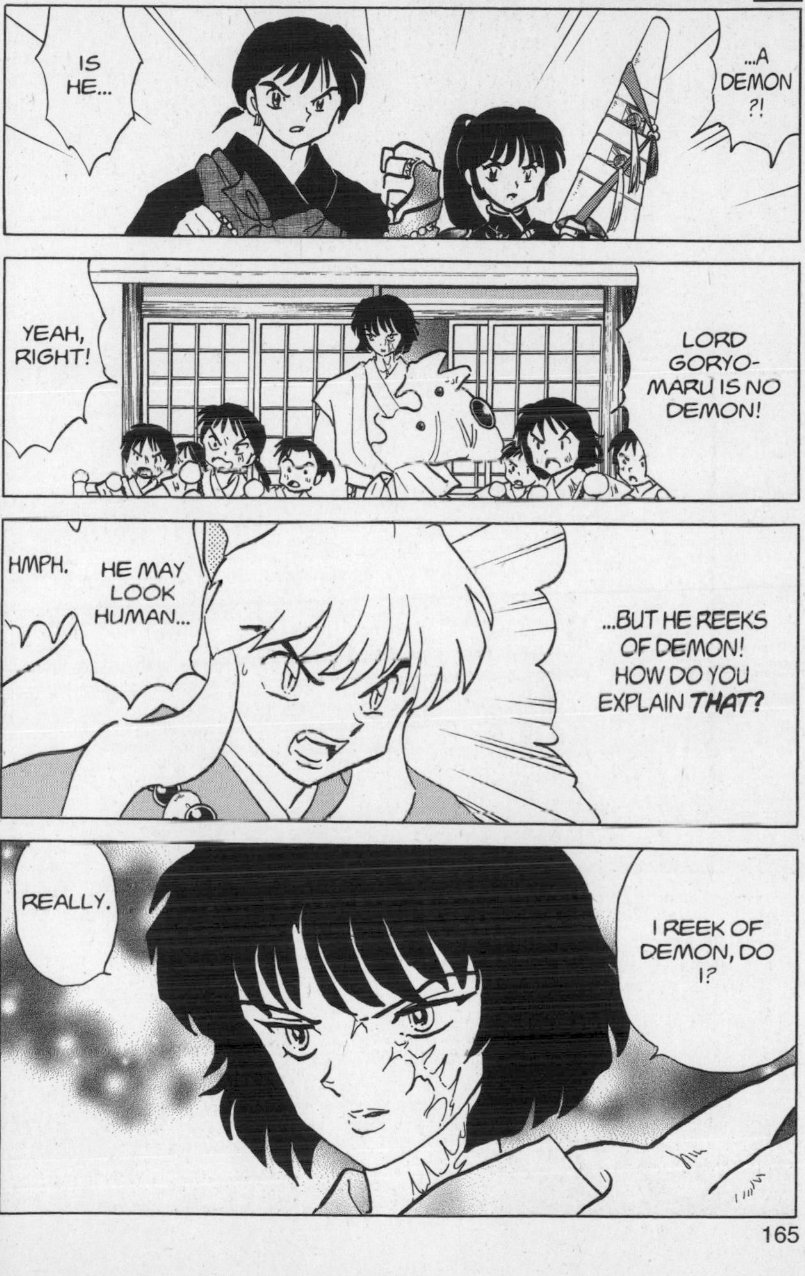
IS HE...
...A DEMON ?!
YEAH, RIGHT!
LORD GORYO-MARU IS NO DEMON!
HMPH.
HE MAY LOOK HUMAN...
...BUT HE REEKS OF DEMON! HOW DO YOU EXPLAIN THAT?
REALLY.
I REEK OF DEMON, DO I?

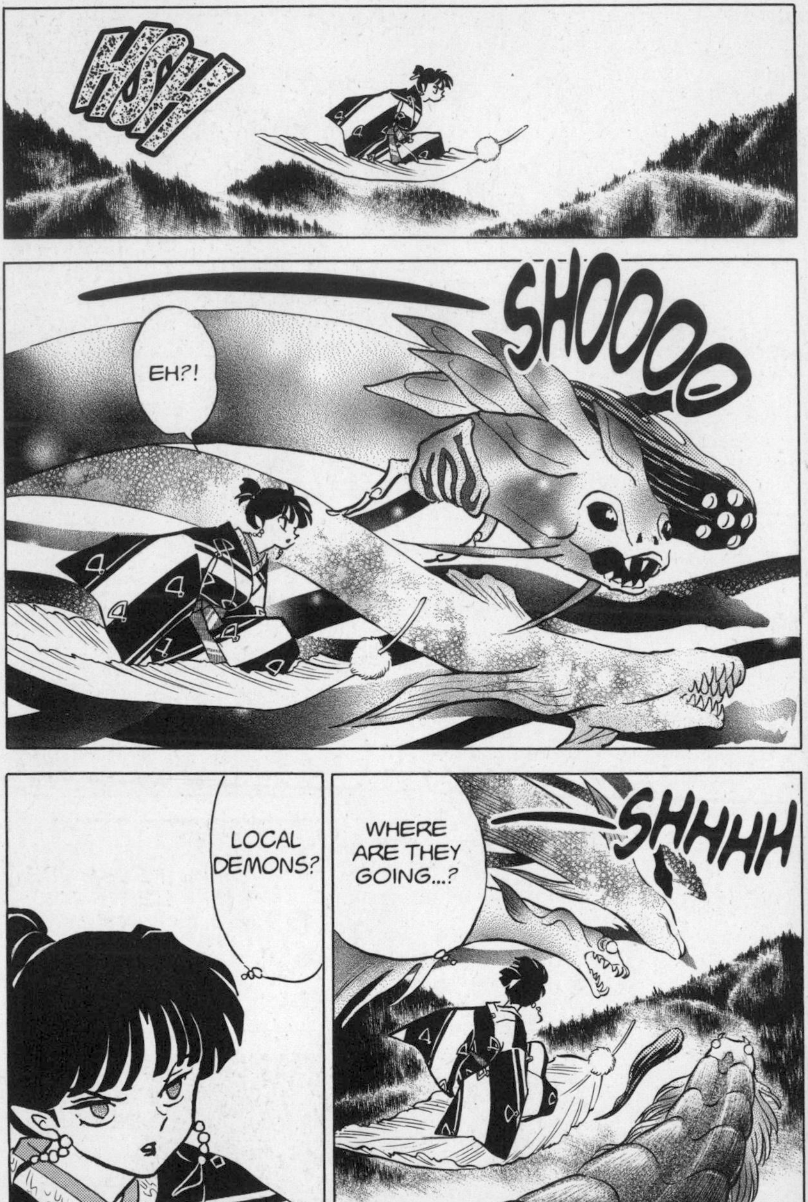
HSH
SHOOOO
EH?!
LOCAL DEMONS?
WHERE ARE THEY GOING...?
SHHHH

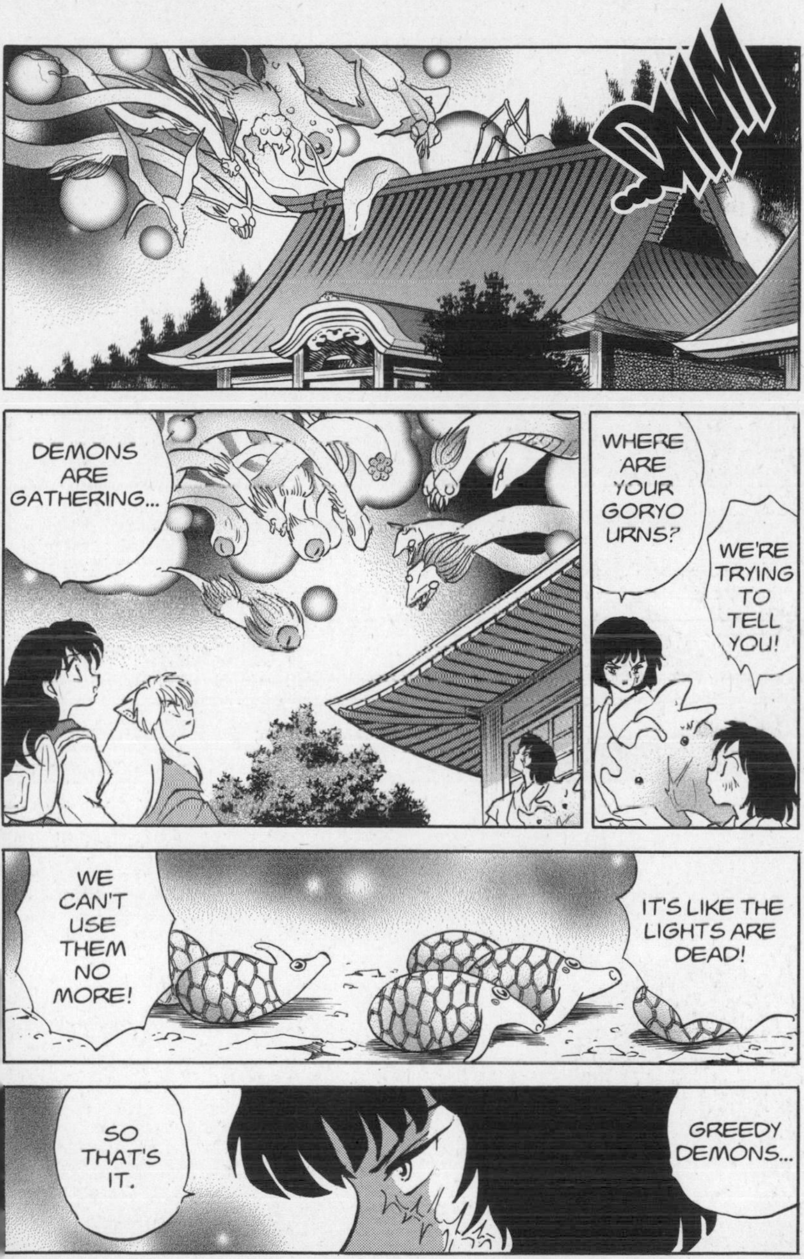
DWM
DEMONS ARE GATHERING...
WHERE ARE YOUR GORYO URNS?
WE'RE TRYING TO TELL YOU!
WE CAN'T USE THEM NO MORE!
IT'S LIKE THE LIGHTS ARE DEAD!
SO THAT'S IT.
GREEDY DEMONS...

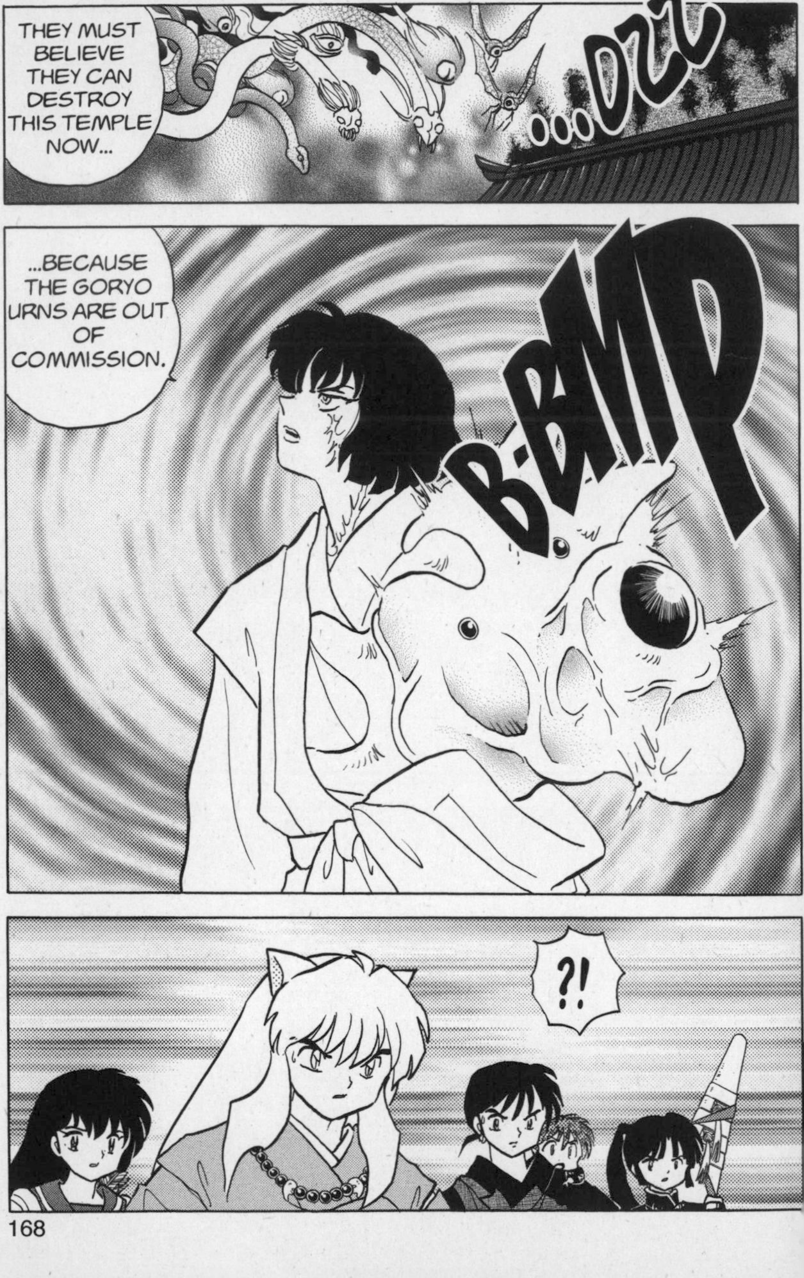
THEY MUST BELIEVE THEY CAN DESTROY THIS TEMPLE NOW...
...DZZ
...BECAUSE THE GORYO URNS ARE OUT OF COMMISSION.
B-BMP
?!

SCROLL 10

THE DEFORMED ARM

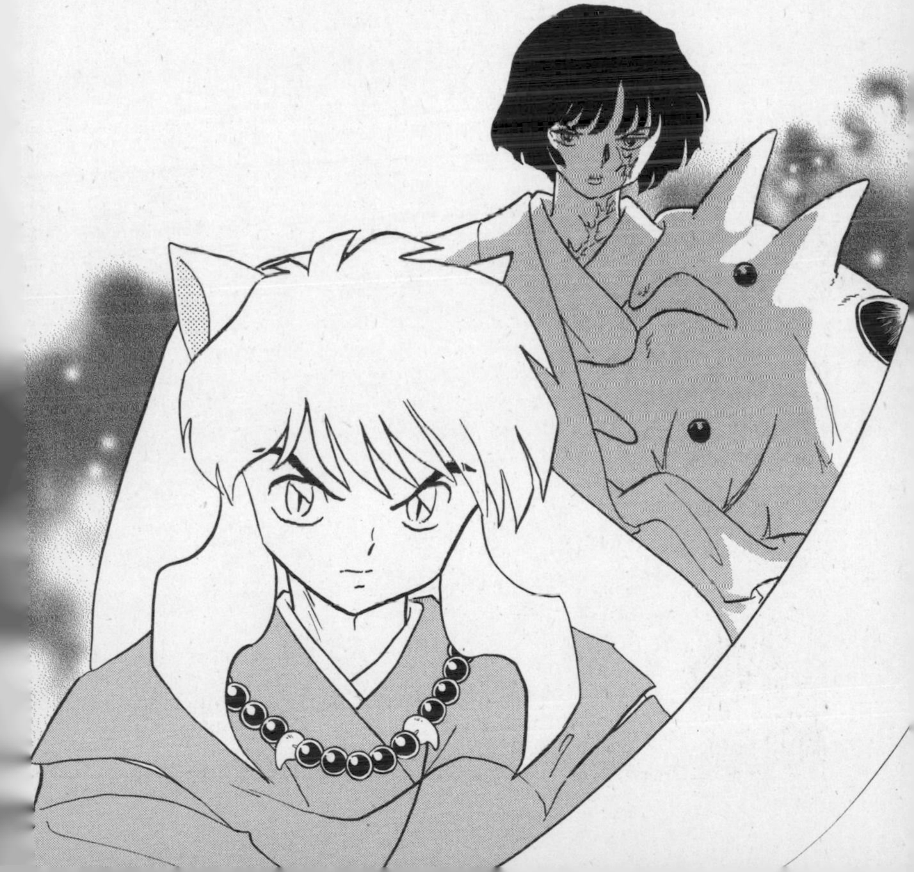

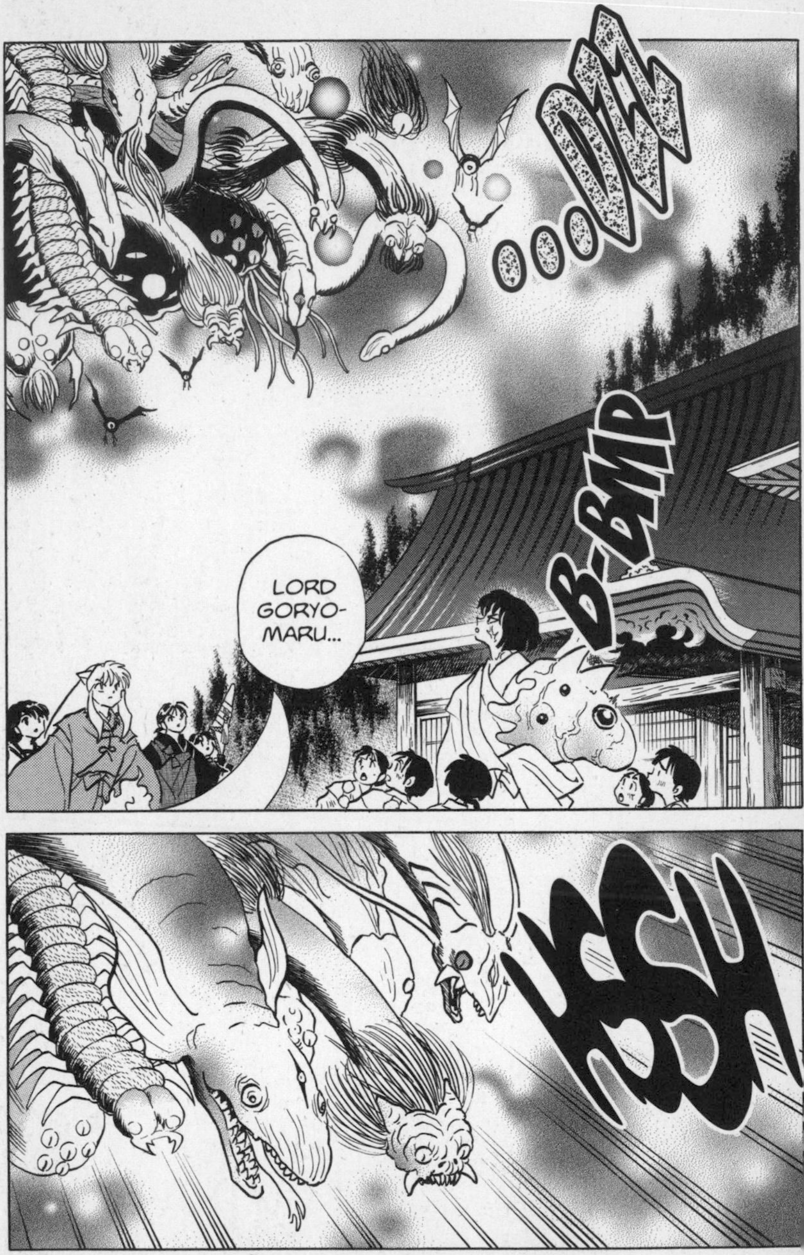
...DIE
B-BMP
LORD GORYO-MARU...

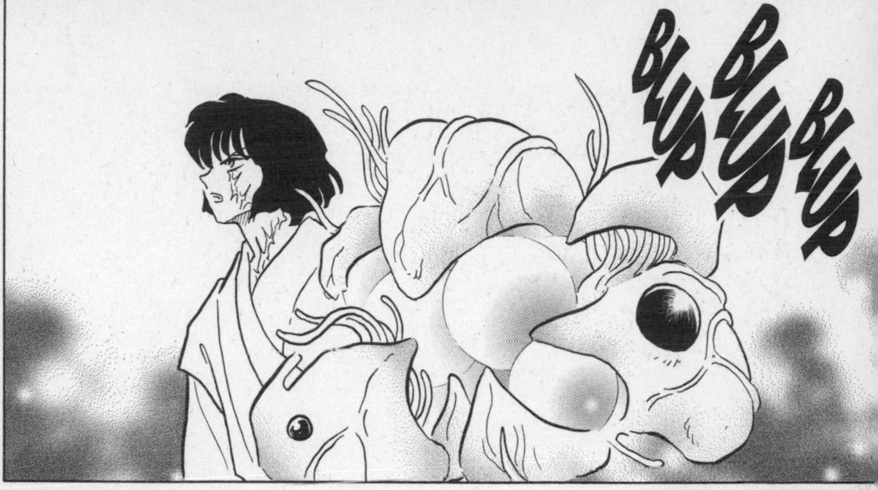
BLUP BLUP BLUP
BLUP
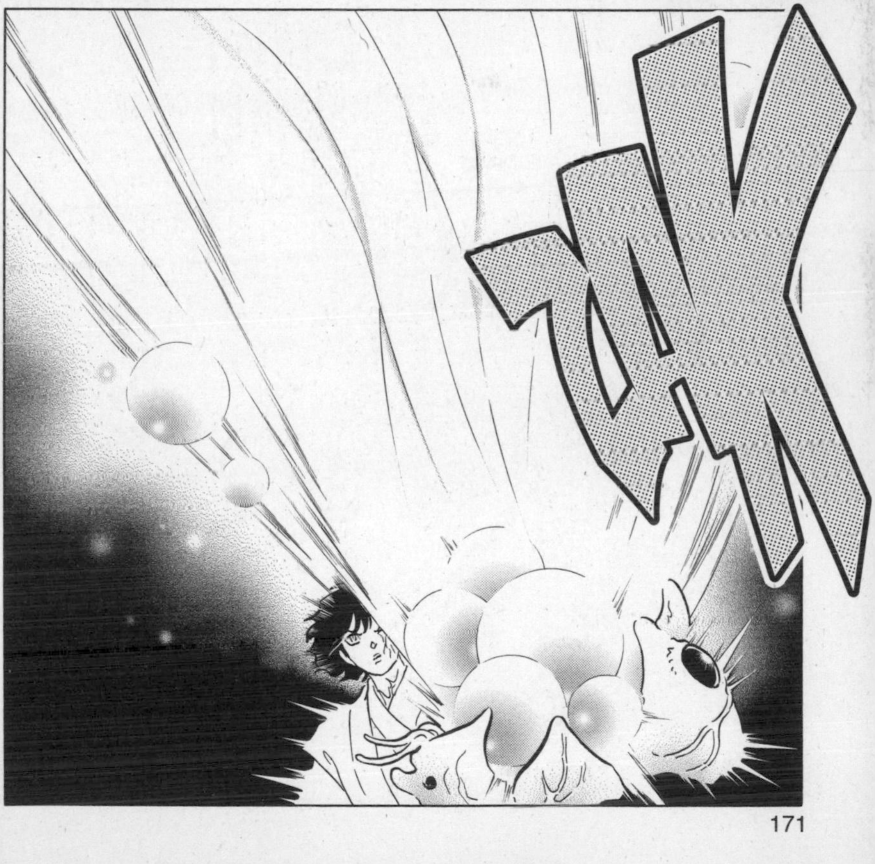
ZAK

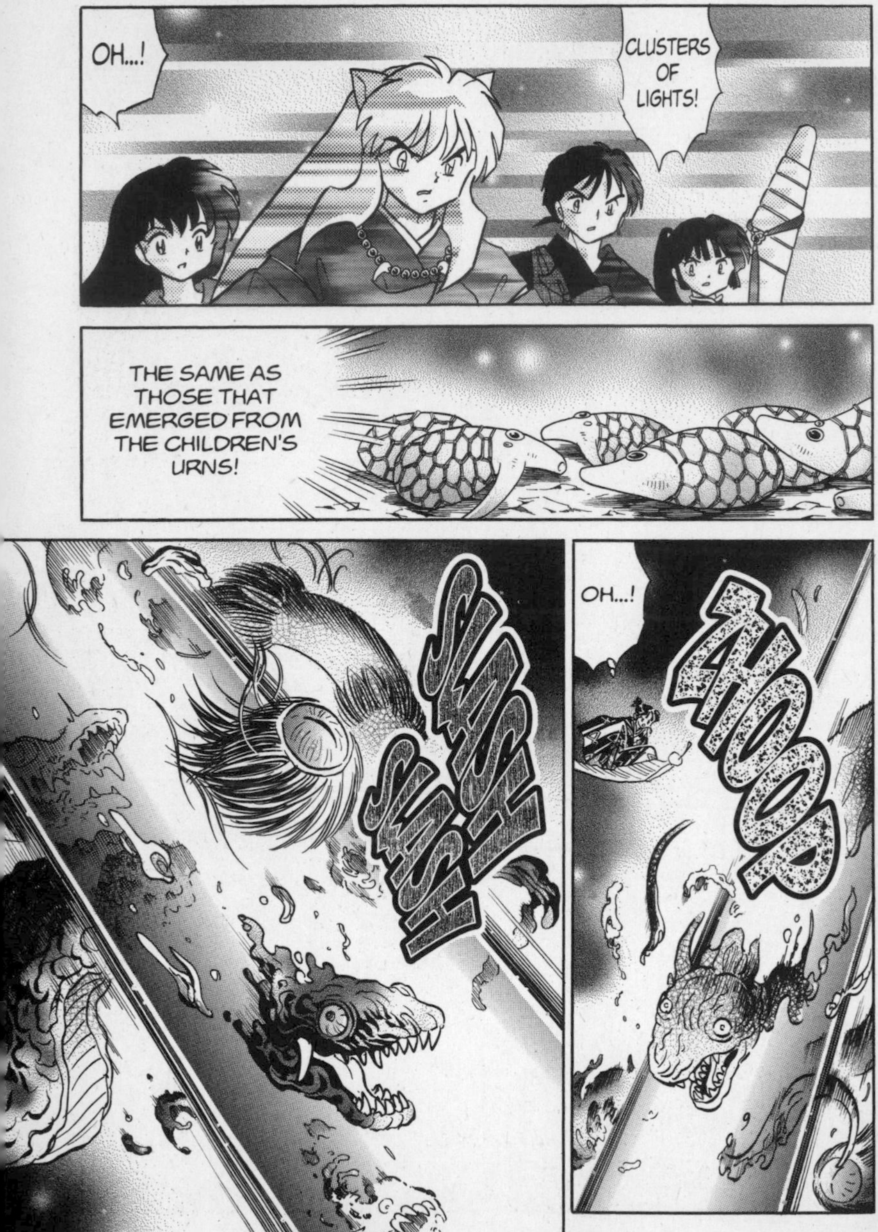
OH...!
CLUSTERS OF LIGHTS!
THE SAME AS THOSE THAT EMERGED FROM THE CHILDREN'S URNS!
SWISH!
SWISH!
OH...!
ZHOOP

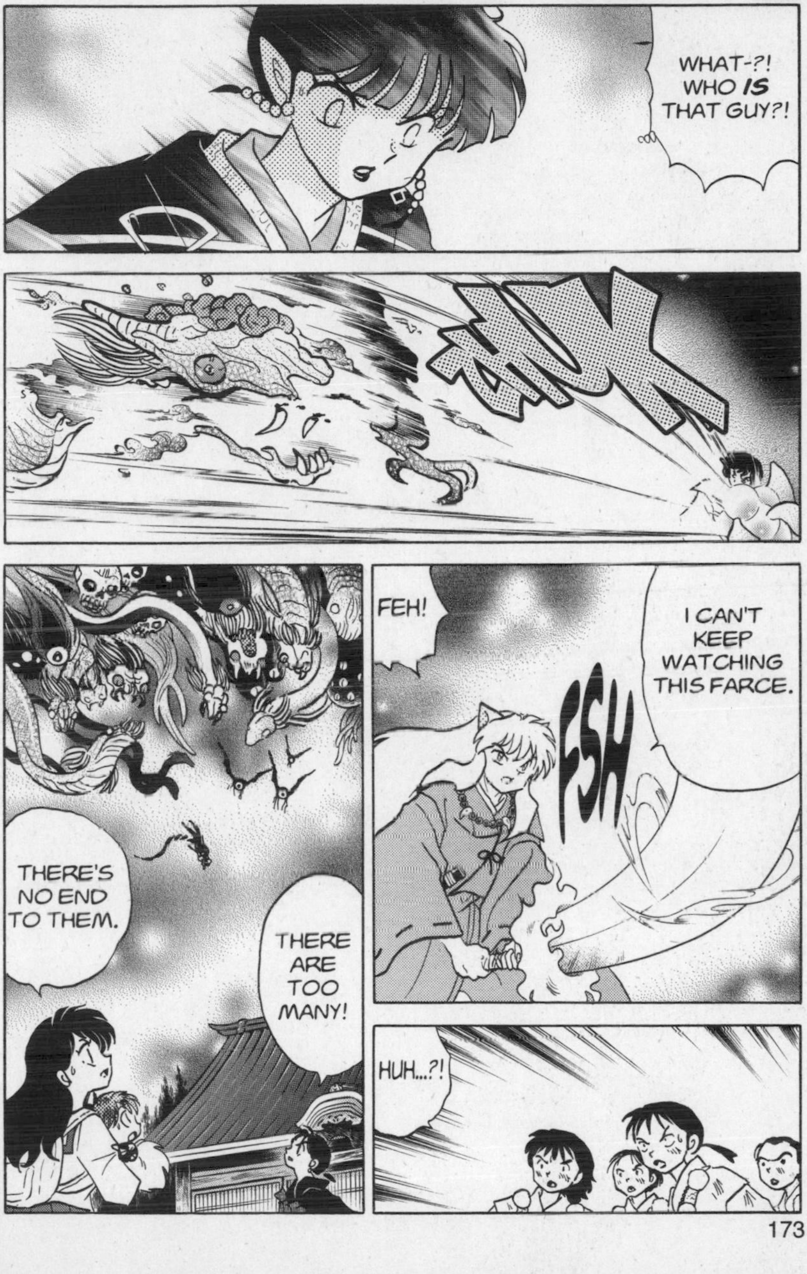
WHAT-?! WHO *IS* THAT GUY?!
CHUK
THERE'S NO END TO THEM.
THERE ARE TOO MANY!
FEH!
I CAN'T KEEP WATCHING THIS FARCE.
FSH
HUH...?!

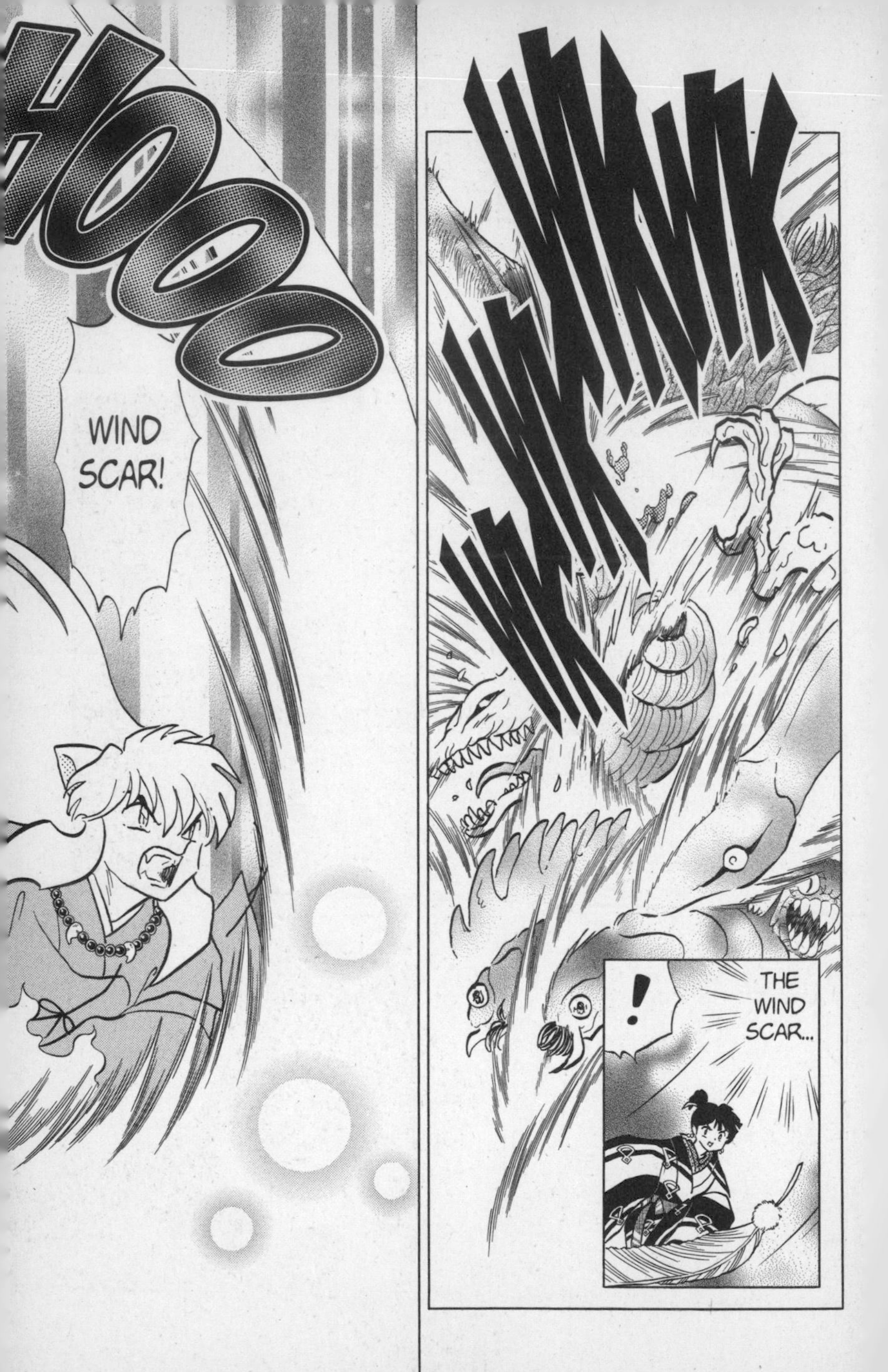
WIND SCAR!
!
THE WIND SCAR...

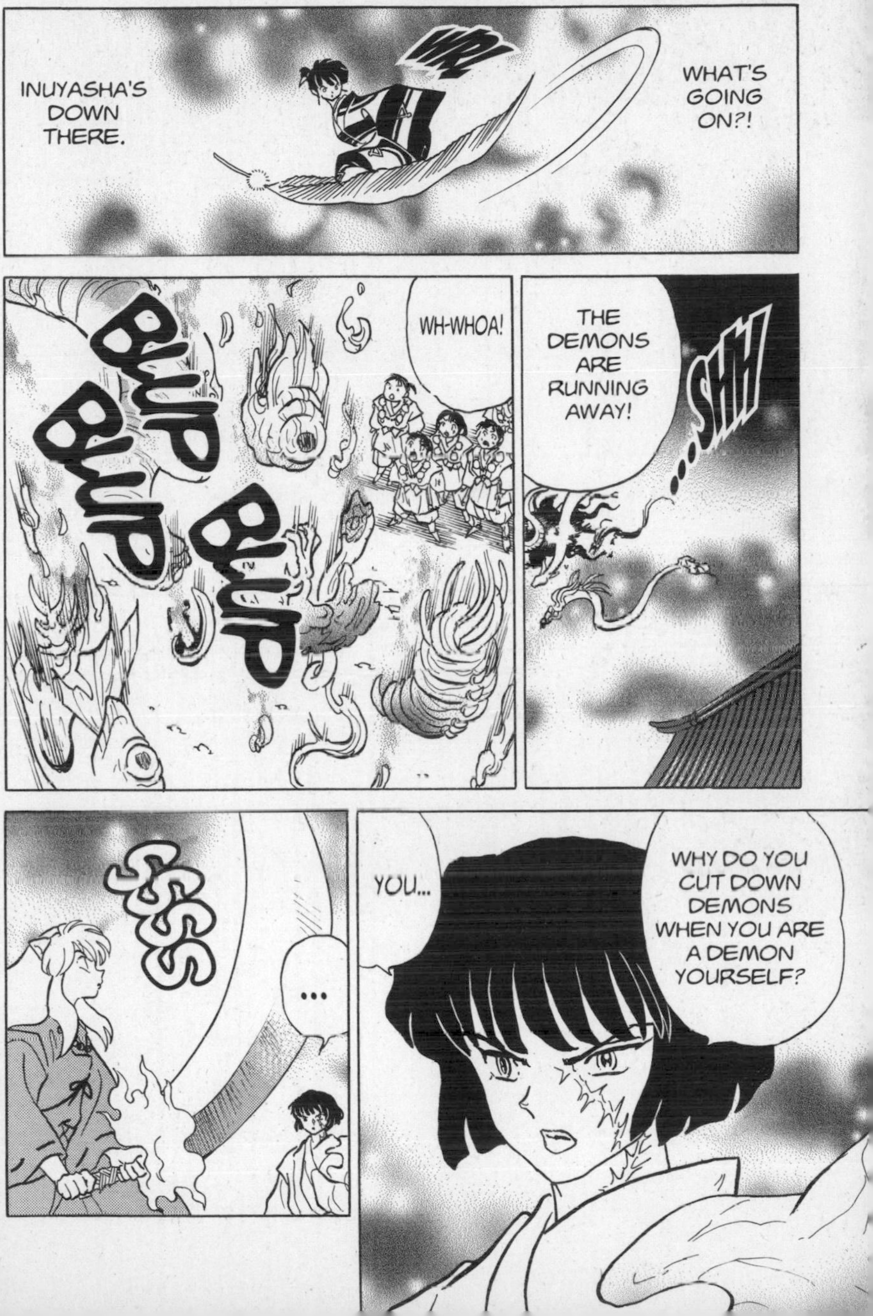
INUYASHA'S DOWN THERE.
WRL
WHAT'S GOING ON?!
BLUP
BLUP
BLUP
BLUP
WH-WHOA!
THE DEMONS ARE RUNNING AWAY!
...SHH
SSSS
...
YOU...
WHY DO YOU CUT DOWN DEMONS WHEN YOU ARE A DEMON YOURSELF?

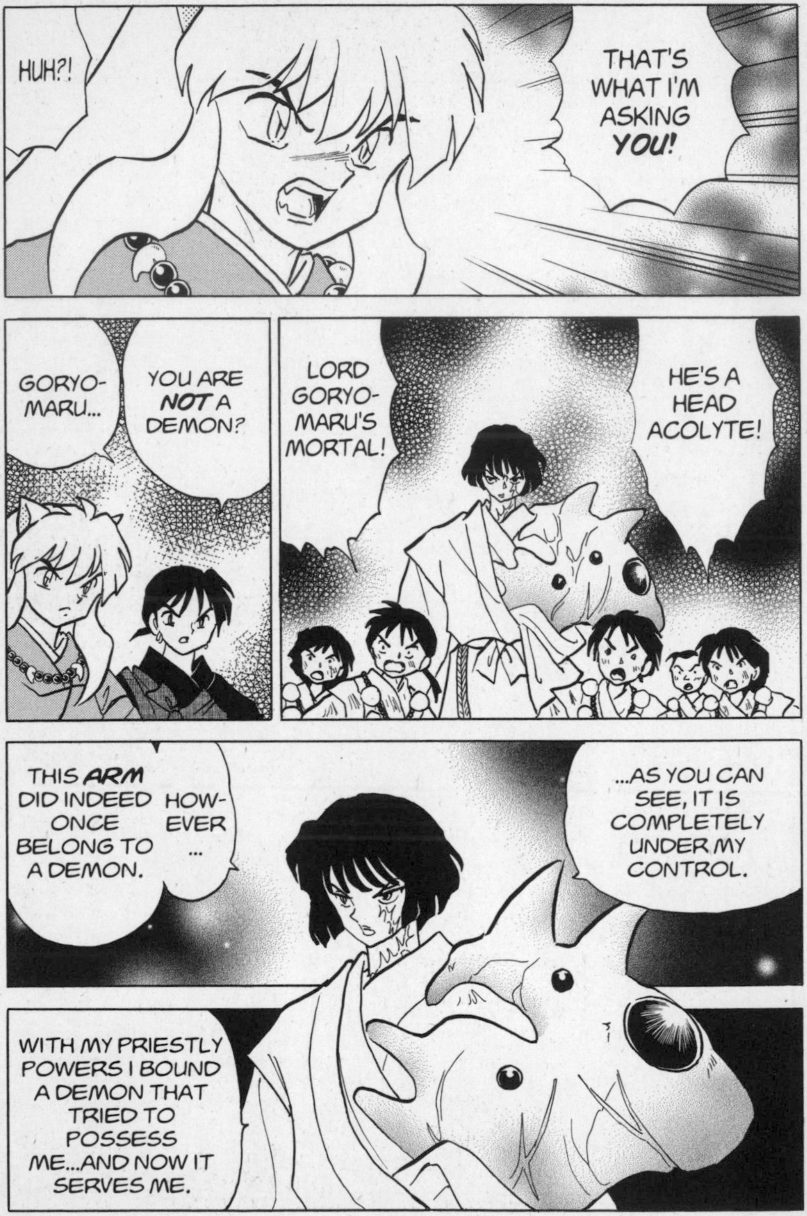
HUH?!
THAT'S WHAT I'M ASKING YOU!
GORYO-MARU...
YOU ARE NOT A DEMON?
LORD GORYO-MARU'S MORTAL!
HE'S A HEAD ACOLYTE!
THIS ARM DID INDEED ONCE BELONG TO A DEMON.
HOW-EVER ...
...AS YOU CAN SEE, IT IS COMPLETELY UNDER MY CONTROL.
WITH MY PRIESTLY POWERS I BOUND A DEMON THAT TRIED TO POSSESS ME...AND NOW IT SERVES ME.

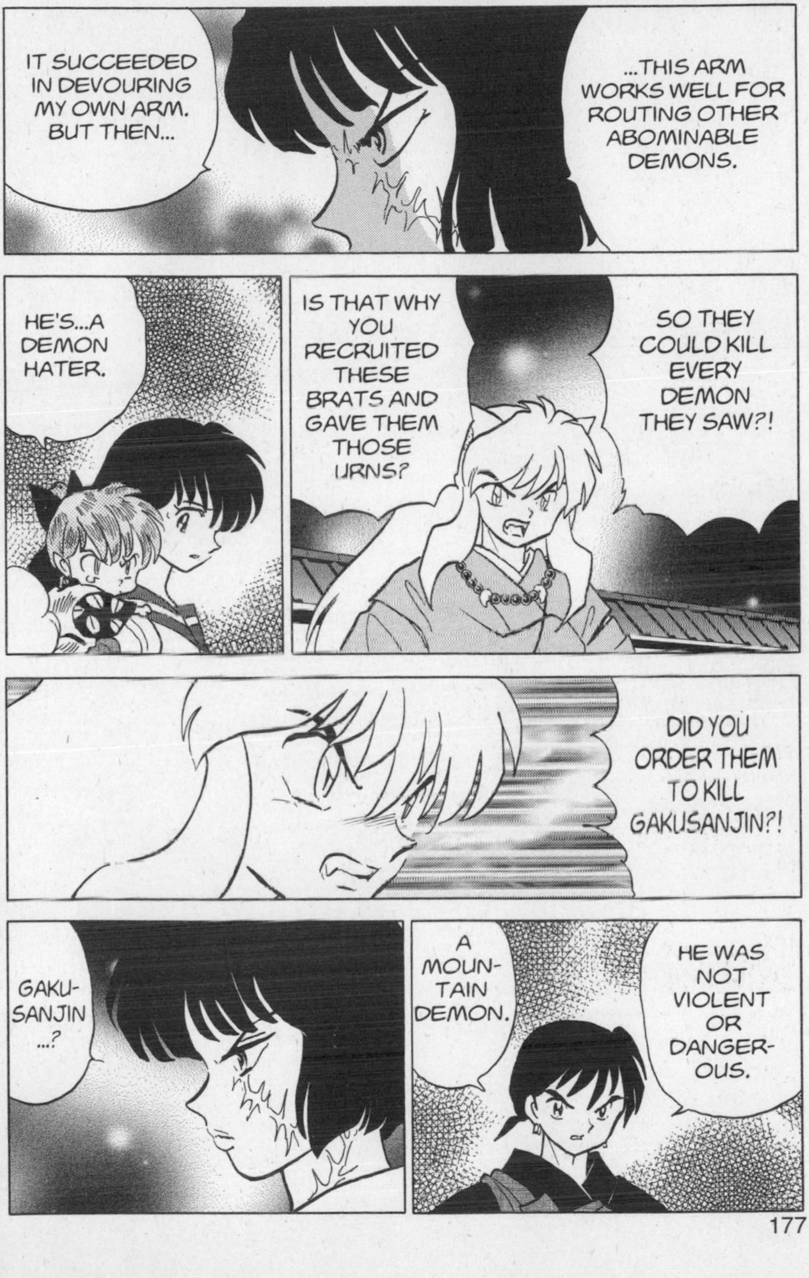
IT SUCCEEDED IN DEVOURING MY OWN ARM. BUT THEN...
...THIS ARM WORKS WELL FOR ROUTING OTHER ABOMINABLE DEMONS.
HE'S...A DEMON HATER.
IS THAT WHY YOU RECRUITED THESE BRATS AND GAVE THEM THOSE URNS?
SO THEY COULD KILL EVERY DEMON THEY SAW?!
DID YOU ORDER THEM TO KILL GAKUSANJIN?!
GAKU-SANJIN ...?
A MOUN-TAIN DEMON.
HE WAS NOT VIOLENT OR DANGER-OUS.

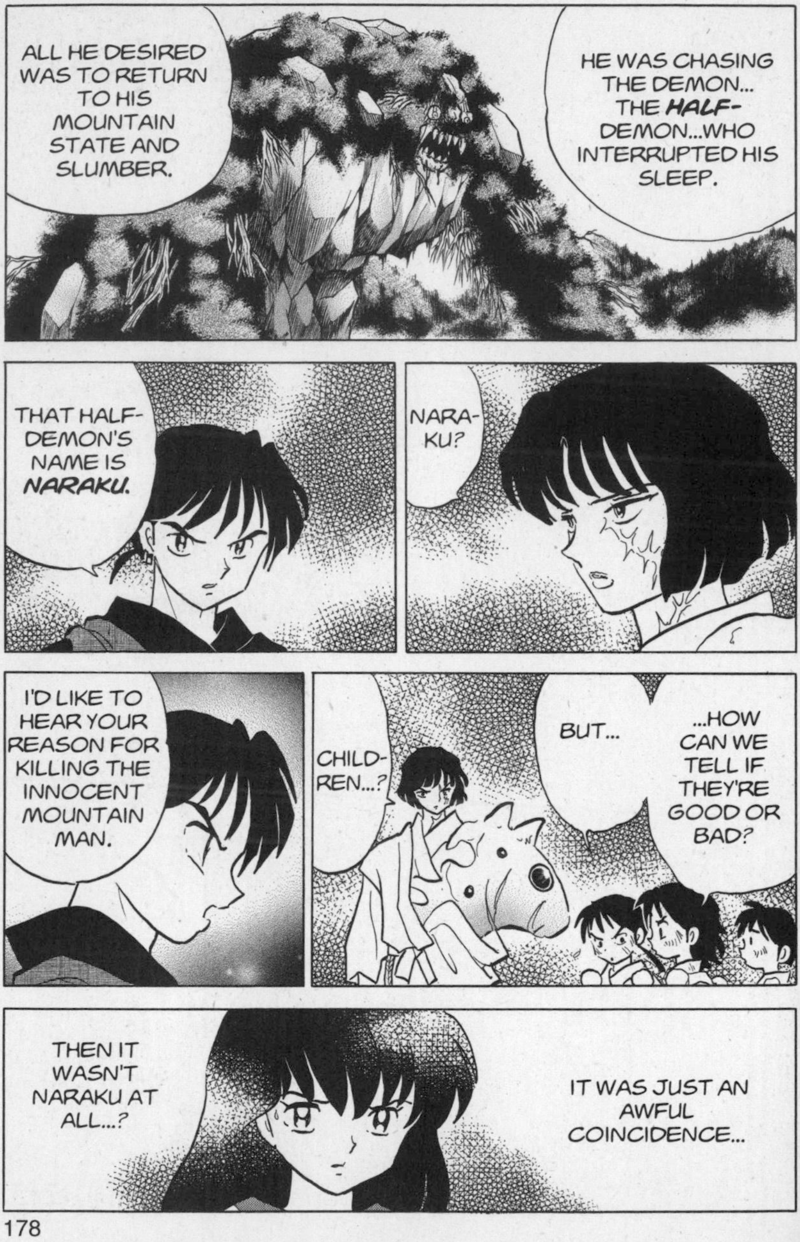
ALL HE DESIRED WAS TO RETURN TO HIS MOUNTAIN STATE AND SLUMBER.
HE WAS CHASING THE DEMON... THE HALF-DEMON...WHO INTERRUPTED HIS SLEEP.
THAT HALF-DEMON'S NAME IS NARAKU.
NARA-KU?
I'D LIKE TO HEAR YOUR REASON FOR KILLING THE INNOCENT MOUNTAIN MAN.
CHILD-REN...?
BUT...
...HOW CAN WE TELL IF THEY'RE GOOD OR BAD?
THEN IT WASN'T NARAKU AT ALL...?
IT WAS JUST AN AWFUL COINCIDENCE...

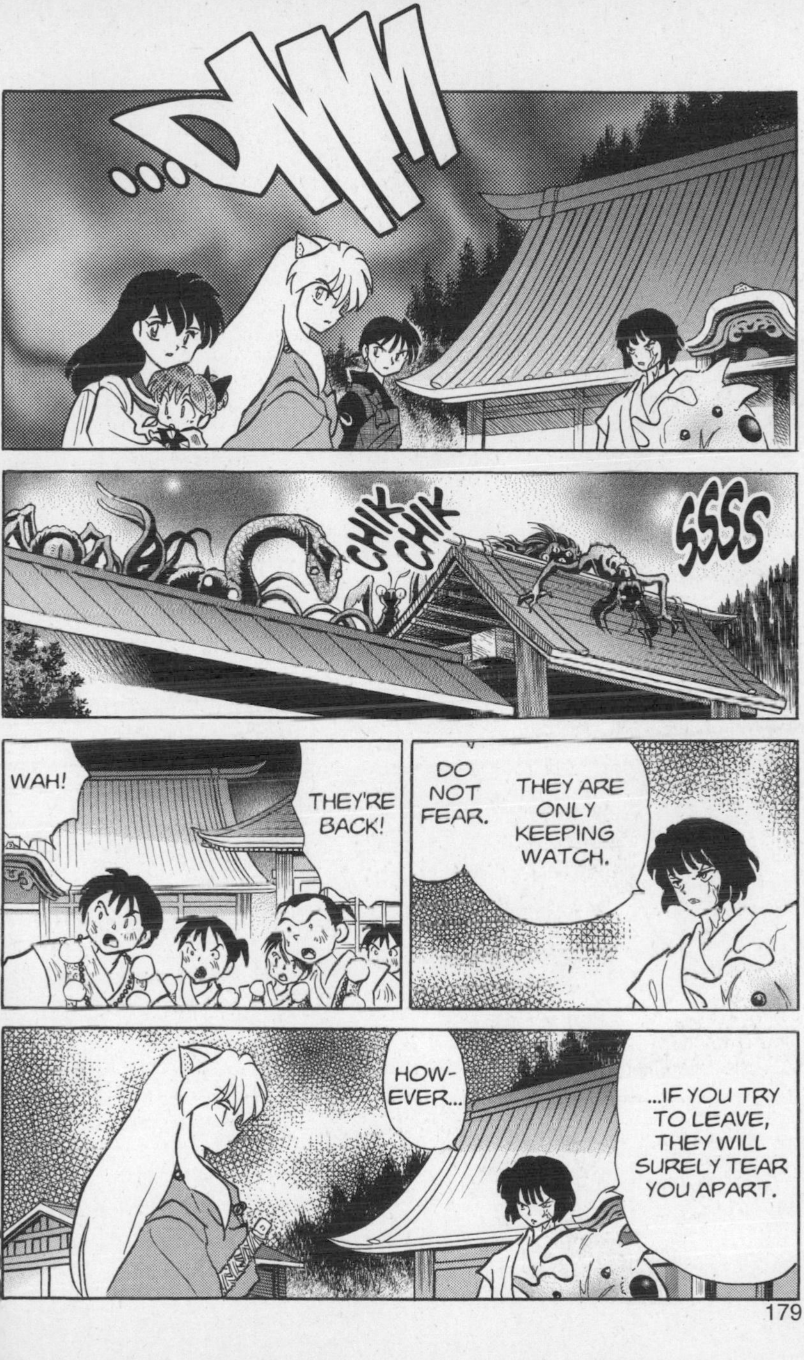
...DMM!!
CHIK CHIK
SSSS
WAH!
THEY'RE BACK!
DO NOT FEAR.
THEY ARE ONLY KEEPING WATCH.
HOW-EVER...
...IF YOU TRY TO LEAVE, THEY WILL SURELY TEAR YOU APART.

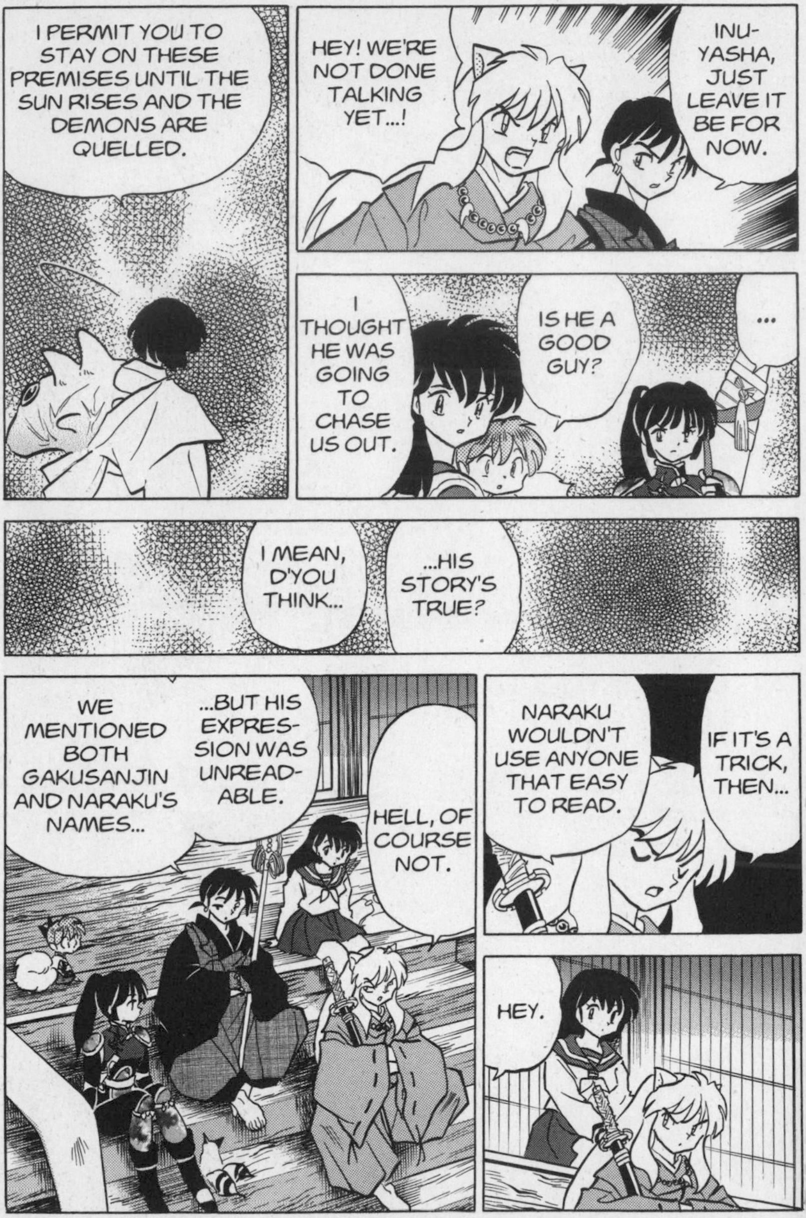
I PERMIT YOU TO STAY ON THESE PREMISES UNTIL THE SUN RISES AND THE DEMONS ARE QUELLED.
HEY! WE'RE NOT DONE TALKING YET...!
INU-YASHA, JUST LEAVE IT BE FOR NOW.
I THOUGHT HE WAS GOING TO CHASE US OUT.
IS HE A GOOD GUY?
...
I MEAN, D'YOU THINK...
...HIS STORY'S TRUE?
WE MENTIONED BOTH GAKUSANJIN AND NARAKU'S NAMES...
...BUT HIS EXPRES-SION WAS UNREAD-ABLE.
HELL, OF COURSE NOT.
NARAKU WOULDN'T USE ANYONE THAT EASY TO READ.
IF IT'S A TRICK, THEN...
HEY.

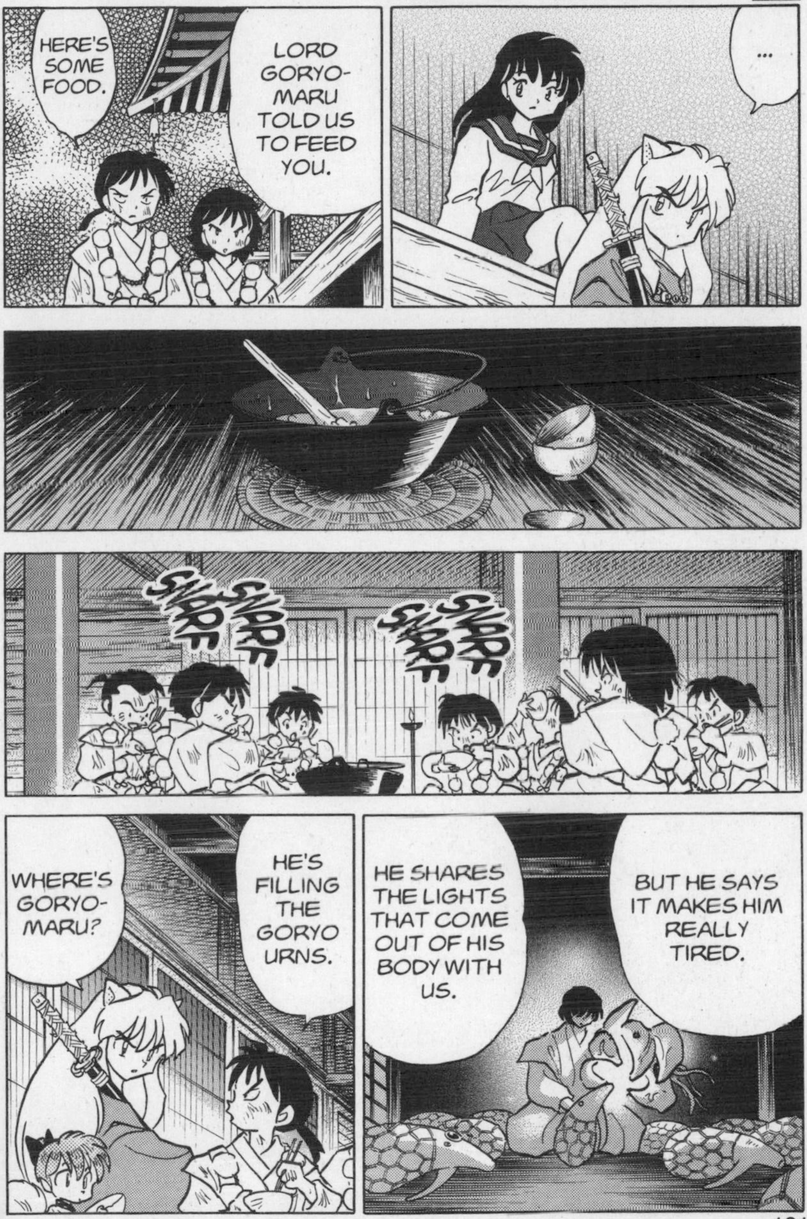
HERE'S SOME FOOD.
LORD GORYO-MARU TOLD US TO FEED YOU.
...
SNARF SNARF
SNARF SNARF
WHERE'S GORYO-MARU?
HE'S FILLING THE GORYO URNS.
HE SHARES THE LIGHTS THAT COME OUT OF HIS BODY WITH US.
BUT HE SAYS IT MAKES HIM REALLY TIRED.

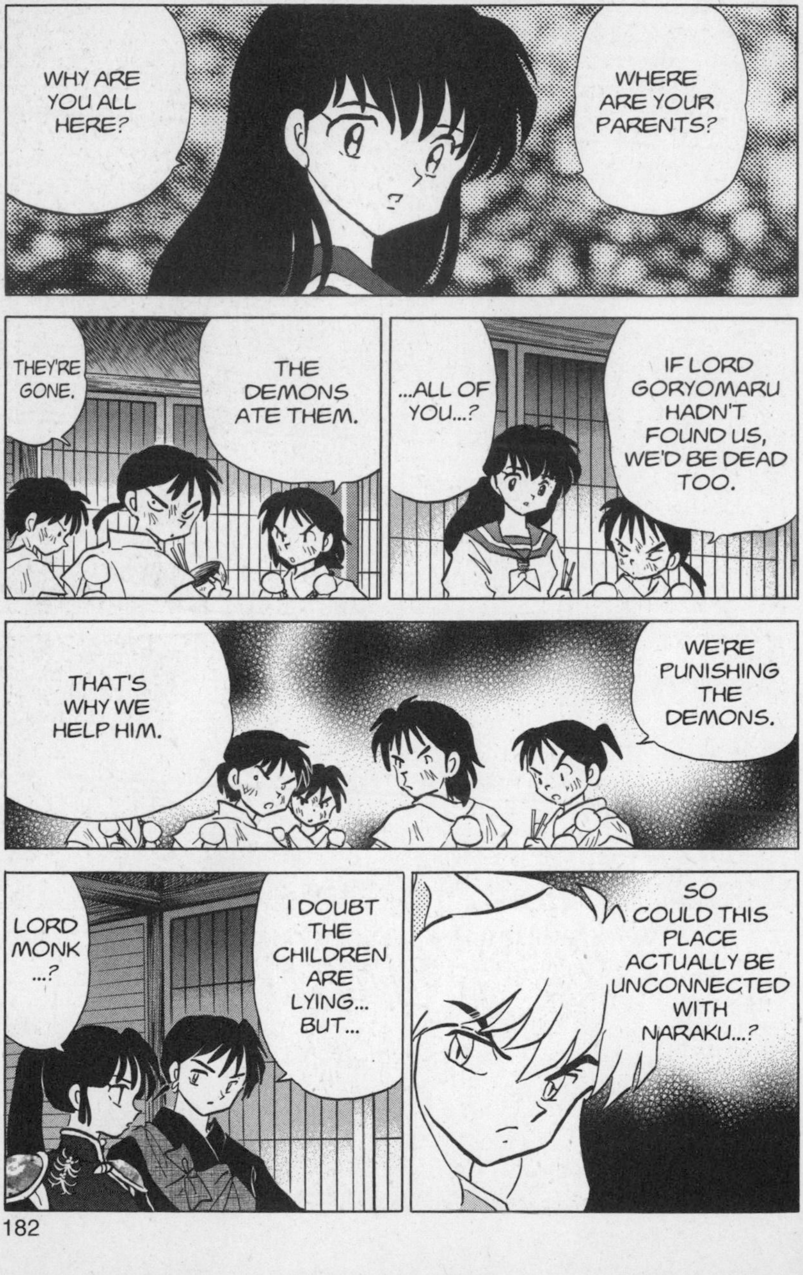
WHY ARE YOU ALL HERE?
WHERE ARE YOUR PARENTS?
THEY'RE GONE.
THE DEMONS ATE THEM.
...ALL OF YOU...?
IF LORD GORYOMARU HADN'T FOUND US, WE'D BE DEAD TOO.
THAT'S WHY WE HELP HIM.
WE'RE PUNISHING THE DEMONS.
LORD MONK ...?
I DOUBT THE CHILDREN ARE LYING... BUT...
SO COULD THIS PLACE ACTUALLY BE UNCONNECTED WITH NARAKU...?

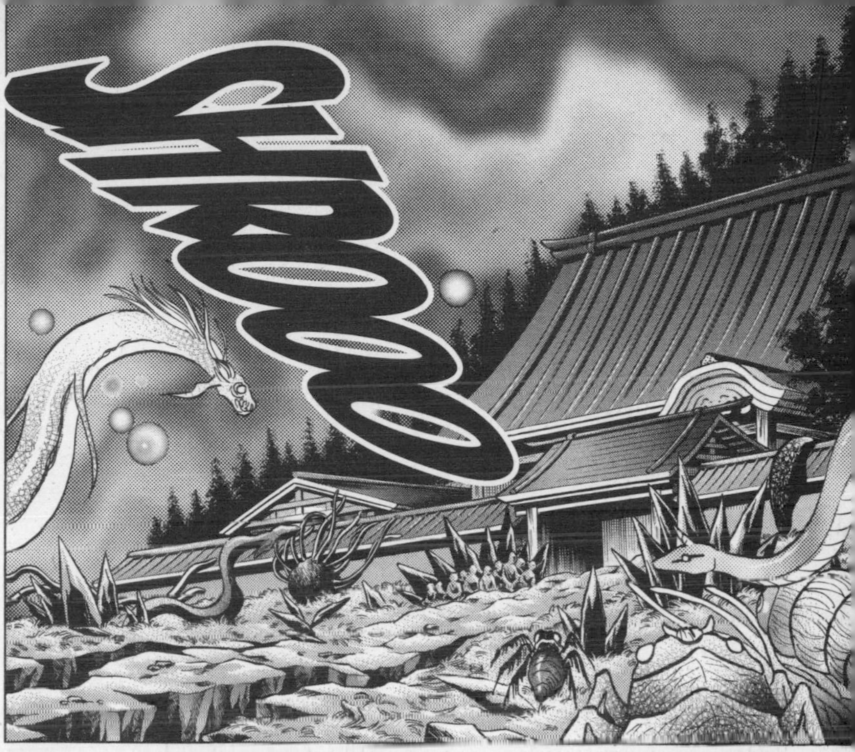
SHROOO
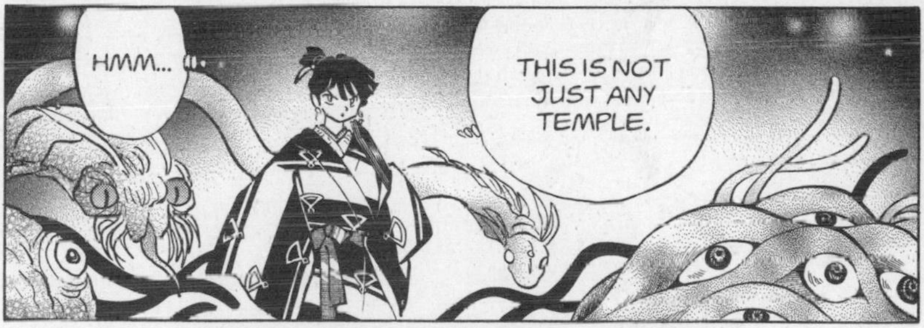
HMM...
THIS IS NOT JUST ANY TEMPLE.
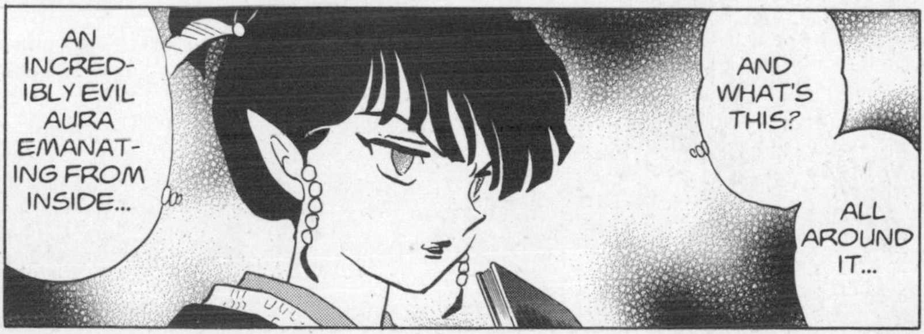
AN INCREDIBLY EVIL AURA EMANATING FROM INSIDE...
AND WHAT'S THIS?
ALL AROUND IT...

...THESE REPULSIVE CARVINGS.

ARE THEY BUDDHIST SAINTS?

THEY DON'T LOOK LIKE THEY'D GUARD AGAINST DEMONS...

...SHHH

...BUT FOR SOME REASON THE DEMONS AREN'T TRYING TO ATTACK THE PLACE.

ZAK ZAK

I CAN'T LET THIS OPPORTUNITY SLIP AWAY.

NARAKU'S HEART'S GOT TO BE NEARBY.

THERE'VE GOT TO BE CLUES HERE ABOUT THAT INFANT!

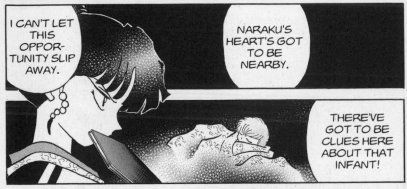

FAP

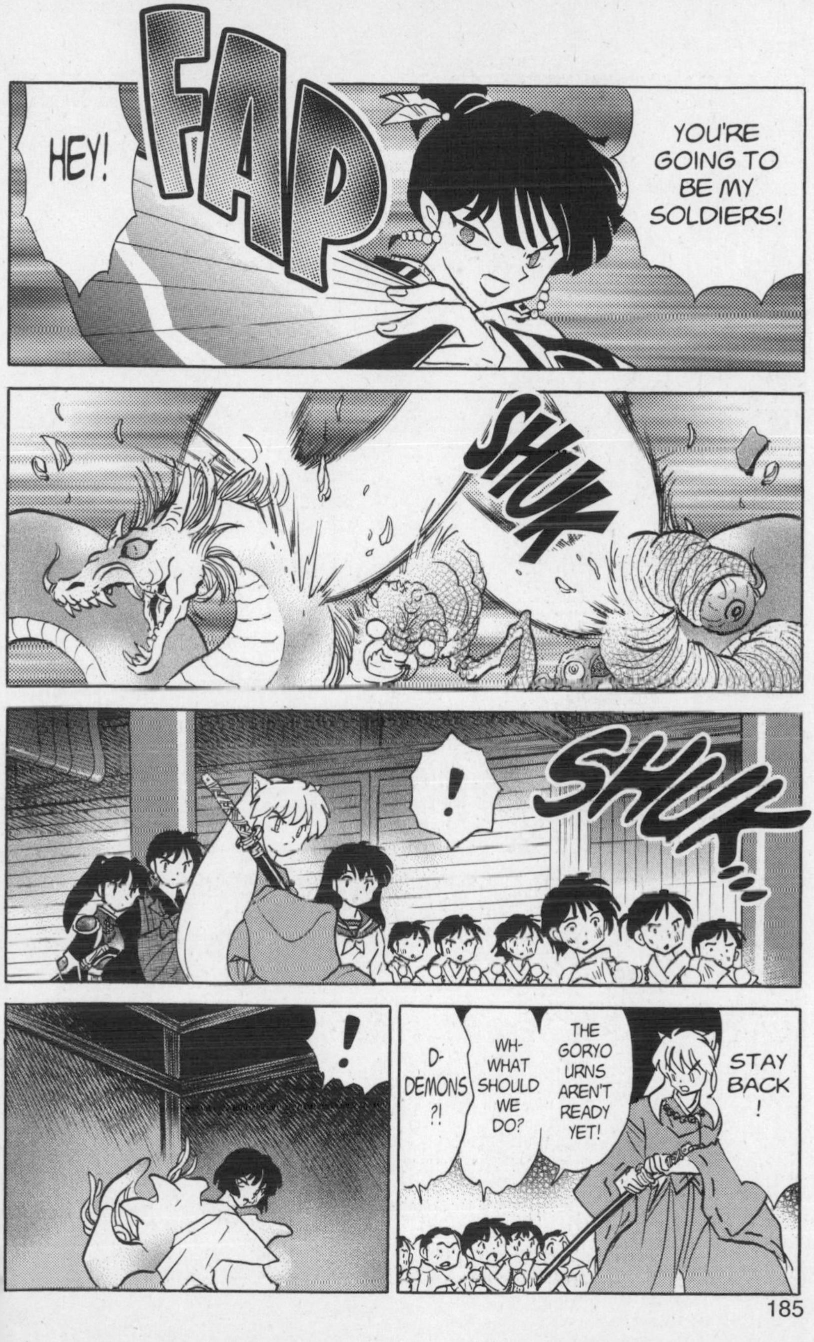
HEY!
FAP
YOU'RE GOING TO BE MY SOLDIERS!
SHUK
!
SHUK
!
D-DEMONS?!
WH-WHAT SHOULD WE DO?
THE GORYO URNS AREN'T READY YET!
STAY BACK!

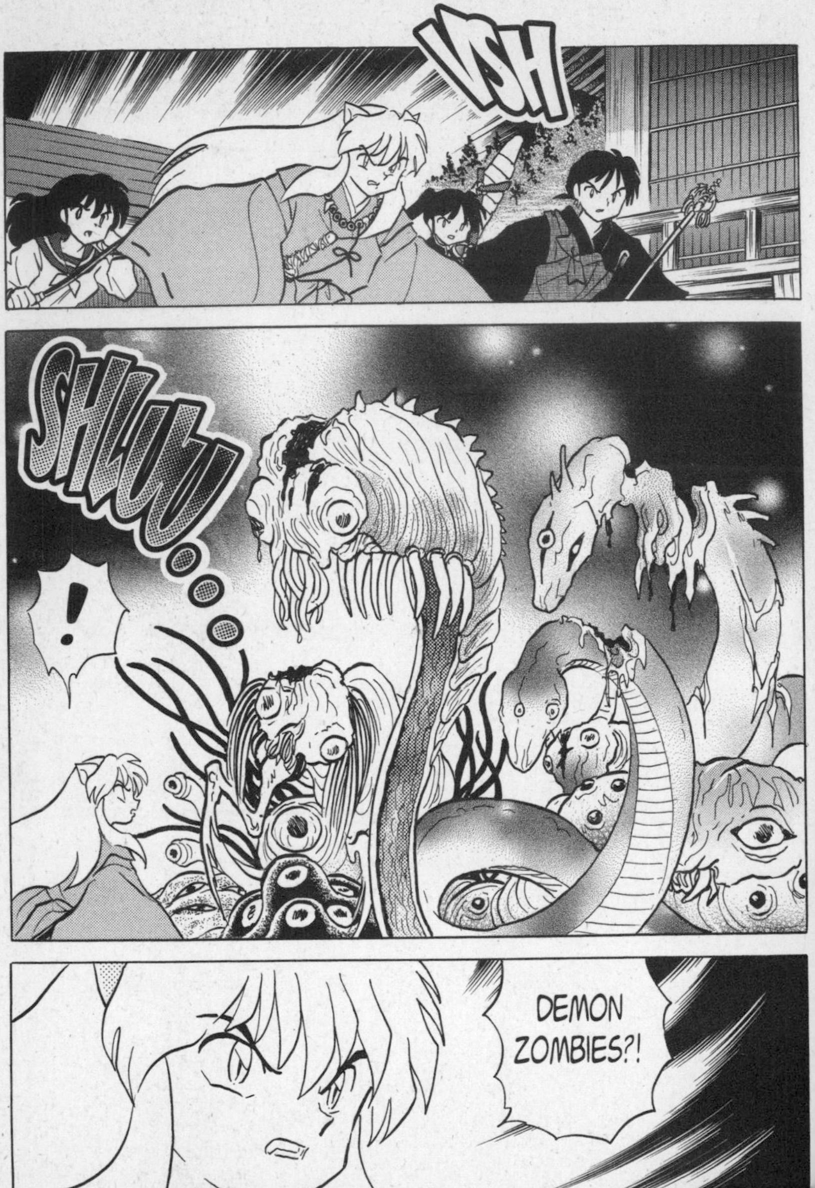
VSH
SHLUUU...
!
DEMON ZOMBIES?!

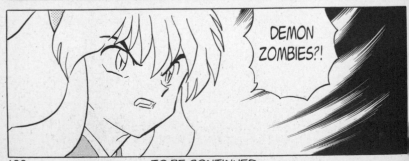

TO BE CONTINUED...

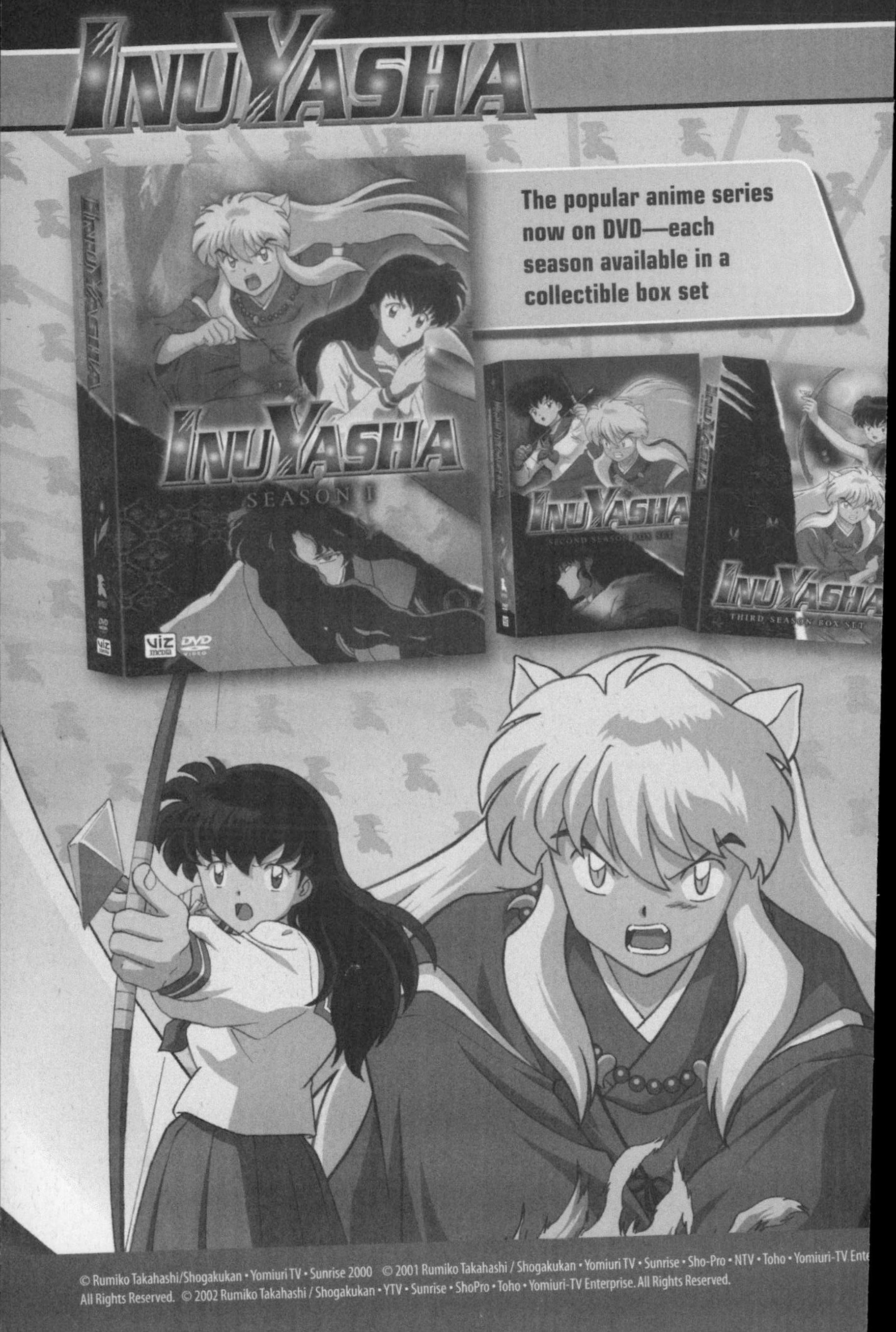
InuYasha
The popular anime series now on DVD—each season available in a collectible box set
InuYasha
SEASON 1
InuYasha
SECOND SEASON BOX SET
InuYasha
THIRD SEASON BOX SET
© Rumiko Takahashi/Shogakukan • Yomiuri TV • Sunrise 2000 © 2001 Rumiko Takahashi / Shogakukan • Yomiuri TV • Sunrise • Sho-Pro • NTV • Toho • Yomiuri-TV Ente
All Rights Reserved. © 2002 Rumiko Takahashi / Shogakukan • YTV • Sunrise • ShoPro • Toho • Yomiuri-TV Enterprise. All Rights Reserved.

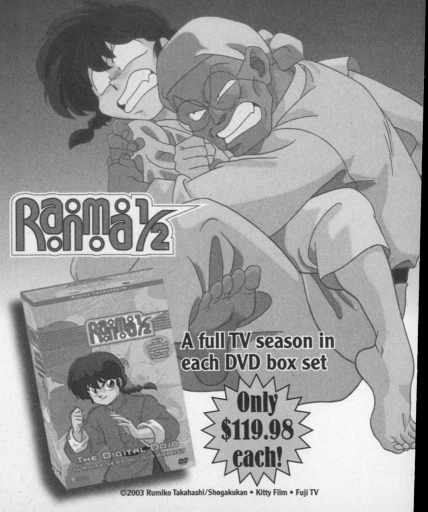

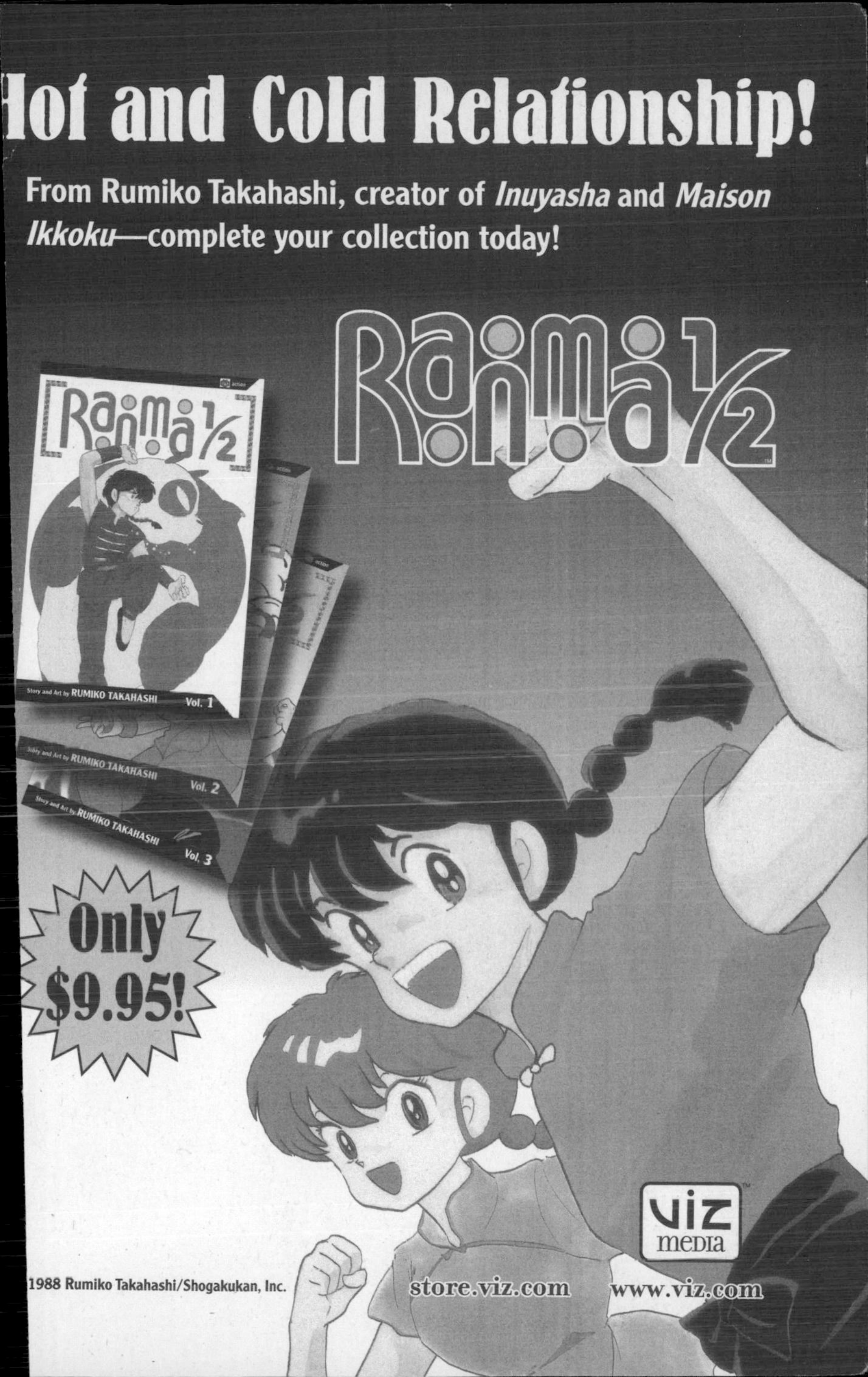
Hot and Cold Relationship!
From Rumiko Takahashi, creator of *Inuyasha* and *Maison Ikkoku*—complete your collection today!
Ranma 1/2
Story and Art by RUMIKO TAKAHASHI Vol. 1
Story and Art by RUMIKO TAKAHASHI Vol. 2
Story and Art by RUMIKO TAKAHASHI Vol. 3
Only $9.95!
viz media
1988 Rumiko Takahashi/Shogakukan, Inc.
store.viz.com
www.viz.com